W9-BZV-163

Redemption Songs

Redemption Songs

Suing for Freedom before Dred Scott

LEA VANDERVELDE

OXFORD
UNIVERSITY PRESS

OXFORD
UNIVERSITY PRESS

Oxford University Press is a department of the
University of Oxford.It furthers the University's objective
of excellence in research, scholarship, and education
by publishing worldwide

Oxford   New York
Auckland   Cape Town   Dar es Salaam   Hong Kong   Karachi
Kuala Lumpur   Madrid   Melbourne   Mexico City   Nairobi
New Delhi   Shanghai   Taipei   Toronto

With offices in
Argentina   Austria   Brazil   Chile   Czech Republic   France   Greece
Guatemala   Hungary   Italy   Japan   Poland   Portugal   Singapore
South Korea   Switzerland   Thailand   Turkey   Ukraine   Vietnam

Oxford is a registered trade mark of Oxford University Press
in the UK and certain other countries.

Published in the United States of America by
Oxford University Press
198 Madison Avenue, New York, NY 10016

Library of Congress Cataloging-in-Publication Data
VanderVelde, Lea.
Redemption songs : suing for freedom before Dred Scott /
Lea VanderVelde.
pages   cm
ISBN 978-0-19-992729-6 (hardback)
1. Slavery—Law and legislation—United States—Cases.
2. Slaves—Legal status, laws, etc.—United States.
3. Slavery—Law and legislation—United States—History.
4. African Americans—Legal status, laws, etc.—Cases.
5. Race discrimination—Law and legislation—United States—Cases.   I. Title.
KF4545.S5V36   2014
342.7308'7—dc23   2013040017

9 8 7 6 5 4 3 2 1

Printed in the United States of America
on acid-free paper

For my best friend, Johannes

And for the remarkable Missouri team—Mel Conley, the late Ken Kaufman, Ken Winn, Bob Moore, Kris Zapalac, Dennis Northcott, and Mike Everman—who helped me find Harriet, and on that journey introduced me to a previously invisible world

CONTENTS

PREFACE

I have been extraordinarily lucky to discover sources that answered questions. While researching the life of *Mrs. Dred Scott*, I found Harriet's master's diary in Minnesota, a first person account of the months that the famous litigant spent in free territory. But in writing her biography, I came to an impasse. After 1840, the diary ended, and Harriet lived in St. Louis for almost a decade before filing suit— the suit that would make history. I went to St. Louis in search of an impoverished and illiterate slave woman who had lived more than one hundred and fifty years ago.

I had a plan. The *Dred Scott* case in the Missouri court did not arise from a legal vacuum. The recorded Missouri Supreme Court decisions indicated that at least six other enslaved persons filed suit in the St. Louis Courthouse. Where there is an appeal, there had to have been a first encounter with the courts, and that encounter must have left some record. It was intriguing to ask how the Scotts learned they could sue for freedom in St. Louis. Who instructed them? Who led the way? How did slaves know that they acquired legal rights by living in free territories? I traveled to St. Louis to find the lower court case records of those other lawsuits.[1] Specifically, I went in search of *Rachel v. Walker*, because Rachel also lived at Fort Snelling and won her suit in the St. Louis court. Was Rachel the link? Did she inform Harriet about how to sue for freedom?[2]

As a legal scholar I was aware that the evolving legal landscape involving slavery was complicated by the westward expansion of the United States. But I had no idea of the extent to which slaves in the western territories actually resorted to the courts in seeking freedom. And I was not alone in that. The historical record simply wasn't available then as it is now. Starting with published appellate cases, I went in search of their beginnings.

In St. Louis, in spring of 1997, I arranged to meet a remarkable elderly St. Louis businessman, with a penchant for local history, who introduced me to Mel Conley, a circuit court clerk. Ken Kaufman had retired after a successful business career, he had lost his wife, and he decided that what he yet wanted to accomplish was to obtain a Ph.D. in history, and so he did. He chose Roswell Field, one of Dred Scott's lawyers, as the subject of his doctoral thesis. When I met him that spring, he was in the process of turning his completed thesis into a book.[3] He introduced me to Melvina Conley, who worked as a data processor in the circuit court clerk's office. Over the years, Mel Conley had stumbled upon a dozen or so cases of slaves suing their masters in St. Louis courts. She came upon a case here and there in the course of her day, looking through the dusty bookcases that surrounded her air-conditioned cubicle. Whenever she found one, she made a point to set the extraordinary document aside in a shoebox that she kept in her desk drawer. As a data processor, Conley's desk was tucked away in an air-conditioned cubicle in an annex to the main courthouse on a floor without even a number.[4] If Kenneth Kaufman had not introduced me to Ms. Conley, I could never have found her, and I would never have become hooked on this work.

From Mel Conley's shoebox, I discovered something few researchers had ever realized before—that there were records that had lasted and there were more than just a few defiant voices seeking freedom in the city courts. I found Rachel's case in much more factual detail than the Missouri Supreme Court had recited in deciding the case.[5] Alas, I did not find any link from her suit to Harriet's, which would have wrapped things up neatly, but I found something even more remarkable. In reading the depositions of witnesses, I was surprised to discover that a black man was subpoenaed to provide testimony on Rachel's behalf.[6] He was never mentioned in the published appellate decision. Could the testimony of black men be taken under oath in court to establish fact? Everything that I read in these cases upended the preconceptions that I had held about slaves, legal status, race, and the courts from my doctrinal understanding of slavery law.[7]

Together, Ken Kaufman, Mel Conley and I searched for additional suits in the dusty side rooms of the St. Louis Circuit courthouse. Someone else found Mel Conley and the precious contents of her shoebox. From his vantage point as historian/conservator of the Old Courthouse, the U.S. Parks Service historian, Robert Moore also discovered Mel Conley's collection of cases.[8] Each of us pursued different in-roads to expanding our discoveries as we began to gather them all. Eventually, the visionary Missouri state archivist, Ken Winn, assembled a small army of dedicated archivists, led by Mike Everman, to locate and preserve other cases in an organized, systematic effort, eventually finding a total of roughly three hundred cases. Over the last ten years I have called Mike Everman, the guardian of the records, to report my discovery of a lead on an additional freedom suit to be located in his warehouse of court filings, based on readings of an old newspaper article, from diaries, or from the Circuit Court

Records Book. As Ken Winn said, "poor housekeeping is the friend of history." The rate of discovery has declined, and I now believe that we probably have found all that can be found.

For more than a century, the documents lay undisturbed tied with brown ribbon, beneath coats of dust, sometimes piled and sometimes shelved haphazardly on irregular bookcases in a warehouse room full of forgotten litigation and unwanted furniture. With the years the once red ribbon had turned brown like old shoestrings, and the handwritten papers showed signs of neglect and aging. Faded, dog-eared, yellowed, and torn, and dried as they had been folded, the pages bore the creases of time. Each time I opened the folds on one of the fragile documents, I feared that the paper would crumble in my hands, and disappear forever, preventing others from ever seeing these histories.[9] I meticulously photographed everything that I could so that I could prove what I was reading.

From the "X" scrawled on Rachel's case, the first official court paper that I opened, I could see that her hand was shaky and unaccustomed to holding a pen. An illiterate young mother known only by a first name, Rachel possessed little but a valid legal claim and courage. She had a baby, John Henry, but she did not own him. Nonetheless, she sued the notorious St. Louis slave trader who was then her master for freedom. No doubt she feared retaliation from William Walker. He was well-known in the community for being ruthless.[10] She must have also known that she and her infant son faced months of life in a dank, dark jail, the only safe haven she could count on, while the court considered her case. The price of pursuing possible freedom was high, higher than we ever imagined, but worth paying, as indicated by the actions of more litigating slaves than modern readers ever realized.

The generations of historians who wrote texts about *Dred Scott* couldn't know until we found these cases that, although the Scotts lost their case, many, many more slaves did succeed in achieving their freedom in the courts. No one, among the most venerated scholars, thought that more than a handful of such cases existed, until Mel Conley revealed to us that she had gathered a shoebox full. Now, these petitions filed by slaves between 1814 and 1860 in St. Louis comprise a remarkably complete collection of freedom suits, perhaps the most complete in any single jurisdiction anywhere in the United States.

These documents provide insight into the heroism, hope, determination, and struggle of slaves who sought liberty in a time when it was not guaranteed.

I read the petitions to hear the voices of slaves who had turned to the courts for justice. Imagine, a slave speaking and signing to the words that she had received *oppression* at the hands of her master! Even today, twenty-first century working people find it difficult to accuse their employers of injustice publicly, and here were slaves calling their masters out! Several of the cases are suits of mistaken identity. Others were true freedom suits where slaves, like the Scotts who had never lived free from legal domination by masters, sought to establish that new status of freedom. The papers also tell the stories of some slaves who were promised their freedom, only to be denied.[11] They also present claims brought on behalf of infants. And they tell heartbreaking stories of family members desperate to purchase their brothers, wives, and daughters.[12]

I thank the Guggenheim foundation and Dorothy Tapper Goldman for supporting this work. The support that I received as a Guggenheim fellow in Constitutional Studies was invaluable in completing this book.

CHAPTER 1

A Metaphor for the Voices of the Subordinate Buried in History

The slave is trained to answer his master, to suit his purposes.
—James Watkins, *Struggles for Freedom*

In suing for freedom, the slave defies his or her master. When one sings a redemption song, one speaks truth to power. But not full truth—the slave is not empowered to tell the whole truth—but enough of the truth to be upsetting to the master, to make a sound discordant with the legitimacy of her master's dominion, and enough of the truth to meet the elements legally necessary to redemption. That much and no more.

At the crux of each of these cases is a story like few others. It is a story told by a slave while enslaved, a person who is normally expected to be neither seen nor heard. It is written from the slave's perspective, seeking the slave's own objective: freedom. Historians of antebellum America have strained to hear muffled voices of a silenced population.[1] Slavery itself created the silence. Yet, here is a chorus of songs.

Each petitioner's story has a structure. There is a pattern to the discourse, and that is what makes it a song. It has a beginning, the petition; a middle, the lawsuit; and an end, the judgment, for that's what must be sung in public. That is the public record of courts, law and legal order. But more than that, each redemption song is situated in the flow of multiple changing contexts: a life, other lives, a social relationship, an economic relationship, a social history, and the history of multiple communities. Each redemption song ends by fading into the quiet of private lives. These lives continue after the public conclusion of final court judgment, but often out of hearing. The public part of the redemption song is part of an even larger phenomenon that itself has beginnings and endings without clear disjuncture. These lawsuits are dramatic and transformative, just like many other songs.

Yet, the redemption song in a freedom suit is unlike other songs. It is not one of rescue, or mercy, or grace; it is a claim of entitlement. In this respect, it is different from other discourses that subordinates voice. Because it is instrumental—intended to redeem the legal right to free status—the petitioner cannot speak fully and freely. Extra notes, and militant tones, will impair the objective and may bring penalties; so the song must be spare, conserving the political economy of the resistance it presents.

Like many other performances, the singer is not alone on the stage. The song can be drowned out by the louder voices or more insistent agendas of others. Free persons can sing more freely than petitioning slaves. They need not be so careful about being in tune or staying on script when singing simultaneously. Free persons can insist that their case be heard in the cacophony. Those singing redemption songs cannot. Thus, the redemption song can be interrupted, but it cannot interrupt the voices of those who are free. For example, the suits of Brunetta and Archibald were drowned out for months by a citywide hunt for murderers and arsonists.[2] Ralph's suit shifted emphasis when the focus changed to imputing the credibility of a white man, his key witness.[3] This new contest devolved into a feud between white men, which was more about them than about Ralph. Dred and Harriet Scott's song was delayed by massive fires and epidemics before it was ultimately killed by two legal reversals: one state and the other federal.[4] Subordinate voices do not necessarily command the authority to maintain attention to their interests, even with appointed attorneys and provisionally recognized claims. Those competing agendas, melodies and noise, though discordant, are also part of the chorus.

Scholarship in many fields has taken considerable interest in the authenticity of subordinates' voices.[5] The slave is trained to answer his or her master, to suit the master's purposes, after all. So most utterances are made to please the master and thus cannot be expected to be from the heart. Still, in these cases, the voices are about as authentic as any historical record that slaves could leave. It must be remembered that slaves were often forbidden from learning to read or write. The cases began with the petitioning slave making a claim to sue as a pauper before some ministerial official, such as the justice of the peace or the clerk of court. Those petitions, signed at the bottom by the "X" of the petitioning slave, led to the assignment of a lawyer. True, the clerk may have coaxed the slave in what to say, or the clerk may have translated the slave's claim into legal language. But often the petition reads as if the clerk simply took down the petitioner's account of what had happened to him or her. Some petitions ramble about occurrences having little bearing on the lawsuit.

The corpus of lawsuits is a chorus of songs. These cases provide a rich context of slave life, patterns of oppression and of survival, as revealed by the slaves themselves in seeking their own objectives. By documenting the lives of subordinated people and their adaptive methods, these stories illustrate how society's least well-off survive and how and why they approach courts in circumstances of widespread oppression. These stories are meaningful today.[6] Although slavery was formally abolished by the Thirteenth Amendment in 1865, the legal system has not completely curtailed social and economic subordination of some working people who struggle for survival. These stories illuminate lessons about their lives as well.

The fact that there are so many full case files in the cache, roughly 300, allows readers to see the variability in slaves' lives. All too often when discussing American slavery, idiosyncratic anecdotes are used to generalize about slaves' experience and motivation. With 300 cases, involving 239 litigants, the detailed pattern is diverse. There are exceptions to almost every generalization. There are more lawsuits than litigants here because some filed suit more than once.[7]

These redemption songs are contested discourse. There is a slave owner as defendant in each of these freedom suits. Although the lawsuit begins as a pattern of call and response, each side introduces witnesses to corroborate its claims. Depositions and witnesses fill in notes to the song.

These cases are unlike most lawsuits about slavery that we have seen because they are the original filings at the trial court level. Until recently, the limits of our understanding were based upon appellate cases. Most analysis was built by reading appellate cases. Most prior work on freedom suits has been directed at those peaks of litigation contests, such as the final opinion in *Dred Scott v. Sandford* from the United States Supreme Court and others from state supreme courts.[8] By the time that cases made it to that rarified level, the facts had been massaged into legal categories by lawyers in the process of appeal. The result of reading an appellate case like *Dred Scott v. Sandford* is to lose any sense of the personal, psychological, emotional, and social context of the litigants' motives. For example, the factual record in the Taney *Dred Scott* opinion is a flattened account, more grounded in prosaic legal fiction than in the complex reality of the particular human motivation of those individuals, however dramatic or mundane. The litigants' motivations, sparked by their lived experience, were expunged on appeal. The legal contest remains but retaining only simplified motivations ascribed to each side. No wonder generations of scholars thought that the infamous *Dred Scott* case was purely a fictitious setup to bring the political question of slavery before the high court. No wonder some earlier scholars couldn't understand why an enslaved man like Dred Scott didn't sue when he first arrived at a place that had a courthouse. No wonder earlier scholars thought that attaining freedom, rather than merely surviving, sufficiently predicted all slaves' motives.[9] Smoothed and refined appellate cases lose the raw authenticity of the songs in the original. The litigants' voices are lost to their lawyers' stratagems. There is not even a quote from Dred, or his co-plaintiff Harriet Scott, in the long Supreme Court opinion. Who could hear their voices muffled by the layers of appeal? Few even realized that the redemption song was a duet, motivated at least as much by the hidden party, Harriet.[10]

Furthermore, lumping together the factual accounts of several appellate cases merely aggregates these simplifications. Since each case has been studio worked by the attorneys, the combined chorus sounds more like elevator music. To actually sense the fresh, raw, authentic, acoustic notes of actual lives, one needs to read the litigants' affidavits. The affidavits and the depositions testify to their experience.

In addition, because the elements in a freedom suit are scripted, one cannot necessarily take even the sworn language of the petition at face value. To bring a lawsuit, slaves needed to allege that their defendant had beaten or imprisoned them, regardless of whether or not they had been beaten by the person whom they named as defendant. One must read dozens of petitions to see where particular statements depart from the required script. It is the departure from script where one finds the details: riffs of fortuity, circumstance, and personality that characterize individual lives. It is only from reading many freedom suits at the trial court level from a single active jurisdiction like St. Louis that larger patterns and departures from pattern can be recognized. Professor Walter Johnson says that he read docket records as "lies," but there are different types of falsehoods in legal documents, some of which are legal fictions which are legally allowed for the formality of bringing the case.[11] Others are false testimony declared out of self-interest. Professor Johnson is right that court records must be examined for their truthfulness. But there is some truth in the legal records. They must be read in the context of their instrumental objectives.

These case files reveal what could not be seen otherwise. Most significantly, the grievances that impelled slaves to file suit for freedom. The grievances explain why the slaves turned to courts when they did. Slave petitioners often had a basis for filing suit long before they actually did. Several describe attempting first to negotiate some better situation or buy their freedom. Some were filed as soon as the person arrived in town and could reach a court officer. While slaves were in transit, they could be hustled from one arriving steamboat to another departing, bound for sale in New Orleans.[12] Filing suit was their only chance to stay in place and claim their freedom. Still others, like the Scott family, waited and filed only after they had lived in St. Louis for some time. Some waited until other family members went first.

Why did some wait to sue? What factors explained the delay? In the range of contexts, one sees that the subordinate litigant needed a trigger. The triggering action was rarely as prosaic as being beaten—slaves were often cuffed for a variety of reasons. Something more was necessary to impel them to go to court. Something changed that made the extreme discomfort of staying in place worth the risk of escalation by angering one's master by claiming freedom. None of the petitions suggest that the petitioner acted impulsively. The risks of retaliation were too high. The decision to sue had to be made with consideration of the chances of winning and the risks of survival. For slaves attempting to sue, the legal system became its own labyrinthine cage. Petitioners were jailed or auctioned off to rough work lives commanded by strangers during the time the litigation lasted.

Sometimes the traps were fully apparent and marked; sometimes they were surprises, such as when the rules changed. There were skeletons and helpers along the path, sometimes at the least expected junctures, as well as people, including other slaves or free Blacks, who could turn on you. One must always read these lawsuits in context of the resources necessary and available for the litigant's survival.

While some slaves chose to fight in court, others—primarily men—chose to run when triggered to action. Protecting children from sale emerges as triggering many lawsuits. Women filed more lawsuits than men, and many of the women were mothers. The law of matrilinearity determined a child's status based upon the status of their mother at the time of their birth.[13] The best way for an enslaved mother to protect her children was to establish her own freedom. That lawsuit usually came first. If successful, that lawsuit could give the mother's children the gift of recognized freedom.

For the most part, these freedom suits were family affairs, whether the litigants sued jointly, in tandem, or in succession. A total of 160 persons, of the 239 litigants for whom we have records, were related to the 38 identifiable families or housemate groups. (There are 11 more litigants for whom there simply are no records at all.) One hundred and fifty-three litigants were women or girls, while 126 litigants were men or boys. Men could run more easily, particularly if they fled alone and without children who would slow them down. For slaves attempting to escape, there were notices posted in the newspaper and rewards offered for men to pursue the runaways with dogs, and bring them back in shackles to a local jail, where they would await their master's "justice." These cases reinforce the adage that men run and women sue.[14] By comparison, men generally outnumbered women in runaway advertisements in the St. Louis newspapers.[15]

How did these lawsuits end? What factors determined success? The ultimate issue of who succeeded and who failed to achieve freedom is much less susceptible to any clear pattern. The variables are too numerous for satisfactory statistical analysis. The litigants' persistence, of course, played a role, as did the quality of their attorneys and the degree of resistance of their owners.

Nor can we always determine success or failure from the last record of the case. We know which petitioners were clearly victorious, and which petitioners died. But what about the others? A significant number of petitioners' suits were dismissed by their lawyers informing the court that they refused to prosecute further.[16] Does this mean that the promise of freedom wasn't enough to sustain the effort, or does this mean instead that some accommodation acceptable to the petitioner was found in another way?[17] Being freed from enslavement was perhaps the most beneficial change of personal status that American law could bestow. Yet these endings show that some subordinated litigants gave up, perhaps unable to hold out for vindication of their rights. Sometimes enduring the lengthy lawsuit encouraged them to settle for accommodation, perhaps with some slight improvement of their situation. To be able to exit slavery, by any means—

lawsuit, self-purchase, or escape—the pathway had to be survivable. These litigants were not suicidal. Survival had to be the more important objective for captive, subordinate persons, more important even than establishing one's freedom.

Owners resisted for the obvious reason of their own personal wealth, and for
more indirect and less obvious reasons as well. Mrs. Emerson seemed more interested in retaining the claim to the Scotts' daughters than to the elderly and weak-
ened Dred Scott. John F. A. Sanford was more interested in winning to please his
revered in-laws than for the money involved. Split-ownership interests affected
owners' motivations and resistance to the lawsuit as well. Slave ownership was
complicated when interests were split between decedents and heirs, debtors and
creditors, owners and hirers, husband and wives. That degree of variability alone
explains some variation of result.

A good lawyer always made a difference, and there truly was a range of lawyer competence and incompetence. Several lawyers gave admirable, zealous legal
services: tracking down witnesses, opposing adversaries' stratagems, and pursuing
appeals. Others were not so conscientious. Some allowed cases to default or worse,
took personal advantage of the slaves whom they were assigned to represent. Some
lawyers failed to make the simplest, most basic efforts to help their clients, such as
showing up in court when necessary. By contrast, the judge seemed to make little
difference to the outcome. There were only six men who occupied the bench of the
St. Louis Circuit Court during this period, and none seemed to leave their mark in
these lawsuits. Each of the six seemed far more involved in other professional matters. Each man conducted the freedom suits in accordance with the law and their
own capacities as managers of their dockets. Large commercial lawsuits usually
took precedence over lowly slaves' suits, but there is no evidence here that any of
the judges behaved ideologically in attempting to influence these cases.

Making the pattern of outcomes less predictable were the rules that shifted
over this half century of slavery in St. Louis. In the common law tradition, outcomes were influenced by precedent, those contests that had gone before. In the
common law method by which case law is made, the rules were shaped by the
litigants' own circumstances through the lawyers' craft. As arguments about law
were won and lost, they altered the terrain for those who came after. More than
a dozen times, masters appealed to the Missouri Supreme Court in contested
attempts to change the rules in freedom suits or alter them sufficiently to be able
to prevail against a slave seeking his or her freedom.[18] Sporadic legislative inter-
ventions changed the rules even more dramatically. For example, in 1835, the
Missouri legislature amended the law to strip away the successful petitioner's
right to damages for the time that they were enslaved.[19]

Nor did the final judgment, after the final appeal, end further litigation. Subsequent suits between white slave owners often occurred after the masters lost.
These derivative suits were occasioned by the significant wealth the master lost

by the slave's success in freeing himself. After a successful freedom suit, what had been a valuable property asset, a human being (ranging in value from 25 cents, in the case of aged or disabled slaves that the master must support,[20] to $500 for a top worker) was totally lost to the master. This financial loss often led the disappointed master to sue others to recoup that loss.[21] Such losses then reverberated into other financial dealings and other lawsuits. These suits that spun off the slave's suit added to the discourse and chorus as well, sometimes revealing more about the nature of transactions that drove the direction of the slave petioner's life.

How does a freedom suit that so upends power relations sit within an otherwise stable system of laws supporting slavery? At minimum, it upsets the economic balance sheet. The larger issue is whether freedom suits' contested discourse is stabilizing or destabilizing to a slave states' laws. The answer seems to be that it depends. The amount of stress that the lawsuit puts on the legal system depends upon the basis for the freedom suit. Slaves filing for their freedom based their claims on one of four possible grounds. Some types of claims were less threatening to the social order and slave state's legal jurisprudence than others. Some suits sought only to return a free black person to their rightful status, and some to uphold a dead master's promise of freedom at his death against the heirs' claims. But some were truly transformational: giving free status and a new independent life to slaves without their master's consent and even over their master's objection. These were the free soil cases.

The 239 St. Louis claims were not evenly distributed over these five categories. One small, discreet group of petitioners claimed freedom because they were Native Americans and Native Americans, like Whites, could not be enslaved. After the practice of Native American slavery died out, this type of case was rarely seen in St. Louis. Only twenty individuals based their claims on their Native American heritage, and eighteen of the twenty were all descendants of the same woman. (That story, told in chapter 3, "The Three Daughters of Marie Scypion," lasted for decades.) The legal basis for Native American freedom in St. Louis was unique to the region west of the Mississippi River, however. It was based upon an eighteenth-century decree by a Spanish colonial governor. Although this legal rule was consonant with parallel U.S. developments, it developed entirely independently west of the Mississippi.[22]

A second group claimed freedom based upon mistaken status. The legal system needed a mechanism to correct errors of classification as long as African Americans could be free. Free African Americans were continuously vulnerable to being mistaken as slaves. Status was usually presumed from a person's color. This type of claim, which sought to recover freedom that had been lost, was common in southern states, but less than 20 percent—only forty-three litigants in St. Louis—made this argument. None of these claimants argued mistake of racial classification.[23] These cases were indeed racist because only African Americans could be enslaved, and were presumed to be slaves, but these individuals did not contest their racial classification. They contested their legal status. When the litigant was successful, the court simply acknowledged the individual's proper status and restored to them their liberty. These suits were not transformative in the sense of providing the plaintiff's first release from enslavement. These individuals, or their mothers, had already enjoyed the privileges of liberty. They sued to regain their proper status.

A third, tiny group of petitioners, just four people, alleged that their master agreed to allow them to purchase their freedom but did not carry through on the contract.[24] They too had the equitable advantage of their master's consent; their master had once consented to their freedom.

The last and largest litigants' group by far based their claim to freedom on their residence in free territory or derivatively that their mother had resided in free territory. These cases were the centerpiece of St. Louis litigation. These cases were fomented by westward migration and national expansion. The rule of freedom by residence, living on free soil, was essentially derived from the story of westward migration of owners with slaves.

In this last and most significant group of cases, the master never intended, consented, contracted, or voluntarily tried to manumit the petitioner. These were not cases of failed or partial manumission.[25] These were not cases of manumission at all. That makes a big difference. In these cases, the petitioners directly opposed their owner-master's volition; they could not pin their claim on a master's willingness ever to free them. They petitioned the state to override their master's wishes.

What Was a Freedom Suit? How the Slave Got to Court and Got a Lawyer

Under the procedure set out by the Missouri statute, the slave began the lawsuit by orally presenting his or her case to a court official: the clerk of court, a justice of the peace, a judge, or a lawyer. This affidavit told the slave's story. The clerk wrote the story down and the slave signed with the "X" customary for illiterate persons.

One remarkable feature of the Missouri statute was that such affidavits, if approved, allowed slaves to be declared paupers, and to be appointed lawyers by the judges who reviewed their affidavits. Slave freedom suits were unique in this regard in Missouri because no other segment of the impoverished public was given a lawyer by simply filing an affidavit and asking the judge to assign one. In most states, *in forma pauperis* suits, as they were called, simply waived the court fees, but in this particular Missouri statute, the slave was actually assigned an attorney.

This meant that the slave did not need to find some willing attorney in order to begin a lawsuit.[26] If the slave claimed circumstances sufficient to bring a cognizable claim, a judge would find an attorney for him. Some slaves did approach lawyers who, in turn, assisted them in filing the necessary affidavit, and other slaves seem to have proceeded to an official on their own. When accompanied by a lawyer, that lawyer was usually assigned to represent the slave. If no lawyer already stood with the slave, the judge could assign almost any lawyer, someone who just happened to be present in court that day, or, at other times, some lawyer to whom these freedom cases were routinely assigned.

The statute did not provide compensation for the attorneys, but nor did it require, like the Virginia statute, that the representation had to be done for free, *pro bono*.[27] Lawyers could not expect compensation from their enslaved client. But that did not prevent some from attempting to extract compensation from their client in one way or another: by carrying a debit on their accounts book in the slave's name, by negotiating with the slave to do work for the lawyer, or by attempting to collect from some free person in the slave's extended family who had the wherewithal to pay.[28] Trading their lawyers their labor was, for the most part, the only thing that slaves had to offer. Slaves were sometimes hired out to their lawyers. Dred Scott was.

There appears to be very little evidence of cause lawyering among the slaves' lawyers. Freedom suits were not brought or advanced by abolitionist societies as they were in several states of the Northeast.[29] Advocating abolitionism in Missouri was a crime after 1837.[30] Even before such advocacy was actually outlawed, abolitionism was unpopular. Among the lawyers who represented slaves in these suits, there is no direct evidence of antislavery sentiment at all. There is no evidence in the local newspapers or in the private papers and letters of the designated attorneys themselves of cause lawyering. Nor does there seem to be crossover activity by those lawyers advancing other antislavery efforts. Most continued to own slaves and to will them to their heirs, rather than free them, upon their deaths.[31] Attorney Edward Bates representing Lucy Delaney proudly stated in court, "I am a slave holder myself."[32] Lawyers who represented slaves are not particularly active in manumitting slaves. Instead, the lawyers who represented slaves most often seemed to be trial lawyers—just that—men who supported themselves by arguing cases on a number of issues and who were sometimes assigned by the judge, before whom they practiced, to represent a slave petitioner.

Situating This Work in the Existing Legal Historiography of Slavery: North and South

Given this large amount of new evidence, and the change of focus that the new evidence permits, it is difficult to join issue with the prior historiography.

Prior historiography of slave law has been concerned with three larger themes, which are not the issue here.[33]

This book does not attempt to address the causes of the Civil War, except to note the obvious—that the *Dred Scott* case was a contributing factor—and to demonstrate something much less obvious: that the decision was the game changer. *Dred Scott* was a major shift in the body of law of the state from which it originated. The decision departed so substantially from Missouri's previous precedent as to conflict with rules applied in more than 200 cases arising previously in the same jurisdiction. The overwhelming lesson of these cases indicated that the Scotts had a very good expectation of winning. Framed by this prior practice, their claim was a relatively simple and easy case. Justice Taney is infamously quoted as saying that black men had no legal rights. In these very numerous cases, black persons had legally enforceable *rights* that white men were obligated to respect. Thus, the *Dred Scott* case can no longer be viewed in isolation as a foregone conclusion that a slave would lose to his master, but as the game changer, the case that repudiated established legal rules applied in at least 200 cases of precedent. With *Dred Scott*, redemption songs were silenced. The Civil War loomed.

Again, in much of the prior work, freedom suits were seen only from the perspective of appellate courts,[34] often as a side issue to studies about manumission and southern ideology. The case law of freedom suits has rarely been the focus of sustained analysis, with the exception of Judith Schafer's pathbreaking parallel work on New Orleans lawsuits, *Becoming Free, Remaining Free*.[35] Several scholars deserve credit for calling our attention to the uniqueness of freedom suits. Judge Higginbotham introduced the surprising fact of Virginia freedom suits in two outstanding law review articles.[36] In 1946, Marion J. Russell reported that 57 percent of the 575 freedom cases, which were decided in state appellate courts, resulted in freedom for the litigating slaves. However, Russell's claim cannot be verified.[37] Nevertheless, this uncorroborated figure has been recited in the literature from time to time.[38] Yet lower court judges did most of the business of freedom suits, and slave's petitions were rarely available for analysis. Fortunately, new studies excavating these unpublished trial court records have been emerging.

In the years before digitization and databases like Westlaw, legal scholars relied upon comprehensive digests like Helen Tunnicliffe Catterall's magnificent work, *Judicial Cases Concerning American Slavery and the Negro* to identify what cases existed on the subject of slavery.[39] Most scholarship has relied on this compendium for data.[40] Catterall's accomplishment of producing five volumes surveying the appellate cases for each American state was extraordinary, particularly considering research tools available in the early twentieth century. Today, more comprehensive searches can be completed in mere minutes by a search engine scouring the entire corpus of published judicial opinions.

Appellate cases like *Dred Scott v. Sandford* were the peak in litigation, but observed without any way to understand of how broadly and with what effect that mountain stretched out at its base. What supported the peak, what was the climb like, and how representative was the case that reached the peak of the hundreds filed and resolved below? Other peaks—leading cases in various state supreme courts—could be viewed in the mountain range, but there was little understanding of what complex social and legal activity supported the peaks below the lofty level, let alone at its base or in the valley floors. Nonetheless, hundreds of petitioners labored every day for years to bring their claims for freedom, each contributing to the mountain that supported the peak.

With new evidence, these cases illuminate aspects previously unseen.[41] They raise questions that have not been framed before.[42] Particularly poignant, is how subordinate people took the lead in pressing their legal rights in suing to establish their freedom in direct contravention of their masters' wishes.

Situating This Work in Existing Western History: East and West

This book's focus is on how redemption songs were sung and how St. Louis handled freedom suits, tolerated slaves suing for freedom, assigned them lawyers,

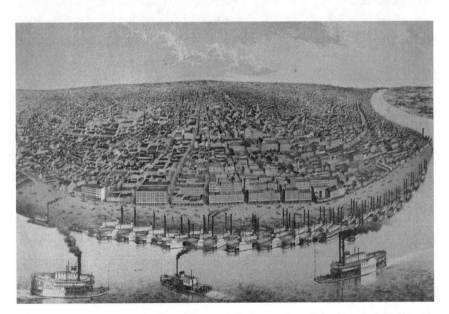

St. Louis Our City. This birds-eye view of St. Louis, a technique popular at the time gives the impression that the Mississippi River wrapped around the City, highlighting the river's importance and the magnitude of the docks. In fact in this reach the river did not bend so dramatically. Missouri History Museum, St. Louis.

and resolved those suits. Ultimately, the question is how did the suits endure in the face of Missouri's slave state norms? This book is paradigmatically about St. Louis and the West, rather than the plantation South or southern ideology. Missouri is not usually grouped among the southern states for reasons that are apparent from the region's history, geography, and economy.

Missouri was a slave state, and it had numerous racist tendencies and laws, but it did not consider itself southern.[43] During the Civil War, it was split over whether to be a loyal slave state or in rebellion. It fought its own internal battle over who spoke for the state in the division between North and South, Union and Confederacy.[44] St. Louis, in particular, did not identify with the South as much as with the West and the frontier. St. Louis called itself "gateway to the west."[45] This self-proclaimed western identity meant that it did not necessarily look to the contemporary South for direction or follow its lead in either ideology or jurisprudence. St. Louis was unrepentant about its slavery, but it hardly considered itself as primarily southern in orientation.

In an era when proximity was key to connectedness, Missouri was not contiguous with core southern states. Its longest, most significant boundary was with the free state of Illinois. It depended upon this neighboring settled area for information and perspective. Missouri responded to its designation as "slave" upon entry into the union by respecting its place in the compromise. It did not seek to influence neighboring Illinois to accept slavery any more than Illinois sought to influence Missouri in its slave jurisprudence. (There appears to have been some peaceable sorting out at the time that Illinois territory was distinguished from Missouri territory. Some slaveholders knowing of Illinois' free designation moved west where they could legally keep slaves.[46]) This long border with a free state, a state that had to be passed by or passed through in traveling west to reach Missouri, provided the geographic basis for most of the St. Louis freedom suits. It was this free state boundary in westward migration that generated the greatest number of enslaved persons eligible to sue for their freedom in St. Louis.

The region of supply was Virginia, which then bounded the Ohio River (since West Virginia had not yet been severed off). More slaves came from Virginia and Kentucky than any other state. Although the St. Louis population exploded during these decades, most migrants, whether staying or passing through, came by way of the Ohio River.[47] St. Louis had strong ties to New Orleans, down the Mississippi River, but more slaves were sent downriver by slave traders than upriver.

With plenty of intercourse between Missouri and Illinois, disputes were bound to arise. The river had been a highway through a unified region long before it became a boundary separating slave states from free. Early settler families continued to maintain households on both sides of the river, retaining their habits of privilege, often taking their black servants back and forth. Even the lawyer community moved back and forth across the river.

These freedom suits do not necessarily reflect southern thinking; they distinctively reframe what was *western* thinking. To say that St. Louis identity was western does not imply that it was any more egalitarian or democratic along the lines of the Turner hypothesis.[48] St. Louis had fully its share of racial exclusions, vendettas, feuds, barbarity, and brutality.

Emphasizing its frontier characteristics does mean that it was engaged in building itself up, inventing certain first generation solutions in the absence of longstanding institutional foundations. Some practices were entrenched but others were not. Emphasizing frontier also means that it was at the periphery, remote from the national metropole in distance, in transit, and in communication.

To be on the periphery meant that it was more remote from the governing center, less controlled by the metropole and less integrated into other states' practices. In expansion, the periphery was newer to the practices and institutions of governance than most of the rest of the nation, hence less bound by institutional practices and more open to alternatives. As periphery to an expanding nation, St. Louis was the bud from which the periphery expanded and moved westward to encompass more settled territories and eventually states into the union.

Its earliest colonial founding tied it to quite different metropoles, France and French cities, like New Orleans, Montreal and Quebec.[49] St. Louis only became tied to the District of Columbia's sovereignty in 1803 with the Louisiana Purchase. The metropole and periphery of St. Louis was also reflected in the nation's military organization and land claim office. Washington, D.C., was headquarters of the eastern army, and St. Louis of the western. Reorienting itself to the U.S. national government in Washington, D.C., made the Ohio River transit corridor even more significant than the great circle of waterways around the Great Lakes to Quebec or down the Mississippi to New Orleans and the sea. Accession to the United States meant accommodating new institutional features of government, like the jury system, the writ of habeas corpus, the common law, and Blackstone.[50] Along with Blackstone and the common law came exposure to the famous British slave suit rulings, the Somerset case and the slave Grace.[51]

The business of St. Louis was as marketplace for the west. It was a place for exchange, and transport, not production, particularly before 1840.[52] St. Louis was the end depot for most westward immigrants. It was the shopkeeper and provisioner of farther westward expansion through river travel, wagon trains, Indian treaty delegations, and military troop movements.[53] It provided a court for disputes arising in vast areas without courts.

Due to its placement as a hub and depot of western river traffic, one would expect that it hosted proportionally more freedom suits based on residence than other jurisdictions, save New Orleans.[54] The evidence seems to bear this out.[55] Disputes brewing elsewhere funneled into the St. Louis courts by gravitating to

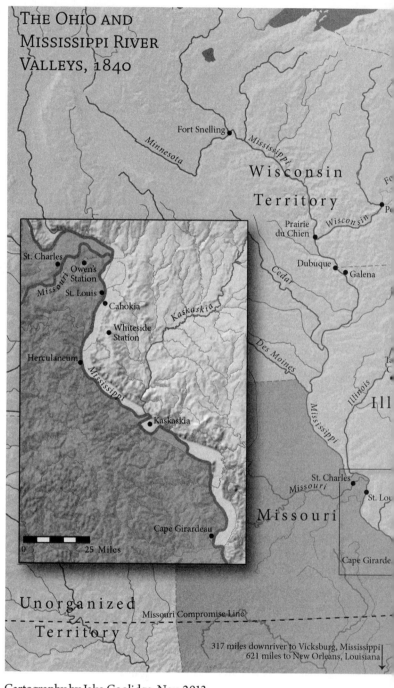

THE OHIO AND
MISSISSIPPI RIVER
VALLEYS, 1840

Fort Snelling

Minnesota

Mississippi

Wisconsin

Territory

Fo

Pe

Prairie
du Chien

Wisconsin

Dubuque

Cedar

Galena

St. Charles

Owen's
Station

Missouri

St. Louis

Cahokia

Kaskaskia

Whiteside
Station

Des Moines

Herculaneum

Mississippi

Illinois

Ill

Ta
C

Mississippi

Kaskaskia

St. Charles

St. Lou

Missouri

Missouri

Cape Girardeau

0   25 Miles

M i s s o u r i

Cape Girarde

Unorganized

Territory

Missouri Compromise Line

317 miles downriver to Vicksburg, Mississippi
621 miles to New Orleans, Louisiana

Cartography by Jake Coolidge, Nov. 2013.

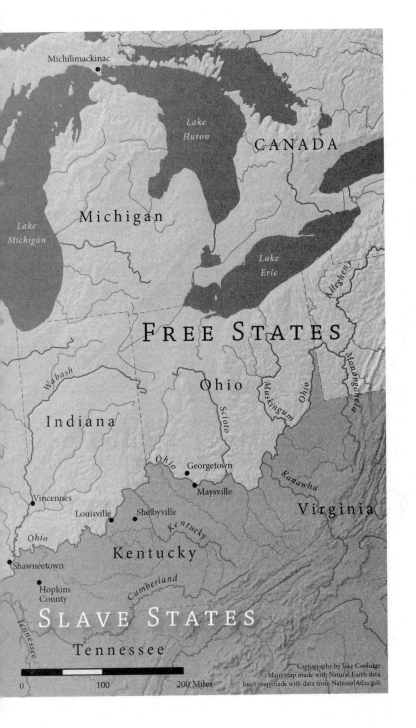

Michilimackinac

Lake
Huron

CANADA

Michigan

Lake
Michigan

Lake
Erie

Allegheny

FREE STATES

Wabash

Ohio

Muskingum

Monongahela

Ohio

Indiana

Scioto

Ohio

Georgetown

Kanawha

Vincennes

Maysville

Louisville

Shelbyville

Virginia

Ohio

Kentucky

Shawneetown

Kentucky

Hopkins
County

Cumberland

SLAVE STATES

Tennessee

Tennessee

0   100   200 Miles

Cartography by Jake Coolidge.
Main map made with Natural Earth data.
Inset map made with data from NationalAtlas.gov.

the transportation hub. Louisville, another mercantile capital on the Ohio River, with a slave market located across from free soil, may well have equaled St. Louis in slave freedom suits, but in the current state of data, it seems not to be the case.

What did it mean that Missouri was a slave state of the West? As a western slave state, Missouri sought to preserve and promote its slavery tradition but not exactly for the same structural economic reasons that states in the Deep South did. Recognizing property in persons serves different purposes in different economic contexts and different labor markets. In particular, slaves were deployed differently in westward migration than they were in the plantation economies.

To the extent that southern slave states perceived that their growing black populations were a problem, exporting them west was often their chosen solution. St. Louis was a likely destination for that export activity. St. Louis had a slave market.[56] On the flip side, St. Louis was a place that owners took slaves when they wanted to emancipate them. The largest collective slave action in the St. Louis suits brought by the 26 slaves of Milton Duty was the result of just such a plan, although the owner died before it could be accomplished. St. Louis was a manumission destination selected over Illinois because it had an existing free black community.[57] By contrast, southern states hosted many more suits over promised freedom in testator's last wills. There were relatively fewer in St. Louis because St. Louis was a population in motion.

Lastly, slaves occupied a different role in the labor market of westward expansion than they did in southern plantation economies. In the South, slaves were sought extensively for agricultural production. Adding slaves could expand the scale of plantation production, at least where the soil could take more intense cultivation.[58] St. Louis did not engage in that degree of production, and the surrounding lands did not yet generate production surpluses.

Frontier slaves were sought instead for the needs of westward expansion. First, slave men were needed to move the cargo to supply the West and provide the muscle for river transportation.[59] Second, in few limited, geologically determined places, slave men were sought for extraction of minerals, either salt or lead. These were jobs that free men did not want to do, jobs for which large numbers of free men could not be hired. And third, slave men and women were sought on the antebellum frontier because labor to provide the basic needs of sustenance could not be hired. Lands were available for settlement in great supply, but labor to make those lands habitable was dear. Slaves were set to work building cabins, icehouses, fences, stills, and fires; chopping wood; feeding, watering, and slaughtering animals; cooking; and laundering. In St. Louis, slaves served the needs of the many travelers in preparing meals, arranging beds, cleaning chamber pots, hauling water and doing laundry.

In even more remote areas than St. Louis slaves provided the labor of basic household sustenance so that the community could gain on the equation of bare survival. Who could build a state, attend court, or form a legislature if all hands were needed to maintain survival? These sites were far from markets for goods and wage laborers. Only with some household members freed from the tasks of maintaining survival could the community build the infrastructure of buildings, roads, governments, and institutions. Work done by slaves permitted settlements to advance faster than the settlements could have developed without them. To be sure, slaves performed similar household tasks in southern states too, but that region's economy was centered upon agricultural commodity production like "King Cotton," rice, and sugar.

Bringing slaves west was also a means of moving finances west. St. Louisians referred to these newcomers as "slave-poor": poor but for their ownership of slaves.[60] There was no easy way to transfer money at the time. Different states printed their own currencies and bank notes during this period.[61] Currency always seemed to be in short supply; frontiersmen and women routinely exchanged IOUs instead of cash. If one wanted to transfer a significant amount of one's inheritance west, moving slaves was a convenient means to do so. Slaves could be sold or rented out to generate income either at any point along the journey or at one's western destination.

Situating This Work in American Law: The Tensile Strength of the Rule of Law

During the five decades of these freedom suits, the St. Louis courts shifted sovereignty twice: from French colonial law to United States territorial sovereignty, which brought the region Anglo-American forms of action. Eventually, territorial sovereignty gave way to statehood. St. Louis was poised at the balance of North and South, but the Missouri Compromise designated Missouri a slave state in the national compromise of accommodation of free and slave states. Although deemed a slave state, Missouri did not adopt entire slave codes wholesale from the other southern states. Instead, it created hybrids of old French colonial practices with newer Anglo-American practices.[62]

Why is Missouri so important in legal history? It was the frontier, it was at the margins of national expansion, and its legal systems were in their protean stage. These cases and this evidence upends many of the conventional beliefs about slavery law drawn from a southern focus by placing slavery law instead in the context of national expansion.[63] Drawing equally from free territory and slave states, St. Louis was not really an extension of southern slave influence. During the period between 1800 and 1850, legal institutions and the city's infrastructure matured. Better transportation and longer settlement brought new industries and more connected markets. During these five decades, the city that was a terminal of the nation's western frontier grew from a small village to a city. During this period, St. Louis changed from frontier as area to frontier border.[64]

By 1820, the city entered the development phase. New immigrants arrived from both the North and the South travelling down the Ohio River, the highway of the nation. Missouri received numbers of immigrating lawyers trained in Anglo-American from both New England and Virginia. The social milieu was dynamic and changing.

Situating St. Louis in the process of national expansion, these cases pose the question, what was the significance of the subordination of an entire class of working people, that is, slaves, in the national expansion of westward movement? Of all the many directions that slaves were moved within the United States, the predominant national migration was westward. Although we have no solid figures on the numbers of slaves brought west, labor market models would predict that the predominant flow of slaves was from east to west. The western labor market needed laborers like slaves, just when the tidewater states had a surplus. St. Louis–bound slaves were brought down the Ohio River west in order to "tame" the West. Slaves were needed as domestic laborers in order to advance settlement at a faster rate than could be done by do-it-yourself yeoman farmers and merchants.

The Ohio River was the main corridor of traffic, with ports at Louisville and Cincinnati.[65] And St. Louis, a short stretch up the Mississippi River, was the main steamboat terminus. With the nation free north of the Ohio River and slave south of the river in the early decades of the nineteenth century, western travelers routinely traversed the lines and often remained a while in free territories in reaching their destination. Many people traveling west brought slaves with them. After all, slavery existed and was only in the process of gradual abolition in northern states in the early 1800s. Thus, St. Louis was a natural cachement place for slaves who had experienced a mixed pattern of residence in free territory, *and* for western legal activity. St. Louis was the perfect storm.

It is pointless to ask whether Missouri was more or less harsh than other slave regimes. Instead, the interesting second- and third-order legal questions here have to do with how the rule of law that recognized slaves' claims to freedom held up in the face of contrary social norms and pressures. Conventionally, the purpose of law is to protect the weak from the strong.[66] The rule of law is expected to hold that line.

The rule of law is subject to different tensions in different contexts. There is little tension (or cognitive dissonance, for either judge or jury) when the enforcement of law generally, or the law of slavery specifically, aligns with social norms. In free northern states, when courts were asked to emancipate slaves held within their jurisdiction, they did so without tension between the result and surrounding social norms. A simple habeas corpus writ was sufficient as a legal procedure to free a slave in the free North. Therefore, when political pressures align with the law's mandates, the tensile strength of a rule of law is not tested. Then the rule of law simply reinforces prevailing political pressures and interests.[67] (It was only when northern judges and communities were asked to actively participate in the rendition of fugitive slaves that a tension arose there between the harshness of the rule of law and prevailing abolitionist norms.)[68]

In St. Louis, all of these cases seeking to free a slave in a slave state test the strength of the rule of law. The freedom-by-residence cases test that most acutely. A steady stream of petitioners satisfied the criteria for freedom by having lived on free soil before arriving at the St. Louis courts in a slave state. The emancipatory rule ran at odds not only with the prevalent social norm that slavery was both legal and desirable, but also with the legal presumption favoring slavery over freedom for African Americans. This conflicting alignment of forces tested the strength of the rule of the law in protecting vulnerable populations.

Still further, different kinds of freedom suits place different degrees of stress upon a state's law of slavery. Cases of mistaken identity do not stress the legal system quite as much; because the case merely seeks to correct a mistaken classification rather than break the bond tying slave to master. Correcting the status of an individual mistakenly categorized has little impact on other master-slave relations.[69] Testamentary cases are similar in this respect. If a master intended to manumit his slaves, there may have been legal obstacles to that manumission, as Andrew Fede has aptly pointed out. Yet the dead master's choices aligned with the slave's desire for freedom. The will indicated the master's volition to manumit.

What makes the freedom by residence cases different is the degree to which the slave's rights conflict with the slave owner's volition. None of the litigants arguing freedom by residence could honestly claim that they had intentionally been taken into free territory with the purpose of effecting their manumission. In freedom-by-residence cases, the slave's desire to win the law suit is in more strikingly direct conflict with her master's wishes.

Here slaves, persons who were the least well-off, typically friendless, and the most vulnerable, were accorded some legal rights by law. Freedom suits (unless they were collusive)[70] were necessarily hostile both to the master's interest and at odds with the prevailing social interest of promoting the number of slaves and limiting the numbers of legally free blacks in the region.[71]

In these cases, in shielding the weak from the strong,[72] the law was under greater stress. It stood against the overwhelming social pressure to bring law into alignment with the exigencies of power, and with social norms. Political considerations pressured that the powerless be returned to their "proper" subjugated place in the social order. The second-order question posed by these cases then is, how long can a court consistently free slaves against the wishes of and to the financial detriment of their masters in a slave state on the nation's periphery? Slave state judges and juries could be expected to frame the equities in keeping with the prevailing power structure. In declaring a slave free by residence, the jury substantially impoverished the slave owner by virtue of legal rule. For some, slaves were the most valuable property that they owned.[73] Still, the law was clear and declaring those slaves free was a legal mandate. How long and how well can the law hold up against the self-interests of the powerful? What is the tensile strength of the "rule of law"?

This large cache of cases from a single jurisdiction, St. Louis,[74] demonstrates slight variations over several decades. Yet, with multiple suits routinely occurring in the same court, one would expect greater stability and consistency of result than in other jurisdictions where freedom suits arose sporadicaly.[75] In many slave states, freedom suits arose rarely, only when a master who had long controlled the slave and promised to free a slave upon his death in his will.[76] Suits that pitted slaves against heirs involved circumstances where title had not necessarily vested in the heirs. The political alignment of promised emancipation at the master's death is less confrontational pursuant to the master's will than a slave challenging a living master who has long controlled the slave and is poised to set the slave to work. The slave manumitted by will could at least invoke the ghost of the dead master's last wishes.

Yet, in no legal system does precedent that runs squarely against social norms, hold without experiencing larger background pressures mounting about its core. And when the rule cannot hold, it can be broken abruptly in a single case, like *Dred Scott v. Sandford*.

For more than thirty years, the St. Louis courts honored the rule that protected the least well-off in their midst against the interests of the wealthy and more powerful. It is amazing is to find so many successful suits decided against the prevailing grain of wealth, race, and class: where people so completely subordinated as slaves sought to use the law to change their status, to sue their masters, and to win their freedom. It required the judge to stand against the prevailing hierarchy and to interrupt the status quo of black persons' presumptive slave status and their continued obligation to work on their masters' behalf. It required the judge to shield and protect the least well-off person based on a legal principle of liberty against someone who otherwise had the legal right to take full advantage of him or her, based on the legal principle of property.

How strong was the rule of law in this circumstance? Surprisingly strong— more than 100 times the court declared freedom. Actually more than 100 times the judge of the St. Louis Circuit Court pronounced the miraculous words that all slave petitioners hoped to hear: "Plaintiff be liberated and entirely set free from the defendant and all persons claiming from, through, or under him." Triumph. Such was the power of law in antebellum Missouri. At the conclusion of successful suit, the judge gave a "judgment of liberation,"[77] effectively separating slave from master. For more than three decades, during a time when law was biased against freedom for servants and people of color, these 100 cases exalted freedom against the backdrop that legalized human oppression and suffering. It is tempting to explain some outcomes in terms of personalities, and within the sequence of cases, several different strong personalities are visible— Leah Charleville, Lydia Titus, David Shipman, the Chouteaus—but whether one slave litigant was aggressive or demure, whether one slave master was an upstanding local citizen or an out-of-state scoundrel, the rule of law usually held. The basic rule of a slave's entitlement to freedom in circumstances where the slave had resided in a free jurisdiction held.

Thus, these cases highlight the strength and fragility of the rule of law to withstand political pressures and continue to protect the least well-off. The sequence of cases shows the method by which legal protections were sustained and in some cases expanded and even strengthened, until the full-blown collapse of this particular law's protection in the *Dred Scott* case.[78] Eventually, in *Dred Scott v. Sandford*,[79] the rule broke completely. Full collapse occurred with collateral damage to other liberties and people, and slaves lost their entitlement to freedom in court based on the usual claim of having resided in free territory.

In terms of the significance to human liberty, the Missouri statute that granted slaves the right to sue stands as significant as the ancient writ of habeas corpus in the Magna Carta. By statute, slaves were able to sue their masters, or anyone else who held them against their will, if they had reasonable grounds to believe they were free.[80] The U.S. Supreme Court would later say that black persons had no rights that whites were required to respect on the occasion of the most infamous Supreme Court case of all time, *Dred Scott*. But, in fact, since 1818 the Missouri court entertained the idea that slaves unjustly kept in bondage had a legal right to sue the very person who held most power over them—their master—and ask to be declared free from that master. If the conditions were met, the courts could legally dissolve the bonds that tied the slave to the master for life, and for the perpetuity of their children's lives.

Although the goal of freedom was always the same, the litigants encountered the courts in different ways. Freedom was the ability to do, go, and serve whomever they wished, and, just as important, to refuse to obey others who had no legitimate claim to them at all, and to remain in place, if they wished to. These cases highlight the various dimensions of freedom and its opposite: the power of enslavement that can be exercised without accountability. Moreover, the cost of anything is the price that must be paid to attain it. The price of freedom, promised to them by law, was surprisingly high for these litigants. As there were many American slaveries in Missouri in the settlement days, so too there were many different reasons to seek freedom. In different surrounding circumstances, with different trade offs, each litigant did not pay exactly the same price.

That these slaves put their trust in courts and American justice represents a breathtaking act of faith. Taking a close look at them allows us to see the potential of a legally benevolent rule, how and why it sometimes succeeds in improving people's lives for the better, and how and why it sometimes goes wrong. In these human courtroom stories, subordinated people worked the system. Sometimes they were successful, and sometimes they got caught or became trapped in it. These voices sound, these songs of freedom. Redemption songs.

CHAPTER 2

Peter's Dual Redemption

The story of Peter and Queen in 1794 is the beginning, the earliest case, the first in several ways. This beginning was told as a matter of folklore in early state and Northwest territorial histories. The tale was most often repeated in the many accounts of "pioneer days," much as a story of origin. Functioning as a story of origin, it was told to valorize the community's beginnings. Hence, it was susceptible to shift according to the standards for valor that themselves shifted over time. Sometimes only the claim of its existence was repeated in different decades.[1] As many stories of origin, it might have just as likely been simply cobbled together from half-truths that are the basic material of folklore. But no one knew for sure if it was actually true.[2] Still, there had to be a first case—so who, when, and where was it? What seeds were contained in that first freedom case that propagated later?

One difficulty of verifying the story of the first slave freed in the Northwest Territory was that the case was so hard to find. It seemed that the original court documents were lost. This was an understandable account of their absence. Many early records from frontier courts of this period were lost. The territory as an American sovereignty was in its infancy. Judges rode circuit, often meeting litigants and holding courts in taverns rather than in courthouses. Courts met in a variety of settings rather than in one fixed place. Papers were fragile and easily subject to disintegration or destruction. (In one case that I encountered, the litigant explained that he had once had a deed to land but it was eaten by mice.) Generations of histories ascribed the story's authenticity to something some historian claimed to have once seen.[3] The search in the literature and footnotes always ended in the same place. An early historian claimed once to have seen an account of this early case decided by one of the first territorial judges.[4] There were two judges; which one was it? This case was sometimes confused with a later case attributed to Judge Symmes, who was the more famous territorial judge.[5]

Where were the court records of the first territorial judges, the honorable George Turner and John Cleves Symmes appointed in 1789 and 1788, respectively? No one knew. One authoritative text stated, "The decisions of the courts were never published,"[6] so in order to find proof of its existence, I had to find the originals, if they still existed, if they ever existed.

To document that such a case actually occurred, one needed at least the litigants' names and the outcome. In search, I contacted all the likely pockets where the early territorial court papers could have come to rest: the Indiana Historical Society, the Indiana State Archives, the National Archives regional office, even the Indiana Supreme Court. None of these institutions knew whether the records had ever survived, but each of them was absolutely certain, and correctly so, that no such record existed in their respective holdings, even when they had some records that would have been contemporary with the ones I was seeking.[7] Of all the several papers that were available in these collections—sales contracts, land sales, probates, and other lawsuits—these records were conspicuously missing.

At stake in the question of how early such a freedom suit existed was how it was handled. How was the Northwest Ordinance interpreted when a slave had first sought protection in the Territory? Did the earliest courts, contemporary with its enactment, recognize that the Ordinance provided an affirmative right to freedom? When did the Ordinance's provision universally prohibiting slavery translate into actually liberating an enslaved person in a specific case? When did the Northwest Ordinance deliver? Post–Civil War accounts of the Northwest Territory have attempted to paint the region as a land untouched by the evil institution of slavery. Many state centenniel histories scrupulously scrubbed the historical accounts of evidence of northern slaveholding to maintain the region's purity—claiming that slavery had never occurred in the Northwest Territory.[8] This was an ethical claim of superiority of the North. The most famous case, Mary Clark's case releasing her from indenture, was heralded as the beacon of liberty.[9] But Mary Clark's case occurred in 1821, more than twenty years after the Ordinance was enacted. The first case, if it existed, if it could be found, would also demonstrate how contemporaries of the Northwest Ordinance and the American Revolutionary War interpreted its provisions as a matter of first impression.

On one frosty day in December 2011, the very same day that my resourceful reference librarian received the final communiqué that we had emptied the last official pocket and the records were not available anywhere, I found everything that I was seeking. That day, legend and folklore took the definite shape of historical fact. I discovered authentic documents in the form of six signed, firsthand, eyewitness depositions, including the ultimate prize: a particularly detailed deposition by the enslaved man, Peter McNelly himself, the first slave suing for his freedom and for the freedom of his wife, Queen. The first redemption song.

The records were discovered where they would never have been expected. They were among the personal papers of a nineteenth-century man who knew their importance and had intended to write the history of these cases himself but never completed the task. The University of Chicago Library holds the William H. English Collection containing the record of Peter McNelly.[10] Even the records' provenance is a little vague about who William H. English was, other than that he was an influential Indiana politician.[11] Apparently, he had handpicked these valuable nuggets from the Indiana official repositories to write a book. He began the book but finished only the first chapters. William H. English never got to the middle, where he intended to discuss the slave cases that he had taken from Indiana.[12] The manuscript was never published. And the original records were never returned to the state. William H. English died in 1895, and his heirs held the records for almost thirty years before donating them to the University of Chicago in 1924. Yet, understood as a collection of research papers of an Indiana politician, their full importance for American history and the law of the frontier was never realized.[13]

There, in his papers, were the lost originals of the territory's earliest court cases, an early ledger of Judge George Turner, and the first slave's suit for freedom brought by a writ of habeas corpus. The English Collection contains the original territorial judge's account books, sent from Judge Turner, hearing cases at one place on the circuit, to Judge Symmes, somewhere else on the circuit; and there was the case of *Peter McNelly v. Henry Vanderburgh*, complete with six corroborating depositions of the circumstances that led Peter and Queen to claim freedom under the Northwest Ordinance of 1787 and details of the kidnapping that resulted immediately thereafter.[14]

Discovering Peter McNelly's identity led to more discoveries: Peter McNelly was not only the first freedom litigant under the Northwest Ordinance, he had also been a soldier in the Revolutionary War. Learning his identity led to a Revolutionary War pension file with additional information about the sweep of his life.[15]

Quality of the Story

As origins often contain the embryonic shape of events that take place thereafter, the story that follows is a microcosm of many elements that become the basic structure of slaves litigating for freedom in the St. Louis cases. St. Louis, the final frontier of slave suits, closed with the *Dred Scott* case in 1857. Almost every major theme of brutality, deceit, subjugation, greed, enforced subordination, family separation, racism, sexual predation and injustice that resonates in the 300 St. Louis freedom suits is present in the account of Peter and Queen McNelly, which took place in 1794. Although brought in free territory, rather than in a slave state, Peter's case reveals the basic structure of redemption songs, how freedom is sued for, what slaves asserted to attain their freedom, and what they risked.

Like the other lawsuits, Peter's story has some veiled beginnings that cannot be fully substantiated. Was Peter born a slave or a free black man? Did the lawsuit change his status or simply recognize it? Unlike some litigants, he never acknowledged ever legally being a slave. And unlike many other slaves, he had a last name. How did Peter and Queen make plans to leave Kentucky? Like other freedom suits, the story has an uncertain ending that tapers off somewhat unexpectedly and somewhat ominously. The story leaves loose ends: beginnings and endings that originate in mysteries and disappear in mysteries, but in the middle is an extraordinarily vivid account of an attempt to seek justice, a redemption song, and the territorial judge's attempt to do justice.

This case is remarkable for its completeness. There are several depositions and each deposition—written independently by a different deponent—corroborates exactly all the others' factual accounts. With five or six complementary accounts, there can be no doubt about the factual accuracy of the events. In many lawsuits, and particularly many contested freedom suits, litigants provide conflicting factual accounts, which require the reader to choose the most believable account from the contradictory testimony. Later freedom suits often contain denials by defendants that conflict with plaintiffs' stories. There are usually disputed facts and standard denials of participation in a kidnapping. Not so in the six depositions in this case file. All six tell essentially the identical story. People who were present at each juncture agreed about what was said and planned and took place. Each deposition is principally an eyewitness account rather than hearsay. The story that is revealed details Peter's struggle, first to get to court to sue for his freedom and then the conspiratorial efforts of five men to kidnap him and his wife in order to keep him from the judge. The conspiracy was organized and carried out under the direction of his putative master, Henry Vanderburgh, who was himself at the time a lawyer and a local authority, a sitting justice of the peace.

Although all the parties agree about what happened in the spring of 1794, there are two slightly differing stories, both recounted by Peter about his early days in Indiana, told three decades apart. Some differences can be explained by ordinary memory lapses. The mind adjusts the accounts of things remembered by knowledge that comes available later. But even more of the difference in Peter McNelly's own accounts is explainable by the very process of singing two different redemption songs of entitlement: one for his freedom, the other for his veteran's pension thirty years later.

What is included in each story depends on the entitlement that the petitioner is redeeming. Each was only a partial account because it was told for a different purpose. The first account, soon after his escape from the conspirators, sought to redeem his freedom and that of his wife. He did not mention that he had served in the Revolutionary War. The second story sought to redeem Peter's rightful claim to a war veteran's pension. He did not mention being kidnapped. As such, for Peter to attain each separate instrumental aim, he had to present a slightly different set of facts and pare others from the whole of his experience. This instrumentalism should be understood as the way that subordinate persons are required to speak about their lives.[16] In order to succeed, they may divulge only those facts pertinent to the redemption, not the more complicated reality. There is a political economy to the songs they sing. This is the paradox of subordinated peoples who tell their stories instrumentally in order to redeem different liberties at different times.

A fully free and independent person is also at liberty to disclose parts or the whole of his life, or even not to speak at all. The free person enjoys this luxury. Those who sing a redemption song, however, must sing those notes that are necessary to the redemption of the specific liberty sought at the time. With the passage of time, it is the modern listener's prerogative to listen through the song, to hear what is sung, and where the silences are and to listen for and consider what is behind the song—to hear, if possible, the human life transcendent.

The basic features of Peter's story, the first, are archetypal. Peter's story demonstrates how hard it sometimes was for an enslaved person to find justice on the frontier simply because it was difficult to locate a court of law. It also demonstrates how easy a group could be gathered to thwart a claim for freedom and how far such measures could be taken when unchecked by legal authority. Unpacked, this first case makes visible some contextual forces that are often only alluded to in the background of some of the St. Louis lawsuits. The corroborating witnesses appear more guileless than later witnesses, who testify with greater attention to possible personal liability. But first, listen to the story told chronologically by combining the corroborating depositions.

Peter knew his last name, sometimes spelled "McAnelly." He knew his birth year, 1758, which he learned from his parents, and where he was born, Louisa County, Virginia. He was once claimed as a slave of a planter, Anthony Thompson, in whose stead he was sent to be a soldier in the Revolutionary War.

Peter stated that he served for three months, returned home to Louisa County, and then re-enlisted for another tour of duty, remaining in the Continental army a total of nine months until Cornwallis surrendered.[17] He did not see battle; he described his war experience as basically being kept in almost constant motion, being marched from place to place.[18] After Cornwallis surrendered, he was discharged from the army and returned to Louisa County, where he remained until about 1790.[19] At some point, Peter McNelly took a wife, a black woman named Queen. They continued to be held in the thrall of Anthony Thompson, in whose stead Peter had served.[20]

Peter's freedom petition stated that he and Queen absconded sometime early in the autumn of 1793 and came into "the Territory Northwest of the Ohio River." Utilizing this terminology of place indicates how very early in the life of the territory this incident occurred. Just six years after the Northwest Ordinance was effected, there had not yet been a designation of this area as Indiana Territory; and Ohio, the first state to be cleaved from the territory, had not yet become a state.[21] The territory lacked adequate courts of law.

At the falls of the Wabash River, Peter and Queen were captured by Indians. Peter's pension application suggests that he was held by the Indians for as long as eight months. Several Indian tribes occupied the Ohio and Wabash River valleys, including the Miami and the Piankeshaw; and with several related tribes in control of the land,[22] two lone travelers, presumably on foot, at some distance from any settlement, would draw notice as they attempted to traverse the distance from Kentucky to Vincennes. No treaty had yet removed the area's indigenous residents.

Capture was a common response by Indian tribes to settler intrusion at the time. In this period in particular, there are many accounts of Indians taking captives. Much as Indians knew that there was value in recapturing a runaway horse, they would recognize that these two individuals held value if taken captive. While horses would have been of immediate use to the local tribes (and the Miami tribe even conducted raids upon settlements to acquire horses),[23] the tribes of this region had little use for domestic servants. Hence, the most profitable thing to do was to bring them back to settlement culture and swap them for something else of value.

The Indians took Peter and Queen to their gunsmith in Vincennes and traded them for two rifles and $10 worth of ammunition. Peter stated this.[24] He knew the price on their heads exactly. In the Revolutionary War petition, he explained how he lost his Continental Army discharge papers during his long captivity by the Indians. He never mentioned his wife in the veteran's petition. In that petition, Peter remembered the gunsmith warmly, with gratitude for his having used his influence and money to free Peter from the Indians.[25] Although the gunsmith may have become his friend in the intervening thirty years before Peter claimed his pension, the gunsmith had no reason to befriend him in buying him from the Indians. Acquiring Peter and Queen was a good trade; they were probably worth more than the two rifles and ammunition. Labor was so scarce in the Northwest Territory that the gunsmith could expect return on his investment.

The Vincennes gunsmith held Peter and Queen for about three weeks until a certain man named Smith, of Kentucky, appeared and claimed them, asserting that he had purchased them from their former master.[26] Accordingly, the gunsmith turned them over upon receiving payment.

Peter was then confined in the guardhouse of a small fort near Vincennes[27] until Smith had a chance to sell the McNellys. It took only one day. As servants, Peter and Queen had immediate usefulness to the frontier settlers. Smith announced to Peter that he had sold him and wife, as slaves, to Henry Vanderburgh, Esquire, of Vincennes. The transaction took place around October 1793.

Henry Vanderburgh had also been a Revolutionary War veteran from New York, although he did not regard Peter as a fellow soldier in the cause of freedom. Vanderburgh was a trained lawyer and must have known full well that the Northwest Ordinance banned slavery. Covert acts that he took later imply that he knew that slavery was prohibited by law. The details of that Ordinance had not yet been worked out. Vanderburgh showed no reluctance about buying the McNellys, though he later denied having done so, publicly claiming that he simply held them for an absent slave owner in Kentucky.[28]

Having been delivered over to Vanderburgh as property, Peter and Queen remained with him for the winter. The record reflects no resistance on the McNellys' part in going where they were assigned at this season. Wintering over with a master was not a consent to enslavement; it was a common circumstance for bound persons in anticipation of seeking freedom. Even if one is thinking of maintaining a claim for freedom eventually, better to work where one was placed over the winter in exchange for food and shelter. Peter and Queen had just experienced the consequence of setting off on their own into the wilderness, only to be seized by Indians and resold to new enslavers. There were not many prospects of improving one's situation over the winter.

One of the first territorial judges appointed by the federal government was George Turner.[29] Judge Turner's arrival to hear cases in Vincennes allowed Peter to seek justice: he sought freedom for himself and for his wife. The papers state, "[O]n the arrival last month, at Vincennes, of the subscribing Judge, he [Peter] applied to him for a Writ of Habeas Corpus [to establish] his and his . . . wife's claim to freedom—and received for answer, that the . . . writ should issue."[30]

Judge Turner's arrival in Vincennes was indeed the first time a federal territorial judge visited since the territory was organized. Only two appointed territorial judges rode the circuit over several hundred miles of unsettled lands that sprawled from the eastern Ohio border to the French villages on the Mississippi River and from the Ohio River north to Detroit on the Great Lakes. The territorial judges held court regularly only in three places, Cincinnati, Marietta, Detroit, and in any fourth unspecified place in the western counties that they could conveniently reach.[31] After 1790, Vincennes was added as a seat of court. Judges' visits were especially noted for their infrequency.[32] Although appointed in 1791, Judge Turner had remained east, attending to his private affairs through 1793. When he finally arrived in Vincennes in the spring of 1794, there was finally someone with authority to redeem the promise of the Northwest Ordinance. This lack of courts to enforce the law was a problem in several remote places where slaves were held contrary to law. In cases like Peter's, it also explained some of the delay of enslaved persons filing suit. But once Judge Turner heard the petition he quickly rendered the habeas corpus in Peter's favor. Awaiting further trial, Peter and Queen remained with Vanderburgh.

Peter's decision to file for his freedom set in motion a conspiracy to thwart his suit by kidnapping the McNellys and removing them from the court's reach. The conspiracy was organized by Henry Vanderburgh, the master who purchased Peter and Queen from the guardhouse at the fort. As one of the territory's few lawyers, and probably one of few men literate in English, Vanderburgh had been tapped to be probate court judge and a justice of the peace. Vanderburgh now made frequent overtures to Peter toward a legal accommodation. He wanted Peter and Queen to become bound to him for a term of years. Peter consistently declined these overtures.[33]

After filing with the court, on May 27, 1794, Peter was sent by his master Vanderburgh some distance away from the household with a carpenter on the pretext of retrieving a load of clay. Thus began the trap for the kidnapping of Peter and Queen and their forcible removal, presumably for sale elsewhere, if they refused Vanderburgh's continuing pressure to indenture themselves to him.

Vanderburgh had contacted two prominent merchants in Vincennes, men of local importance, to arrange and carry out the kidnapping. Toussaint Dubois was a fur trader in partnership with French fur trade merchants in Vincennes, Detroit, Kaskaskia, and St. Louis. He traveled frequently. As a courier, he carried messages and occasionally transported slaves west to sell to other masters.[34] The other man, Joseph Baird, was the brother of a minor court official and assumed his brother's role during his absence. Both these men were established and respected in the community, and they then contracted others to provide the muscle.

Vanderburgh contacted Baird and Dubois together, asking them to arrange to forcibly kidnap Peter and Queen *because* they had applied to the territorial judge for their freedom.[35] Not only did Peter make this claim, but it was exactly the way that both Baird and Dubois explained their participation in the mission. Lawyer Henry Vanderburgh carefully said the least that implicated himself in the kidnapping scheme, but with four eyewitnesses and no denial by Vanderburgh, the story holds up very well.

Vanderburgh assured Baird that he would be held harmless for his participation in the kidnapping. "No proof would be made of his having purchased the...Negroes." Vanderburgh also reassured Baird's doubts. "Do not be uneasy: I will make you secure."[36] A third man, Nathaniel Ewing, who was also present at the trading house when the plan was proposed, agreed to join in. Baird and Dubois were offered $100 to accomplish the deed, and Dubois engaged three more persons to assist them in it. The fur trader Dubois dealt with many lesser fur traders, so he easily tapped three of the retainers who worked for him: Henri Renbeau, Jean Baptiste Constant Jr., and an Indian from the Piankeshaw nation, to do the unpleasant work. Their payment was negotiated in advance.[37] The depositions were quite explicit about the division of payment that Vanderburgh provided for kidnapping the McNellys, guarding them, and transporting them beyond the court's reach.

Even with five able-bodied men involved and Henry Vanderburgh's continuing ability to direct the day-to-day duties of Peter and Queen as servants, the conspiracy continued to expand. Dubois ordered another store clerk in his employ, Joseph LaMotte, to assist Baird in whatever was necessary.[38]

The plan initially separated Peter from Queen and took each captive separately. Peter went along with the carpenter, traveling with a horse and cart into a prairie. The carpenter's participation was part of the ruse to get Peter away from the house. On the way, "there suddenly appeared in view three persons": Baird, LaMotte, and Nathaniel Ewing. The three men seized Peter, bound his arms with rope, and, since Peter was unwilling to accompany them, the men tied the rope fast to the tail of Baird's horse. They then dragged Peter forward into the woods—telling him, in Peter's words "exultingly and sneeringly, that he must now go before the Judge."[39] The carpenter was then sent home.

Once captors and captive arrived in the woods, in a place under some cover, Peter was disengaged from the horse's tail, though his arms remained bound. Baird mounted the horse and left, leaving Peter guarded by the others. After an hour, Baird returned on foot accompanied by Renbeau, leading Baird's horse, and on which Peter's wife, Queen, was mounted. She had been forcibly seized outside the Vanderburgh house.[40] Queen had put up quite a fuss about the matter.

In the intervening hour, Vanderburgh had visited Dubois's home and drawn him out to take a walk to put the plans in motion. On the walk, the conspiracy continued to grow. The two encountered Abner Prior and included him in the impending task of luring Queen away from Vanderburgh's house. Vanderburgh, Dubois, and Prior got Queen to leave the house peacefully. The three walked Queen away from the house. Vanderburgh accompanied them for some distance and then left, ordering Queen to go on with the others. It was then that Dubois told Queen that he was taking her to the River Du Chi, at which she expressed "great unwillingness." Notwithstanding, he was able to place her on his own horse and set out.[41] At some distance from town, Prior turned back while the others proceeded. Both acts of segregating Peter and segregating Queen were supported simply by the presence of additional men, who were socially friendly with the kidnappers but not actively involved in manhandling the victims. Once the group of men succeeded in isolating the victim from the settled area, the additional men simply peeled off, as they were no longer needed. The involve-ment of these extras was perhaps insufficient to be charged with kidnapping, yet their presence prevented the captive's escape.

Upon meeting with Baird in the woods, Dubois delivered over the woman, saying, "There is the girl"; "do what you please with her"; and then he left.[42] "Do what you please with her," when spoken while turning over possession of a cap-tive woman into a larger group of hostile men, is provocative language indeed. There is no evidence the men acted upon the language, but it implies that the boss gave his permission for debauchery.

According to plan, Peter and Queen were taken twelve miles from Vincennes to a house in a stockade outpost called White River Station. There they could be sequestered while the court was in session the following day. By being absent when called, Peter would find his case passed over, or even dismissed.

Dubois's three henchmen brought Peter and Queen to the stockade. Peter was then bound in cords and Queen tied to a chair. The owner of the house, Moses Decker, untied her soon afterward. Decker had his own black servant woman whom Queen could probably help with the housework.

A new attempt was made to force Peter and Queen to sign legal documents binding them to serve Vanderburgh for a term of years. Vanderburgh was per-sistent in attempting to legalize his control of them. The carpenter arrived with a paper sent from Vanderburgh drawn up to indenture them for five and a half more years. They were offered nothing in exchange but a counter-threat.[43] Peter was told that if they did not sign, Vanderburgh had a boat ready to take them to New Orleans for sale. The McNellys had no choice but to put an "X" to the paper.[44] Dutton and Baird then quickly mounted horses and returned to Vin-cennes with the signed indentures.

Vanderburgh had also sent warning that Judge Turner might visit White River Station. So the three henchmen were ordered to take Peter and Queen farther away, across the White River, and to stand guard over them until fur-ther notice.[45] On the opposite bank of the river, "they bound Peter to one tree, and his wife to another, [where] they remained from . . . noon till about one o' clock in the afternoon of the next day—a prey to the tormenting musketoes [sic], which during this period were so insupportable that he [Peter] often-times begged his oppressors to kill him, and put him out of pain."[46]

Consider his predicament. The preceding day, Peter had suffered severe emotional torment from deceit, abuse, and captivity, and he witnessed the forced capture of his wife. Yet it was prolonged exposure to the elements and to the insects while immobilized that prompted him to request death rather than life. Particularly in wilderness situations, immobilizing an individual and leaving them exposed and unsheltered was torture enough to move someone to the breaking point of requesting death.

After some time, the party returned to the stockade still holding Peter and his wife as prisoners. "Baird, Renbeau, and Constant alternately act[ed] during their duresse, as centinels [*sic*] over them by night and day."[47] At Vincennes, Vanderburgh was sufficiently concerned that Peter might escape that he ordered Baird to fetch a pair of handcuffs and return to see that Peter was manacled. Vanderburgh ordered them held prisoners until he came himself or sent someone.

Peter remained handcuffed until midnight of June 6, when, disengaging one of his hands, he was able to make his escape. He climbed through the roof of Decker's house, got outside the stockade and walked the twelve miles back to Vincennes. The next morning he presented himself before Judge Turner.

Although Peter had to leave Queen behind in order to make his escape, his departure left her even more vulnerable. A traveler who was at the station took an interest in buying Queen. On the morning after Peter's escape, as Baird prepared to set out for Vincennes to tell Vanderburgh, "Richard Levins of Jefferson County, Kentucky" told Baird he would purchase Queen if he and Vanderburgh could agree upon her price.[48] Levins accompanied Baird "to treat" (meaning "to deal") with Vanderburgh in person at Vincennes. Vanderburgh met them, again covertly at Dubois's home, and again went outside to negotiate Queen's sale.[49] Upon purchasing Queen, Levins returned to the stockade late the next night, after the residents were asleep. Queen was sleeping next to Moses Decker's black servant woman. Levins took Queen away. The next morning, when Queen was found missing, "the other wench" disclosed that "Dick Levins took her away in the night." Levins was thought to be traveling toward Green River along Pigeon Creek. This is where Queen's story ends. We don't know whether Peter ever saw her again.

Shortly after Peter reappeared in Vincennes, Judge Turner declared them both free.

Rather than return Peter to Vanderburgh, it seems that Judge Turner offered Peter the protection of his own lodgings. Some efforts were taken to bring Queen back. Judge Turner directed a habeas corpus to Vanderburgh, ordering him to produce her. Peter McNelly requested that two additional charges be filed against the conspirators. He pressed a case against them for his own false imprisonment and for "man-stealing his wife."[50] When Vanderburgh refused to produce Queen, Judge Turner jailed him.

What happened after Peter got to court is a common pattern in other freedom suits: white men continued to battle each other. The judge's continued recognition of Peter's right to freedom led to an increasingly broadened set of vendettas between the judge and Vanderburgh. In many freedom cases, after the decree, the liberated slave litigants are forgotten—as long as they keep their heads down—and the fight ensues on other grounds among the white men who had

The handwritten flyleaf of Judge Turner's notes reads as follows:

McNelly & Wife v. Vanderburgh} Hab:Cor:ad pub;

Vanderburgh committed on refusing to produce Queen the wife, on to enter into recognizt[*sic*] for that purpose

Same v. Same: Writ of false imprisonment Dam: 3000 dols

Witnesses: Joe: LaMotte; Moses Decker—; Joseph Baird; Toussaint DuBois; Henry Renbeau; Jean B. Comptant Jr.; Abner Prior

All except Prior & Renbeau recognized to give evidence in action below – viz:

U.S. v. Same: Manstealing of P. McNelly & wife

McNally to prosecute 500 dol.

Witnesses above

Decker; Baird; DuBois; Constant 200 dol each Eact to be of the good behavior to term

U.S. v. H. Rambeau} aid of abetting in the manstealing above.

Recognzt Reambeau to be of the good behavior to stand trial next Col 500 dol

Sureties for above purpose} J.B. Constant & Diometre Payyette }each in 250

The above witnesses

been adversarial, though not necessarily opposing parties, in the lawsuit. This second round of litigation attempts to adjust the social, and perhaps financial, balance sheets among the free white men who won and lost in the preceding round. Owners who lost control of their slaves seek others to hold liable for their losses. Losing parties accuse the judge.

The vendettas escalated as Judge Turner promptly reported the situation to the territorial governor: "[C]ertain persons here have lately been guilty of a violent outrage against the laws. They were employed by Vanderburgh to seize and forcibly carry away two negroes, a man and his wife, who are free by the Constitution of the Territory...."[51] Turner also noted, "The outrage was accompanied with some acts of cruelty toward the unfortunate blacks."[52]

"I have caused several of the offenders to be apprehended, but others of them were encouraged by Vanderburgh to resist...and in one instance, this was actually done by drawing a knife upon the sheriff.....[T]he offenders...have since surrendered themselves, and, full of contrition for their misconduct, have amply exposed the machinations of Judge Vanderburgh in this nefarious business.... There is reason to believe that [Abner] Prior was privy to and aiding, in this transaction."[53]

Indeed, Turner was correct that some participants were contrite. One wonders, though, whether they would have been sorry had they not been caught. Baird expressed being "sorry for the part he took, but that he was deluded and seduced to the measure by the fair speeches of and assurances of support and other encouragement from...Vanderburgh."[54] Joseph LaMotte, upon being told that he had done something wrong, said, "Yes, Sir, but I was ordered upon it, and should not of myself have undertaken it."[55] But Toussaint Dubois reacted defiantly and, clapping his hand on his left breast, exclaimed, "Twas I that sent 'im, Sir."[56] No wonder all the major negotiations in the matter took place at Toussaint Dubois's home. He continued unrepentant, and later evidence shows he continued to transport slaves across Indiana to Illinois.[57]

As Turner correctly targeted Vanderburgh as the perpetrator, he announced to Governor St. Clair that he planned to "impeach Vanderburgh before the Territorial Legislature," because he had not "repented." Judge Turner wished to act, lest he "try to elude the punishment that may await him in case of conviction...."[58]

Judge Turner received no support from the territorial governor for his plan, however. Governor St. Clair refused to back him up. By return post, St. Clair sent the judge a letter announcing his own position regarding slavery in the Northwest Territory, a position that would form the basis for new generations of "French slaves" to continue to be held enslaved in the Northwest Territory.[59] (These slaves' redemption story is taken up in chapter 6).

Governor St. Clair wrote, "[T]he affair of the slaves is, I am afraid, a source of discontent that will not very soon be stopped. Permit me, sir, to offer you my opinion upon the subject,...that the declaration in our Constitution, that there shall be no slavery nor involuntary servitude in the Territory, applies to, and can be taken advantage of only by, those slaves who may have been imported since the establishment of that Constitution."[60] (Notably, both Judge Turner and Governor St. Clair described the Northwest Ordinance as a "Constitution.")

Did Governor St. Clair think that the Ordinance applied to Peter McNelly or not? Peter's circumstances do not match the governor's conditions. Because Peter entered the territory after 1787, he was not a slave held before the enactment so as to remain so; nor was Peter held by those French residents whom Governor St. Clair sought to appease. The French residents had argued that the Northwest Ordinance not be applied retroactively to require them to forfeit their property rights.[61] Peter and Queen were not imported: they entered the territory of their own volition. Governor St. Clair should have supported Judge Turner in every instance. Did the Vincennes-based sale to Vanderburgh violate the Northwest Ordinance? St. Clair again waffled.

> Slavery was established in that country when it was under the dominion of France. It was continued [under] Great Britain; and, again, under Virginia,...until [ceded] to Congress...there is also a clause in that cession about continuing to the ancient settlers, and those who had settled under Virginia, the benefit of their ancient laws and customs....Slaves were

then a property acquired by the inhabitants conformably to law, and they were to be protected in the possession of that property. If so, they are still to be protected in it.[62]

So far, St. Clair had assessed the situation of persons long held in slavery by the earlier French residents, but that analysis simply did not apply to Peter and Queen, or Vanderburgh who was from New York. That analysis spoke only to the political pressure on St. Clair from the numerous French residents, whom he had to govern and who might resist his authority.

> [It] must be construed to intend that, from and after the publication of the said Constitution, slaves imported into that Territory should immediately become free; and by this construction no injury is done to any person, because it is a matter of public notoriety, and any person removing into that Colony and bringing with him persons who were slaves in another country, does it at the known risk of their claiming their freedom.[63]

St. Clair then highlighted the political pressure animating his decision. "I have troubled you with my thoughts..., because I have heard that there is great agitation among the people respecting it; and they should be set at rest, because it was formerly brought before me by some of these people to whom I gave my opinion nearly as I have now stated it to you."[64]

Indeed, St. Clair had assured the territory's French inhabitants that their slaveholding was not affected by the ban on slavery precisely because their slaveholding preceded the Ordinance. St. Clair agreed with them that applying the ban to them would be illegal as an *ex post facto* taking of their property.[65]

Without the backing of the territory's chief executive, Judge Turner was vulnerable. The enslavers turned their enmity on the judge who had redeemed Peter's entitlement to freedom. The white men fell out further among themselves.

Upon hearing that Peter was protected in Judge Turner's lodgings, Abner Prior called the judge "a N——judge" within earshot of others, and Judge Turner then sued him for slander. Judge Turner also accused Prior of other misdeeds, such as selling liquor to the Indians. Both Prior and Judge Turner dug in and escalated their conflict. A tirade of angry letters and insults ensued.[66]

Vanderburgh charged Judge Turner with misfeasance in office. Vanderburgh turned the tables on Judge Turner, attempting to get *him* impeached. Vanderburgh spread rumors around Vincennes that the judge had protected Peter so that he could have a servant himself.[67] This seems entirely unlikely.

A habeas corpus sent to Vanderburgh to bring Queen before the court was finally returned by the sheriff. "Queen is not forthcoming."[68] Judge Turner continued to jail Vanderburgh for contempt.

Only the unrepentant French trader, Toussaint Dubois was not targeted by the judge. Perhaps the judge, unlike the governor, saw American settlers as the primary subject of governance or reform. Or perhaps Judge Turner had his hands full with the embattlements on all sides and no support from the governor. Judge Turner's time in office was eventually undermined by French residents as well as by Vanderburgh. When the judge later visited Kaskaskia and Cahokia on his circuit, he angered the residents there by requiring court to be held at one site "where convenient" rather than stretching his circuit and travel yet further, to visit all the villages where the French residents had been accustomed to having court held under the *Ancienne Regime*.[69]

In the end, the escalation of accusation and counter-accusation completely masked the original claim, the freedom suit that lay at the heart of the animosity. Judge Turner, who upheld the meaning of the Northwest Ordinance as emancipatory, was forced to resign under the shadow of congressional impeachment. The impeachment was fostered by Vanderburgh and tacitly supported by Governor St. Clair. The House of Representatives received a report from the attorney general charging Turner with demanding bribes and levying fines without trial.[70] The following year, Judge Turner modestly requested that any hearing on the allegations be conducted while he was in town so he could respond. Congress denied even this modest request, and Judge Turner simply resigned during the winter of 1797–1798 rather than endure the impeachment proceedings held in his absence. Turner returned to Philadelphia.

Vanderburgh remained in the Knox County jail for some time, apparently increasing his prestige with his neighbors. Judge Symmes freed Vanderburgh from contempt for failure to produce Queen, and Vanderburgh quietly slid into political power and higher judicial office, unscathed by the brutal conspiracy that he had perpetrated upon Peter and Queen. With consummate nerve, Vanderburgh went after Peter McNelly the following year, this time succeeding in getting him to indenture himself for five years for a payment of $250. Without Judge Turner to turn to, this second document indenturing Peter was probably accomplished by coercion. There was no mention of Queen at all.

All later evidence suggests that Peter remained in Vincennes,[71] and there is some indication that Queen may have rejoined him, or, if not, that Peter later found another wife. Entries for later censuses show Peter "McNeely" as the head of a household in which a black woman resided, who was roughly his same age.[72] But in his Revolutionary War petition, as he is redeeming his pension for war service, he made no mention at all of Queen, or his freedom suit, or his kidnapping and torment by Vanderburgh's men. By 1840, with his freedom secured, he had a different promise to redeem. Disclosing those sensational facts would only complicate the Revolutionary War veteran story. A redemption song must be performed with the economy of effort and not generate additional resistance.

After the War of 1812, most of the principal conspirators against Peter and Queen had become heroes of the new war against the Indians and the British, or they had died. Vanderburgh and Dubois had counties named after them.[73] Peter McNelly still lived in Vincennes, and he was recognized in the census of 1840 as a Revolutionary War veteran. What did happen to Queen?

CHAPTER 3

The Three Daughters of Marie Scypion

All men talk of liberty, but the savages alone possess it.
—Missouri Supreme Court Judge Tompkins, in *Marguerite v. Chouteau* (1828)

Most people, and certainly most important historical figures, have pedigrees. A person's pedigree, the identity of their parents and grandparents gives them a certain social capital, opportunities, inheritance, and connections. Rather than a pedigree, an enslaved person had the kind of provenance that property has, a chain of title. Not only did legal title bind the slave to the master—the master owned the slave—it bound subsequent masters to respect each other's property rights. The judgment of liberation under Missouri law was absolute; it broke all links of the chain of title. When a slave was declared free by the court, the decree included freedom from "all claiming from, through or under the defendant."[1] This language came directly from the Missouri statute that provided the means by which slaves could sue for freedom and it set the terms of the judgment of liberation.

In a chain of title created to pass ownership from one master to the next, each link in a chain is conditioned and qualified by the means deemed legitimate to legally transfer title. Whether a property transfer is valid depends on the sovereign's rules. Property must be recognized as such by the sovereign in order to be property. And when sovereignty changes, so too does the possibility that some means of transfer in a chain of title will no longer be recognized by the new sovereign government.

For slave petitioners in free states, asserting freedom was a relatively easy assertion of the here and now. There they simply asserted that they were enslaved by someone, and sought release. Freedom was presumed in free states, so a simple writ of habeas corpus could do the trick. In slave states, like Missouri, asserting freedom was much more difficult. Missouri recognized slavery, and its law presumed that persons of color were slaves.[2] Slave petitioners had to know the details of their chain of title in order to prevail. Knowing the times and places of one's ownership and how that ownership changed from one master to another were factors that could militate either for or against success. Most important, one had to name the appropriate defendant in order to break the chain of title completely and secure a judgment of total liberation.

This presented a practical difficulty. Almost all slave litigants in St. Louis were illiterate.[3] Thus, slave litigants needed to rely on memory because they could not record their own past, or even the correct spelling of their owners' names. Yet they had to be able to remember and recite the story of their origins—their chain of title—in order to select the right target against whom to establish and redeem their freedom. For those who had been owned and controlled for a long time by a single master, the target for suit was obvious. But often the frontier slave was handed off from one household to another as necessary. Sometimes a slave was assigned to different households within an extended family, or hired out as needed, residing at different locations on the frontier under different sovereign's laws. Then it was far less obvious who was the slave's true master and the proper defendant to name in the suit. Also, when a slave master died, there was almost always some uncertainty about who inherited the slave, and who would become the next owner and link in the chain of title and, hence, the proper party to sue for freedom.

In the case of Marie Scypion's daughters, the chains of title were as entangled and attenuated as any chain imaginable, although she and her daughters lived within a limited sixty-mile radius their entire lives. One tangle was changes of sovereigns over the area. The sovereignty of the area changed over them, like successive waves washing over the soil. These sovereignty changes occurred, of course, without consent of the area residents. Their masters, powerful over their slaves, were colonials, and the big decisions of sovereignty were not made democratically or even locally: they were made in the capitals of Europe by treaty.

Another tangle was that members of the Scypion family were subject to control by so many different owners over their lifetimes. Ownership claims were conditional upon dozens of potentially legal or potentially invalid transfers, each depending upon the property rules of changing sovereigns. In their family's cases, the puzzle of their chain of title reached perhaps the greatest degree of legal complexity.

The legal complexity was also an obstacle for the feuding members of the extended family that claimed the Scypions as slaves. For decades before the three Scypion sisters staked claims for their freedom, various members of the extended Tayon family battled one another and outsiders for control of the Scypions. These skirmishes added further layers to the accumulated pattern of successive transfers, domestic placements, gifts, loans, hiring out, bequests, marriages, French prenuptial marriage contracts, deaths, wills, and even in this devout Catholic family, a marriage separation. Marie Scypion's chain of title was tangled and confused, and, consequently, so were her daughters', and the chains that continued to bind their children. But ultimately, after these many transfers had been litigated for decades, none of those transactions mattered. What would matter—the one factor that cut through all the many transactions—was more akin to a pedigree. It was their bloodline, their maternal ancestry. Marie Scypion's three daughters could trace her maternal line back to an Indian woman. After four decades of dispute, that conclusively made them free.

The Scypion sisters' maternal grandmother, a woman named Mariette, was a member of the Natchez tribe. The significant *legal* moment that determined their fates occurred well before Marie Scypion was born. In 1769, when the Spanish controlled the region, a colonial governor issued a decree that banned Indian slavery. And long afterward, by the received Anglo-American tradition, once slaves became free, they were forever free, as were their descendants.

This next redemption song spanning three generations is the account of Marie Scypion's three daughters and their children, all descendants of a Natchez Indian woman. This redemption song is confusing, almost chaotic, because of the series of attempts by the Tayon family members to lay claim to the Scypions. This dispute is the earliest of its kind on record in St. Louis. It began even before the Louisiana Purchase, but it was not resolved until ten years after Missouri had become a state.

As early as the 1700s, the French settlers had routinely enslaved Indians, and they had periodically imported large numbers of African slaves through the port of New Orleans and up the Mississippi River to serve them in the first European settlements in the valley. Thus, in the middle ground of Illinois country, French settlers held African as well as Indian slaves.[4] And for generations, African and Indian slaves intermarried and had children, like Marie Scypion.

Marie Scypion's mother, Mariette, was Natchez. The Natchez once lived in the Mississippi River valley near what is now Natchez, Mississippi. The tribe was conquered by the French moving up the Mississippi valley in three wars in the early 1700s.[5] Mariette was on the losing side of the wars of conquest. She may have come to the French settlement seized as a slave by virtue of French victories in those wars, or as a refugee to the settlement when her tribe was destroyed. The Missouri Supreme Court later described her situation chillingly: "[S]he was of the Natchez nation and made a prisoner by the French in the war which terminated in the extinction of that nation."[6] Mariette then survived as an enslaved servant. Enslavement was her means of survival. She lived at Fort Chartres, a tiny fortified French settlement on the east bank of the river, across from present-day St. Louis before that city was founded.[7]

Indian slave Mariette and African slave Scypion had at least three children. Their daughter Marie-Jean Scypion was said to belong to the village priest, and through gifts to cousins she was given to the priest's niece,[8] a young woman who married Joseph Tayon. Belonging to the village priest may or may not have meant legal ownership in the Illinois country. But it did mean that the village priest had the authority to direct where Marie Scypion worked if she wished to survive.

In Illinois country, it was not uncommon for slave marriages to pair Indian slave women with African slave men. There were more subordinated Indian women "sauvagesses" than Indian men in these settlements.[9] Yet, this pairing of black fathers and Indian mothers had legal consequence. Since a child's status followed the rule of matrilineality, having an Indian slave mother made all the difference in the world.[10] Under the rule of matrilineality, the mother's status, whether free or slave, determined the child's status; the father's was irrelevant.

Fort Chartres disbanded in 1765, and most community members moved to the higher ground on the river's west bank to found St. Louis.[11] LaClede and his stepson Chouteau led the migration. Joseph Tayon's family followed, taking along the part-Indian, part-African girl Marie-Jean Scypion. Tayon's association with the Chouteaus would be close and lifelong, an association that would influence the fate of Marie Scypion's daughters. As the town miller, Joseph Tayon was very important to the new settlement. He dammed the water source to create a pond and built the community's first mill. He later sold the pond and grist mill to the Chouteaus, and in time, even the pond became known as Chouteaus' pond.[12] Yet decades later, Joseph Tayon would still be remembered by toasts raised to him as the man who built the first St. Louis mill at a time when milled flour was in short supply.[13] The Chouteaus would be embroiled in resisting slaves' redemption songs for the next century,[14] influencing even the Dred Scott case.[15]

Auguste Chouteau laid out the town in a grid of streets running along the river bank. St. Louis also built a fortification, much as all French forts had. Old Joseph Tayon lived just a block from the Chouteaus. With his social standing in the community, he was chosen to be one of the city's syndics, or village overseers.

Five years after St. Louis was founded, the colonial governor issued a decree that would give the Scypion family their claim to freedom. In 1769, the new Spanish governor, Alejandro O'Reilly from New Orleans, decreed an end to the practice of enslaving Native Americans.[16] Seeking more peaceful relations with Indian tribes, the decree angered the many settlers, who had grown accustomed to depending upon their Indian slaves. In the Illinois County, there were said to be more Indian slaves than African slaves.[17] Since the decree had no immediate enforcement, those settlers with Indian slaves interpreted it in different ways, according to their liking. Some thought that it meant that Indian slaves were immediately free, while others thought that it would take effect only in the next generation, and still others thought that Indian slaves would become free only upon their master's deaths. In short, Governor O'Reilly declared an end to Indian slavery, but he did not prescribe a means of enforcement, how soon the institution should end, or what means of transfer of Indian slaves from master to master were forbidden. There was some community consensus that Indian slaves could not be sold from owner to owner. As with the early Northwest Ordinance prohibition, under a prohibition but without enforcement, old patterns of behavior could persist without scrutiny. Residents easily retained persons in slavery because, without effective administration or judicial processes, there was nowhere for wrongfully enslaved persons to turn.

Marie Scypion, like many Indian slaves, simply remained in her situation. A year later, in 1770, the local lieutenant governor completed an enumeration of Indian slaves in St. Louis, the newly Spanish seat of government.[18] There, in the household of Joseph Taillon, were four Indian slaves, seemingly comprising two separate families, a woman named Marie-Louise, baptized and age thirty-five, her two unnamed sons, ages thirteen and eleven, and an eleven-year-old girl, Marie-Rose, also a baptized "savage" girl, who cost her owner "400 livres in silver." The implication is that this girl was not Marie-Rose's child, but was purchased separately. (Scypion was not listed in the census enumerating Native American slaves since he was African.) The 1770 St. Louis census listed 69 Indian slaves in a total population of roughly 500 persons, more than 10 percent of the population.[19] Twenty years later, St. Louis had doubled to 1,000 persons. The population was roughly two-thirds free white and one-third enslaved.[20] Census takers no longer noted who was of Indian origin.

Though Marie Scypion remained with the Tayon family, it appears that she retained a committed belief that she was free, a belief that must have been conveyed to her children. Remaining in place seems to have been a purposeful means of survival, given her options. If one fled, one encountered an uncertain future. If one remained in the community, whether free or not, persons without means were assigned to do work for persons of means in order to maintain their existence.

Marie-Jean Scypion had three daughters: Catiche, Celeste, and Marguerite, born within the Tayon household. Catiche was the oldest, born when Marie Scypion was barely thirteen, and Marguerite, nicknamed, Sourie or little Mouse was the youngest. Their fathers are unknown, perhaps the same man or different men, perhaps the master or other men in the household or community. Celeste was referred to as a mulatto.[21]

In the custom of French colonial slaveholding, as each Scypion daughter grew old enough to be separated from her mother, seven or eight years old, she was assigned away to be a servant for one of the master's several children, as they married and formed their own households. Celeste was given to Helene Tayon Chevalier, Catiche to Marie-Louise Tayon Chauvin, and Marguerite to son Francois Tayon.[22] The Tayons had several older married children, too, but these younger three of Tayons' eight children formed households at the right time to receive Marie-Jean Scypion's daughters as domestic servants.[23]

These customary casual assignments of slave children to the master's children created some legal confusion.[24] Was the assignment a loan or a gift? Once a slave child moved into the newly formed household, it was no longer clear who owned her. Was Celeste now the property of Helene Tayon Chevalier, or was she there only on loan? The slave children changed hands without designating formal transfers in the chain of title. This placement, which began informally, evolved into a full dress legal battle. Tayon family members and their Chouteau relatives litigated this very issue over the lives of the Scypion sisters for decades before the Scypions litigated their lineage on their own behalf.

Although the Tayon sisters, Helene and Marie-Louise, appear to have regarded the Scypion sisters as entitled to freedom, the older generation, specifically, their father and his cronies, did not. Not only did old Joseph Tayon continue to insist that the Scypions were slaves, he insisted that they were *his* slaves. He listed them in his household inventory. When his wife died, he insisted that she had no legal authority to give them away to their children. In essence, he maintained that the Scypion sisters were only on loan to his adult children's household, that he was their owner.

Joseph Tayon's claims made at his wife's death in 1799 undermined the stability of Celeste and Catiche in the homes in which they had grown up. Sisters Celeste and Catiche had grown accustomed to the respective households of Tayon's daughters, where they had been servants since childhood. By then, both Celeste and Catiche had borne children of their own. Both of their mistresses, Helene Chevalier and Marie-Louise Chauvin, not only favored their servants' freedom, they also appear to have shown interest in their well-being. They sought doctors for the servants when they were ill. They stood as godmothers in the baptisms of their servants' children, and they saw to proper Catholic burials when necessary.[25] This was more respectful treatment than the Chouteaus usually accorded their slaves.[26]

At his wife's death, Joseph Tayon, now eighty-five years old, decided to disband his own household and go to live in the home of Pierre Chouteau Sr.[27] He said that since his wife's death, he "could no longer manage his affairs competently."[28] This decision shows how essential the mistress was in maintaining a household, even when that household had the labor of domestic slaves. Still, even with slaves at his disposal, Joseph Tayon preferred to move to another established household. In breaking up housekeeping, Joseph Tayon proposed to divide his own estate among his eight children. To do this, he petitioned the proper authority, commandant of the region, to allow him to accomplish the distribution. During this time of colonial governance, the local law was a mixture of customs and practices that had taken root under the French and the newer gloss of rules during Spanish sovereignty. Under colonial law, a petition to the governor was simply that: a request for an executive order. What validity that property division would have when the administration changed would have to wait to be determined by the next colonial governor or the next sovereign regime. It might hold fast, or it could be undone by a later regime. The territory did not come under U.S. sovereignty until 1803, three years later.

It is noteworthy that Joseph Tayon, the widowed family patriarch, chose to move in with the Chouteaus, rather than one of his daughters. Pierre Chouteau Sr. had married Tayon's granddaughter, though she had already died. Chouteau's second wife now ran the household and raised her husband's four young children. Pierre Chouteau's household was a different household order. Tayon's choice may have been a matter of a more accommodating house with Chouteau's growing wealth and importance in St. Louis,[29] or a matter of compatibility. Tayon seemed to get along better with Chouteau, than he did with his own younger children with whom he persistently fought over the ownership of the Scypions.[30]

When Helene's husband Chevalier died, about the same time, she moved her household to the smaller village of St. Charles on the Missouri River, about 25 miles away, taking along Celeste Scypion and her children.[31] The widow Helene was childless and much younger than her husband, but she did not remarry, as many widows did. She had sufficient wealth on which to live, a Spanish land grant that her husband had been given. Her brother Charles was the head man in St. Charles. He and her husband had long been close friends and fellow militia members.[32] Charles may even have arranged their marriage.

In gathering his assets to divide his estate, Joseph Tayon took one step too far. He attempted to sell the Scypions. The governor's edict forbade sale of Indian slaves. The colony's new governor, replacing son Charles, discouraged old Joseph Tayon from his proposed sales. Not only did Tayon face official resistance, but his two daughters, Helene and Marie-Louise, stepped forward to insist that the Scypions could not be sold. They were *servants*—just that—servants, rather than slaves. They argued alternatively that even if the Scypions were not free, then Celeste and Catiche were given to them by their mother and hence were not their father's to sell. The mistresses actually moved the court to declare their servants, Celeste and Catiche, free.[33] It's not clear that there was ever any legal ruling on this.

In the initial family dust-up, it appears that the old man backed down, and the Scypion sisters remained where they were, but the elderly servant Marie-Jean Scypion and one daughter, Marguerite, moved to Chouteau's mansion along with Joseph Tayon.

With the freedom issue raised, other Chouteaus grew concerned about the dispute. The extended Chouteau family still held several Indian slaves in service.[34] Freedom for Celeste and Catiche could potentially upset several Chouteau servant relationships. Auguste Chouteau, the town's founder, confronted Marie-Louise Chauvin one day, asking whether there was talk of freedom among the slaves. Learning that there was, Auguste Chouteau punished his own slaves, having them tied and whipped until the discussion stopped. He later bragged of this success.[35] (The beatings were followed by a mysterious allegation that a Chouteau servant woman attempted to set the house on fire.)

This flare-up in 1802 was the first of three decades of skirmishes among members of the Tayon–Chouteau family over the Scypion family and five decades of Chouteau resistance to freedom suits. Chouteau masters engaged in successive waves of suppression when angered by their slaves' petitions for freedom. As different masters claimed control of the Scypion family, it can to be expected that the Scypions were roughed up. Dominance was effected by threat and physical control. Their bodies were the subjected to capture by competing claimants. Sheriffs, deputies, and others, acting at different times under different orders, physically seized Scypion family members time and again. They were detained in holding facilities, such as cellars and jails, while the litigation between contending masters continued.

The elderly Marie Scypion died in 1802, always maintaining her right to freedom. In her final illness, she was removed from the Chouteau household to Madame Chauvin's home, near St. Charles, where she was cared for by eldest daughter Catiche and given a respectful Catholic burial.[36] It was then up to her three daughters to take turns in litigating for freedom.

Joseph Tayon was persistent, however. With the transfer from French to U.S. sovereignty in 1803, he saw a new opportunity to approach another authority to obtain permission to sell the Scypions. An interesting feature of the French and Spanish territorial legal system is that it relied primarily upon the local commandant's decision as law. It had no appellate process and little precedent.[37] (There was, of course, a colonial law called the Code Noir, but it was unclear that it applied to Indian slaves.) Thus, under Spanish or French authority, there was never a final definitive determination of the Scypion sisters' status. There was no gold standard declaring them once and finally free. With each change of colonial governors, someone like Joseph Tayon could again request permission to sell the Scypions, even if he had been refused before.

This time, widow Helene Chevalier and Madame Chauvin responded by drawing up written legal documents declaring the Scypions to be free. Normally, such an emancipating effort by owners would be dispositive. The legality of these documents would be in question, however, if Helene and her sister lacked authority to manumit the Scypions.

The newly minted territorial commander under U.S. sovereignty delayed Joseph Tayon's contested request until an American court could be organized to hold trial. Nonetheless, Joseph Tayon, who already held Marguerite, somehow seized Celeste and Catiche and kept them, pending the legal action. Joseph Tayon was then well into his eighties and could not have acted alone. The family may have expected him eventually to give up, but he did not. Pierre Chouteau Sr. backed him and would continue the battle after Tayon died.[38]

Celeste, Catiche, and Marguerite filed habeas corpus petitions to wrest themselves from Tayon's control. Even the habeas corpus action was a new American import to the area, which had no habeas corpus under French or Spanish law. Finally in 1805, two judges heard the cases and took testimony from many witnesses. At issue was whether Marie-Jean Scypion was actually Indian at all. The dead woman was described by different witnesses as either brown, black, or red black with long wooly hair.[39] Since she had adopted French manners and wore a handkerchief on her head like most French women, witnesses could not tell for sure. The objective was to determine her race from her appearance.[40] Almost ten witnesses, who remembered her at different stages of her life, described Marie's features, running them through the racial typology of Indian to African. The tribunal eventually released the Scypion sisters from Joseph Tayon's constraint. The 1805 habeas corpus proceeding indirectly implied their freedom from Tayon, but it did not guarantee it.[41] It went no further than to suggest that Joseph Tayon's constraint was illegal. It did not declare the Scypions absolutely free from servitude or provide any legal finality. The dual interpretations were played out by the parties. It would take twenty years before a Missouri Supreme Court acknowledged this subtlety and eventually rendered a final outcome in the Scypions' favor.[42] For the next twenty years, the Tayon family continued to fight over the bodies and services of the Scypion sisters and their children.

After release, both Celeste and Catiche resumed living and working for their former mistresses, women who had testified to their freedom.[43] Whereas the Tayon sisters insisted on their servants' freedom, their brother Francois, who held Marguerite Scypion, did not. He yielded to his father's wishes. Yet, even Marguerite was released a week later and joined her sisters in St. Charles.[44]

By late 1805, the entire Scypion family lived in the village of St. Charles, across the Missouri River, presumably with or near widow Helene Chevalier. All seemed to go about their lives freely—that is, until Old Joseph Tayon made his next move. He seemed to be obsessed with the idea of controlling the Scypions.

After being rebuffed by the U.S. territorial court, Joseph Tayon took another tack. Instead of appealing to higher authority, Tayon appealed to lower authority, the sheriff charged with keeping peace in the locality. On May 9, 1806, Joseph Tayon asked the county sheriff to round up all of the Scypion descendants, alleging that they were slaves running at large. Whatever independence the Scypions enjoyed seemed to irritate Joseph Tayon. Backing him again, this time to the extent of a $4,000 bond was the wealthy and influential Pierre Chouteau Sr., with whom Tayon resided.[45]

The sheriff swept up thirteen Scypion family members: Celeste and her five children, Catiche and her three children, and Marguerite and her two.[46] For roughly a month, all thirteen were confined in some sort of jail, but on June 29, pursuant to the sheriff's writ, the Scypions were sold publicly at auction on the church steps in the village of St. Charles. The priest gave permission to hold their auction there.

Notice of Auction of members of the Scypion family, July 3, 1806

Know all those to whom this is presented, seeing that I, Joseph Tayon, Senior, residing in the city and district of St. Louis in the Territory of Louisiana, after having posted notice, and having fixed notice at the entry of the Church in this city, and by that means having announced that on the 29th of June of the present year, by permission of the priest and at the door of the said Church, held a public sale for cash, and in piasters gourdes, to the highest bidder and to the last bidder, of several fine slaves belonging to me. In conformity with which and by means of which, it has been adjudged that several of the slaves have been transferred and transported to Mr. Pierre Chouteau as follows: First, for the sum of 400 piasters gourds, one mulatto woman named Marguerite, aged about 25 years, with her son, named Antoine, aged about 3 years, and her daughter, named Elizabete, aged about one year; Secondly, for the sum of 200 piasters of the same money, one griffe slave named Paul, aged about 6 years; and thirdly for the sum of 560 piasters of the same money, a mulatto woman aged about 34 years and called Catiche, with Carmelite, her daughter, 4 years of age, and lastly, her son, aged one year. All this total 1162 piasters gourdes, which I receive having herein affirmed, and to my satisfaction from the hands of the said Mr. Pierre Chouteau, and to whom, by these presented, I give full and total receipt and discharge, acknowledging that the said slaves are well and duly and legitimately sold to the said Mr. Pierre Chouteau for him and his heirs to possess and dispose of at their pleasure and will as property belonging to them and by them legitimately acquired, promising to guarantee them against all trouble, debts, mortgage settlements from which evictions entail, and all other impediments in general whatsoever, and to contravene the terms of the present contract. In testimony of which, not knowing how to write, I have made my ordinary mark and do this in the above stated city, district and territory, this 3rd day of July in the year of our Lord 1806. Written, signed and delivered in the presence of George Tayon and M. P. Leduc

---

What old Joseph Tayon was unable to do on previous occasions, he achieved by a writ directed to the sheriff suggesting that slaves were *running at large* in the streets of St. Charles. Tayon and Chouteau described them in the writ simply as African American slaves rather than Indian descendants, and the sheriff never asked otherwise. By naming them and claiming them as African, Tayon slipped the knotty legal question of their combined Indian-African heritage. Tayon invoked the simple municipal notion that if a master's slaves were running at large, the sheriff was authorized to sweep them up to aid the master in restoring control and public order. Thus by resort to the simple municipal authority of keeping the peace Tayon achieved his purposes without the legal complexity.

The Scypions might have tried for a habeas corpus petition again, but they had just done so, only to have the sheriff re-arrest them for running at large. The Scypions' predicament exhibits the ephemeral nature of habeas corpus, which can have the effect of a revolving door. The writ seemed to have little precedential value the next time the victim was constrained, particularly when constrained by another. The writ invoked the justice of the peace's authority and required that the person be brought to court and, if appropriate, ordered released, though that did not ensure the victim against recapture by other men or other measures.[47]

At the auction on the church steps, the Scypions were purchased by masters connected by family or business to Pierre Chouteau Sr. The extended Chouteau family were the wealthiest French-speaking masters regularly seeking slaves in the area. The Chouteaus required their slaves to speak only French within the households, and French was the Scypion family's "mother tongue." Pierre Chouteau Sr. himself bought Marguerite (who had already spent time in his household) and Catiche, as well as Celeste's son.

Indeed, this kind of wholesale dispersal of slaves by auction among the extended Chouteau family is a pattern that was repeated over the next half century. Each time that a household was disbanded or extinguished by death of the master or mistress, Chouteau family slaves could expect to be sold at auction among other Francophone households.[48]

Celeste and her baby girl went to Charles Tayon, Helene's older brother, who was once commandant under the Spanish.[49] Charles may have bid on Celeste in order to keep her with Helene. He purchased no one else, and Celeste was allowed to remain with Helene.[50] Celeste's other children were all sold separately.[51] After the auction, most of the Scypions were taken back to St. Louis, where the Chouteaus resided.

For family members to purchase servants whose enslavement was contested, with the sales proceeds going to Joseph Tayon, meant to take the side of Tayon and Pierre Chouteau Sr. against the claims of Tayon's daughters, as well as counter to the Scypions' own assertions of freedom. While Marie-Louise Tayon Chauvin eventually folded under Chouteau's continued pressure and yielded Catiche to him, accepting money for the sale, the widow Helene Chevalier did not take this action lightly.[52] Helene set herself at war with much of the rest of her family. She would seek to retain Celeste and recover Celeste's children from extended family members for the rest of her life. (And years later, after she died, her former lawyer and her estate's administrator would continue to litigate over them.) The strong-willed woman who survived her

elderly husband and permitted her servants to run at large seemed to be totally
at odds with her family on this matter. The extended family had sided with the
patriarchal directives of Joseph Tayon and Chouteau. When Joseph Tayon died
at age ninety-two in 1807, Pierre Chouteau Sr. stepped forward, litigating to
resist the Scypions' claims of freedom.

Over the next twenty years, practically every form of legal action to recover
property was applied to Celeste's family as they were wrested from one claimant to another. Trespass, replevin, trover, and foreclosure were all distinctive
legal writs, and each one was deployed over the bodies of the Scypions. In each
contest, the issue was who had relatively better claim to the enslaved person.[53] It
was not until after Missouri statehood that the Scypions petitioned the courts
for themselves. Being the subject of litigation for so long, they were familiar with
the courts. They knew that the courts were powerful enough to remove slaves
from their possessors. When the Scypion sisters claimed freedom as their own,
they were litigating the ultimate contest: the claim that they had absolute title to
themselves.

During these twenty years, an entire generation, as Widow Chevalier attempted
to reclaim Celeste's family, Celeste's youngest child, Sophia grew to maturity and
became a mother herself. Sophia appears to have made a stable pair bond with
another slave named William, since the church records contain two separate baptisms of children born to Sophie and William.[54]

Attorney, and later judge, Matthias McGirk represented Helene Chevalier in
getting Celeste's children back. In payment for his services, Widow Chevalier
signed a contingency fee agreement. The agreement assigned the value in her
ongoing litigation against the Chouteaus over the Scypions to Matthias McGirk.
The agreement provided: "[F]or value received I may recover in 4 replevin actions:
one v. P. Chouteau Sr. For Paul; One v. Sylvester Labaddie for Antoine; One
v. Maria Antoinette Honey otherwise Labaddie for Sophia; One against J. P.
Cabbane for Clarisse [sic]."[55]

It appears that McGirk used the transaction not merely to enrich himself
but to leverage the freedom suits on behalf of Celeste and her children. Matthias
McGirk hated the Chouteaus, and only a champion of this stature would be
able to see them released from the Chouteaus. This strange transfer of interest in
the case outcome gave him standing in the further disputes.

By 1821, when Missouri finally achieved statehood, the Chouteaus had
prospered tremendously in the fur trade and in real estate. They controlled
a far-flung frontier empire. St. Louis was their base of operations. They were
the wealthy powerful aristocrats of the village that had grown into a town of
about 4600. Although the Scypions had repeatedly undergone reassignments
within the Chouteau extended family, most Chouteau houses were located

near each other along the same St. Louis main street. Only Widow Chevalier continued to live in St. Charles. Thus as the Chouteaus' domestiques, most of the Scypions lived near each other.[56] Both Chouteaus and Scypions attended the same church mass in the Cathedral that the Chouteaus financed. Their babies were baptized by the same succession of priests as the Chouteaus' children.

When Madame Chevalier died in August 1823 without a will, her inventory listed Celeste and six of her children and grandchildren, assessed together as worth $1500.00. Included were youngest son Auguste, Antoine, Paul, and Sophie and her two children.[57] One man, Devance Chauvin, probably a nephew of Madame Chevalier, hired most of them as servants. Another Chauvin nephew was her administrator. Sophie and her two children were assigned elsewhere to a Mr. Eakhart. Each year for the next several years, the estate included a payment for the hire of Celeste's family as slaves.[58]

Now with the assignment of the contract, McGirk was a creditor, who had higher priority on the order of distribution of assets than even the heirs. Thus, a new round of litigants lined up: her new administrator continued the fight for Celeste against other members of her family, who had taken and sold away Celeste's children, and against McGirk, the creditor. Yet the recovery of Celeste and her children by the estate's administrator would have given the administrator

The original LaClede-Chouteau family mansion pictured above was inherited by Auguste Chouteau. His brother Pierre Chouteau, Sr., built a similar one for himself. The slave cabins were within the yard enclosed by the stone wall, set behind the mansion. Missouri History Museum, St. Louis

his own fractional interest in the estate (for assuming the tasks as administrator), and the rest would have gone to her closest kin by the rules of intestate succession. In the new lineup, McGirk as contract assignee of Madame Chevalier sued Administrator Lefrenier Chauvin, Helene's nephew.

Celeste waited until after Helene Chevalier had died to bring her own suit. This may have been fortuitous, or it may have suggested that Celeste saw her own interests best fulfilled in Helene Chevalier's household. Helene had always declared Celeste to be her servant, not her slave. Yet Helene Chevalier probably could more effectively use the courts to recover Celeste's children than Celeste herself could do. In 1825, when Celeste brought suit, she had to be able to name the correct claimant as a defendant. To some extent, that required sorting out the claimants among the feuding family over three decades, and four changes of sovereignty between her mother's birth and Celeste's lawsuit.[59] Changes of sovereignty like these could also disrupt chains of title if the successive sovereign opted not to respect property rules of the previous one. Had successive sovereigns adopted their predecessor's laws regarding slave title? Only litigation would decide. In addition, rules of property ownership sometimes changed within sovereign regimes. Did a French colonial prenuptial marriage contract accounting for slaves continue to be recognized under Missouri law? Generally, the legal solution is to trace title back to some definitive point of departure, which renders all intervening events either relevant and material or irrelevant and legally void in determining ownership. But tracing back was a nightmare.

The successive layers of legal events—the Tayon's marriage, Madame Tayon's gifts to her daughters, long residence in their households, the posthumous effect of Madame Tayon's marriage contract, Joseph Tayon's decision to divide his estate prior to his death, the habeas corpus proceeding in St. Louis, the arrest by the St. Charles sheriff, and the sales at the church door—provided a legal thicket. With possession and sovereignty significant to determining legal title, the Scypion family's status was a mess. Each detail may or may not have been legally relevant for later regimes, so each was a source of obfuscation for litigious parties. Some forms of slavery were acceptable under the legal regimes of all these jurisdictions, but the law of slavery as property was not constant.

From 1825 to 1830, all of the Scypions were in court as plaintiffs suing for their freedom. Sadly, no copies of these multiple case files remain. When the cases were transferred to other counties, the initial filings went with them, and so all of the cases' files have been lost. We can only view the litigation as it is reflected in other collected documents, such as Madame Chevalier's probate, the St. Louis Circuit Court Record Book that made daily notations until the cases were transferred out, and some transcripts of appeals.

The several suits lined up against two principal defendants. Celeste and her children sued Helene's estate administrator,[60] and Marguerite and Catiche and their families sued Pierre Chouteau Sr.[61] Altogether three sisters, their twelve children, and three grandchildren were plaintiffs in the courts arguing for their own rights to freedom. Sometimes the various suits were lumped together, and at other times different persons among the eighteen individuals were styled as independent plaintiffs. The greatest degree of antipathy among any of these suits was evident in Pierre Chouteau Sr.'s opposition. The issues were the same in all the cases, though, and the Scypions appear completely unified in their common effort. Celeste's family was represented by the McGirk brothers, Matthias and Isaac, the same lawyers who had once represented Helene Chevalier in attempting to get Celeste's children back, and had taken an assignment interest for that work.

Different cases came to trial unpredictably at different rates of speed. Some trials were won and others lost, some delayed and continued, and some appealed. Lawyers for the Scypions argued that they could not get a fair trial in St. Louis (because of Chouteau family influence). Venue was shifted from St. Louis to two different neighboring counties. Of the Scypions's cases, Marguerite's case was appealed to the Missouri Supreme Court twice.[62] Catiche appealed once.[63] And although Celeste did not appeal in her own right, the two opponents who contested their own interests in her family and their wages did.[64] Two of Celeste's grandchildren (Sophie's sons) had been assigned to masters in St. Charles, so William and Edward sued in St. Charles County Court.[65] Marguerite's sons Francois and Michel had their cases transferred there as well.[66] The other cases were transferred to Jefferson County, the county south of St. Louis. According to historian William Foley, in November 1836, the parties finally agreed to consolidate all the cases in one jury trial, five against Pierre Chouteau, and the three against Helene Chevalier's estate.[67]

One difficulty in following the lives and litigation of Marie Scypion's three daughters is the exclusive reliance on slaves' first names and the repetition of first names in the community. French Creoles seemed to use and reuse the same small collection of first names, both for family members and for their slaves. By the 1820s, several other slave women were suing the Chouteaus for freedom as well.[68] The only way to keep the persons and their litigation distinct is to identify each woman either by the distinctive name of her mother, or by the names of her children.[69] Thus, Celeste who was Marie Scypion's daughter was Celeste, the mother of Paul, Sophie, and Antoine, not Celeste, daughter of Judy, and mother of Celestine.[70]

In late 1828, Catiche petitioned Jefferson County Court. The lawsuit proceeded under then Judge William Scott, (who would cast a negative vote for slave freedom suits when later appointed to the Missouri Supreme Court hearing the *Dred Scott* case.)[71] The judge instructed the jury along the terms of the last state supreme court's ruling, and the jury ruled for the Scypions but awarded them only a single penny in damages.[72] Pierre Chouteau insisted on appealing the result again.

The McGirk brothers, Matthias and Issac, both lawyers, appear to have put something of a pincer move on Pierre Chouteau. One brother represented the Scypions in their freedom suits, while the other brother went after Chouteau to obtain back wages for all the time that he had employed Celeste's children against the wishes of Widow Chevalier. On February 22, 1830, Pierre Chouteau gave up; he came into court and confessed judgment to the damages action for replevin of Paul.[73] Chouteau then turned Paul over to Helene's administrator, and paid one cent in damages.[74] The case, *Matthias McGirk v. Lefreniere, administrator of Chevalier*, was then appealed to the Missouri Supreme Court on which Matthias McGirk was a sitting judge.[75] Chauvin had obtained only one cent from Chouteau, so a fraction of that was what McGirk was owed. McGirk insisted that the value of Paul's wages surely exceeded one single cent. So McGirk filed an appeal to the Missouri Supreme Court on which he himself sat, and McGirk lost. The court's ruling appears to be a slap at McGirk, their fellow judge. It is surprisingly ironic, since it posits that Pierre Chouteau, known to one and all as Missouri's richest man, might have been shown to be insolvent, rendering the one cent damage award appropriate. In lawyerly style, Justice Tompkins wrote for the court that not knowing the circumstances that were before the lower court, the supreme court had to uphold the amount on any conceivable basis that lower court could have found.

> [Y]et it does not appear to us that Chauvin, by a diligent prosecution of the suit against Chouteau to final judgment, could have recovered more than one cent damages. The plaintiff gave evidence before the Circuit Court, it seems, that the services of Paul, during the time he was detained by Chouteau from Helene Chevalier, were worth several hundred dollars. Evidence, we are told, was also given of the amount of damages....But we are not told that this was all the evidence given before the Circuit Court. For anything we see on the record, Chauvin might have given evidence to the court that Paul's services during the time of his detention from the intestate were worth nothing ..., *or that Chouteau himself was insolvent*. Where we are not precluded by an entry on the record, we are bound to presume everything to sustain the judgment of the Circuit Court.[76]

How odd to have to presume, contrary to what the judges could take judicial notice of, the clearly erroneous fact that Pierre Chouteau was insolvent; he was notoriously among the richest men in the entire region.

In October 1834, the Missouri Supreme Court decided Marguerite's case. In a 2:1 opinion, the court declared that the Spanish governor's edict meant that children of maternal Indian descent were free.[77] (This was Marguerite's second trip to the Missouri high court.) Not yet content Pierre Chouteau tried to appeal to the U.S. Supreme Court, dragging the dispute out until 1838. He was finally informed that the U.S. Supreme Court had no basis for jurisdiction over something that was a matter of state law. The cases were remanded again to determine if Marie Scypion really was of Indian descent.

A Jefferson County jury found Catiche to be free and Pierre Chouteau relentlessly appealed yet one more time. Matthias McGirk got the last word. Sitting on the Missouri Supreme Court, with the consent of only one other judge, he affirmed the jury verdict giving Catiche and Marguerite freedom, and freedom particularly from Pierre Chouteau.

Sophie died before the final result. Helene Tayon's probate papers mention the care provided to her by the note: "Sophie, daughter of Celeste buried in Catholic cemetery was paid for by Chevalier estate, including a hearse, catholic ritual, coffin, burying clothes, sperm candles, carriages." The entry also notes that a wealthy, free black riverboat pilot, Jacque Desire, made the funeral arrangements and took charge of Sophie's two children.[78]

Helene Chevalier's estate also paid the costs associated with the lawsuit brought in Jefferson Circuit Court for Celeste and her children.[79] Other bills and items in Chevalier's estate suggest that she took relatively good care of Celeste Scypion's family. Each ministration to Celeste's family identify them individually. A final entry in the Chevalier estate, payment for medical attention, indicates that a doctor visited Helene Chevalier's place in St. Charles and ministered both to her in her last illness as well as to the ailments of the slave children in the house.[80]

Celeste reached freedom, though several of her family members died before it was over. Celeste's enslaved life spanned the last two decades of the eighteenth century and the first three decades of the nineteenth. By the 1840 census, Celeste Chevalier headed a household consisting of three younger men and one younger woman.[81] Who were they? Who survived? What happened to Celeste's sisters and their children?[82]

Counter to expectation, it appears that Marguerite, the little Mouse, continued to work for the Chouteaus after the lawsuits had established their freedom. "Cypion Margueritte" is named in the 1842 probate of the widow Marie-Therese Cerre Chouteau. Marguerite Scypion was decreed free in 1836. Did she still work in widow Chouteau's family as a free woman, was she still somehow in the thrall of an enslavement that she had resisted, or did the widow's inventory simply still stubbornly claim to own her as a slave? Or with the Chouteau's propensity to use and reuse names, was this a different person entirely?

One mulatto man named Francois remained with Madame Chauvin through-out her life. Her will makes a point of freeing Francois in 1852.[83] Francois or Frank was born in 1813, which made him the right age to be Catiche's son of the same name. He too should have been granted his freedom in 1834, but did he stay on with the masters into whose household he was born?[84]

The Scypions' lives were marked by uncertain legal rules and entangled lives and domestic practices. Their cases clarified the law in Missouri. In succeed-ing cases, petitioners could reliably win their freedom by demonstrating that they had a Native American mother or grandmother somewhere in their pedi-gree. Yet only two similar lawsuits took place in St. Louis thereafter.[85] Without documentation of their Indian ancestry, witnesses and juries were again invited to examine the petitioner's features for racial type.

CHAPTER 4

Winny and Her Children

In 1824, three years after Missouri's statehood, Winny's case established the legal rule of freedom by residence. This basis was different and its scope much broader than the bases upon which Peter McNelly or the Scypion sisters prevailed. Because of the rule's breadth, many more enslaved people—those who had been in intermittent transit through the Northwest Territory lands—could establish freedom in St. Louis. The rule of freedom by residence meant that a slave became free by residing or working in a jurisdiction where slavery was banned. This rule did not apply to runaways, however. The slave had to be upon free soil with their master's consent. That is, the master must have taken the slave to free territory or allowed the slave to be assigned to free territory. Thereafter, the slave was deemed free. Slavery did not re-encumber the former slave, even upon return to a jurisdiction where slavery was permitted. The slave might need to redeem that freedom in a court of law, but once free, forever free.[1] The rule's purpose was designed at least as much to punish the master for bringing contraband slave property into free lands as to emancipate the slave.

The massive westward movement of settlement people into American territories is often imagined as entirely independent and voluntary migration. Symbolically, in American popular culture, the event is sometimes equated with the essence of liberty.[2] The forced migration of accompanying slaves like Winny is a jarring counterpoint to this image of voluntary relocation. The story of Winny and hundreds of other accompanying slaves coerced by their masters to move west undermines the grand theme that westward movement was free from constraint and liberty-enhancing. Peter and Queen did set out for western lands on their own volition. Winny was moved by her masters, taken first to free territory and then to a slave state, where she sued decades later.

Winny's path to St. Louis and her case are more typical of the freedom cases. What marked Winny's westward movement for success is that she had lived on free soil. Winny's case established the rule.

Winny was born in the Carolinas, at a time when the distinction between North and South Carolina was barely recognized. It is not clear exactly when she was born. Winny's masters brought her to the region of present-day Illinois, long before it mattered whether that region was considered North or South. Then the major rivers functioned more as highways of passage uniting a river valley than as boundaries separating jurisdictions. Still, by 1787, the Northwest Ordinance proscribing slavery governed the northern shore, and by 1792, Kentucky was a slave state that stretched the length of the southern shore. It was Winny's sojourn north of the river, with the Whiteside family as they moved west, that made all the difference to her destiny.

In 1793, the Whiteside household settled at a fortified village, named for their family, called "Whitesides Station," that had been built ten years earlier on the road between the early French settlements of Kaskaskia and Cahokia, east of the Mississippi. Unlike the neighboring French villages, newly founded Whitesides Station was described as a "family fort," primarily occupied by several Anglophone families who had traveled down the Ohio bringing along slaves as part of their travelling households.[3] Winny's household remained on the Illinois side for only three or four years while she was a young girl.

Those years that the Whitesides spent in Illinois country were anything but peaceful. During that time, the fortified settlement and the larger Whiteside family were involved in a series of violent skirmishes with the surrounding Indian population.[4] Several Whitesides were killed in raids by and against the surrounding tribes. Not content with this new location, Winny's master moved his family farther west to another fortified village on the Missouri River.

Little is known about John Whiteside or why he made this move, while many Whitesides remained east of the river.[5] Yet, with this move, the John Whiteside household left American sovereignty to settle in what was then French colonial sovereignty, where African enslavement was fully accepted as legal. In 1799, the only extant laws concerning slavery in the jurisdictional locale were some remnants of the Code Noir and the colonial decree prohibiting Indian enslavement.[6] Winny's later claim for freedom would be based upon the three or four years she spent in Illinois while the fortified settlement was under siege.

The Missouri village where John Whiteside resettled was originally called Marais des Liards, or Cottonwood Swamp. The timber provided planks to construct the wooden fort.[7] John Whiteside acquired several arpents of land in the countryside in 1799. In the customary French colonial ownership patterns, the village had common fields.[8] The population of Marais des Liards then consisted of 337 whites and 42 slaves.[9] The territory was in the hands of Spain and, accordingly, John Whiteside acquired a Franco-Spanish sounding moniker: "John Whitesides dit Juan Wedsay."[10] Whiteside's new name showed the mixture of French and Spanish cultural influence there. The addition of "dit" was a French custom to distinguish what he was locally called from his formal name. The name Juan indicated the Spanish influence.

John Whiteside never relocated again and he died in 1803, the same year that the Louisiana Purchase was made. The Northwest Ordinance had banned slavery only in the lands northwest of the Ohio River no further west than the Mississippi River. (There was no proscription west of the Mississippi until Missouri entered the Union pursuant to the Missouri compromise directing the states north of the specified latitude to be free states.)[11] Slavery as an institution continued in the Louisiana Purchase, as it had in the river valley for more than 200 years.[12] Occasionally, additional African slaves were brought upriver from New Orleans.

After Winny's master died, little changed for twenty-year-old Winny and her two children. They remained with the widow, Phebe (often spelled Feeby), and her two sons on the same farm. It is hard to imagine that Winny had other options. She continued to serve the widow, as she had during all the family's relocations. Winny now had two sons: Jerry and Daniel.[13]

Ten years after John Whiteside's death, his widow, Phebe remarried. This marriage, to Fielding Pruitt,[14] did not work out. Soon after the wedding, Phebe left her new husband and sought to secure her property as separate from his. She moved in with one of her now grown sons.[15] In the decade since John Whiteside's death, the family had never formally probated his estate; the property had never been formally transferred to the heirs. In the course of the dissolving of her second marriage, Phebe insisted that her short-term husband relinquish his interest in her most valuable property: her slave woman Winny and her children. Phebe went even further and relinquished her own interest in Winny and her children to her grown sons, Thomas and John Whiteside Jr. Given the timing, Phebe's transfers of interest seemed be motivated by a concern that her second husband might attempt to claim Winny. (Fielding Pruitt signed in accordance with her wishes and moved on to marry someone else.[16])

Concluding formal action on John Whiteside's estate required an inventory of the property that he held at his death, including Winny, Jerry, and Daniel. From 1803 to 1814, Winny had borne four more children, Jenny, Nancy, Lydia, and Sally,[17] roughly one baby every two and a half years. By 1822, she had borne three more, Hannah, Lewis, and Malinda, and by 1825, she had Harry and Lorinda as her babies. Winny's adult life must have been one of almost continuous pregnancy, child birth, and weaning. Winny's family continued with the Whitesides, although Phebe lived with her sons and no longer headed a household of her own.

Winny was almost forty years old by the time she first filed suit, and her family numbered ten. Her petition is undated, it claims a date in 1815, but it was likely first filed in 1818.[18]

What precipitated Winny's suit? It was not statehood, though statehood furthered the opportunity by setup of courts. It must have been something more personal, something that made suing worth the cost of angering the Whiteside family with whom Winny had lived without interruption since childhood. Winny's petition alludes to no specific cause at all. It states no other traumatic event: no beating, no abduction, and no imminent threat of sale. Instead, the precipitating events seemed be the death of all three remaining adult members of the original Whiteside family whom she had served for more than thirty years. Within less than five years, both Phoebe's adult sons died.[19] While they lived, Winny may have felt a connection and a sense of dependence, a personal sense of stability making her home with the Whitesides. After all, a slave did not have a household but must have considered some place home.

For a slave, the death of a master meant change. The death of both Whiteside sons and later Phebe meant even greater instability.[20] Nothing would continue as it had before. Four of Winny's older children already worked for neighboring farmers in the county.[21] With the death of the Whiteside sons, Winny's family was now under new ownership.

In the frontier practice of prompt remarriage, each of the sons' respective spouses quickly took new husbands. Through the legal rules of inheritance and coverture, the new husbands became owners—authorized to control and dispose of—their spouses' inherited property.[22] Winny and her family were now legally under the domain of the new husbands, who were strangers to them. Accordingly, these two men, Charles Hatton and Michael Sandford, probably had no reason to care about the welfare of Winny and her family, other than the work they could do or the value that they could bring at sale.

Even before Phebe's death, Winny's legal status was the subject of some question in the community. Phebe and a neighbor, Frances Collard, had quarreled about whether Winny was free or enslaved. Phebe insisted that Winny was a slave, and neighbor Frances claimed that she was free. Frances Collard's deposition is one of the earliest dated documents in Winny's court case file.[23] There is no inkling of what sparked the argument between the neighbors. Yet when Winny was ready to sue, neighbor Frances Collard, who had also once lived in Illinois country, was ready to assist her by filing a deposition on her behalf in court.[24]

Following their mother's lead, son Jerry filed suit against new husband Charles Hatton, and daughter Jenny sued Robert Musick, a neighboring farmer where she was assigned.[25] (Musick may have been married to a Whiteside girl, maybe even Phebe's daughter. The Musicks and the Whitesides had come west together, and the families intermarried. At the time of her death, Phebe lived with the Musick family.[26])

Although the Whitesides had accumulated property in land and livestock, the most valuable assets in each of these Whitesides' successive estates were still the slave property of Winny and the several children she had borne.

Winny's 1818 Petition and Subsequent Lawsuits

Winny's original petition appears to have been lost. Its text can only be found where it was transcribed for the Missouri Supreme Court on appeal, now available in the on-line Missouri Supreme Court Database. The petition is undated, but is said to as have been filed in 1818. It reads:

"That since she has been living in This Territory she has had the following children, to wit: Jerry, Daniel, Jenny, Nancy, Lydia, Sarah, Hannah, Lewis and Malinda. And your Petitioner is informed that by reason of having been held in Indiana, she and her children born since are free. And your Petitioner further showed that she and her children Hannah, Lewis, and Malinda are now claimed as slaves by Phebe Prewitt, that Jerry is claimed as a slave by the representatives of Thomas Whitesides deceased, Daniel by John Whitesides, Jenny by Robert Musick, Nancy by Isaac Voteau, Lydia by John Butler and Sarah by Michael Hatton."

This dispersion of Winny's children set up lawsuits by each of them against the persons who held them. It appears that most of her children first filed in 1818, and sometimes again in 1821, 1825, and even 1826.

Winny went on to have more children, born after the 1818 filing. Since these children were not covered by this filing, but were entitled to freedom as well, additional lawsuits had to be filed for each of these children. Harry and Lorinda were plaintiffs in their individual suits, and a man named Alexander Clark stood as their next friend.

Jenny sued Robert Musick first and after she prevailed against him, Robert's father Ephraim Musick stepped forward to claim that he, rather than his son, was her true master. Jenny's later suit was against Ephraim Musick. Jenny's later born child, Winetta, is also the plaintiff in a separate suit.

In 1820, the value of Winny and her children was $2,350, whereas the value of John Jr.'s house was a mere $600. Slaves were in such demand in Missouri in the 1820s that the value of a single, particularly valuable slave, such as eldest son Jerry, equaled all other assets these productive farmers had acquired.

After filing for freedom, Winny's suit was continued through several terms of court, until a jury decided in her favor some time in 1822. The jury awarded her $167.50 for the duration of her false imprisonment, notably "on the same principles *as any other plaintiff* might recover" in such an action.[27] The ruling seemed to take the heirs by surprise. Because the result was financially significant and novel enough to be questioned, the heirs appealed, and within two more years the Missouri Supreme Court had fully affirmed freedom for Winny and all of her children.[28]

In the entwined social web of small frontier communities, Rufus Pettibone, Phoebe's lawyer now with an ownership interest in Winny's family, had actually become a judge of the Missouri Supreme Court by the time of the appeal.[29] Appropriately, Judge Pettibone recused himself from deciding the case in which he himself was a party.[30] He must have been somewhat surprised, though, when his colleagues, the two remaining justices, ruled so strongly against his interests. Not only did they rule in Winny's favor, they even socked the defendants with the obligation to pay for Winny's defense of the appeal. And further, they awarded Winny and her children damages for their enslavement, on the false imprisonment theory.

During the argument, the heirs fell back to the following procedural position: since Winny had never sealed her freedom by bringing suit while she lived in Illinois, the change in her status was never final and hence her status as a slave was maintained (or revived) when she returned to a slave territory. As an alternative claim, the defendants urged that Phebe and John Whiteside never actually owned Winny at all, but that she was a gift to the now deceased Whitesides' sons from their grandfather.[31] The argument implied that John Whiteside had no authority over Winny when he had taken her to Illinois. (This argument that the chain of title went off on some other spur of family ownership became a defense commonly deployed in later freedom suits.)

With Judge Pettibone's recusal, two judges remained, one of whom was Judge McGirk. (Matthias McGirk was actively involved in the Scypions' freedom suits transpiring at the same time.[32]) McGirk cast his vote, but he did not write the opinion. The opinion quoted the Northwest Ordinance, "that there shall be neither slavery nor involuntary servitude in the said Territory," and deemed those words to be so clear as to be unmistakable.

> We did not suppose that any person could mistake the policy of Congress in making this provision. When the States assumed the right of self-government they found their citizens claiming a right of property in a miserable portion of the human race. Sound national policy required that the evil should be restricted as much as possible. What they could, they did....
>
> This court thinks that the person who takes his slave into said territory, and by the length of his residence there indicates an intention of making that place his residence and that of his slave ... does, by such residence, declare his slave to have become a free man.[33]

With these words, the Missouri Supreme Court defined a new legal basis for freedom for those slaves who had lived in free territory while forced to move westward: freedom by residence. To reside on free soil was to become free. Residing on free soil extinguished all of their owner's property rights in them. Once free, the former slave was forever free, even upon return to a slave state. This path to freedom was limited, however. Runaway slaves who reached free territory did not gain free status.[34] Nor did slaves who merely alighted on free soil while traveling through from one slave state to another. The slave had to prove residence for some duration on free soil, perhaps by proving they had done work there. Westward travelers who remained for a while with their slaves were deemed to have declared their slaves free by dint of their own indication. No additional procedural step was necessary to seal the slave's emerging status; freedom could be redeemed by Winny, even in a slave state, like Missouri, long after the fact of her residence in Illinois. Freedom could be redeemed by Winny even though she had never enjoyed the privilege of freedom while on free soil.

This was an extraordinary opening in the otherwise tightly sealed, perpetual bondage of enslavement. Free territory was not a place of asylum, because runaways could be sought after and returned. If a slave was taken to free territory, it not only had the potential to protect the slave against removal, it transformed one's status. Crossing that boundary with one's master and remaining a while made the bondsman free. The rule was as simple as a children's rule in a game of tag. Even more, if one reached this free space with the master's indication of residence and one left this safe place, one was still safe, even from one's master. The bondsmen carried that new protean status of freedom, even when she returned to a place where slavery was legal and legally enforced. And by the principle of matrilineality, all of her later born children were free as well.

What was extraordinary is how unique this rule was. There were very, very few ways that a slave could participate in an act of his or her own emancipation. American slaves had no right to purchase their freedom, as did slaves under Spanish colonial law.[35] American slaves could not hope to attain freedom by good deeds, unless the favor sprang from a master's generosity, his gratitude, or his mercy. Yet, in the right circumstance, a slave could be declared free in the legal system of a slave state. A lawsuit taken against the master's unwavering desire to retain the slave broke the bondage and truly transformed the slave's life circumstances, because many petitioners, like Winny, had never lived as free in their entire lives. Thus, this was the singular legal means that overrode the master's volition: the slave taken into free areas attained freedom by these acts of migration.

Winny's case created something relatively novel to the law: a public basis for severing a private relationship, against the will of the stronger party. Manumission could arise only from the master's prerogative, not from public recognition of entitlement, or desert. And there was no overriding public recognition of mercy in law or custom, not even punishingly harsh treatment, that would break the slave's bond against the master's will. A master's barbarity toward a slave could in some states expose him to public criticism or criminal sanction, but it did not break his hold on the slave.

Though freedom by residence was a public policy basis for emancipation, it was still expressed in terms that mollified the master's opposition and reconfigured it in terms of the master's own consent. The court emphasized that it was the master who had moved the slave there and the master must have known that freedom would result from entering free lands. Hence, the master consented to the slave's freedom as a consequence of voluntarily taking the slave there. In effect, the loss was of the master's own doing.

Winny's case went even further. The two judges said yes to freedom, yes to attorneys' fees for the appeal and court costs, and yes to money damages for her treatment being wrongfully enslaved. Winny's case was a three-rule sweep. The court could have left the decision at ordering Winny's release. Charging the master to pay the former slave money went beyond emancipation. The heirs continued abuse of Winny's freedom resembled a tortious injury, so Winny's attorney requested compensation for the injury she had sustained by being wrongfully enslaved. The heirs argued that damages should be minimal, nominal, if awarded at all. Winny won this argument, too. Damages were to be computed as wages and injury. The measure was the worth of Winny's labor *"and any ill-treatment during the time . . . held in slavery* [as] evidence in aggravation of damages."[36]

With this phenomenally favorable ruling, Winny's several adult children refiled suits seeking compensation. Daughter Jenny sought $85 against her former master. Nancy and Jerry asked for $500 each.[37] Jerry was awarded $175 based on a calculation of his time. Winny herself received the $167.50 that the jury had awarded her, which, in 1820s Missouri, was enough money to buy a farm.

For at least a year Winny and her children were permitted to enjoy their freedom. But then Pettibone and Musick made one more attempt to seize Winny and Jenny and their young children. The plot was thought to be to sell them South. In early May 1825, the two women immediately brought habeas corpus petitions before the Missouri Supreme Court, rather than the local judge. They summoned several area neighbors to stand as witnesses.

Judge Pettibone died shortly thereafter. His probate shows that he did not keep Winny and the young children. His probate inventory states "1 Negro Woman Winne [*sic*], aged about 40 years, 1 Negro boy Harry 4 years old. 1 Negro girl Lorinda 2 years old. The above negroes taken out of possession by order of the St. Louis Circuit court—they having commenced suit for their freedom—also for freedom of Lindey [*sic*] who is appraised at $200 as a 7 year old girl."[38]

Winny and Jenny escaped their disappointed captors attempts to re-enslave them. Winny did not buy a farm, though. It seems that like many women without farming husbands, she gravitated to the city and became a washerwoman. By 1830, it appears that Winny and her daughter Jenny set up households on the south side of St. Louis, next to Widow Keesucker's boarding house.[39] Living near to a boarding house was a good location for laundresses because it gave them a dependable customer base. Winny headed a household of three persons: herself and a boy and a girl both under ten, presumably Harry and Lorinda. Jenny headed a household consisting of herself and a young girl, presumably her daughter Winetta. Caveats, of course, must be made. Without a last name, it is difficult to trace any slave woman and impossible to be certain. Moreover, Winny was a common name given to slaves in the area at the time. (Another different Winny also sued for her freedom in 1820.[40])

There is still more evidence that Winny remained in St. Louis though. When Missouri required all free blacks to take out licenses in 1835, a sixty-year-old woman, named only "Winny," registered on the same day as two younger women with names similar to her daughters.[41] The 1840 city directory lists a free black woman, "Minny [sic] Whiteside." We don't know where or how she lived, though it seems she and her children were able to receive the best outcomes for bonded people of her time. They were adjudged free and compensated for their injury.

And they left a silver path for the lucky few who had resided on free soil.[42] It was a forty-year-old woman, girlhood survivor of Indian wars and mother of many children, whose circumstance established the rule of freedom by residence in the fledgling state created by the national compromise on slavery that bore its name, Missouri.[43]

Winny's lawsuit set the standards for three decades of freedom suits that followed. Thereafter, freedom by residence was recognized in Missouri, until the court overruled itself in *Dred Scott*. Although the jurisprudence was not unknown in places far from Missouri, the 1824 Missouri opinion had been written without any citation to prior interpretative authority of the consequences of residing on free soil or the effect of the Northwest Ordinance. *Winny v. Whitesides* took on a life of its own as precedent for the freedom by residence rule. It even influenced the Supreme Court in the free state of Illinois, which had been slow to give full effect to the Northwest Ordinance within its own borders.[44]

Thereafter, slaves bringing suit for their freedom routinely requested $500 as damages. The legislature later revoked the law on damages,[45] but Winny and her family received compensation, and her case established the reigning favorable precedent.

CHAPTER 5

The Kidnap of Lydia's Children

Lydia Titus's free family was kidnapped from their home in Illinois. This kidnapping took place even after the family had lived in peace and freedom on their own Illinois farmland into the third generation. The widowed grandmother lived with her children and grandchildren. On one fateful day in May 1832, white men, claiming to be acting with the authority of the law, appeared at her home to kidnap her entire family from their farm home in the Illinois countryside. Her adult daughters, working across the river in St. Louis, were also seized. Eighteen years after she had established her freedom in Illinois and she and her husband had registered as free persons, a new generation of Mitchells kidnapped a new generation of Tituses and smuggled them across the river to St. Louis in an attempt to return them to bondage in the South. This second generation threat demonstrates that even at home in a free state, there was no guarantee that the heirs of a former master wouldn't try to re-establish ownership rights in a later generation. It happened to Lydia's family very suddenly and unexpectedly on a summer night in 1832. As a result, the validity of her freedom was tested once again.[1]

This 1832 St. Louis lawsuit was Lydia's third redemption song. Her quest for freedom had begun in 1808. The Mitchells had made one failed attempt to re-enslave her in 1825. In 1832, she was forced to engage in the redemption song again for her children's sake.

Lydia first encountered the law's majesty in 1808 in what was then technically Indiana Territory, when she initially sued for freedom.

As a young mother, she was brought to the Illinois country with six other slaves by Elijah Mitchell. Mitchell came from Kentucky and he was considering relocating west, either in Illinois or Missouri. He stopped at a place within five miles from present-day Harrisonville, Illinois, and there he rented some land for two years.[2] (The local community was not very literate, and hence there is considerable variation in spelling of the names of many people in this story.)

Old-timers later testified that Elijah Mitchell didn't know the local custom that slaves could be held in Illinois only for a short time before they would be deemed free. "[Mitchell] was ignorant of our laws...." Mitchell's neighbor warned him that if his slaves stayed over sixty days, they would be free according to the law. (Some masters even thought to remove their slaves from the state periodically in order to preserve the status.) The custom was based on an Indiana territorial law, and, at the time, all of Illinois was part of Indiana Territory. The "Act concerning Negros and Mulattos of 1807" provided that slaves brought into the territory had to be indentured within thirty days of entry, or removed within sixty days.[3] Failure to engage in the legal formality could result in their freedom. This statute does not appear to have been designed as much to secure freedom as it was thought to accommodate continued bondage and the terms of the Northwest Ordinance and to penalize the master's failure to indenture.

Mitchell thanked the man for his concern, stating that he had already been in Illinois longer than that and did not intend his black servants to be slaves forever. He trusted that they would remain with him for his natural life and that he did not intend that they remain slaves after his death. According to Ichabod Badgely, "[T]he old wench [Lydia Titus] had been a mother to his children in raising them, and he knew she would not heard [sic] him."[4] That may mean that Lydia had been their mother figure in the absence of their own mother.[5]

True to his expectation, Lydia did not seek freedom until after Mitchell's death, a year later in 1808. Then she and a slave man named Bob filed suit against Mitchell's widow for freedom in Illinois. Lydia and Bob prevailed in their lawsuits, though it took some years, and Lydia eventually received her free papers at age thirty-one in 1814.[6]

Bob and Lydia's suit for freedom in 1807 was one of the first trials undertaken by the territorial Court of Common pleas that was newly established in the old French village, Cahokia located on the Mississippi. Nine years after Peter McNelly's suit in Vincennes, this freedom suit coincides with the first establishment of a new court system in this region of the Illinois country under the American regime.[7] During the course of the dispute, sovereignty changed, but not the governing law. The Illinois Territory was separated from Indiana Territory, although the same basic laws, including the Act Regarding Negroes and Mulattoes, was deemed in force in Illinois Territory as well.[8] To alleviate any doubt, the Illinois territorial legislature later re-enacted it for good measure.[9]

It is not clear that anyone counseled them; Bobb and Lydia simply stepped forward and asserted their own claims for freedom. (Lydia and Bob had a lawyer but how he was appointed is unclear.)

Elijah Mitchell's probate and the freedom suits occurred simultaneously but in the tribunals of two different villages some 50 miles apart. Mitchell's probate was done in Kaskaskia. Bob and Lydia sued in Cahokia. (The sheriff charged Mitchell's estate for the freedom suit's court costs.) Mitchell's widow, Jinsey, appears to have been illiterate, but she had strong ideas about the estate's management because she often found herself at odds with a series of co-executors appointed to help her administer the estate.

Mitchell left no will. Although Elijah Mitchell claimed that Lydia had raised his children, no children are mentioned as possible heirs in these proceedings. Did Jinsey, his wife, work to exclude Mitchell's children? Whether Mitchell had any other legal heirs would come back to haunt Lydia and her family.

Exactly how many slaves Mitchell held is unclear. One old-timer thought there were as many as seven, but he could name only five: "Bob, Lyd, Hester, Matilda, and Vina."[10] Elijah's November 1809 probate inventory lists at most three: an unnamed Negro girl is appraised at $200 on one scrap of paper, and one Negro man worth $350 and a Negro woman worth $400 on another. The inscription reads, "[T]his is a List of the property apprised for the widow Mitchel as nere [sic] as we can recolect [sic]."[11] Later suits against the widow suggest that she might have been hiding assets.[12]

The probate file suggests that the widow was quick to sell off two of Lydia's young daughters. Four-year-old Matilda and two-year-old Vina were sold to a Kaskaskia attorney John Rector for $150 and $120, respectively.[13] What could possibly interest anyone in purchasing children so young? The girls could not have done productive work. Instead, they required care. And who cared for them? John Rector was an attorney, not a farmer.[14] Rector did not keep the little girls. He resold them rather quickly to William Christy, a storekeeper. Matilda and Viny would reunite with their mother later.

Widow Jinsey Mitchell formally indentured only one slave girl: Hess, age eight.[15] Why Hess was indentured and the younger girls sold makes less financial sense because an eight-year-old slave child could garner a sale price as an independent human commodity of value.[16] A plausible answer is that Jinsey indentured Hess because Hess belonged to her—that is, Jinsey brought her to the marriage. Thus, Hess was probably not Lydia's daughter. It appears that Hess never rejoined Lydia's household. Eight-year-old Hess was indentured for what was then the legal maximum: another twenty-four years.[17]

A remarkable insight into the freedom suit is a single slip of paper in the probate. It lists the court fees as $7.04 for the suit. A full-scale jury trial was conducted on the matter in April 1810.[18] Old-timers remembered the lawsuit.[19] Drawing eleven witnesses and twelve jurors, the lawsuit must have created quite a stir in the small community. Bob and Lydie won.[20] When Lydie formally registered as a free person on May, 21, 1814, she could do so because she had won the lawsuit. In 1814, Lydie is listed as a woman with a very black complexion, five feet nine inches tall, thirty-one years of age, and the wife of Nathan Titus, who came to Illinois with the Ogle family.[21] The very same day two more family members were registered. Husband Nathan Titus and Lydia's eight-year-old daughter, Vincy or Vina. Vina had been sold away from her mother as a toddler.

Lydia must have known where to find her. Vina's freedom is based on her mother's successful lawsuit.

Bob and the girl, Hess were no longer part of Lydia's family nucleus.[22] Jinsey Mitchell had also moved on, marrying a constable in Monroe County, presumably taking Hess with her.[23] (There is no 1832 record that Hess was ever released, but the Monroe County records are missing.)

Shortly after Lydia registered freedom papers for herself and Vina, daughter Matilda filed suit for her own freedom across the river in Missouri. Matilda, who was sold away from her mother at age four, was now twelve. Matilda had been sold three times before she found herself working for a Missouri tavern keeper. By 1815, twelve-year-old Matilda worked for Isaac VanBibber in St. Charles, Missouri, and she sued him for her freedom there.[24] (Matthias McGirk, involved in the Scypions' lawsuit and a judge in Winny's case, was her lawyer.)

Matilda claimed freedom based on her residence in the free territory of Illinois. One wonders whether Lydia, her mother, was behind this. Lydia's freedom papers six months earlier may have allowed her, or even impelled her, to seek out Matilda in Missouri and encourage her to file suit in order to return to the family. The young Matilda won her suit and did return to the Titus family in Illinois. (VanBibber then sued Christy for the money that he had paid for her.)[25]

By 1820, the extended Titus family had taken their place in the Turkey Hill settlement of free black farmers in St. Clair County. There was some strength in numbers. Two Titus brothers settled not very far from the Ogle family farm, the masters who had brought them to Illinois and then freed them. They were prepared to dig in as pioneers on their own land, and within two years of registering their freedom, both Nathan, who went by "Nace," and his brother acquired adjoining land grants in the fertile area known as the Great American Bottom in the Mississippi's flood plain. Nace Titus took out 160 acres and brother Sam 320 acres.[26] Nace Titus earned his livelihood primarily by raising livestock. In close proximity to the growing city of St. Louis, he could sell his stock to local butchers.

Nace and Lydia's household was comprised of nine people of color, including children Matilda, Vina, and Mahala.[27] Later-born children included Mary Ann, Nathan Jr., and little Sam.[28] Brother Samuel Titus had his own expanding family on a farm nearby. All were free from bondage or indenture; the younger children were free born in a free state. This degree of independence secured by free papers and even land ownership should have been enough to guarantee their personal security.

Nace did not survive the decade, however. He died in 1822, and Lydia administered his estate.[29] Joseph Ogle, who had freed Nace, stood as security for Lydia. Nace's estate included more than twenty head of livestock: cows with calves, heifers, oxen, mules, and horses. Much of the stock and household goods were sold to a "W. Clark," who seems to have been a friendly neighbor and may have purchased the items to help out. (A William Clark would

Lydia Tituses' family must have occupied a log cabin much like this self-sufficient African-American family. Florida State Archives

stand as "next friend" for some of Lydia's grandchildren in the later lawsuit.) The household inventory also included a rifle, bullet molds, and a wagon. Lydia kept the farm.[30]

In 1825, things changed dramatically. Three white men, Elisha Mitchell (perhaps Elijah's son), William DeGraffinreind, and Daniel Winn, attempted to take Lydia captive presumably to re-enslave her.[31] Elisha Mitchell made his first appearance in this suit, but not his last. Lydia went to court, and it appears that this got them to back off, at least for a while.

Forty-seven-year-old Lydia did not remarry; no man her age shared her household. There were seven people in her household in 1830, including three boys and three girls, all a generation younger than she was. Vina, now twenty years, old had already left home. She now went by the more formal name "Lavinia." She lived on her own in St. Louis, where the 1830 census recorded her independence.[32] Vina's presence may have been known in the streets of the city because she owned a horse—which was common for black drayman but uncommon for black women in the city. Yet, Vina had grown up in a family that raised livestock, as her mother still did.

It was on November 10, 1831, that Vina was seized in St. Louis. She was accused of being a runaway on a charge brought by a man named Martin

Mitchell. Vina was taken before a justice of the peace and was committed to jail as a runaway slave.[33]

Her arrest seems to have led to her family's abduction shortly thereafter.[34] But Martin Mitchell could not be found in St. Louis a month later, when the sheriff attempted to serve him with a summons to testify. This probably occasioned her release. She was seized again from the streets of the city a few weeks later, however. Younger sister Mahala, too, was arrested in St. Louis, by the same man, who it was said "pretends to be acting as attorney in fact for the executor of her mother's owner's estate."[35] Elijah Mitchell's Illinois estate had long been finalized, but there could have been some lingering proceeding over property assets or debts in Kentucky, where Mitchell had once lived.

In what must have been a coordinated effort, a team of kidnappers descended upon Lydia's farmhouse and seized her remaining children and grandchildren, six months later, on May 22, 1832. The kidnappers were led by an imposing man who also held public office. Alexander P. Field, none other than the then Illinois secretary of state. The other men joining him were identified as Mitchells.

Alexander P. Field was a domineering personality and a man of substantial physical presence. He stood six feet four inches and was strongly built. He was both charismatic and subject to extreme passions. He used his strong voice to advantage.[36] He was a buddy to the other young lawyers on the circuit, including his pal Abraham Lincoln. Yet, everyone who described him referred to his sarcasm, which his detractors described as "ugly," effected with "a sardonic smile playing around his lips." What most characterized his life was his virtually unprincipled shift between political extremes. "[A] man of strong feeling, [he] was very ultra in the avowal of his political sentiments."[37] He could zig and zag from one extreme to the other, embracing each with fervor. His political stump speeches were considered devastating, yet he switched political sides at least

Alexander P. Field, Illinois Secretary of State, 1829–1840, participant in kidnap of the Titus family, and equally surprising, for a time attorney of record with partner, David Hall, in the Scotts' freedom suit.

four times in his life. Because the politics of his era often divided men based on their views of slavery, he crossed over that divide each time that he switched his allegiances. He had come into authority by frontier nepotism. His uncle, the governor, appointed him secretary of state. He practiced law at the same time that he served the state, and was said to pay more attention to his private practice than to his official duties.[38] He used both his physical presence and his official position in overpowering Lydia's family.[39]

By coincidence, a white man named Nathan Cole witnessed the events that evening at Lydia's house. Cole was a butcher, established locally in St. Louis and Illinoistown. He was probably present for the purpose of buying livestock from the family. He had a slaughterhouse in Illinoistown, just opposite St. Louis and not far from the Tituses' home.[40]

Cole described the kidnappers' surprise attack as brutal. A. P. Field was clearly in charge, and claiming authority for removing the Titus family from their home. The others in the party were Field's clients. Cole tried to intervene to stop the attack, until he discovered that Field was armed. Field drew his weapon on the group and informed Cole that he would be arrested if he interfered. Field made no attempt to keep his roles distinct. Threatening arrest invoked official state authority. This was on top of his physical domination of the situation, with a weapon, and his clients present to help seize the Titus family. According to Cole's affidavit, Field "turned Bully and made indecent threats against Cole's life" to discourage him from interfering.[41] Field directed Lydia to lie down or she would be tied down if she tried to interfere with her family's removal. Before her eyes, armed men seized, bound, and smuggled her children and grandchildren out of her home.

Only Lydia Titus was not seized. Perhaps this was because at age fifty, she was too old to be valuable for sale, or maybe she was too feisty to transport, or possibly it was because she had registered freedom papers in the Illinois courthouse. Lydia sprang into action, pursuing her kidnapped family and their abductors, and seeking justice. Lydia seemed to know that they would be taken to Missouri.

The next day she was in the St. Louis courthouse to sign habeas corpus papers seeking their whereabouts and their release. The habeas corpus petitions asked that her family members be found and returned to the court from wherever they were. By Lydia's side, swearing to the truth of the facts, was meatpacker Nathan Cole.[42]

The men had taken six of her children and two grandchildren. As Lydia recited in their respective petitions, Mary Ann, Sam, and Nathan Jr. were born after Lydia's freedom judgment, and lived with her at their Illinois home "in the uninterrupted enjoyment of their liberty" until Field and Mitchell forced them to Missouri as slaves. Their captors threatened to remove them further, out of Missouri. Her three youngest children and her two grandchildren had never been enslaved, so their treatment was all the more outrageous.

Her family was found on the road to Herculaneum, a small lead mining town south of St. Louis, which was another steamboat stop on the river. The sheriff of Jefferson County, responding to the habeas corpus writ, took both the captives and two of the kidnappers into custody. Attorney A. P. Field was no longer with them. Having delivered the Tituses to his clients, he had gone on to other matters on his busy schedule.

The captives were jailed for their own protection. As the sheriff stated, Mary Ann was "put in the gaol of Jefferson Co for safekeeping and has been by me detained for no other purpose, but her personal safety."[43] The others were similarly jailed.[44] Their captors, H. C. Russell and Mitchell, were charged with kidnapping and also jailed.[45]

Once the family was rescued from their captors, they were transferred to St. Louis. Eight parallel cases were filed on the same day by Vina, Mahala, Sam, Mary Ann, Nathan Jr., Matilda, Michael, and Anson against different combinations of the four defendants: Alexander P. Field, Elijah Mitchell, H. G. "Martin" Mitchell, and H. C. Russell. (There is considerable confusion about the Mitchells' first names. Henry G. Mitchell was arrested under the name of Martin Mitchell. Martin was the name of the man who first had Vina arrested as a runaway.) Lydia's adult children sued in their own names; Lydia sued as next friend for her

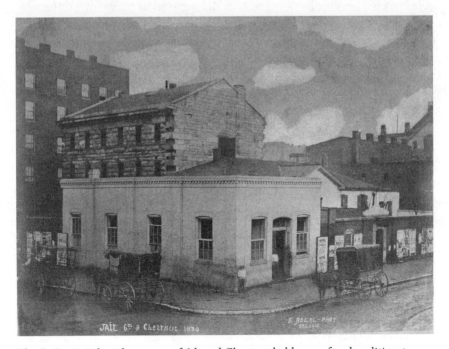

The St. Louis jail at the corner of 6th and Chestnut held many freedom litigants while they awaited trial. The jailor's office is in the foreground. The cells occupied the three-story stone building behind the office. Missouri History Museum, St. Louis.

underage children and her grandchildren. Then William Clark stepped in as next friend for the grandsons, who were Matilda's children.

Who were these enslavers, where did they come from, and how did Alexander P. Field come to represent them? They had no presence in St. Louis, and scant presence in Illinois. Other than Field, none of these persons appear in any of the other local litigation of the era.[46] Nor do they seem to be connected to the widow Jinsey Mitchell, now Mrs. Masterson. St. Louis seems only to have been a transit stop on their way south, with the objective of removing the Tituses to Kentucky.[47] The place of their discovery, on the road to Herculaneum, suggests an attempt to smuggle them out of state without being noticed. Anyone in pursuit of the captives would look first in St. Louis and search the docks. Herculaneum was a less obvious transport depot, where fewer steamboats stopped mostly to pick up lead for transport.

Most likely the kidnappers were from Warren County, Kentucky, and were Elijah Mitchell's descendants.[48] The 1830 census identifies several Mitchells living there, including one household headed by Henry G. Mitchell and another by Martin Mitchell.[49] (Elijah Mitchell's Kentucky county of origin is unknown.[50])

Responding to the kidnapping, and the law's presumption of enslavement for African Americans, forced the Tituses to prove again their right to freedom. A lawsuit with eight plaintiffs and four defendants was unwieldy, so the suits were consolidated. Only the suit of Mary Ann against Field and Elijah Mitchell would go to trial.[51] The other cases would be resolved according to the outcome of her suit.

But while the case was pending, several of the brothers and sisters were hired out. On May 30, 1832, Mary Ann was brought before the judge, and the St. Louis County sheriff was ordered to hire her out for the duration. The defendants refused to enter into recognizance as required by law, so the judge directed the sheriff to hire the Tituses out. The practice seems odd, but while they were imprisoned, they were running up charges for the jailor. Thus, the county's typical response was to seek to hire out freedom petitioners. Despite the fact that grandson Michael was only a child, the court ordered him hired out as well.[52]

Attorney Gustavus Bird represented the Tituses. He handled freedom suits expertly. In July, the lawyers went to Illinois to both Monroe and Madison County to take depositions from witnesses.[53] The depositions pitted neighbors against one another in what appears to have been a long-held neighborhood grudge over whether Lydia should have ever been adjudged free in the first place. Some said that the old master, Elijah Mitchell intended to free his slaves at his death;[54] others claimed he did not, as if Elijah Mitchell's intent was even relevant to legally determining the family's status. The real issue was not Mitchell's intent, but the family's prolonged legal presence in free territory. Plaintiffs called two of their neighboring farmers as witnesses. Curiously, neither one could be found to testify.[55]

A. P. Field cleverly sought to evade the action against him by claiming that he was merely acting as an attorney in representing his clients, rather than engaging in a trespass as a principal party. He did not represent himself or his codefendants in these law suits.[56] The testimony reiterated that Field was armed, claimed to be the responsible person, and "he fell foul of Lyd and threatened to tie her."[57]

Matilda, Lydia's oldest daughter, who had already won a freedom suit against VanBibber in Missouri when she was twelve, invoked that judgment.[58] Matilda's son Michael was assisted by William Clark, probably the same man who had purchased goods from Nathan Titus's estate sale.[59] The case is styled "Michael, a boy of color, son of Matilda, by next friend William Clark." Matilda and Michael later took the last name "Clark."[60] Two decades later, Michael registered himself under the name Michael Clark, son of Matilda Clark.[61] Another census similarly lists the only "Anson" as Anson Clark.[62] Was William Clark the children's father? No marriage license can be found linking Matilda to William Clark.

One great sadness of the whole affair is that despite the family's eventual victory and release, three family members did not survive the ordeal. Mahala, who was hired out, died first, in January 1833. Her brothers, Sam and Nathan, were reported to have died by May. "Suggestion of death of plff, suit abates also attested to by Nathan Cold [*sic*]."[63] Cholera swept through St. Louis that year, and may have caused their deaths.

On May 3, 1833, the jury of twelve white men ruled in Mary Ann's favor, declared her to be free, and assessed the damages as $250.[64] The redemption came almost a year after the kidnapping. Marry Ann was awarded damages for her injury. The stipulation brought freedom as well to the other surviving plaintiffs. While Matilda and Lavinia also received $250 in damages for their ordeal; the children Michael and Anson were awarded only a single penny. No damages were awarded posthumously for the deaths of Nathan, Sam, and Mahala. In their death, so too, ended their claims against their kidnappers.

Although two of their captors were arrested for kidnapping, no charges can be found in Jefferson County. Were the Mitchells ever actually indicted for the crime? We don't know. No kidnapping charges can be found in the Illinois records either. But who would attempt to indict the powerful Illinois secretary of state?

Lydia's family had excellent representation in Gustavus Bird. Although Bird often represented individuals who had no capacity to pay, Bird did not work for the Tituses for free. Upon winning the freedom suits, he asked Lydia to pay him $125 for his legal services. On the day that the family was freed, Lydia initialed a written note promising to pay him that amount.

When she did not pay him in the weeks that followed, he sued her on the note for the amount adding an extra $25. Fearing that he would not be paid, Bird sought an order demanding that she post bond for the amount. He stated that

Lydia was still in town but was preparing to leave the jurisdiction, presumably finally to return home to Illinois. When she did not—or could not—post bond, Lydia was thrown in the same jail from which her children had been released only a month earlier. While her children were initially imprisoned for their own safekeeping, and subsequently because no bond was paid, Lydia Titus was now imprisoned as a debtor. The sheriff's return states, "Executed this writ by arresting the body of the defendant and securing her body in the common Jail of St. Louis County on the 4th day of June 1833."[65] How long Lydia remained in jail is unclear. The case did not go to trial until six months later in December, and then the jury awarded Bird the full sum of $125, but not the additional charge that he had requested.[66]

Bird's suit for his fees was further confused by peripheral legal skirmishes over Lavinia's horse. In the intervening months, Lavinia sued another free Black man, Jerry Duncan, for having taken her bay horse. Lavinia eventually dropped her claim against him without pursuing it to trial or filing criminal charges.[67] These contemporary events suggest further speculation. Jerry Duncan's brothers were also Gustavus Bird's clients in freedom suits, and when Lavinia sued Jerry Duncan, Gustavus Bird, who had just won Lavinia her freedom, represented Jerry in the dispute over the horse, rather than Lavinia. What motivated this dispute over the horse? Was Jerry attempting to enforce Bird's claim for services, or was Jerry acting on his own? We don't know. Jerry Duncan was the only Duncan brother ever suspected in other theft charges.[68]

The value of the bay horse would hardly have resolved the larger debt. But the value of Lydia's homestead in Illinois did. After receiving a judgment on the debt in the St. Louis courts, Bird crossed the river to sue on the debt in Illinois, the site of the homestead. This action appears to have forced Lydia to sell the homestead, since she conveyed her entire homestead to a buyer for $300 within days of Bird's filing the claim against her in her Illinois county.[69]

Lydia had won back the freedom of her family but at a tremendous price. Three of her children had died in the ordeal while they were coercively hired out awaiting trial, every family member had spent time in the jail, and in the end Lydia had even lost the farm to pay her lawyer.

After that, the family seemed to break up. Lavinia and Matilda worked as washerwomen in St. Louis.[70] By the time he was twenty, Michael was going by "Michael Clark, son of Matilda Clark, a free woman." He was registered as formally free at age 20.[71] He and his brother remained in Illinois. His registration indicates that the obligation to continually redeem one's liberty was an ongoing feature of the lives of African Americans as long as there was a presumption that an African American was a slave.

The white men at odds in the case responded as white men of status usually did. Nathan Cole sued A.P. Field. Cole did not sue A. P. Field for the surprise assault, threaten him with criminal prosecution, or challenge him to a duel. Instead, the tension between the men manifested itself by A. P. Field talking publicly and derogatorily about Nathan Cole's reputation within days of Cole attesting to Field's involvement in the abduction. Cole then used Field's public statements as a basis to sue him for slander, and he did.[72] Cole successfully sued Field for defamation to clear his name and to get his revenge. Butchers were respected tradesmen. Cole was in partnership at the time. Field had tried to drive a wedge between Cole and his partner by telling Cole's partner that he should be sorry to be in business with Cole—that he was a rascal and perjurer who should be "cropped."[73] Cole won his case against Field and was awarded $500, twice the amount that any of the Tituses received for their injuries and loss of liberty.

CHAPTER 6

John Merry, Also Known as Jean Marie: Free Born

There are no slaves in France.
—French maxim that predates the French Revolution

The Ordinance was construed to operate prospectively, and not to operate
on the French slaves in the Territory at the time.
—Illinois governor John Reynolds

Thirty-six-year-old John Merry based his claim for freedom on the fact that
although his mother was a slave, he was born in the free territory of Illinois. His
suit paved the way for the suits of his wife and children by raising a distinctive
legal issue about birthright freedom. The issue was simple and direct: was the
child of one of the original French slaves (still recognized as property of their
masters because that property preceded the Northwest Ordinance) a free person or a slave? John's mother was one of the original French slaves that Governor St. Clair had exempted from operation of the Northwest Ordinance.[1] Even
in 1825, years after Illinois statehood, there were still 238 persons registered as
slaves living in Randolph County, Illinois, where John Merry's family lived. Illinois had done nothing to emancipate them.[2] But what about the children of these
exempted slaves?

Governor St. Clair's original decree exempting the French and the slaves that
they then held was expedient at the time. It was done in response to Tarvideau's
lobbying and made concrete in the correspondence surrounding Peter McNelly's case,[3] but it was not at all forward looking. Successive waves of American
territorial jurisdiction had washed over the region east of the Mississippi River
since George Rogers Clark wrested military control of that territory from the
French in 1778. The French communities remained and were allowed to retain
their slaves. Did each new sovereignty "grandfather" in the exception accorded
to the French for their slaves and their descendants? From the Virginia Territory
(1778) to U.S. territory (1787) to the Northwest Territory (1787) to Indiana

Territory (1800) to Illinois territory (1809) to Illinois statehood (1818), sovereign power over the region had been linked in succession. The French right to retain their slaves, authorized by the Northwest Territory's first governor, St. Clair in 1794, could have been extinguished as simply too tenuous a carryover to protect as a property right at the point of any change of sovereignty.[4]

Yet, there was no political inclination to do so within the area. So African Americans continued to be held as "French Slaves" in Illinois. Many of the governors, judges, and lawyers, like John Reynolds, held slaves themselves under the French exception.[5] Reynolds had married Julian Dubuque's daughter, a woman who as a French descendant expected to continue to own slaves. Others indulged themselves in the privilege of keeping slaves under a spirit of self interest that if the French could hold slaves, why couldn't they, as Americans, enjoy that privilege as well?[6] And after all, the distinction between a legally fully indentured servant and a slave was merely a matter of a piece of paper and taking the slave before a clerk.

The indenture process was viewed as a way to retain bondsmen within the technical language of the Northwest Ordinance.[7] Governor John Reynolds described the process of transforming the Illinois bondsman from slave to indentured servant. "The owner might go with his slaves before the clerk of the court of common pleas, and make an agreement with his negroes to serve the master a certain number of years, and then become free. The children were to serve their masters—the males until they were thirty-five years old, and the females to thirty-two years." Reynolds acknowledged that this "proceeding was intended by the legislature to introduce a species of slavery...."[8]

The only advantage that the piece of paper offered the enslaved was the possibility of release at the end of the specified term of years. Even that was a possibility, not necessarily a guarantee, because there was no state enforcement of the release.[9] Release at the end of the term was precariously dependent upon the master's good will and his respect for the legal term limit in the face of his self-interest. Still, bondsmen viewed indenture as some improvement over practices in the territory before. Peggy, a released indentured woman, described the circumstance as making some difference, "all that came on first were slaves—we had then no indentures."[10]

John Merry was born to a slave woman who continued to be the property of her owners when the Americans established jurisdiction over the French settlements in southern Illinois. There were three major French colonial enclaves at Kaskaskia, Prairie du Rocher, and Cahokia on the Illinois side, north of the juncture of the Ohio and Mississippi Rivers, when the state of Virginia first established its claim to jurisdiction over the area by George Rogers Clark's conquest.

It was estimated that in 1800, the country consisted of 100,000 Native Americans, 4,875 whites, and 135 African American slaves.[11] In the 1800 census, Kaskaskia had

47 slaves and there were 60 in Prairie du Rocher.[12] Thus, most of the slaves of African descent living on the Illinois side of the river, were located near one of these enclaves. By 1810, there were 129 in the county containing Kaskaskia, and 40 in Cahokia. Not all the slaveholders in the area were French. They had been joined by a few enterprising Americans, like the Morrison family, who had moved west as traders and also bought slaves locally or brought slaves with them. Still, since these slave arrangements had begun under the French regime, describing them as "the French slaves" of Illinois is not far from the mark.

Virginia's claim to the Illinois county was ceded to the federal government before the United States enacted the Northwest Ordinance prohibiting slavery. The cession document had specifically reserved the rights and liberties of the territory's inhabitants, including their right to hold slaves.[13] In dealing with the French settlements, Governor St. Clair had seen this concession as a political exigency and he interpreted the Territorial Ordinance as not intending to emancipate "the slaves they were in possession of and had obtained under the laws by which they had formerly been governed, but was intended simply to prevent the introduction of others."[14]

None of these documents, pronouncements, or interpretations necessarily extended to the second generation, which was John Merry's circumstance, a child born of a French slave in free territory. Nor were they clearly repudiated by the Ordinance's language. John was born to a slave mother in the Trottier household and later acquired by the Jarrot family. Nicholas Jarrot was a significant Cahokia resident who owned several slaves.

Susette, who became John Merry's wife, had been a slave west of the Mississippi river where slavery had always been and continued to be legal. She was taken to Illinois after her owner died and she was bequeathed to Nicholas Jarrot. Jarrot was prominent enough in the community to be appointed a justice of the peace in 1809 (though he soon resigned). Upon bringing Susette to his household in the free Illinois territory, Jarrot wisely had her indentured as a servant for a term of fifty years.[15] Although Jarrot held several "French" slaves in his lifetime, Susette was the only one whom he formally indentured, presumably because she had not been born in Illinois, as the others had. Most owners of French slaves in Illinois did not bother to formally indenture them, or their children, nor did anyone require them to. Pierre Menard, for example, never indentured a single one of his many slaves, although some he had acquired from Missouri slaveholding relatives, just as Susette had been acquired. Most owners of French slaves simply ignored the indenturing process, seeing slaveholding as a privilege that preceded the American claim to the area; they continued to buy and sell persons across the Mississippi River and hold them and their children in perpetual slavery unbothered by subsequent legal constraints.[16]

During Jarrot's lifetime, he gave several slaves away to his children.[17] At his death, his estate still contained seven slaves, including John Merry and his family. John, his wife Susette, and their child were listed in the 1821 estate of Nicholas Jarrot, valued together as worth $900.[18] Under the French *Code Noir*,[19] black enslaved families were not to be separated or sold away from one another. That code was no longer law in the state of Illinois when Jarrot died. Still, Jarrot's estate made a point of listing John's family together and appraising them together anyway. The Merry family members were sold together twice eventually ending up into the hands of Pensonneau.[20] In the meantime, Susette had another child.[21]

John initiated efforts toward freedom by offering to buy his family's way out of slavery. Ultimately, he would end up as a captive defensively litigating his freedom in two slave states, though never in Illinois. He would base his claim, however, on his birth there. John Merry's lawsuits would extend the principle established in Winny's case, freedom by residence, to freedom by reason of birth. John Merry's family were not the last remaining slaves in Illinois. They were, however, the first family to raise this legal issue. A simpler way to freedom was to get one's master's consent by purchasing one's freedom. So John first tried to negotiate. He told his new master, Pensonneau, that he would not work for him, but he would pay him the price that he had paid for his family. He offered him money and some horses in exchange for the freedom of his family.[22] The agreement was that John would pay Louis Pensonneau $450 over three years, $900 in total, their full appraised value. He gave his master the down payment of $230 immediately, $200 in cash and $30 in the value of two horses. John said that Pensonneau then "liberated" him, which perhaps means simply that he released him, and he left for St. Louis to earn the rest.[23]

There are many ironies in the river crossings in this story that run contrary to stereotypical expectations about slave and free territory. One would expect that freedom-seeking slaves would only choose to migrate *toward* free lands —and never from a free state to a slave state. The first irony in this story is that as a recently "liberated" Illinois slave, John Merry left Illinois for an urban area in a slave state where he could expect to earn the money necessary to complete the purchase of his freedom. The fact of the matter, however, is that St. Louis offered much better opportunities for earning a living. As a person of color, John Merry was not alone in moving to St. Louis, a slave jurisdiction, to earn money. Lavinia Titus had done so. Several other Illinois freed people found themselves drawn there because of the better economic opportunities. In another example, a couple whom Illinois Governor Edward Coles freed— individuals who were even given their own plots of land—chose to work at higher wages for a white farmer in St. Louis, rather than trying to scrape by on income from their own farm in the rich Illinois soil.[24] A second irony, not only did St. Louis draw free Blacks because it provided better economic opportunities, as John's treatment will indicate the slave state of Missouri actually offered slaves more receptive venues to litigate their freedom than did Illinois at the time.

Despite the contractual agreement and taking the down payment, Louis Pensonneau refused to honor the agreement, and came after John Merry in St. Louis to reclaim him. He had him jailed and, further, shipped downriver in chains to New Orleans for sale. To be shipped to New Orleans for sale was the circumstance most feared by slaves.[25]

When Pensonneau seized John Merry, he told him that he had always intended to cheat him and that it was his right to do so. Another witness verified that this had always been Pensonneau's plan, "Perceneau [sic] told her that he intended to get out of the said Negro Jean Louis [sic], all he could, and then send him down to New Orleans."[26]

Under Illinois law, specifically the Illinois black code, John Merry's contract was not legally enforceable. The Illinois code rendered all contracts between masters and servants during the time of service void.[27] If John Merry was a servant for life, it would mean that he could never engage in an enforceable contract with his master for his liberty.

Pensonneau personally saw to John Merry being manacled and placed in irons aboard the steamboat *General Brown* at the St. Louis docks. Still in chains, John was transported downriver and then transferred to a slave trader in New Orleans for resale. Though in January 1825, John Merry had believed he had a contract for his family's freedom, he had left his family, had relinquished prospects, money and his horses, and was in the process of working off the rest, by May, he found himself in New Orleans resold as a slave to a man that the Missouri courts called "Andrew Sheckoni."[28]

Andrew Sheckoni was, in fact, a Louisiana plantation owner named André Cexnaider, a name that was subject to multiple spellings, even in Louisiana. In New Orleans, John Merry's name was transcribed as "Jean Marie." Cexnaider had a plantation outside New Orleans in the parish of St. John the Baptist, Louisiana, and he was in the process of acquiring more slaves. Within five years after buying John, he had acquired nine slaves.[29]

But John Merry did not remain with Cexnaider or at the Louisiana plantation. After some time he managed to escape and make his way back upriver to Cahokia, the village where he had been born, and presumably where Susette and their children still lived. Susette's indenture had also been sold to Pensonneau, which meant that essentially Susette had been sold to him. Once John Merry was discovered at Cahokia, Pensonneau seized him again. This time he employed a St. Louis part-time deputy sheriff, and sent John back across the Mississippi River to be jailed in St. Louis.[30] The slaveholding Pensonneau brothers controlled one of the few ferries between Illinoistown and St. Louis.[31] Pensonneau then sold John Merry again, from his jail cell this time to two local men who understood the value of French slaves from Illinois.

Louis Menard and Dr. Clayton Tiffin purchased him and bailed him out of jail, claiming him as a slave. Menard's relatives continued to own the largest number of French slaves in Illinois. Dr. Tiffin was married to Nicholas Jarrot's daughter,[32] the man who had once owned John Merry. Dr. Tiffin still held slaves from his late father-in-law's provenance, so he may have seen acquiring this man as a natural extension of his slaveholdings.[33] Acquiring this man would keep him in the next generation of the Jarrot family.

Upon his release from jail, John Merry sued both Dr. Tiffin and Louis Menard for his freedom.[34] While the case was in litigation, John Merry could not legally be removed from the court's jurisdiction, so he would be safe from extradition to Cexnaider in New Orleans and kidnapping by Pensonneau.

In April 1827, the suit went to a full trial, with eight witnesses.[35] John Merry was represented by Joseph Charless, Jr.[36] The jury decided against John Merry, however, and the freedom litigant immediately appealed to the Missouri Supreme Court.[37]

Many of the lawsuit's legal arguments involved peeling back the layers of earlier sovereignty to see which laws stuck and had become imbedded in the legal firmament and which had been overwritten by newer legal regimes. Since 1787 Virginia Act of Cession ensured protection for its inhabitants' right,[38] this, the Illinois slaveholders argued, protected their right to own not only those who were enslaved at the time, but also the progeny of those slaves. There was no doubt that John Merry's mother was a slave, and despite residing in Illinois, her ownership was secured to her French masters. The argument's extension was that slavery was a hereditable circumstance. The child of a slave mother, resident of Illinois, should be a slave as well. The Illinois courts had never entertained this question. The enslavement of successive generations of "French slaves" had been complacently accepted in Illinois. The legal elite continued to enjoy its advantages.

The Missouri high court rejected the slaveholders' argument. The Court wrote that the cession act was "completely satisfied, by securing to them the enjoyment of such rights as they then had [one generation], and not that the things or objects that might then happen to be." Again Judge Matthias McGirk, who wrote Winny's case and worked behind the scenes for the Scypions, wrote the opinion.[39]

The Missouri Supreme Court declared the important principle of birthright freedom. The Court wrote,

> The whole of these instruments, taken together, are unable to create any doubt in our minds, as to the meaning of the sixth article of the ordinance. The express words in the cession act of Virginia...are completely satisfied, by securing to them the enjoyment of such rights as they then had, and not that the things or objects that might then happen to be. Property should be so throughout all future time. This man [John Merry] was not then born, and when he was born into existence, the law forbid slavery to exist; and at the time of the making the cession act, this man, John, was not property; and at the time of his birth, he could not be property.[40]

As a newborn in a land of freedom, John was free. "No words are to be contrived, unless a doubt arises; here there is no doubt. The ordinance is positive that slavery cannot exist, and shall we or any other court say otherwise."[41] This notion of birthright freedom appeared to be a relatively new legal development. There was not a lot of precedent that the Missouri court could cite for this proposition.[42] Illinois courts had never so held. French slaves in Illinois were a relative anomaly.

Accordingly, the Missouri Supreme Court declared, "John is free."[43] These were stirring words for the high court of a slave state to issue in 1827. This holding was extremely important in dismantling the perpetuity by which generations of "French slaves" had been held in Illinois since Governor St. Clair exempted them.

Thus, in this case the courts of a frontier slave state, Missouri, took a step ahead of Illinois at this time. Illinois continued to respect "French slave" owners' claims, and many of these same men were still influential in Illinois law and politics.[44]

John Merry's victory did not mean that all French slaves in Illinois were free, however. Even the Missouri Supreme Court was not willing to go that far. (The following year, the Missouri Supreme Court ruled against Theoteste, who was a generation older than John Merry, reinforcing the notion that the older French slaves in Illinois continued to be enslaved.[45]) The line drawn between original French slaves and their later-born children meant that the French slave population in Illinois could not be perpetuated in bondage by reproduction. John Merry's mother, had she still lived, would have remained enslaved, but her children born after the Northwest Ordinance would all be free by virtue of "birthright freedom."

Despite the ruling, French inhabitants of Illinois did not allow their slave populations to dwindle; they continued to bring slaves in from their Missouri cousins.[46] As long as they indentured them, as Merry's wife Susette had been indentured, the group could continue to expand by adding slaves from outside Illinois borders. Illinois residents, who were members of old French families, continued to move their slaves back and forth among family members as required.

Despite declaring "John is free," the Missouri Supreme Court remanded for retrial. Why re-try the case, when the high court had declared the legal conclusion? Because under the language of Winny's case, John could go further and press for compensation. The retrial of John Merry's freedom suit could not be held until August, when the term of court reconvened, since the St. Louis Circuit court rarely sat during the heat of the summer.

Nonetheless, John Merry must have held a big party on his victory. He had good reason to celebrate. During the summer of 1827, he was charged with running a disorderly house because a party held at his house drew the attention of others. Persons in the house were said to be "hallooing, cursing, singing, tipling and misbehaving."[47] It sounds like quite a celebration!

The misdemeanor charge seems to have been the result of a backlash directed at John Merry and prompted by his recent victory. Complaining witnesses were none other than the same part-time deputy sheriff who had dragged him across the river to the St. Louis jail and other witnesses called in John's freedom suit.[48] In this misdemeanor prosecution, John Merry was accused of keeping a "common, ill-governed and disorderly house, [where] for his own...gain, certain ill-disposed persons of evil name and fame, and of dishonest conversation, as well slaves as a free persons...come together unlawfully...."

John was still under the indictment for running a disorderly house when his freedom case came to trial. Susette and his children, John Jr., age eight, Angelique, age two, and Edmund, just an infant, appear to have joined him in St. Louis, according to inferences drawn from the events that followed.

Two court proceedings affecting the family, argued by the same attorney, occurred on the same day in March. First, the prosecution dismissed the disorderly house misdemeanor, and, simultaneously, Merry's wife and three children filed suit for freedom.[49] Joseph Charless Jr., who represented John Merry, also took Susette and the children's case.[50] Ironically, the very disorderly house charges against John Merry—that he had allowed slaves and free persons of color to commingle—fit the status distinctions of members of his own family residing in the same house. Susette's presence and her continued status as a "slave" or indentured servant living with John Merry, declared free by the high court, could have been used as grounds for the charge. There is no explanation for why the misdemeanor was dismissed, but so it was.

Susette Merry and her children brought suit that day against a man named John Reynolds.[51] Susette alleged that she had been sold by Pensonneau to John Reynolds, but Reynolds couldn't be found in the county to receive service of process.[52] It seems that this suit also figured in the backlash against the recent ruling. The evidence suggests Susette sued none other than the prominent John Reynolds, lawyer, judge, and soon to be governor of Illinois, who lived just across the river in Illinoistown.[53] This John Reynolds, the most noteworthy man with that name in the area, then resided only five miles from St. Louis in the same town as Pensonneau. He had grown up in the area where John and Susette had been enslaved, so she could hardly have been mistaken about his identity in naming him. But Reynolds could not be found when the sheriff looked for him.[54] With Pensonneau's ferries crossing the river regularly, and John Reynolds living on the Illinois side, Reynolds had a convenient means to leave and a place outside the jurisdiction to retreat to.

Generally, when the sheriff could not find the defendant on the first attempt, the routine procedure was to search for the defendant again, or even a third time, before the suit was dismissed for lack of a defendant. No second summons was ever sought, however. By the time that a second summons would have issued, Susette and her children had been kidnapped and taken to Illinois by more Illinois residents, acquaintances of John Reynolds from the old neighborhood.

This event reveals yet another irony: persons of color living independently in the chief city of a slave state, and filing suit for freedom, were kidnapped in order to return them to involuntary servitude in the free state of Illinois. Yet, that is what happened. A grand jury found that Moses Whitesides and Jacob Judy, both Illinois residents, forcibly captured Susette and the children intending to move them out of state so that they could not pursue their freedom suit.[55]

The sheriff was ordered to arrest the men on conspiracy to interfere with Susette's lawsuit. A grand jury, convened in November, indicted the two Illinois farmers, charging them with conspiracy in the kidnapping.[56] The prosecuting witnesses were the Merrys' attorney and other leading St. Louis citizens.[57]

The identity of Susette's kidnappers links back to John Reynolds. The families of all three men had known each other for two generations.[58] Moses Whitesides and Jacob Judy were brothers-in-law. More fittingly, each kidnapper was planning to relocate, moving north to set out for Illinois lands further removed from the settled areas. Either man would have found it useful to take along an unclaimed servant. Judy moved up the Illinois River north to Peoria,[59] and Moses Whitesides was preparing to move to the lead mining, boom town of Galena farther north on the Mississippi.[60] Galena is exactly where John Merry Jr. later turned up. Even John Reynolds visited Galena that year on his campaign tour.[61]

Paradoxically, these three Illinois men had stronger legal claims to Susette, who had been indentured in Illinois than anyone had to her husband, John Merry. No one had bothered to indenture John Merry, as he could have been as a servant's child. Susette was indentured in Illinois and indentured still when she attempted to sue for her freedom before being kidnapped. According to her indenture papers, Susette was bound until 1867, for another thirty-seven years, in all likelihood a period exceeding her expected lifespan.[62]

Their children had an even more complicated claim to freedom, since the principle of matrilineality bound them to their mother's status, rather than their father's newly proclaimed free status. The children were born in Illinois, and therefore like their father should be free-born, but the children of servants could themselves be indentured. John Merry's children were the children of a still indentured Illinois servant, Suzette. Illinois law provided that they too could have been indentured until they came of age, but such papers were never executed. At least, none can be found of record. In any case, though free born in Illinois, underage children of an indentured mother had little basis for claiming their freedom until they became adults.

After the grand jury indicted the kidnappers, Susette and the children and the kidnappers disappeared. Even after a different jury was convened in August and John Merry's second freedom case was tried, Susette could not be found. Her lawsuit dissolved with her disappearance; there were no further entries in the daybook or the case file. This time, John Merry won his suit, which was no surprise; the high court already declared him free, although he was awarded only 1 cent in damages for all his injuries.[63]

John Merry was next seen back in New Orleans, again being forced into slavery by André Cexnaider, the man who had purchased him from New Orleans trader years earlier.

Under what circumstances did he return to New Orleans? There are two possible divergent explanations. First, he may have been in pursuit of his family, fearing that they had been forced down the same path that he had been when kidnapped. That would draw him to New Orleans in search of them. The other explanation was that he too was kidnapped, again, just as his family was kidnapped, but that he was shipped south to the man to whom he had already been sold. By November of the same year that he was declared free in St. Louis, John Merry was again in New Orleans, and it appears that Susette and the children, swept up by kidnappers, were taken to Galena, Illinois. John Merry's troubles continued.

John wasted little time suing again, this time taking Cexnaider to trial in New Orleans.[64] It had been a tumultuous year. Almost a year to the day that John Merry had filed suit in St. Louis against Tiffin and Menard, he sued for freedom a second time in New Orleans against André Cexnaider. Although he had escaped Cexnaider's clutches once before, he was again in his grasp. At the same time,

John Reynolds, the man sued by Susette and implicated in her continued captivity, was elected governor of Illinois.

The case file for John Merry's New Orleans lawsuit duplicates his Missouri case, but now he also had the further favorable Missouri appeal and jury verdict to substantiate his claim. His legal victory in St. Louis, the gold standard in establishing freedom, had not protected him from recapture, but it certainly made it considerably easier for him to parlay the Louisiana case to victory.

Freedom suits never seemed to occur easily, however. In New Orleans, John Merry encountered the inevitable and unfortunate delay of court proceedings and a recalcitrant, and somewhat vengeful, defendant pulling every trick to delay the trial still further and apply pressure on John Merry to cave. The fact of his freedom was documented by the Missouri courts' records. Full faith and credit required that Louisiana respect the Missouri decision, not only on the legal issue of children of "French slaves," as a matter of precedent, but also the judgment that this very person was free, as a matter of *res judicata*.

John did win his case, but not without considerable aggravating delay. Cexnaider prevented John Merry's release from jail on bond. During the four-month pendency of the proceedings, Cexnaider alleged that John Merry could not be trusted because he "is so much addicted to running away," that he might run away during the pendency of suit. As a result, the court denied John bail, requiring him to remain in the New Orleans jail for the duration.

When the New Orleans trial court finally ruled in Merry's favor,[65] Cexnaider delayed his release still longer by appealing. The appeal detained him until the Louisiana Supreme Court could affirm the decision and ultimately release him about March of 1830.

Thirty-five-year-old John Merry, married, and the father of children had won his freedom twice over in two separate slave states. But his victories were not without hardship. His enjoyment of his freedom had been interrupted by repeated kidnappings and time spent in jail awaiting the slow-moving machinery that eventually released him.

While his father engaged the New Orleans courts, John Jr. was in Galena, still treated as a slave. John Jr. was removed from Galena by a man named William Campbell, who claimed to have bought young John and was intending to take him to Washington, D.C. John feared that, like his father, he was actually destined for New Orleans for sale. When the steamboat stopped at the St. Louis docks, as all upper Mississippi River boats did, young John Merry remembered the lesson and filed suit for freedom.[66] In 1832, John Merry's son, John Jr. now a boy about twelve or thirteen years old, sued for his freedom to interrupt his removal from the area.

The case record identifies him as Susette's son. A woman named Susan signed an affidavit for young John, but she never appeared again in the suit.[67] Was this

his mother, Susette? Did she find the exposure too dangerous? Susette's term of indenture had not expired. John's suit proceeded instead with the help of another adult, Margaret Sarpee, as his next friend. The witnesses that young John called are exactly the same cast of characters whom his father had sued for freedom, particularly Dr. Clayton Tiffin, and his wife, daughter of the late Nicholas Jarrot. Who was Margaret Sarpee? The last name is probably a misspelling of "Sarpy." The Sarpy family lived next door to the Tiffins in St. Louis. Although the Sarpy's were a prominent St. Louis Creole family, there is no Margaret listed as part of the family in the genealogies or church records.[68] So it is more likely that Margaret was a black servant in the Sarpy family than a free white family member. John Jr. was formally declared free eighteen months later.[69]

This might have been the end of the story, but the last recorded chapter occurred only a year later. John Merry—Jean Marie, the elder—now a man of forty-four, died near St. Louis at the house of a woodcutter named Joseph Montaigne. In three trials and two trips to the supreme courts of different states, John Merry had broken the link of heritable status that chained the children of "French slaves" residing in Illinois to bondage. The death of this man, a man who had been kidnapped twice, was sudden and suspicious enough to prompt a coroner's inquest. The inquest was inconclusive, however; it stated that John Merry, persevering litigator of freedom, was killed by "visitation of the Almighty."[70]

It is not clear whether Susette died or was ever released from indenture, but a young man named John Merry, of the appropriate age, was listed in the 1840 St. Louis census as a boatman, free from the scourge of enslavement and kidnapping that had so affected his parents and the years of his early life.[71]

CHAPTER 7

David Shipman

The Daughters of the American Revolution of Tazewell County, Illinois, sought to memorialize a Revolutionary War soldier who died in that small county near Peoria.[1] To that end, in 1921 they publicly printed his entire one-page will.[2] The will provides several important bequests, including one to Moses Shipman and his sons. The will does not mention, however, that Moses Shipman is notable because he is a former slave of David Shipman, and not his relative. Nor does the will mention how David Shipman freed his slaves, their extraordinary flight together from Shelbyville, Kentucky, to Indiana to Illinois in the 1820s, or the kidnapping that took place in Tazewell County, Illinois, that attempted to drag Moses' family back to St. Louis and enslavement. This is the story of their redemption. In this story, their former master, David Shipman, acted honorably in the redemption of their freedom, in an admirable manner even perhaps surpassing his participation in the Revolutionary War.

Little is known about David Shipman's adult life in the border state of Kentucky, except that he owned a grist and sawmill and he seems to have befriended some free persons of color early on. One free man of color trusted him sufficiently to make him the designated recipient of his land after his wife's death.[3]

By 1820, Mr. and Mrs. David Shipman were already considered elderly and had no children—although a nephew, Stephen Smith was raised in their household. They lived on a creek in Shelby County, Kentucky, not too far from the Ohio River.[4] By 1826, David Shipman's financial fortunes had declined and he owed roughly $1,800 to merchants and other creditors in the town of Shelbyville.[5] When the creditors sought foreclosure, two of Shipman's several slaves were seized and sold to pay some of his debts.[6] Faced with further foreclosure and execution of debts on his remaining slaves, David Shipman asked his adult nephew Stephen Smith to provide security for him, deeding him a mortgage on his land and other property.

Sixty-year-old David Shipman was said to be very weak, and often unable to ride, but nonetheless, he managed to ride fast enough to save the rest of his slaves from his creditors. Always intending that they be free, Shipman decided to flee to free territory in order to manumit his remaining slaves, and save them from possible foreclosure. David Shipman proceeded across the Ohio River, accompanied by his seven slaves, and once he reached Jefferson County, Indiana, he signed final manumission papers for them. Present at the courthouse to receive their freedom papers were Moses and wife, Milly, her three children as well as two more young slave men, Harry Dick and William.[7] David Shipman, the elderly miller, left behind his wife, the mill on a small Kentucky acreage, and some livestock.

The departure of David Shipman and his slaves was done secretly, although perhaps not from his wife. Mrs. Shipman who suffered for a time, because she too was elderly and unwell, later joined him. After emancipating his seven slaves at the first stop, Indiana, the entire group then continued on to Illinois, presumably in an attempt to cover their tracks from possible creditors.

They eventually reached Tazewell County, Illinois, where there was a Quaker settlement, and they settled with the intent of residing permanently. Over the winter of 1826–1827, Shipman rented a farm, and in the spring, they put in a crop. Shipman announced to his neighbors that the black persons in his household were free and that all intended to stay permanently. His neighbors later corroborated that Shipman's former slaves were indeed permitted to go about as they pleased and live as free persons.[8]

Shipman's nephew, Stephen Smith, who had stood as security for Shipman's Kentucky debts, was dissatisfied with Shipman's departure and with the prospect of levying upon the real estate and livestock remaining in Kentucky to cover the debt. Smith himself planned to move west to St. Louis, and for traveling west, slaves were always more portable wealth. Bringing slaves from Kentucky to St. Louis was a favorable means of transferring wealth to the west, whereas a farmstead in Kentucky would tether him to that site. Stephen Smith pursued his Uncle Shipman's whereabouts and found him in Illinois. Smith confronted his uncle, and Shipman acknowledged the debt and offered to repay whatever was due. Shipman insisted that he had left sufficient real estate behind in Kentucky for Smith to execute against if he chose to call in the debt sooner than Shipman could pay cash. The land in Kentucky consisted of twenty-six acres and a grist- and saw-mill. Also at the mill site were six horses, a yoke of oxen, ten cattle, 30 sheep, and 30 hogs that could have been foreclosed upon.[9] But Smith wanted the slaves.[10]

Although Smith found his uncle and the freed people in January 1827, there was little way to seize the former slaves he sought during the winter. But in early May 1827, with the help of unnamed others, Smith took a skiff up the Illinois River as far as Peoria and seized five of the manumitted former slaves. Two of Milly's children were not seized with the others; they remained at the farm. En route downriver, Moses successfully got away from the skiff, escaping the kidnappers' clutches and traveling back to sound the alarm, because not long after the seizure, two men set out from Peoria by canoe in pursuit.

The trip downriver to St. Louis took less than a week. On May 8, while Smith had the slaves onboard the skiff docked at the city's wharf, the two men from the

Quaker settlement who had trailed him from Peoria, overtook them, entered the boat and reseized the group, intending to escort the freed people safely back to their home in Illinois.[11]

With the resulting dispute, each of the five freed people sued to re-establish their freedom. The very following day, the seized former slaves filed suit for freedom from Stephen Smith in the St. Louis Circuit Court.[12] The group now consisted of Harry Dick, age seventeen, tall, thin, dark complexion, with a speech impediment; Billy, about eleven, of black complexion and large, full eyes, who was said to show his teeth when he laughed; Milly, a yellow woman in her mid-twenties, "neat and cleanly in her dress and appearance"; Milly's son, little Davy, a well-fed two-year-old; and Milly's six-week-old baby, who had recently been born in Illinois. Smith also filed a counter suit insisting upon his mortgage claim to the slaves. He also sued the two rescuers for the trespass of boarding his skiff and "stealing his negroes."[13]

One remarkable feature of this petition is that, rather than having it penned with an "X" by the petitioners, it appears that Milly, Harry Dick, and William knew how to sign their own names, or someone helped them sign their names. These attestations are not the names neatly written by the scribe, with a space for the signer to write only an "X," framed by the words "his mark." This attestation is rare, and it is perhaps the only complaint filed during that era that was signed by freedom seekers able to pen their own names.[14] Each of the names appears to be in a different hand. It suggests that Shipman's former slaves were being taught to read and write. Sadly, in later filings, however, after being held in jail for some time, they do not write their names again. In the later filings, Milly's and Harry Dick's affidavits were marked by the customary sign of an "X." Perhaps without practice or reinforcement during their isolation in jail, they had forgotten how to write, or had been deterred from doing so.[15]

Rather than releasing the group on their own recognizance or to Shipman, the act of filing suit landed the five persons of color in jail.[16] Over the next five years, the dispute would involve two appeals to the Missouri Supreme Court.[17] During this time, Milly and her children spent most of the time in jail, and seventeen-year-old Harry Dick was hired out, conscripted for hard labor at Letcher and Bobb's brickyard. The jailor declared, "[I]f he was to get any money for the fees of the family of negroes [being kept in his jail], it would be from the hiring of Harry Dick."[18]

The brickyard of Letcher and Bobb was the rough-and-tumble workplace for many slaves hired out as temporary workers, and the brickyard was often the scene of fighting, brutality, and even death.[19] Letcher and Bobb often leased slaves from their masters and occasionally became involved in lawsuits over them.[20] Under Harry Dick's leasing arrangement, the brickyard owners paid the sheriff $7 a month for the privilege of working Harry Dick, as the suit slowly moved forward in the courts. It is not easy to say whose circumstances were worse, those freedom seekers left to rot in the St. Louis Jail, or those like Harry Dick assigned to hard labor in the open-air brickyard. The brickyard owners had little incentive to treat their leased slaves decently. Under the rental agreement, the brickyard owners were supposed to provide food, clothing, and shelter for their hirelings, but appallingly, Harry Dick was left without clothing. The sheriff took it upon himself to sue Letcher, arguing that Harry Dick was "in want of clothing, or naked," counter to the terms of hiring that hirers had signed. If he was unclothed, he probably received little in the way of food either.[21]

At some point young William or "Billy", the boy with large full eyes, was hired out. Surprisingly, he was hired out by the defendant's lawyer, Henry Geyer who represented Stephen Smith in opposing William's freedom.[22]

It was not until late March 1828 that the combined cases came to trial. The jury did not look favorably on the petitioners' claim and ruled in Stephen Smith's favor.[23] (The same decision was applied to Harry Dick, William and little David.[24] Ominously, Milly's infant was never mentioned again.) When Milly's attorneys appealed, the case made its first trip to the Missouri Supreme Court. On appeal, the high court ruled in favor of David Shipman the elder, as the legal owner of Milly and the others. The high court viewed the dispute as principally a contest between respective white men with ownership interests in the debt, rather than a straightforward freedom case. The court wrote, "[B]y contract, the right of possession remained in [David Shipman] for an indefinite time, and Smith had only a lien on her to secure the payment of debts; which lien Shipman might, at any time, have defeated, by paying those debts."[25] As far as Milly's rights, the court was less than benevolent. It declared that it was "not disposed to view the deed of emancipation with much favor." This makes little sense because the Missouri Supreme Court should have been obligated to give full faith and credit to the Indiana court's action manumitting her, whether it was "disposed to view those deeds with favor" or not. The court seemed to be stuck on the question of whether the several slaves had adequately "purchased" their freedom, rather than been given their freedom. The court stated, "A slave [like Milly] cannot be regarded as a purchaser for a valuable consideration, a slave having nothing to give."[26]

A much more significant constitutional provision was not considered in the litigation. Despite the principle of freedom by residence, the U.S. Constitution provided its own exception in Article IV, section 2: "No person held to service or labour in one state, under the laws thereof, escaping into another, shall, in consequence of any law or regulation therein, be discharged from such service or labour, but shall be delivered up on claim of the party to whom such service or labour may be due."[27] If Steven Smith had a valid claim to the slaves who fled with David Shipman and were emancipated in an Indiana court, then neither their emancipation nor their residence in free territory would render them free.

This Missouri Supreme Court ruling still did not resolve the case, however, because the Missouri high court had failed to speak exactly to the issue of whether Milly had rights against Stephen Smith. On April 13, 1829, the case was tried before a judge, who ruled for Stephen Smith just as the jury verdict had gone before, and the case was appealed again.

This time the appeal focused upon Milly's rights, particularly her rights vis-à-vis Smith, the mortgagee. Short of finding that she had a right, the court hedged by saying that by living in a free state with her owner's permission, Milly had acquired a "sub modo right to freedom" from her owner that released her from mortgage and his mortgagee.[28] In this opinion, written just a year later, the court turned its scorn upon David Shipman, who was described as "base enough to emancipate the slave to injure and ruin his security [Smith]" and "little below that of a felon." The judge, writing the opinion in favor of Milly, drew a dissent from Judge Wash, who argued that Shipman had only a *qualified* property right in Milly once he signed the mortgage and hence *could not* free her.[29] This language of "sub modo" rights to freedom and "qualified" property rights demonstrates the degree to which both judges were hedging their claims rhetorically, in an area without clear legal rules.

Three years after their kidnapping from Illinois, the court declared the litigants liberated and entirely set free from Stephen Smith.[30] Finally, the court had recognized their right to freedom duly bestowed by their master in the Indiana courthouse.

However, just a month later, on July 6, 1830, the *Missouri Republican*, which had taken no prior interest in the case, reported on its further developments:

> KIDNAPPING—We are credibly informed that an outrageous act of this kind was committed in Illinois, a few weeks since, by one Stephen Smith, and several accomplices, upon two black boys, named Harry Dick and William. Suits for freedom had been brought in the Circuit Court here, by Harry Dick and William against Stephen Smith, some two years ago. They were strenuously litigated; when after several trials, they were finally decided in April last, in favour of the slaves, who were deemed by the judgment of the court, forever free from Stephen Smith and all persons claiming under him. A few weeks ago, Harry Dick and William left this place for Tazewell County, in Illinois, and were pursued and seized by Smith, and put on board a steam boat and taken to the South, whether to Kentucky or further down the river, is never [*sic*] known.
>
> It is hoped that editors of papers in Kentucky, Tennessee, Mississippi, &c. will, for the sake of humanity, publish this notice.... Those who wish to ascertain the right of these boys to freedom, are referred to the records of the Circuit Court of St. Louis County, Missouri.[31]

The further drama of this second capture by Stephen Smith leaves us wondering; it does not play out in public sources. We do not know how Harry and William made it back to Tazewell County, but they did. This story appears to have ended happily with the freedmen returning there to a free life. The 1830 census taken later that year suggests that Milly made it back by then. David Shipman's entry shows that his wife had joined him and there were seven free people of color living in the household next door. They continued to live with, David Shipman—or, more accurately, he continued to live with them. They took care of him in his old age. The 1840 census indicates that elderly David Shipman was still alive, over seventy years old. His wife had died, but David Shipman still lived near Peoria with a free black family of ten, composed of seven free men and three free women.[32] And when David Shipman died, he left an estate to Moses and his sons.

The probate is remarkable for a further point. Not only did David Shipman leave property to Moses and his sons, the estate was permitted to pay out to Moses and his sons wages for the care of David Shipman and his wife up until the times of their respective deaths. David Shipman's estate compensated Moses's family for their care in their old age. Such a contradiction to the Missouri Supreme Court's claim in their freedom cases that a slave had nothing to give and nothing to expect for his services! Their former master did not expect them to work for free in return for their manumission. They were free and free persons are entitled to wages.

The black Shipman family seemed to flourish. Moses became a miller in Tazewell County. Harry had married in 1842,[33] and his household contains some younger members named Shipman. The 1850 census also lists Harry, as a mulatto laborer age forty, born in Kentucky, his wife, two young children, and a collection of young mulatto men who share the last name of Shipman.[34] There is even David Shipman, age twenty-four, who must indeed be Milly's son, the child who survived the ordeal of kidnap and lawsuit. The youngest Shipman boy listed in the census would have been born some time after the captives' release. Milly no longer survived. Moses Shipman remarried, presumably after Milly's death.[35] When the time came, even young David Shipman found a bride in Peoria.[36]

As for the elderly David Shipman, he died in 1845.[37] The Daughters of the American Revolution of Tazewell County published his will for posterity, to link their county to the founding of American liberty. First and foremost in his will, he left to Moses Shipman and his sons a wagon, four head of horses and steers, three cows, and two heifers. He left the family silver to his nephews back in Shelbyville, Kentucky, as well as that tract of land, which Stephen Smith must never have foreclosed upon.[38]

His will left one other specific devise: that the rest of his property be left for the clothing and education of George Shipman, when he became of age. The identity of young George Shipman is not clarified. The 1850 census for Peoria, Illinois, lists two possible recipients of David Shipman's patronage, both young men named George Shipman, both mulatto.[39]

As for David Shipman's Revolutionary War service, his pension was questioned because he had not served a full six months.[40] The D.A.R. claimed him anyway.

CHAPTER 8

The Duncan Brothers: Black and White

In 1842, Robert Duncan's death marked the end of an era: the white Duncan brothers lost control of the river island, a base from which they had smuggled slaves into and out of the upper Mississippi River valley.[1] Duncan's Island, as the wooded sandbar came to be known on city maps, was close enough to the city to be convenient but sheltered enough by trees and water to provide cover. It had been their staging area for smuggling the family's slaves for the previous two decades. By 1842, the black Duncan brothers had succeeded in redeeming their freedoms. This song is sung by two male choruses, one black, seeking to redeem their freedom, the other white, resisting by legal and illegal means.

A somewhat rogue band of bachelor brothers, the several sons of white Kentucky farmer, Jesse Duncan Sr. had reconnoitered slaves at Duncan's Island. From Kentucky, where they first inherited slaves from their father, they had sent their slaves to work at jobs of hard labor in the West, places where the bondsmen could earn wages for them, first to salt-mining counties in southern Illinois, and then farther into the interior, to the lead-mining country, deep in free territory. Almost all of their slaves were men, whom the Duncan brothers rented out, often for the hard labor of mineral extraction. Whenever these enslaved people sought their freedom, the brothers seized them, moved them across state boundaries, always threatening to carry out the ultimate penalty, to sell them south.

Generally, the Duncan slaves were not sold outside the family, although the Duncans occasionally bought additional slave men to add to their holdings. The white Duncans basically lived off leasing out their slaves for wages. Since labor was most scarce and yielded the highest return on the frontier, they kept moving their slaves west.

Both sets of brothers, white and black, were named Duncan. The seven black Duncans became increasingly well established as hard-working, church-going, free black persons of respectable standing in the St. Louis and Galena communities, at the same time that the six white Duncan brothers declined in capacity, wealth and social status. The former slaves' rising success, as more of them gained their freedom, runs counter to the declension, demoralization, and degradation of the brothers who once were their white masters. The black Duncan brothers gradually and steadily worked their way to freedom, eventually achieving stability and buying property, while the white Duncan brothers ended their wastrel lives in poverty and grand schemes that never worked out.

This story of redemption begins in 1819 with the division of the family slaves in accordance with father Jesse Duncan's will. The family had come to Kentucky from Virginia, bringing slaves with them. Jesse Duncan Sr. had settled a homestead with a small blacksmith site and tobacco fields in Hopkinsville, Kentucky. Like other Kentucky slaveholders, he also hired out his slaves for wages at the salt mines, just across the Ohio River boundary that separated the free Northwest Territory from slave Kentucky. At his death in 1819, he divided his eleven slaves among his eight sons and daughters. With this cast of the die, the fates of eleven enslaved people were determined as they were allocated to Jesse Sr.'s children. Ultimately, most of them found their way west, to establish their freedom in the St. Louis court.

The provisions of the will give some insight into the family structure.[2] There was no surviving Mrs. Jesse Duncan Sr. Robert, presumably the eldest, was

---

Slaves assigned in Jesse Duncan's Will, 1819.

To sons Coleman & James, tract of land "on which I now live."

To Coleman, 1 horse, 1 bed, 3 negroes: Joseph, Shadrach & Milly.

To James, 1 bed and 2 negroes: Simon & Gilbert.

To Jane, 1 negro woman, Silla, & her increase.

To Polly, 2 beds, 1 horse, 2 negroes: Nancy & Abraham & their increase.

To William, $500. to be paid to him in a wagon & horse, if said wagon & horse should not amount to $500., balance to be paid by executors at expiration of 3 years.

To sons, John, Jesse, and Robert, "3 negro fellows: Winston, Jonathan & Jere, if they can agree on division of said negroes. If not, said negroes are to be sold & proceeds of sale to be equally divided at expiration of 3 years which time son Robert is to take charge of said negroes… and keep them hired out for the purpose of raising money to pay my debts."

appointed executor. By the time of his father's death, Robert already lived in St. Louis, but returned to Hopkins County, Kentucky, to administer the will. Robert and the two youngest brothers, John and Jesse Jr., were to divide up three slave men between themselves, with the stipulation that Robert care for the three slaves until the brothers could decide how to allocate them. Jesse Sr. left the farm and more slaves to sons Coleman and James, presumably the next oldest brothers, who remained in Kentucky. The youngest brothers, John and Jesse Jr., remained at the homestead as well, each given a slave, to be managed by Robert.

The two Duncan sisters were provided for in being married off. Within the year, Jane Duncan married Benjamin Duncan. Duncan was a very common name in Kentucky.[3] Benjamin Duncan may have been a cousin; he did associate and get into trouble with the brothers sometimes (as did brother-in-law Metcalf),[4] but there were so many Duncans in Kentucky that he may have been no relation at all. Sister Jane received a slave woman that she brought to the marriage.

Sister Mary (known as Polly in the family) received a pair of slaves, a man and a woman. She became the second wife of Isaac Metcalf, a man much older than she was, after Metcalf's first wife died.[5] Although her younger brothers had sometimes tormented neighbor Isaac Metcalf, once he married their sister, they all became tight. Metcalf became part of the Duncan clan. Only one brother, William Duncan, received no slaves. Instead, he got cash, a horse, and a wagon. William was the only Duncan brother to marry and have children. He had nine children in all, though later it seems he abandoned them in order to join his brothers near St. Louis, where he died.

The Duncan brothers, growing up without a mother or father in Hopkins County, Kentucky, were truly wild boys. The Kentucky court record reflects numerous incidents of fighting and feuding with neighbors. Two brothers burned down a neighbor's smokehouses, others charged their horses and wagons through a neighbor's dooryard simply to rip up the place, and occasionally some physically attacked their neighbors. It was not that they moved as a pack: with four of them in Kentucky, they did not have to. They seemed to engage in mischief, threats, and violence in twos or threes, and they backed each other up when the need arose. Collectively, they terrorized some neighbors so significantly that their victims were afraid to sue for justice. One woman, upset that the Duncans had beaten up her husband, filed suit on her husband's behalf. Very, very quickly the victim had the lawsuit dismissed, insisting that it was filed by his wife without his consent, and implying that he wanted no further trouble from the Duncans whatsoever.[6]

Each bachelor brother had a slightly different profile, but as a clan, they appear to have coordinated their joint endeavors.[7] One brother would bring others into his big plans. Whenever a big plan failed and money was lost or someone threatened to foreclose on a debt against one brother by levying upon a slave, the others quickly resisted the foreclosure by shifting the slaves around, claiming that a different brother owned the slave about to be foreclosed upon. This shell game of intentionally obfuscating who owned which slave appears to have successfully confounded their debtors more than once.

Each brother was susceptible to a slightly different vice. Brother John, one of the youngest, was given to drink and succumbing to others' influence.[8] Once when drinking, he willingly signed his entire pay check over to the tavern keeper, who was plying him with liquor. Young John was a follower among the brothers. He followed his teenage brothers into trouble in his youth, and in his adulthood he became completely dependent upon them, perhaps due to alcohol.

Brother Coleman was given to gambling and risk-taking. Although he seemed always ready to take advantage of someone, he seemed to be equally susceptible to being cheated by others who set up opportunities for him.[9] Coleman was often in the middle of some scheme that went awry. Once in trading horses, he was convinced that the horse that he acquired was the foal of a prize racehorse. When it turned out not to be true, he got angry about being cheated. He responded by abandoning the horse, turning it out to fend for itself until another neighbor picked it up as a stray. He later sued the neighbor to get it back. Coleman responded to disappointed schemes by physical assaults and retaliatory lawsuits.[10] Coleman was the most litigious of the Duncan brothers, and he seemed to relish it. He was involved in so many lawsuits that it is surprising that he had time for anything else. His practice was to personally show up at depositions and stare down opposing witnesses until he got his chance to ask the witness the most intimidating questions he could imagine.

Everyone seemed to like brother Jesse Jr. He might have become a smarter, more responsible leader among the brothers, but he died young. The incident seemed to be an event noted as important whenever one of the brothers testified, but an event that was never explained.

It was brother James who was the all-round clever mastermind of schemes and the tough guy. James became the gang leader in kidnapping and smuggling the family slaves. Early on, he and younger brother John were charged with arson. In response, James actually took the offensive and sued the complainant for slander. Who dared to accuse James of arson?[11] Over time he gained a reputation as a more clever swindler than brother Coleman. Coleman's schemes usually blew up in his face; James sometimes succeeded. The brothers were not averse to ganging together to beat someone up, and their weapon of choice was something called a French dirk. But the Duncan brothers not only fought things out physically, they were also strongly disposed to lawsuits and intimidation.

The white Duncan brothers were as litigious as they were contentious. James was involved in resisting at least twelve freedom suits in the frontier courts, ranging from Galena, Illinois, to St. Louis to Belleville, Illinois. Wherever the brothers settled, the court records are peppered with additional acrimonious disputes brought by and against the Duncan brothers. Battling others seemed to thrill them.

Eldest brother Robert Duncan left the family early, perhaps when the others moved to Kentucky. Robert had established himself on the island near St. Louis by taking up with the ferryman's wife and eventually throwing him over, usurping both the wife and his land. A knockdown, drag-out fight ensued between Robert Duncan and the ferryman, Calvin Adams. Robert enlisted the help of his slave to fight off Adams. It led to criminal charges against all parties, but it was Duncan's slave, ordered to fight by his master, who took the blame. The fight led eventually to the territory's first divorce, when Sally Adams left her husband and stayed on to live with Robert Duncan.[12] Sally Adams had not been faithful to her husband before Robert came along. Calvin Adams had sued other men for sleeping with her, but this time her relationship to Robert Duncan stuck and she even came to be known as Mrs. Duncan in time, although more in custom than in law.[13]

Local folks described Robert as illiterate and unrefined, although they thought him "honest in his dealings." This reputation for honesty may have been overstated. Robert, at least, did not have the same record of fighting and litigating as his younger brothers had. After fighting Calvin Adams. Robert did not show up in the periodic arrest records for gambling, like his younger brothers often did. But from the remoteness of the island, who knew? Maybe he simply grew out of it sooner. Robert never joined civic organizations, churches, or clubs. He had no real occupation or obvious means of support. Robert seemed to survive by staying under the radar. Robert was said to own "a quantity of negroes."[14]

"Duncan's island was a landmark on the river, off the lower part of St. Louis. Steamboats were in view when they turned the head of Duncan's island."[15] The island was a somewhat mysterious place; it was the site of an unexplained suicide and the unexplained death of one or two of Robert's hired slaves.[16] The island was well situated for clandestine transfer. During the Duncan brothers' heyday, the island was a particularly useful refuge. It was remote from surveillance and had easy access to navigate a river escape. One could easily launch a canoe and cross the river from any side of a sandbar island. The Duncan brothers were well aware of where legal jurisdiction ended and played off those limits to their advantage.

If the white Duncan brothers formed something of a clan, the several people who were owned as slaves by them formed a countervailing social network among themselves, akin to a family, to help one another. Several of the enslaved men were indeed brothers: specifically Jonathan, Gilbert, and Vincent.[17] Shadrach and Swansey were brothers, or at least as close as brothers; and perhaps all five were related. Their claims of freedom did not depend upon a free mother, so a mother's identity was not part of their song. It can't be ruled out that some of these men may have been Jesse Duncan's children, and hence blood brothers of the white Duncan brothers who sought to enslave them. Ralph was not a brother of any of the others. Very little is known about Joe. The last to sue was Milly, who had a child and was probably a sister of some of the brothers but, remaining behind in Kentucky, she had long been separated from the others if they were kin.

If not related by blood, the Duncan slaves, as persons serving in the same household, were housemates. They were bound in a common household past: they had been owned simultaneously by the same master, and they used that past to connect to each other and free themselves.

As manumitted and emancipated slaves tended to take their master's names, so, too, one after another took the last name "Duncan." Thus, St. Louis gained two different families of Duncan brothers, the white Duncans and the black Duncans, separated by race and experience of servitude. From 1829 to 1835, almost fifteen lawsuits were brought by the black Duncan housemates against the white Duncan brothers in three different legal jurisdictions.

Freedom suits against the Duncan Brothers in three different places

4 lawsuits in Galena, Illinois—all filed May 11, 1830
Lawsuit 1. Raphael v. James Duncan
Lawsuit 2. Swansey v. James Duncan
Lawsuit 3. Gilbert v. James Duncan
Lawsuit 4. Joseph v. James Duncan

5 lawsuits in Belleville, St. Clair County, Illinois
Lawsuit 1. Gilbert (Colored man*) v. Coleman Duncan, (1831)
Lawsuit 2. Joseph (n----) v. Coleman Duncan, (1831)
Lawsuit 3. Swansey (free negro) v. Coleman Duncan, et al., (1831)
Lawsuit 4. Ann (free nig) v. James Coleman, et al., (1836)
Lawsuit 5. Milly (colored lady) v. James Duncan, et al., (1836)

7 lawsuits in St. Louis.
Lawsuit 1. Vincent, a free person of color v. Jerry, a free person of color. (1829).
Lawsuit 2. Vincent v. James Duncan. (1829).
Lawsuit 3. Ralph v. Robert, James, & Coleman Duncan (1830). (1833).
Lawsuit 4. Joe v. Coleman & James Duncan. (1830).
Lawsuit 5. Jonathan & Gilbert v. Coleman Duncan; Edward Tracy; Chas. Wahrendorff. (1831).
Lawsuit 6. Coleman Duncan v. Jonathan Duncan. (1832).
Lawsuit 7. Milly v. James Duncan. (1835).

---

* These descriptions were part of the case names.

The first Duncan slave to receive his freedom was Jonathan. Jonathan was a tall black man with a scar on the back of his head. He was manumitted by Robert Duncan shortly after Robert administered the estate. (This was also one of the first registered emancipations in the city of St. Louis.)[18] In dividing their allotted three slaves, Robert took Jonathan, Jesse Jr. took Jerry, and John took Winston, later known as Vincent. Robert then brought Jonathan, and probably Jerry, with him to St. Louis. In all likelihood, Jonathan achieved his freedom by paying off his master. Robert was not known to be magnanimous or a benefactor of anyone. Yet, bringing Jonathan to St. Louis, he may have accepted an offer to buy out Jonathan's bondage. The will stated that Jonathan could be sold. Twenty-three year-old Jonathan, emancipated in 1822, remained in the city as a dairyman, selling and delivering milk to households and to the steamboats on the levy. Within a year of his emancipation, a city map shows that he owned a small piece of land outside the city that was suitable for pasturing a few cows.[19] Somehow Jerry Duncan, too, managed to be manumitted, but there is no documentation of how.[20] He simply appears as a freed man in St. Louis several years later. Vincent, assigned to youngest brother John, had been earning wages for his masters by working at the salt mines. He was left there to continue to generate income.

While freedman Jonathan acquired pastureland behind the town back from and above the river, Robert lived near the water, close to the bridge on the southern edge of town, but as the great river meandered and moved, he laid claim to more of the sandbar off the shore of the city[21] that was accreting into an island.[22] "Old residents state that as the accretions to the sandbar formed and grew into an island, old Bob Duncan built a shanty on it, in order to hold possession by pre-emption."[23] Many people from town procured their firewood from the driftwood that lodged on the island. Some of the city's old French residents made a living by cutting the timber from the island into firewood and split rails.[24] Robert maintained control; he permitted some taking of wood, but took action against others.[25]

Interestingly enough, both Robert and Jonathan gained their foothold in the community by taking up with a landowning woman. As Robert gained the island by taking up with Sally Adams, Jonathan similarly came into property. Jonathan seems to have achieved his start in St. Louis by taking up with a wealthy, free woman of color, named Fanny Klinger. The June 1823 tax rolls list very few persons of color, but one is Fanny Klinger, who owned cash, a house, and cows. It is not clear where she came from. Almost nothing is known about her, except that among wealthy free persons of color in St. Louis at the time, hers is the only name that is not obviously Francophone.[26] There were very few free men of color in St. Louis in 1823, the year that Jonathan was manumitted, and even fewer who were not Francophone Catholic. (Religion seemed to be a barrier to marriage even among St. Louis's African Americans.) Though Fanny was twenty years older than Jonathan, they married. Fanny is repeatedly listed as Jonathan's wife in several land deeds.[27] The fact that there is no record of any land conveyances to Jonathan in the early years suggests that he acquired these lands by his marriage to Fanny, who owned lands as early as 1823 when she was identified as a woman of property. It is also entirely possible that Fanny Klinger purchased Jonathan's freedom buying him from Robert Duncan. She had the wealth to do so. Thereafter, Jonathan Duncan was a man of status, always listed prominently in the city directories as a dairyman.[28] In 1835, when free blacks were required to register for licenses, Jonathan Duncan, age thirty-six and fifty-six-year-old Fanny (now surname Duncan) registered the same day, listed by occupation as dairyman and milkmaid, respectively. Over the next twenty years, as a free and independent black man, he achieved financial stability and social respectability. He was the base from which other Duncan slaves could leverage their own freedom and gain independence.

Thus two men named Duncan—one, white Robert, living a subsistent existence close to the river but with no identifiable means of earning a living, and the other, black Jonathan, with his dairy on higher ground—became the St. Louis focal points for subsequent contests of continued captivity and freedom among their respective brothers.

It was six years later, February 10, 1828, before another of the Duncan slaves, Shadrach, was emancipated in St. Louis by Coleman Duncan. During this period, Coleman was spending time gambling in St. Louis.[29] Coleman had debts in both St. Louis and Kentucky. Why free Shadrach? Perhaps on Shadrach's promise of payment, and simultaneously to avoid losing Shadrach by foreclosure to his creditors. Emancipating a slave avoided foreclosure (as David Shipman knew.) While Coleman was in a weak position with regard to his creditors, he was still in a controlling position with regard to his slaves. He could free Shadrach, knowing that he could collect continuing wages from him in payment for his freedom. Shadrach became a drayman in St. Louis. He had managed the Duncans' horses and wagons back at the homestead in Kentucky. He married a black woman, whom he later saw emancipated, and they began a large family of their own.[30]

Though Jonathan, Shadrach, and Jerry were freed as young men, the others, their fellow housemates, were not as lucky. Four Duncan slaves continued to be worked in the salt mines in Illinois. Duncan slaves had been worked there earning slave rent for their masters ever since the family moved to nearby Hopkins County. Every aspect of their service there was examined as a basis of contest in the freedom suits. For a slave to work in Illinois for an extended time with his master's consent was the event that bestowed freedom upon them.

Notwithstanding the Northwest Ordinance's ban on slavery,[31] many slaves were set to work at the Illinois salt mines near Shawneetown. The inland nation needed salt as a foodstuff and as a preservative for settlement so far from the sea. Thus, Congress treated the saline lick as a natural resource of sufficient importance to be run as a government-leased monopoly. The secretary of the treasury leased the lands laden with a substance as necessary to life on the frontier as water was. Mountains of salt, measured in thousands of bushels, were manufactured at the saline lick.[32]

To accommodate the inland nation's urgent need for salt, Congress made an exception to the Northwest Ordinance's ban on slavery permitting slaves to be hired by their masters to work the saline.[33] The law provided that slaves could labor in Illinois temporarily, as long as sixty days, without a change in their status as slaves. Thereafter they had to be removed from the territory for a time in order to remain slaves. Thus, the law accommodated the ban on slavery with the need for slave labor by permitting slaves to be worked there "temporarily." Any one slave's work there was temporary, lasting only sixty days, but cumulatively—with the hundreds of slaves working at any one time—the salt mines were an island of legalized slave labor in a territory that otherwise banned it. The continuous manufacture of salt was accomplished by continuously recycling slaves into the area from slave states. Many government lessees kept as many as twenty slaves at work. So prevalent was the labor of African Americans that one salt field was known disparagingly as "Nigger Spring" and "Nigger Furnace."

The work of boiling off salt in huge kettles, vats, and furnaces was so hot and so hard that a sufficent number of white men could not be found to do the work. Slaves were considered suitable. Hired slaves worked alongside hired white men, although the hired slave generally performed the heaviest, hottest, and most unpleasant work. The process involved chopping down trees, hauling the lumber to the site, and chopping it into firewood to fuel the boiling of salt vats, building wooden slurries for saltwater, attending to the salt flats, and shoveling out the pits. Slaves like the Duncan slaves were cycled into the saline and back to slave territory every sixty days so the owners could preserve their bondage, all to produce the salt needed to preserve the meat that fed the frontier.

Five Duncan-owned slaves, Vincent, Joe, Gilbert, Swansey, and Ralph, worked at the salines. Ralph did not originally belong to the Duncans, but he was swapped to the Duncans from the neighboring Gordon family. Accordingly, Ralph continued to call himself Ralph Gordon.

Vincent was the most enterprising and proactive of the Duncan slaves sent to the salines. He sought to prolong his stay in Illinois territory by seeking extra work. Vincent was a large black man (some called him stout) with an afflicted left eye. Some said it was a scar; others said he had a blemish on his eye like a birth defect. During his stay at the salines, Vincent worked as a carpenter for the Funkhauser salt-making crew and for a tavern keeper.[34] At one point, Vincent worked every day for about two years with a white man named Hume, who chopped the wood. Vincent tended the fires.

While at the salines, Vincent worked an extra salt flat for his own income on the side. He leveraged additional independence from his masters by convincing them that he had to stay on at the salines to finish his own salt flat before returning to Kentucky, as he was asked to do for one of the routine returns to the Duncan homestead. To stay within the sixty-day legal limit, the Duncan family usually took their slaves to the saline after planting season or after harvest until the New Year. Then they would return with a wagon to fetch a load of salt, the slave men, and the slave rent they had earned. Vincent, however, cleverly came up with excuses to avoid returning in the wagon to Kentucky. His independent streak bothered the white Duncan brothers, but Vincent was owned by John. Vincent was able to cajole his young alcoholic master into letting him stay.

Vincent feigned a lack of interest in freeing himself to serve his purposes of staying on. A witness recounted hearing a conversation between Vincent and John Duncan, when John tried to retrieve him. John jokingly remarked that if Vincent remained at the saline too long, he might get his freedom. The sloe-eyed man's shrewd reply was that he did not know that he would want it.[35] Nonetheless, he begged John for just a little more time to wrap up his affairs. His extended stay at the Illinois salt flats later became the basis of his freedom claim. Eventually, Vincent had refused to return to Kentucky so often that the older Duncans seized him by force. Vincent was tied up and transported first to Kentucky and then west to St. Louis.

Once Vincent got to St. Louis, he was sent to work at Letcher's brickyard. (Harry Dick was probably working there at the time.) Brickyard work was also furnace work and as grueling as the salt mines: shoveling clay, packing and lifting forms, and stoking the oven fires. The Duncans regarded Vincent as having bad character, and their good friend, Mr. Letcher, was thought to have a firm hand in running slaves.[36] Vincent must have resisted effectively because he stayed only one day at the brickyard. Eventually it was arranged that Vincent work for James Clemons, drawing a wagon for his dry goods store. Again earning money on the side, while paying the Duncans his slave rent, Vincent bought his own pair of horses and wagon and ran deliveries around the city. It was not until 1828 that Vincent first sued for freedom, the first of several freedom suits by the Duncan slaves.

Ironically, Vincent, the first of six Duncan slaves to sue for freedom, filed against Jerry Duncan, a free black man who had been his former housemate and perhaps his brother.[37] This is one of the strangest pairings of petitioner and defendant in all of the freedom petitions. Jerry had hired Vincent's labor for a year. Was this arrangement between former housemates and this lawsuit amicable or hostile? Coleman Duncan was in St. Louis at the time and again running up gambling debts.

Other documents suggest that Jerry was an opportunist. He took the bay horse belonging to Lydia Titus's daughter when she was imprisoned.[38] She had to sue him to get it back. He was later discovered with property stolen from a store.[39] If there was any black Duncan brother with a somewhat tarnished reputation, it was Jerry. Jerry never achieved the same standing in the free black community that the others did. So, was the lawsuit an afterthought or planned by Vincent and Jerry?[40] During the pendency of the lawsuit, brother Jonathan, the dairyman, agreed to keep Vincent's horses and dray safe.[41] Did Vincent suspect that Jerry would take them?

Jerry Duncan had no means, or perhaps inclination, to defend against Vincent's suit, and so he defaulted. Jerry's default did not render Vincent a free man, however. Jerry did not own Vincent: he had only rented Vincent's life for a year; it was John Duncan who owned it. But John, the alcoholic brother, was back in Kentucky, so Vincent next sued James, who was in St. Louis at the time, and exercising some control over Vincent.

In response to the lawsuit, James Duncan kidnapped Vincent. He forced him to the riverbank near Duncan's Island and attempted to smuggle him out of the jurisdiction. He had men and a canoe waiting. This was the second time that Vincent had been strong-armed in an attempt to move him across state lines in order to control him. James Duncan would use this tactic repeatedly in the years to come. What was surprising was that this time James was caught red-handed.

Vincent's attorney suspected the kidnapping attempt and sought a habeas corpus writ to stop it.[42] The sheriff's deputy found the group at the river's edge. Vincent was handcuffed, hidden in the brush. He was guarded by a man, holding a dirk, who worked for James. Letcher, the brickyard owner, was also there hiding in the brush. James was sitting in a canoe on the Mississippi River safely watching the encounter from a distance. The lawman declared that he was not there to arrest James but simply to serve an order on him. On cue, Letcher emerged from the brush and asked whether James was at risk in coming ashore. The deputy said he was not; so James Duncan came ashore and accompanied the captive Vincent to appear before the judge on the habeas corpus writ.[43] The Duncans were sternly warned that any attempt to remove Vincent again meant contempt of court.

Vincent was represented by Gustavus Bird, the very able attorney, who won back the Tituses their freedom. Vincent's claim was based on freedom by residence, because Vincent's residence in Illinois had exceeded the sixty days permitted under the salt mine exception. The claim was good, the evidence was solid but the verdict went against him. The clerk scribbled on the flyleaf of the papers in Vincent's case: "The wiley art and seducing strategies of the slave."[44] The testimony had demonstrated how Vincent had tricked his masters into letting him stay on in Illinois. Vincent's appearance may have biased the jury against him as well. Vincent, with one scarred eye, might have appeared evasive in court. The clerk indicated that he did not think Vincent was trustworthy. His attorney appealed; the Missouri Supreme Court reversed, finding error, and Vincent's case was remanded for a second trial.

Back in Kentucky, the Duncan brothers continued to litigate over the slaves and debts that they had there. Any attempt to collect money from one of the brothers allowed them to trick their creditors by shifting slaves from the debtor brother to another. James Duncan got into two lawsuits in Kentucky over slaves. One involved a slave named Clarisse, whom he had rented,[45] and another was a long, drawn-out lawsuit over Isaac, a slave boy, whom he had purchased in St. Louis to take back to Kentucky and "grow" into a more valuable work slave.[46]

In 1827, the white Duncan brothers made plans to pull their slaves from the salines and move them farther west. The law permitting slave hire at the salines was expiring. (The slave Milly continued to work at the Duncan homestead, where John and Coleman still lived. She would be the last Duncan slave removed from Kentucky.)

Five men—three white men and two slaves—set off from Hopkinsville, Kentucky, in 1827, headed west for the lead mines. Aboard a leaky flat boat floating down the Ohio were enslaved Joe and Ralph, along with Jesse Jr. and two friends. The plan was to ride the current down the Ohio until they reached the Mississippi River, where they could take passage on a steamboat headed north for the lead mines of Galena. Slaves were needed in this boomtown, filled with an influx of fortune seekers, to extract the lead. The flatboat commissioned by Coleman was ill-fitted for the strong river current, however, and it capsized before going very far, leaving the five men in the middle of the Ohio River, struggling to shore. Upon reaching the shore, they began walking to find the next steamboat landing to get steamboat passage. (A new lawsuit against the builder of the leaky boat was added to Coleman's string of lawsuits.)

Upon arriving in Galena, Joe and Ralph were put to work for Jesse Jr.'s gain. We have no description at all of Joe. Ralph was relatively nondescript, of medium height, but without distinctive features as far as anyone could state. Slaves were customarily identified by scars or disfigurements, but Ralph had none. Perhaps Ralph had kept his head low and avoided the blows and scars to the head and face that seemed to afflict other Duncan slaves. Once Ralph achieved his freedom, he would slip invisibly beneath the radar again.[47]

Apparently, four Duncan slave men were moved from the salines to Galena. Everyone who mined in the Galena area needed a digger's permit. There were just two digger's permits registered under the name of Duncan in 1828, both the same date, but neither was for Joe or Ralph: one permit was issued to Swansey Duncan and the other to Gilbert Duncan, men who it seems were brought to Galena by James.[48]

The four slave men worked near the lead mines for almost a year, before some incident prompted them to sue for their freedom in Galena, as Vincent continued to do in St. Louis. The incident may have been the death of Jesse Jr. In mid-July 1829, probate papers were granted in Kentucky to James for his younger brother's estate.[49] James next appeared in Galena. His presence in town is evident from the small mining town's court docket. James was in town reasserting his control over the family's four slaves, gaming, and generally raising pandemonium. Jesse Jr. had leased Ralph from his brother Coleman, but now it was up to James as Jesse's administrator to regain control of the slave property in Galena.

The local Illinois record books show a splash of four freedom suits brought against James Duncan in the second week of May 1830.[50] Four suits were brought under the names Raphael, Swansey, Joe, and Gilbert, all identified as men of color, all against James Duncan, all to establish their freedom.[51] None of the men were indentured in Illinois; all were claimed as slaves by the Duncans. Even though many black servants were brought to Galena in circumstances suggesting involuntary servitude,[52] a direct suit like this should have led immediately to their release because the indenture procedures had not been followed in time. On two successive days, James was in court, not really defending the lawsuits, instead personally filing his disclaimer to the men's services. He moved to dissolve the injunction ordered against him. To the petitioners' disappointment, all four cases to establish their freedom were dismissed, not because the four men weren't entitled to freedom, but because James told the court that he was not their true owner. He was not the man to sue; brother Coleman was. Again, the white Duncan brothers used this shell game of switching up ownership among themselves to confound the Galena court. The cases were dismissed because "the said James Duncan... renounced all claim to the services of Swansey" and to the others.[53]

But James' plan was sneaky. James Duncan renounced his claim to the men in Galena court in order to have them released, only so he could kidnap them and whisk them out of the jurisdiction on the next steamboat. This man, who had waited offshore in a canoe to covertly move Vincent beyond the court's reach, used the same trick on Swansey, Ralph, Gilbert, and Joe, this time successfully transporting them to St. Louis. (James could not have overpowered four men alone, even with the element of surprise, but he always seemed to find help in these kidnapping efforts.) The four men had filed assault claims against James too. All were dismissed, presumably because the complainants did not show up. By fall, the state's attorney in Galena brought an indictment against James Duncan for kidnapping, which was never resolved.[54]

The St. Louis court files continue the story. The kidnapped men sued James Duncan again, only days later, in St. Louis. Within days of having their suits dismissed in Galena, three new suits were brought in St. Louis against James Duncan.[55] (The fourth man, Swansey did not file.)[56] These suits added to Vincent's suit still on the docket. Of these three new suits, only Ralph's would go the distance of full-scale litigation. He alone reached redemption by litigation, and by doing so, his successful suit breathed new energy into Vincent's faltering one.

In his petition, Ralph alleged that James forcibly took him from Illinois to St. Louis, threatening to take him back to Kentucky. He sought the court's protection to make sure he was not further removed from justice. Before the St. Louis court could order his protection, however, Ralph and Joe decided to protect themselves by going into hiding. James Duncan sought to have them arrested as runaways.

Brother Coleman Duncan must have found Gilbert, Swansey, and Joe and smuggled them across the river again to Illinois. Again, attorney Gustavus Bird, who secured Vincent from kidnapping, anticipated this move and tracked them down in Illinois. Bird filed suit on their behalf, against Coleman across the river in St. Clair County, Illinois.[57]

Ralph, however, evaded Coleman and remained in hiding in St. Louis. A few weeks later, he came forward. The sheriff reported, "Joe & Ralph have surrendered themselves to me, are in jail, claim to be free men, hired out until end of trial."[58]

Gilbert's and Swansey's cases never went to trial because they got help from two of the emancipated black Duncans. Jonathan, the dairyman, offered to buy Gilbert's release. Shadrach, the drayman, came forward to help Swansey. Jonathan attempted to buy brother Gilbert's freedom. The tall black man explained to attorney Charles Wahrendorf that his brother was presently in town and that he needed his help to negotiate Gilbert's release or he would be sent south. Jonathan persuaded the attorney to lend him some of the purchase money.[59] James and Coleman agreed to sell Gilbert, and Jonathan signed a note to buy his brother's freedom. However, when Jonathan learned that an Illinois court in Galena had already deemed his brother Gilbert free, he stopped payment to the white Duncans. On March 12, 1831, Jonathan and Gilbert sued Coleman, as well as the lawyer, to cancel the note and to have the money advance returned. Coleman countersued.[60] Jonathan accused Coleman of fraud by contracting to sell Gilbert knowing full well he was free, all the while threatening that if Jonathan did not buy him, he would be sent south and sold.[61]

It's not clear why Jonathan acted only on Gilbert's behalf—perhaps Jonathan and Shadrach arranged to divide their efforts each to help another. Jonathan and Shadrach did cooperate in later Duncan family matters. But the fact that Jonathan supported his brother Gilbert, more fully than Vincent, suggests several things. Was Gilbert more vulnerable under the direct threat? Vincent seemed able to take care of himself. James Duncan's attempt to kidnap him had failed, and they were under a court order not to do so again. Vincent had outwitted his enslavers before. Or was Jonathan helping his brother Vincent financially as well? Was Jonathan underwriting part of Bird's fee for representing his brother? Bird did charge Lydia Titus for his services, when he knew there was money. Jonathan owned property. Did Jonathan assist Vincent by paying his attorney?

Spring 1832 shows a slave named "Swanston" formally emancipated by Shadrach Duncan.[62] The terms of this deal are not apparent. Swansey had filed suit in St. Clair, Illinois, but never in St. Louis. Swansey did become free from these masters. Two months later Swansey was alive and well and kicking up a fuss in Galena. He was cited for disturbing the peace.[63] It might even have been a celebration like John Merry's. Swansey remained in Galena.[64]

And Joe? What happened to Joe? A year later an entry in the St. Louis docket book reveals his death. The entry simply reads "Apr 7, 1831_ Joe dies."[65] This particular quest for freedom ended badly. Joe was probably in the Duncans' control on the island when he died. The sheriff said that Ralph and Joe were hired out, and documents show that Ralph was there.

Ralph Gordon, on the other hand, did not get assistance from any of the free black Duncans. He was not a brother to those men. Ralph and Joe had been held together since the ill-fated flatboat trip north. They fled and turned themselves in together. But Ralph had never been a housemate of either Jonathan or Shadrach, the two in a position to help. Ralph came into the family after they left Kentucky. They had shared the same group of Duncan masters, but they were strangers to one another. They did not experience that enslavement together. There was neither a kinship nor an experiential bond. Neither a brother nor a homeboy, neither one appears to have helped Ralph in any way.

Ralph, too, tried to buy his own freedom by offering the Duncans $100 in cash and a note for $200 if they would only release him, but they refused. Ralph was remanded to the possession of none other than Robert Duncan on the island, where he was set to work for a year before being hired out to a stonemason for the rest of the lawsuit's duration.

Those That Remained to Sue

With Joe dead, Swansey free in Galena, and Gilbert's freedom secured by Jonathan, two freedom disputes remained. Still pending in the St. Louis courts were *Vincent v. James Duncan* and *Ralph v. Coleman Duncan*, and a third case yet to be fulminated. Vincent's and Ralph's suits were allied by their work experiences (both had worked the salt flats, and both were claimed by the Duncans) and by the respective attorneys in both lawsuits. Two of the city's most able attorneys squared off against each other. Gustavus Bird represented enslaved Ralph and Vincent, as he had the Tituses. Edward Bates, later Lincoln's attorney general, represented their masters. These estimable lawyers pursued testimony in four counties in Illinois, two counties in Missouri, and one in Kentucky. They litigated this pair of cases to the Missouri Supreme Court three times in all.[66] This was a coupling of redemption songs played out in full legal complexity. These two Duncan slaves' lawsuits defined new easier evidentiary rules for achieving freedom on the frontier.

To establish their residence in Illinois, the petitioners sought witnesses from the principal men at the salines. Bird gave a full effort to these freedom cases. He struck the first blow by seeking court orders to examine witnesses simultaneously in Kentucky and Illinois. This was an extraordinary escalation of effort in the service of slave freedom suits. Vincent appears to have traveled with Bird to southern Illinois to find and depose the witnesses. It was important that the witnesses see Vincent to recognize him if they were to testify to remembering him. Bird probably bought Vincent's hire. It is not clear whether he could have arranged it otherwise.[67]

One saline master had no recollection of Vincent,[68] who stood before him, though he testified that he had hired a number of hands at the salt mines. Vincent and his attorney had better luck with Robert Funkhouser.[69] Funkhouser had known Vincent since about 1820 when John Duncan hired Vincent to him and drew his wages. Vincent was assigned to Funkhouser for as long as he chose. Funkhouser said Vincent stayed at least two years, John taking his wages the whole time. Funkhouser also said that Vincent's brother Gilbert worked with him part of the time.[70] Vincent and his attorney found a man with whom Vincent worked the furnaces as well. The man also said that Vincent never left Illinois for two full years.

Despite solid evidence and Bird's skilled advocacy, a second jury ruled against Vincent. Vincent, it seems, was shown to be more clever than his masters. The very cleverness that allowed him advantageously to trick John Duncan when he attempted to retrieve him disadvantaged him to the observers in court. Vincent had lost both jury trials despite the evidence. Attorney Gustavus Bird did not give up; he simply redoubled his efforts in Ralph's case. Vincent may not be able to win before a jury, but if the appropriate rule was established in Ralph's case, Vincent might win based on that. The battle over the Duncan slaves shifted to Ralph. Ralph, the nondescript slave, was a more acceptable plaintiff than devious-appearing Vincent.

The star witness for Ralph was John Steele, a local newspaperman and former schoolteacher who had seen both enslaved men at the salines. He was hired to teach school in the Kentucky valley where the Duncans lived. Steele had boarded with the Gordons, and hence knew Ralph. Steele testified to seeing Ralph first at Shawneetown. Steele accompanied Ralph's master, Mr. Gordon, back to Kentucky after he had dropped Ralph off to stay and work. Gordon had explained to Steele the routine of hiring Ralph out during certain seasons. Ralph had been given a note by his master, a sort of pass that allowed him to obtain some credit and to travel at will. Ralph's note allowed him to work there as long as he paid his slave rent.

Once the schoolteacher testified on Ralph's behalf, Steele's own character and family became the major focus in the lawsuit. Was John Steele credible? John Steele edited a St. Louis paper called the *Free Press* and was reading law as well.[71] John Steele was adventurous and enigmatic. Several witnesses were called solely to discredit him.[72] Steele was principally criticized for leaving his wife and children in Kentucky while he pursued his career in St. Louis.[73] Others were then called simply to rebuild his character and reputation. "I should believe [John Steele] in a court of justice," one testified.[74] Altogether eight people in Kentucky were asked to give their opinion about the former schoolteacher's character.

The critical legal point of contention was whether Ralph's masters had expressly assented to his extended stay in Illinois by giving him the note. On appeal, the Missouri Supreme Court held that the note was sufficient proof of assent. "The master who *permits* his slave to go to the state of Illinois to hire himself commits as great an offense against the ordinance of 1787 as he who *takes* his slave along with him to reside there."[75] Ralph won.

The third time around, Vincent finally won freedom when the jury was dispensed with and the case was tried to the court. While the litigation ensued, James Duncan was gaining a reputation for gaming both in the city of St. Louis and in Galena. This was the Duncans' next big scheme. An anonymous writer provided a tip that James was promoting faro (card) games in town. In Galena, too, he was indicted with sixteen other persons. His name led the list.[76]

Ralph won no damages for his enslavement. (The Missouri legislature had limited damages in freedom suits since Winny's case.) He did pursue the return of the wages that he had earned while hired out. On this, Ralph also prevailed, receiving $153, though his attorney had to make another trip to the Missouri Supreme Court to secure that victory.[77] Ralph's victory provided the basis for Vincent to win.

By the June term of 1834, the white Duncan brothers had lost Ralph as well as Vincent. They were out the amounts they had expected to be paid for Gilbert, and, as if to add insult to injury, they were assessed court costs and forfeited Ralph's $153 impounded wages.

Ralph and Vincent's success seemed to inspire another, unrelated slave to sue the Duncans. In one of the more curious filings, a slave girl sued Robert for her freedom. This young woman was not part of the Duncan brothers' inheritance, nor was she ever in Illinois. Robert Duncan had bought her in St. Louis years before. She claimed to be the child of a free mother from Pennsylvania. It seems that she was influenced to sue by Ralph's victory. After all, she served Robert Duncan, while Ralph was hired out to Coleman, both probably living on the island pending the judgment in Ralph's case.[78]

James must have left the city because by the following spring he was moving the last of the inherited slaves to Galena. This time the slave was Milly, a domestic servant also inherited from their father. Removing Milly from Kentucky indicated the dismantling of their Kentucky home. Milly was brought to Galena in July 1834 but she was soon moved across the river to the Dubuque mining area.[79] There were certainly people to hire her in Galena, but James must have found that it was too difficult to hold Milly in slavery there. After all, she must have known Swansey who was free and worked on Galena's main street. Somehow Milly crossed the river to return to the Galena court anyway and she too filed suit. James kidnapped her, before the suit could be heard, taking her to an out of the way little town in Missouri.

By October 8, 1835, the persistent Milly had made her way to court in St. Louis to sue for freedom again. James Duncan fled. He could not be found in the county when the sheriff attempted to serve the summons. He crossed the river again, retreating to the Illinois side opposite St. Louis. Did James force Milly with him when he fled? Just days after the St. Louis suit was filed, Milly's attorneys pursued the action by filing suit against James Duncan in St. Clair Illinois.[80] This time there were two petitioners, Milly and her daughter, Ann.[81] James seems to have taken one or both of them with him. But the Illinois sheriff could not find James Duncan there either.

These filed freedom suits were never resolved. Milly's St. Louis suit was struck from the docket for lack of a defendant.[82] What happened to Milly and daughter Ann? No one by either name ever showed up later in any of households maintained by the black Duncans. The only trace appears two decades later, pointing to Galena. One of the very few black women listed in her own right in the Galena city directory for 1854 was a woman named Ann Milly, a laundress running a boarding house for black riverboat men.[83] Was it Ann, taking her mother's name for a last name? Of course, Milly was a common name, more common than Ann, and it may be wistful thinking to hope that Milly's Ann had found her way to independence in the community where Swansey and his growing family lived free.

The white Duncan brothers clearly resented losing. They had their chance to get back at the judge. When one of Judge Wash's slaves sued him for freedom, James made a point of stating his willingness to testify against the judge, even if it was to help free the slave Alsey. Alsey had worked at the same tavern in the salines, where Vincent had. To show his spite, James Duncan stated that indeed he knew Robert Wash "to his sorrow [and] would give $100 to see said Alsey get her freedom...since Wash had given decisions against him in similar cases."[84]

And what became of the black Duncan men? Ralph Gordon disappeared without a trace after his successful trial. Vincent, Shadrach, Jerry, and Jonathan remained on in St. Louis. Vincent, a drayman, later became a waiter.[85] Vincent never married or accumulated property, but he died peacefully of old age in 1859.[86] Jerry Duncan married and had several children. He worked as a store servant, living above the store. He made the newspapers when a search for his daughter turned up stolen goods in his lodgings. His daughter was even more sensationally accused of throwing a white child in her care down a well.[87]

Shadrach and his wife Jemima had six children; one son he named Swanston, and one Joseph. Shadrach Duncan even acquired a slave of his own, whom he finally emancipated in his will in 1851. He even sued a slave trader who attempted to take his slave away.[88]

Jonathan was undoubtedly the most successful of all of the black Duncans. Jonathan Duncan actually bought a log cabin and founded the first African Methodist church there in the same year he was manumitted. He was a church leader and "exhorter" in the congregation, remaining with the church until 1850. He owned many properties in his lifetime. One was between 6th and 7th Streets, on an alley called "Clabber Alley" for the sour milk clabber from the dairy. The neighborhood was home to many African Americans, both free and slave, in the 1850s, including Dred and Harriet Scott. After Fanny died, he no longer ran the dairy, and he moved to upstairs rooms in the neighborhood. He remarried, this time a younger woman from Maryland. With his wealth, he continued to stand as security for licenses for free persons of color. Several people he vouched for were ministers of the African church.[89] Jonathan Duncan, who had begun his life as someone else's property, had, over the course of his life, acquired sufficient property of his own to secure financial independence for himself and for others. Jonathan, former penniless slave, was financially solvent enough to post bond for other freedmen.

The white Duncans' story is just the reverse. By the early 1840s, all of the brothers' lives ended in poverty, each dying debt- and bedridden within a few months of one another. Their Kentucky homestead and eleven slaves had been frittered away in get-rich schemes. Only Robert's estate contained anything of value: two slave girls, and five pieces of land in the St. Louis area that had become quite valuable as the city grew.[90] The island was claimed by Robert's common-law wife, Sally. Robert Duncan's last remaining slave girl sued for freedom.[91] The only asset that Robert's younger brothers had was their inheritance from him.

Sister Mary Duncan Metcalf, now widowed herself, survived them to come to St. Louis to collect what little remained in their estates. In a twist of fate, she sold the last interest in their estates to Jonathan and Shadrach, her father's former slaves. What was the possible point of these transactions? There were no specific properties mentioned. The six transfers simply said "real and personal property from the estate".[92] To make the conquest of the white Duncan brothers permanent, Jonathan and Shadrach bought out the little Illinois land remaining in the estates of their former masters. Was this done to ensure that no ghost heir would ever step forward and threaten the black Duncan brothers, as the Titus family once had been seized?

Swansey changed his last name to Adams and lived out his life as a respected water deliveryman in Galena. (Did the name "Adams" link him to some past, or was it just a fine-sounding presidential name? Shadrach also went by Shadrach Adams at one time.[93]) A photograph of Swansey taken in the late 1870s shows a lean,

Swansey Adams, the water delivery man, on a Galena, Illinois stereopticon. Scott Wolfe, Galena Historian, Galena Illinois

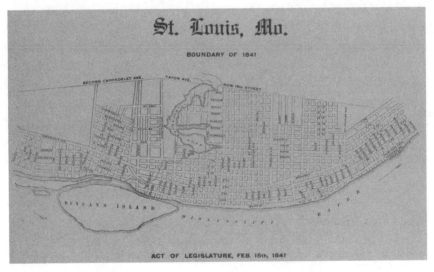

1841 official map of St. Louis showing the prominence and location of Duncan's Island. St. Louis had a population of 16,469 that year.

dark-skinned man wearing a workman's apron and holding two buckets of water.[94] Swansey married, raised a family, owned a home and ran a business in Galena.

Galena histories tell a very different story of Swansey, as if he lived in isolation, disconnected from the brothers, lawsuits, and the other kidnappings. The Galena story focused solely on Swansey. As that story goes, he was brought to Galena in 1827 from the Shawneetown salt mines by James Duncan, and was put to work at the diggings in Hardscrabble, Hazel Green. (The lead mining permits corroborate this.) When Swansey refused to leave Galena with James Duncan, he was kidnapped. (The case files corroborate this, too.) However, the Galena story never mentions the other Duncan slaves or the lawsuits at all.[95] Nor do these stories mention Shadrach's help.

The hero of the standard Galena account is a white man, William Hempstead, a local merchant who is said to have followed on the next steamer, bought Swansey from Duncan, and brought him back to freedom.[96] Swansey was said to have repaid Hempstead by working off the debt. Yet, as a free man, who had spent a year in Galena, Swansey owed nothing to Hempstead or anyone else. This account may have some shreds of truth, but William Hempstead's benevolence seems highly doubtful. Hempstead revealed a much more ominous side to his dealings in Eliza Tyler's case, a story told in chapter 10.[97] Hempstead's involvement in several slave trades between St. Louis and Galena had much more to do with financing slave trafficking than with emancipation.[98]

And what became of Duncan's Island? A young West Point engineer named Robert E. Lee began work on the problem that Duncan's Island was causing for the St. Louis harbor and river navigation in 1840.[99] And eventually it washed away.

CHAPTER 9

Leah Charleville

Leah's redemption song is that of a survivor. She left behind a story of pluck and independence, but also a tale of dubious manipulation of other people. As a survivor, the light-skinned Leah found herself living in a somewhat unsavory netherworld of duplicity between legality and illegality. She left dozens of secrets hinting at the quality of her life scattered across the civil and criminal records of two states. She was able to play off two free black men as her lovers at the same time. While she attended church and allowed her children to live with the minister, she kept house for a ring of thieves at her boarding house. She was familiar with what the courts could do for her. She turned to them time and again, when necessary, not just to guarantee her freedom, but also to leverage her independence and her children's.

Leah's story is important not for the rules of law it created—none of her cases were ever appealed—but for her savvy use of the courts to leverage her situations by asserting freedom. In fact, Leah made two trips to court to secure her own freedom and two trips for each of her children.[1] Each case was resolved fairly expeditiously, and it does not appear that Leah ever spent much time in jail while awaiting a verdict. She and her children always won these disputes at the lower court under the existing rules. She used those rules to redeem her entitlement to autonomy as a free person.

Yet, in the end, it was a sensational criminal trial that sealed her fate and caused her to disappear, leaving her teenage children to finish their own court battles. In that incident, Leah was implicated as an accomplice to the crime, though she was not charged, convicted, or exonerated. The widely publicized criminal trial revealed her means of survival and exposed her as complicit in a variety of petty crimes. After that exposure, she disappeared.

Leah's first encounter with the courts occurred in Ohio when she was barely twenty, though she was already the mother of a two-year-old child and pregnant with another. She was then living in Kentucky, but her first step to redeeming her freedom was to cross over the river highway to the Ohio side. At the time, she was nearing the birth of her second child.

The young pregnant slave woman and her toddler arrived in Georgetown, Ohio, about 1817 with a white man who was not her master. The man immediately took her to the home of his brother to stay. The man was Peter Grant, a tanner from Maysville, Kentucky.[2] He told his brother that he had brought Leah to the Ohio county seat in order to establish her freedom. Jesse Grant hosted Leah and her two-year-old son for the time it took to establish her freedom.[3]

How did Leah attract the tanner's assistance, and why did he choose to help her? There is no indication. Grant did not have her master's permission and risked being charged with illegally transporting a slave across state lines. Unlike the Underground Railroad that aided and protected escaping slaves from the reach of the law, Peter Grant brought Leah to court to redeem the freedom that she was legally entitled to, because of her prior residence in Ohio.

Leah was owned by Arthur Mitchell, a hatter by trade; she was his only slave.[4] Arthur Mitchell had moved his small household back and forth across the Ohio River, always taking Leah with them. Ohio was a free state by 1817, carved out of the free Northwest Territory, and by her residence there, she was entitled to her freedom. Mitchell then moved her back across the river to Kentucky, continuing to claim ownership.[5] Mitchell and Peter Grant probably had a business relationship, since they both dealt in furs and leather. Mitchell, as a hatter, probably purchased hides from Peter Grant, the tanner in the tiny Kentucky town. Peter Grant took the hatter's pregnant slave woman back to Ohio to establish her freedom.

To take away a man's slave was actionable and certainly likely to disturb local sentiments. There was even a risk for his brother in harboring them.[6] Yet Jesse Grant, living in Ohio, took in these travelers immediately, seemingly without question. Jesse Grant deferred to his older brother, to whom he had once been apprenticed. Jesse owed him his livelihood. Jesse had his own tanning business on the north shore of the river.

Arthur Mitchell pursued Leah, accompanied by his own brother, a carpenter, for support, and perhaps for muscle. The Mitchell brothers seemed to know exactly where to find her. All the parties turned to the Ohio courthouse to resolve the dispute.

What motivated Leah to seek out the Ohio courthouse at that particular time? It was not to get away from her master. She was quite willing thereafter to return to his Kentucky household. Could it have been the fact of her pregnancy? Why was she willing to travel so near to her delivery? Quite likely the impending birth of another child in the slave state of Kentucky prompted her to get her papers so it would be clear her baby was born to a free mother. So then, why did she not file earlier, with her first child's birth? Perhaps because little Archibald was born in free territory, where clarifying his status was unnecessary. One does not know her exact motives, though one might expect that she feared that her children would be slaves if her own freedom was not officially declared, and this second child was born in Kentucky. Although enslaved people, uneducated and illiterate by state design, would not know the legal rules and consequences with precision, they may still have been attuned to circumstances of jeopardy. Leah may have sensed her next born would be in jeopardy, and her late-term pregnancy provided motivation to cross the river then.

Her local host did not attend the trial, though he later provided important testimony supporting her when events took her to Missouri. The Ohio court declared Leah and her son to be free persons, and gave her a legal document, which she had the presence of mind to keep.[7] By now, Leah was in an advanced state of pregnancy. The ultimate resolution was amicable: Leah's freedom was established. And, surprisingly, she agreed to return to Kentucky with Arthur Mitchell and remained in his household. Returning to a slave state with her former master seems counterintuitive, but her freedom and that of her child were established; she had in her possession a court paper that said so. Thus, Leah left the home of Jesse Grant, from all appearances voluntarily, to return to the slave state of Kentucky, with the former master whom she had just sued for freedom.

Her host, Jesse Grant, would stand as witness for her again, but he would become better known to history for a different reason. His four-year-old son Ulysses, probably playing with two-year-old Archibald in the tanner's cabin, would grow up to become president of the United States, Ulysses S. Grant. Jesse Grant was known to have antislavery sentiments, though his involvement in aiding Leah is not generally known.[8] Peter Grant, who brought Leah to the Ohio court, was the future president's uncle. Could Peter Grant have been the father of Leah's child? The paternity of slave children is almost impossible to establish.

By 1830, the hatter Arthur Mitchell moved west to Missouri, taking with him his family of nine as well as Leah and her two children. The census that year lists Arthur Mitchell as the head of a household with only three slaves who match Leah's family's demography perfectly: a young woman between twenty-four and thirty-six, and a boy and a girl, both under ten years old, presumably her son Archibald and daughter Brunetta.[9]

After some years in St. Louis, Arthur Mitchell was preparing to move back east again, and this time Leah was making her own plans. Leah seemed to be intent on making her own money, which she claimed could have been a large sum had Mitchell not interfered. Leah turned to the courts again, this time in St. Louis, alleging that Mitchell had interfered with her *earning capacity* by constraining her to prison.[10] This is a far cry from the average freedom petition, which is typically framed as humbly begging the court for release from a bullying master. This is a person relatively confident not only of her freedom, but also of her ability to earn money and large sums of it. Leah claimed she had been prevented from earning $700 and thereby sued Mitchell for $800 in damages. One wonders what sort of work the attractive, light-skinned Leah expected to do to earn such a high wage.

To secure her earning capacity, she sued Arthur Mitchell, the man she claimed was interfering with her income. Her free status had already been established in Ohio a decade earlier, and the Missouri courts were obligated to give that decision effect. When service of process was delivered to Mitchell, he refused to hear it read to him, not because he seemed offended by the suit, as some defendants responded, but because he was hard of hearing. He took the paper and read it himself, calmly acknowledging the contents.

There were no further filings in the case. Within six months, the case was discontinued, and again, apparently amicably. Leah came into court to dismiss the suit herself. "Now at this day come the said Leah in her own proper person and says she will not further prosecute her action against Arthur Mitchel but voluntarily suffers the same to be discontinued."[11] Though Leah was illiterate, she carried a copy of her Ohio habeas corpus papers in order to prove her free status; she knew what was necessary to call forth proof of her status.[12] She was also willing to use the court to press back against a master's constraint if and when he interfered with her earnings. Of note is the fact that Leah appeared in court "*in her own proper person*" rather than by a lawyer. Leah clearly had control of her case. Slaves in freedom suits were rarely noted as appearing in court on their own behalf, and in no other case in which a freedom litigant dropped the charges.[13] She probably agreed to dismiss her case because she had gotten what she wanted.[14] Her former master, the hatter, gave up, for he returned east again to the Ohio River valley, and Leah and her children remained in St. Louis.[15]

In time, Leah married a free black riverboat man who was several years older than she was. Peter Charleville was a local man, probably a descendant of early French slaves of the Charleville family.[16] He worked the steamboats traveling up the Missouri and the docks at various warehouses in St. Louis. Although there is no certificate documenting their marriage, the community regarded them as "married." Peter and Leah occupied a two-story house on South Third Street where Leah took in boarders and did washing for the guests at the hotel next door.[17]

There was a steady stream of black riverboat men who came in and out of Leah's house. The young, attractive, yellow woman found herself approached by different men coming into town, offering to pay her for more than washing. Free black riverboat men had the rowdy reputation of sailors when arriving in town, looking for liquor and looking for trouble. And the relative freedom, irreverence, and license that free black riverboat men enjoyed raised resentments among whites in St. Louis. In fact, one black boatman had been burned alive while tied to a tree by a mob in a shocking incident of racial brutality.[18]

Leah's house provided a place to stay for itinerant boatmen between jobs on the river and meals for an even larger group of local free blacks who worked nearby but slept farther from town. Like many St. Louis boarding houses, her house appears to have consisted of only two upstairs rooms, one where she and her husband slept, and the other occupied by the lodgers. Downstairs she offered meals. Her boarding house at 21 South Third Street seemed to be a frequent meeting place of roustabouts.[19]

As Madison, one of her boarders told it, the atmosphere at Leah's house was casual.

> I...went to the house of Leah to board. Leah is a colored washer woman, the wife of Peter Charleville, both free, living on Third Street below the National Hotel.... Ennis boarded there, but slept with a girl, up near the North Market.... After I went to Leah's I bought a bed of Mr. Shaw and gave him five dollars for it. This I took into a room in Leah's house, made a present of it to her, but was to sleep on it as long as I staid [*sic*] there.[20]

Thus, Leah exchanged a free place to stay for the gift of a bed. A bed was better than the pallet of old clothes and rags that usually served as the communal sleeping arrangement for poorer folk. Having a bed there did not mean that Madison had it to himself, however. Other boarders could expect to share Madison's bed with him.

Leah attended the African church from time to time, but her children, Archibald and Brunetta, actually lived with the minister, rather than with their mother at the boarding house.[21] It is not clear how Leah's children came into the custody of the senior black minister of the African Church. The record fails to reveal any official guardianship papers. Yet the children may have been placed with Reverend Meachum informally, either because he was asked to take charge of the children by Leah or, in the unofficial way that municipalities removed many children from their parents, because he was seen as a more responsible member of the community. Leah herself may have wanted her children placed with him in order to learn a trade, to learn to read, or to keep them away from the surly rough-and-tumble circumstances of her boarding house. Or she may have simply wished to make more room for paying boarders. Archibald and Brunetta lived with some sixteen African Americans, ten free and six slaves, at the Meachum's house on Second Street.[22]

In a curious twist of fate, Leah's children filed papers to sue the minister, John Berry Meachum, for their freedom in 1840.[23] Archibald and Brunetta, then aged sixteen and fourteen, sued Reverend Meachum for grievances concerning their treatment. Their initial filings in July did not seek freedom per se, but only to alter the conditions under which they worked. They sued under the last name "Barnes," rather than Charleville, the name their mother Leah now went by. Who was Barnes? Barnes is a clue that leads nowhere: possibly the name of their father back in Ohio or another St. Louis "husband" of Leah's before Peter.[24] Leah is never known to have used the name "Barnes." Peter Charleville assisted the children in the lawsuit as guardian ad litem.[25]

The defendant, Reverend John Berry Meachum, was one of the most significant and established free black men in St. Louis. Meachum was successful, over fifty, large in stature, and married with grown children. He was not only the energetic minister, founder, and central figure of the black church, but he ran a successful business making barrels.[26] The industrious and persevering Meachum had found a profitable niche in the western markets as a master cooper. Barrels were in demand for shipment particularly in St. Louis, the shipping hub for the West. All kinds of shipments departing St. Louis required new barrels. As a minister, he enjoyed a large following among Free Blacks and slaves alike in the city. He preached each Sunday and at funerals.[27]

Meachum was a complex literate man who was committed to raising up the black community. Meachum was a self-made, "can-do" man. Having raised himself by his bootstraps by buying his way out of slavery, he endorsed that method to attain freedom.[28] Meachum had gone on to wrest other members of his family from enslavement by buying them.[29] Meachum did not advocate immediate emancipation. He could not have preached abolitionism in St. Louis at the time; it was illegal to do so and punished as a crime.[30] But he also did not advocate achieving freedom by any means other than earning and paying for it. He did not assist slaves suing for freedom. Instead, he found himself as a defendant in three freedom suits, even before Archibald and Brunetta sued him.

The freedom suits arose because from his shop's profits he financed the purchase of slaves, with the understanding that they work off their debt to him to finance their own self-purchase. He usually permitted these persons to find their own work by hiring themselves out for a price.[31] Not everyone whom he purchased agreed with the program, however. This is where his principles came in conflict with the interests of slaves who he owned, people whom he expected to pay him back for their freedom.

Reverend Meachum had freed half a dozen slaves by this working-off method.[32] In the mid 1830s, two slave women he purchased sued him for freedom, claiming they were already free under the freedom-by-residence rule before he bought them. He strenuously resisted their freedom claims in court.[33] Coincidentally, both of these women were named Judy: one Judy (also known as Julia) Logan, and the other known as Judy LeCompte.[34]

In 1835, Judy Logan and her young son sued Meachum for freedom.[35] Judy Logan's case raised a new legal issue which placed Meachum in even more of a racial contradiction. Testifying for Judy was a man of color named Louis. His status, as free or enslaved, was unclear.[36] At issue was a black man's ability to testify in court against Meachum. Meachum objected to Louis's testimony on the basis of Louis's race. Meachum appealed to the Missouri Supreme Court, seeking to exclude Louis' testimony, and he lost. When the Missouri Supreme Court allowed Louis's evidence, it actually opened the door for freedom suits to be substantiated by the testimony of persons of color.[37] This may not have seemed like a major advance for people of color, but it was. Other black house-mates were likely to be in the best position to bear witness to the petitioner's circumstances. To have barred testimony based on a witness's race would have meant that freedom petitioners would have to prove the facts of their case with only white witnesses.

Almost simultaneously, Meachum was sued by another Judy, a very dark skinned woman who had resided in a different Indiana settlement, Vincennes. This Judy, too, had been sold from person to person (even trafficked by Toussaint Dubois, the man who had kidnapped Peter and Queen McNelly). Judy LeCompte was eventually sold to Meachum.[38] She sued him and won her freedom as well.

Thus, by the time that Brunetta and Archibald sued, the minister had already been drawn into other freedom suits as the enslaver and lost those suits. Fourteen-year-old Brunetta's lawsuit could not have played more wisely into Reverend Meachum's philosophy of black assimilation of middle-class values however. Meachum lectured mothers to teach their daughters morality—"teach them to be decent and modest in their deportment."[39] Brunetta's complaint was that the tasks that the Reverend Meachum assigned her jeopardized her decency and modesty. The impetus to Brunetta's suit was her working conditions: she didn't want to sell milk at the steamboats in the early morning hours anymore. As a teenage mulatto girl walking alone in the early morning hours, she found herself continually harassed by the rowdies on the dock.[40] Her mother, Leah, seemed to know how to manage these approaches—even to exploit them for gain—but young Brunetta found them uncomfortable. She claimed that when Meachum sent her to the wharf to sell milk onboard the steamboats, she was "exposed to insults of the grossest character from various members of the crew of different vessels." Brunetta's daily trip to the wharf coincided with the time that drunken boatmen returned from a long night of carousing. Her petition stated that Meachum had other persons in his service (her brother among them) "who are more fit than she is for these errands." Brunetta had even sent Meachum a written request "couched in the most respectful language through her step-father, Peter Charleville, stating the inconveniences she suffers in the employment. But, Meachum indicated his intention to pay no regard to her request. The hardship of which she complains is of a serious nature to her... she is exposed to wanton insult which Meacham could easily spare her through no cost to himself."[41] Brunetta begged to be excused from this task which exposed her continually to sexual harassment.

Her brother, Archibald, stated no grievance of his own. His separate filing seemed simply to support his sister. Reverend Meachum defended both claims, arguing that Brunetta and Archibald were his slaves. (The minister's 1840 census entry does list a boy and a girl in the slave column of ages comparable to theirs.[42])

Brunetta won, although the only relief that she sought was to avoid being sent to the docks at daybreak to sell milk. Brunetta was present in court to get the satisfaction of the judge's ruling, but she was in the sheriff's custody rather than there independently. The court ordered Meachum to relieve the petitioner from the grievances that she complained of and find her other employment. She was "remanded to [his] care and custody."[43]

Things must not have worked out as hoped at the minister's house because Brunetta and Archibald returned to court just two months later, this time seeking to establish their independence from him. It appears that the minister had disciplined them, perhaps in retaliation for the bother and embarrassment of taking him to court. This time, sister and brother filed identical suits alleging cruelty on his part. Archibald claimed that Meachum treated

The St. Louis docks where hundreds of slaves were brought with their masters and where Brunetta was sent by Reverend Meachum to sell milk. Missouri History Museum, St. Louis

him with great inhumanity, harshness, and severity, and even threatened to remove him from Missouri.[44] (The last charge was highly unlikely.)

This would have been a good time for Leah to present her Ohio habeas corpus paper on their behalf, the document that demonstrated that Leah was free. But it wasn't proffered, so the lawyers went to Ohio to get Jesse Grant's testimony.[45] (Only Leah would have known who to get this evidence from; Archibald had been a toddler and Brunetta hadn't yet been born.) Although Peter Grant was now dead,[46] Jesse Grant, who had sheltered Leah and toddler Archibald while they awaited the Ohio courts' decree, was available to attest to the tale of her freedom. On May 10, 1841, Jesse Grant appeared in response to a summons at the Ohio courthouse to testify about the previous freedom case. He supported their side of the story.

While the teenage siblings' freedom suits were pending and awaiting Jesse Grant's deposition, a calamitous event took place that rivetted the town's attention and catapulted Leah into the limelight in a much more unsavory way.

On the night of April 17, 1841, an enormous fire burned down one of the city's leading financial houses. A fireman died fighting the fire. But when it was extinguished, it became clear that the fire had been set to cover up the murders of night watchmen in the course of an attempt to rob the safe. The events of that evening ignited the town's curiosity in the succeeding days as every newspaper reported whatever news could be found.

Attention came to focus on Leah's house and several persons who regularly gathered there.[47] Identified as important witnesses were Leah; her husband, Peter; the barber Edward Ennis who had begun to sleep at the house; and Madison, who brought the bed.[48] During the weeks it took to round up all the accomplices, intense scrutiny focused on Leah's boarding house. Edward Ennis was a free black barber who worked at a barbershop close by. The Maryland-born Ennis was a dandy and man of the world. Ennis had no criminal record, but he had been picked up at one point on charges of being in the state without a license. He simply paid his fine, sent for some papers from Maryland, left the state temporarily, and then returned, again unlicensed, as if nothing had happened. Many free Blacks lived without licenses in St. Louis, but few were arrested, so the fact that the authorities had noticed him must have meant that he had sufficient swagger to be noticed.

The record reveals that six men who met regularly at Leah's, including Ennis and Peter, ran something of a spree of robberies, but this particular robbery went terribly wrong when the four robbers encountered a security guard and had to kill him and then set a blaze to cover their tracks. Ennis was arrested on suspicion of knowing about the robbery and counseling the robbers to flee, although he was not suspected as participating in the robbery. After the robbery, the thieves had retreated to Leah's house, where Ennis persuaded them to leave town in different directions and then lie low.[49]

Under arrest, Ennis eventually went public with his side of the story. He admitted knowing of the crime and finding the murder weapon, a bloody crowbar that had been used to kill the night watchman before the fire was started. Ennis threw it in the privy behind Leah's house, fearing that he would be implicated. In fact, the gang later claimed that Ennis furnished them with items, such as this, as burglary tools. Peter Charleville attempted to mask his association with the robbers by being helpful to the police, publicly offering to go after one suspect. He said that he could recognize the suspects since they met regularly at his house. As Ennis and Peter attempted to distance themselves from the incident, apprehending the suspects' and the anticipated trial was the talk of the town.

Eventually, the four confessions revealed that this particular group who frequented Leah's house, barbers and boatmen, had been involved in robberies up and down the Mississippi River. Peter and Ennis were often accomplices. While Brunetta and Archibald's freedom cases were pending, the men had often planned their capers at Leah's house, discarded evidence behind her house, and divided up the spoils with her.

Although Leah, Peter, and Edward Ennis were not prosecuted, they became the star witnesses. Leah's involvement in these episodes depends upon whose story you believe. She appears to have been the gangster's moll.

The confessions of the four men convicted, and later executed, describe the shadow community in which Leah operated. Peter, Leah, and the dandy Ennis occasionally suggested the targets to rob, but most robberies were carried out by the foursome of Madison Henderson, Charles Brown, Alfred Amos Warrick, and James A. Seward. Peter joined in sometimes as lookout, and he more often fenced the goods. Peter was said to be less reliable in the operations, because he was not too bright. Of the four robbers, one was a slave—Madison worked along the river with the permission of his New Orleans master. Released to earn his own way as long as he paid his master his slave rent, he stayed at Leah's house for several weeks at a time when he was in the city.[50]

Ennis now boarded at Leah's and shared Madison's bed in the boarders' room. Ennis claimed that he and Madison did not share each other's confidences. "We were merely together as boarders and were not in the habit of confiding our secrets to each other, we had none to confide; neither of us married; never confided to each other our courting scrapes."[51] However, the confessions of the convicted murderers tell a much different story.

Ennis was clever, but always wisely kept his distance from the robberies; he was involved in planning, scoping out the target, furnishing crowbars, and

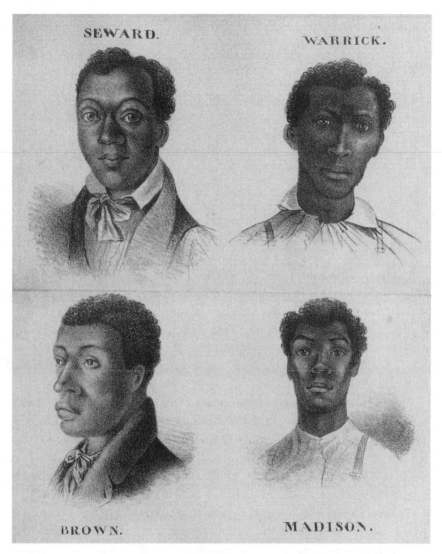

SEWARD.   WARRICK.

BROWN.   MADISON.

These four men convicted of arson and murder frequented Leah Charleville's boarding house where they planned robberies. Missouri History Museum, St. Louis.

dividing the spoils, but he never accompanied the men during the heists. "Ennis generally knew of our plans and consulted with us frequently, but seldom went along."[52] Leah usually covered her tracks by attending Meacham's church on the Saturday nights when the heists took place. She could be seen there, thus providing herself with a convenient alibi. Apparently Ennis had moved from Madison's bed in the boarders' room to Leah's across the hall. One man recounted that "about this time Peter did not stay very much at Leah's for he thought Ennis was too intimate with her."[53]

Ennis and Warrick were barbers at different shops.[54] Seward was a gambler from New York; he had studied bookkeeping and mastered the gambling techniques of games of chance. He boarded at Leah's but slept at Warrick's barbershop.

Both Brown and Madison seemed to be full-time thieves and con men involved in opposite dimensions of the slave trade. Madison had worked with his master hustling African Americans into slavery in the South. Madison bragged about being a very good con man, using lies about fortune and freedom to get African Americans to trust and accompany him, only to lure them into his master's trap, where they could be transported across borders and sold to new slave buyers. Madison also had many robberies to his credit in New Orleans, Galena, and St. Louis.

Brown by all accounts was the smartest of the group, (having studied at Oberlin) the most political, and said to be the most ruthless of the group. It was claimed that he never feared killing someone or setting fire during a heist. Brown claimed to be an Underground Railroad conductor, but he mostly worked to be paid rather than for principle. He befriended Madison, the con man, because he had hoped to turn him on to helping him with slave smuggling for pay to free states.

The city newspaper covered the scandalous trial of four suspected murderers, which dragged Leah further into the limelight. One of the accused asked Reverend Meachum to bear witness for him, but Meachum claimed never to have seen him before.[55] After the heist, Leah and Peter had gone to church and Warrick saw her there up at the altar proclaiming.[56] All the while, Leah's children were suing the minister for their independence.

The social order of the group suggests that Ennis spoke mostly to Madison, who carried the directions to the gang.[57] They had developed a list of eight to ten robbery targets, but some were discarded as too risky.[58]

After robbing several small stores, the gang wanted a big score. They had pulled off a couple of successful heists in Galena, but they did not want to mess with small towns anymore and they were getting tired of petty robberies. They wanted a score so large that they could live off of it for the rest of their lives. They began to target financial institutions with larger amounts of money on hand. Ennis wanted the gang to rob a bank in Alton, Illinois, across the river, but they refused. Peter and Ennis had suggested one target on the wharf, where Peter was working. There was good money, $1,800, in the store and Peter knew who had the key. Afterward, Warrick said, "I went directly up to Peter's house, and when I rapped, Peter opened the door and let me in.... He replied, that was nothing—colored people would never be suspected—all we had to do was to be cautious. I gave him the money. He got a light and divided it with Leah, Peter, himself and me. He gave Peter and Leah their's in bed."[59]

Was Leah implicated in the illegality? It was said that she and Peter always got their cut. Her boarder Madison claimed that she was in on it. Madison indicated that Leah sometimes tipped the gang off to likely targets by observing who had brought money with them to the hotel next door. Doing laundry for the nearby hotel, Leah could find out where the hotel guests stored their money while they were in town. On one occasion, Madison testified, Leah told "Ennis and myself that a gentleman from the south had made her certain propositions, that when she refused to gratify him he put his money in his pocketbook and put it in his trunk—that he had a large sum." In this account, Leah seemed to be luring the man in. She then reported where his room was and what time he left for supper, so that they could steal the trunk. Madison took the trunk to Leah's house, but when it was opened they found no money inside.[60]

It was Ennis and Peter who had urged the counting room that was to be the big score. Peter said the vault was downstairs. The goods were always taken to Leah's house to divide up. "[S]he and Ennis took charge of them. In these things Peter Charleville had but little to do. he [*sic*] knew of them but he was too simple to be trusted far." Yet Peter sometimes helped Ennis take the goods to St. Charles to sell them. In one heist, there was a plan that "Peter and I should take a parcel of goods up the river and sell them.... I spoke to Peter about the trip up the Missouri, and he professed to know so much of the country that I entertained no doubt of our success."[61]

"We went to Leah's and divided the money, but upon making the division, the gold and cup was gone...they had been left [behind]."

All four men were convicted of bank robbery, murder of the two night clerks, and arson.[62] The prosecution was swift. One prisoner was tried and convicted each day for four consecutive days. Each was assigned a separate defense attorney. In each case, the verdict was guilty in the first degree. Some jury deliberations took no longer than five minutes to convict. The judge ordered each man to be hanged. "On July 9th, you will be taken hence to the place of public execution, there between the hours of ten o'clock in the forenoon of that day and four o'clock in the afternoon, be hung by the neck until you are dead."[63]

The local newspaper interviewed the prisoners in jail awaiting their executions. The newspaper hired an artist to sketch their portraits, and sold the pamphlet to the public. Even a national newspaper covered the events and mentioned Leah and Peter by name.[64]

After the public spectacle of the hanging, with notoriety and under the shadow of unsavory reputations, Leah, Peter, and Ennis disappeared. It is not clear whether they went separate ways or whether Leah left with either her husband or her lover. Although Peter Charleville had proudly listed his name and address in the 1840 city directory, like other up-and-coming free black residents, his name does not appear in city directories thereafter.[65]

More than a year after the hangings, the circuit court got down to the business of declaring Leah's children free, based on Jesse Grant's affidavit. The decision drew little fanfare.[66] It was eclipsed by the scandalous events that had preceded it. The minister did not appeal.

Although Leah disappeared, she left her children the legacy of freedom and knowledge about how to use the courts to leverage their working conditions. Archibald too disappeared, but Brunetta, the baby whom Leah carried when she first crossed the Ohio River to establish freedom, continued to live out a long life in the city of St. Louis. She bore several free children of her own. Brunetta gave birth to her first child at seventeen, within a year of gaining her independence from the minister. Her second child arrived just a year later. The children were given the last name of Finley.[67] Fifteen years later, in 1860, the census shows Brunetta, now named Thompson, living as the wife of a man from Santa Domingo. Her sons, still carrying the last name Finley, remain in her household, and there are now two younger children with a different but familiar and surprising last name. These young children are named "Barnes," the same last name that Brunetta and her brother took in all the freedom cases.[68] One implication is that Brunetta gave these babies her maiden name, and that they were born after the time she was with Finley and not yet with Thompson. But where did the name Barnes come from? Like her mother, Brunetta did not remain with just one partner.[69] But, unlike her mother, she and her children remained respectable residents in St. Louis.[70]

CHAPTER 10

Sex and Servitude in Women Litigants' Cases

Among the multiple indignities that slaves experienced, one experience sets the lives of slave women apart. To be subjected to a slave master's sexual desires without consent and to suffer the continued subjugation of bearing children to be owned by that master has few parallels in the human experience of dehumanization.[1] Yet the historical data demonstrates, and the genetic data now establishes, that the practice of masters using slave women as concubines for sex was widespread in antebellum America. Frontier Missouri was no different.[2] Although many Missouri slave owners intentionally sought to own paired slave men and women, expecting them to be each other's partner, others did not.[3] A number of the slave mothers litigating for freedom seemingly had no stable partner. Some of their children were identified as mulatto, distinguishing them as different from their mothers or other slave children who were identified as black.

For most mothers and children litigating for freedom in St. Louis, there is almost no information about the children's fathers. That information was legally irrelevant to the freedom cases. The rule of matrilineality made motherhood crucial to the case and fatherhood legally irrelevant.[4] More generally, information on the paternity of a slave mother's child is rarely recorded anywhere: not in census data, baptismal records, or even in criminal record files. Sex with a slave woman, even rape, was not an event that was noted, unless the woman killed her assailant.[5] Yet the fact of sex with one's master and the consequent circumstance of bearing one's master's child certainly affected the slave woman's psyche, and perhaps the emotional register of her freedom song as well. What we do not know, that which lies beneath the surface, is how many of the petitioning women sued men who had once held them as concubines. Similarly, we do not know how many litigants were suing their own fathers or brothers.

Among the legal contests between slave women and their masters, it seems highly likely that some women litigants were contesting not just the authority of their masters, but also the sexual power that that authority gave them. Similarly, the master's exhibited resistance could in some instances be the product of the challenge that the suit brought to that sense of masculine prowess. That fact would inflect the legal contest for freedom with a tension and strain distinct from other petitioners' desires to rid themselves of their masters.

But if that tension was part of the courtroom drama, such accounts are largely absent from this battery of cases. Why? Was the revelation of such information suppressed? At least some portions of the white population believed it to be sufficiently scandalous to suppress. One St. Louis man who provided in his will for the manumission and education of one of his young slave girls made the denial explicit in his will: "[S]he is not my daughter."[6]

The critical audience in the court proceeding was the all-white, all-male jury. Was sex between a master and his slave woman sufficiently commonplace as a practice that it drew no notice? If the practice was commonplace it may not have distinguished the litigants in any sensational way from the white male slaveholders who sat on the slave mother's jury. Would revealing such information move the jury to empathize with the slave woman as a victim? Or would it move the jury to side with the master more strongly, since the woman who had received his "favor," and perhaps special treatment, now had exposed their liaisons and acted against his interests? Were these stories suppressed at the time? Or were they simply so well understood that they did not draw comment? We have almost no evidence from the legal record.

Certainly, a master's sexual interest was a part of slave women's motivation. Rather than even enter such a relationship proposed by her master, Harriet Jacobs acted defensively by seeking other lovers and ultimately by hiding until she could run away. Some women who found themselves in circumstances as enforced concubines might have been led on with promises of freedom—at the master's death—for themselves and their children. One woman in Solomon Northup's famous account was.[7]

In these stories sex and servitude come through so rarely, each presents very, very differently. Yet in two cases, a slave woman's sexual experience with her owner, her belief that she was free, and his subsequent betrayal give rise to the freedom suit. One master was black and the other was white. Eliza Tyler contested a master to whom her black former lover had sold her. Hence the confrontation between the slave concubine and the man who betrayed her did not occur in court. The betrayal had occurred offstage, though it overshadowed the legal contest. Hester challenged her white master, father of her first child, directly in her lawsuit. Yet he did not appear in court. He remained coolly out of state, in New York. He let his lawyers do his talking. Hester had to confront the slave dealers to whom he had sold her. (What we cannot know is how often such a situation of concubinage lay in the backdrop of the litigants' histories.) We can go with only the information that is discernible when women themselves made statements. Masters usually did not reveal their dalliances.

Whether the master who held the woman as a concubine was white or black, the relevant factor in the redemption song is that the woman's intimate partner gave her reason to believe that she was free and then betrayed her by selling her. Hester Williams was betrayed by her white master who had given her freedom in writing. Eliza Tyler was betrayed by her free black master, whom the community regarded as her common-law husband while they lived together in free territory. He attempted to sell her into prostitution.

There were also women whose sexuality became apparent in their stories. Leah was a free agent with different men. Could it be that Peter Grant or Arthur Mitchell had been her sexual partner? There is no evidence at all. There simply is no evidence about the father's identity for most slave children. On the other hand, there were only two couples who filed for freedom together. Tempe and Laban sued very early in the series of freedom suits. Harriet and Dred Scott remained loyal to each other, and fought together for freedom for themselves and their children.[8] These relationships seem to have sustained them during the litigation.

Eliza Tyler's Redemption

Eliza Tyler did not plan to sue for freedom; she was not even aware that she would become involved in redeeming her freedom. She was betrayed by the African American man with whom she lived as husband and wife.

Born a slave in Virginia, Eliza was brought to St. Louis by her master, and sold to George Taylor who took her to Galena, Illinois, late in the summer of 1834. (Given Taylor's name and the last name "Tyler" that Eliza took for herself, Eliza might have gotten her last name from him). In Galena, George Taylor sold her to a free black man from Kentucky, Perry Bark for $400. Perry Bark had once been shot in the leg, walked with a limp and did odd jobs for various merchants in town.[9]

It was not uncommon for free black men to purchase their future wives from slavery. Shadrach Duncan and Swansey Adams had both purchased their wives before freeing and marrying them. Thus, after having arrived in free territory and having been purchased by an eligible free man of color, Eliza could well have considered herself to be akin to a mail-order bride.

The tiny lead mining town had been experiencing a boomtown economy for five years before Eliza arrived in 1834. Newcomers described it as the "new El Dorado of the west."[10] Despite being in a free state, slaves brought up the river to work in Galena often acquired ambiguous legal status. With the constant mobility of persons moving into and out of the town looking for a quick fortune, many brought slaves with them. It was still possible to indenture slaves in Illinois at the time.[11] Slave laborers were in demand in Galena, whether available temporarily or for an extended period of time. With most working people who were attracted to Galena hoping to claim stakes for themselves, there was a great need for people who would take work as servants for others. The Duncan brothers took their four slave men there to work the mines. James Duncan had brought Milly there and then took her across the river to Dubuque, just as Eliza Tyler was arriving. Galena was where John Merry's captive wife and son were taken after they were kidnapped to quell their lawsuits. (Ironic though it is, Susette and John Merry Jr. had greater protection in the St. Louis courts in a slave state than they did upriver in Illinois.) Slave women were frequently brought to Galena to serve as maids on steamboats and domestic servants for the households and boarding houses that provided lodging for the influx of lead miners, adventurers, and speculators. Eliza's actual status while living in Galena was no more obvious to the community than Perry Bark's own. Perry Bark was said to "pass as a free man of color" in Galena.[12]

Eliza would remain in Galena for only one winter. The twenty-three-year-old worked as a servant in the household of two relatively successful local merchant families, the George W. Campbells and the Morehouses, who lived together in the log house that also served as their place of business.[13] She passed as the wife of a free black man named Perry Bark, the man who had purchased her.[14]

Eliza seemed to respond to the arrangement without objection. She and Perry lived in town, not out at the diggings where life was much harder and more isolated. And although Perry Bark and Eliza did not formally marry, to live together publicly in town as man and wife would present them to the community as married by common law. One witness testified specifically that Eliza passed as Perry Bark's wife.[15] To be known in the community as married would have given Eliza some security about her living situation.

In spring, on April 25, 1835, believing herself to be free and free to travel, she left Galena, where she had lived for only the winter, with a plan to visit her family members who remained in St. Louis.[16] What Eliza did not know when she left was that her visiting trip was actually part of a ruse to sell her south into slavery.

Days before she left Galena, she had caught the eye of a man named Nelson Campbell, a slave trader from Iberville parish, Louisiana who owned numerous slaves. Eliza was described as a very light skinned, mulatto woman with a freckled face. Campbell was only visiting Galena. (There were several different Campbell families in Galena; there is no evidence that Nelson and George W. were related despite having the same last name.) Nelson Campbell concluded that Eliza was worth at least $600 and perhaps more than $1000 if he could buy her and take her south.[17] It was such a high price for a slave woman in 1835 that it raises questions, but Eliza's appearance was special.[18] She was a "yellow woman" in the parlance of the time; and yellow women sold for higher prices. The implication of his assessment of her worth and her youth and complexion is that Campbell intended that she become a woman of fancy in some brothel in Baton Rouge, New Orleans, or some other town. Nelson Campbell even claimed that he had been "intimate" with her when she had been George Taylor's slave in St. Louis, before coming to Galena.[19]

Campbell came to an agreement with Eliza's common-law husband, Perry Bark, to buy her for $400 and deceive her into traveling south. To conclude the agreement, Perry Bark asked his boss, to write out the deed of sale for him and to arrange for and manage the transfer of physical custody of his common-law wife to Campbell. Nelson Campbell negotiated through Perry's employer as his agent because as George said, Perry Bark was "ignorant and unqualified for business." Thus, the respectable Galena merchant drew up a deed for his servant to sell his common-law wife.[20] Nelson Campbell was sufficiently unsure about the legality of purchasing Eliza that he actually consulted with a lawyer in St. Louis before paying over the money.[21]

The plan was for Nelson Campbell to take possession of her in St. Louis, which was the transfer point between steamboats plying the upper river and those traveling south to New Orleans. Campbell did not want her to be told about the plan. He would have a boat in port for New Orleans when she arrived from Galena so she could be taken easily from boat to boat.

In St. Louis, William Hempstead would see to her delivery to Campbell. Hempstead had merchandizing stores in both Galena and St. Louis, and he moved between them sometimes in partnership with George Campbell. This particular year he was in St. Louis. His St. Louis firm served as transfer agent for George Campbell's firm. In addition, he seemed to be something of a Galena middleman for slave owners who brought slaves to Galena to sell and who could not immediately find buyers for them. William Hempstead sold a black man into the service of a steamboat master.[22] Hempstead had bought William Henry from someone who brought him to Galena and sold him again to Captain David Bates to work on Bates's steamboat. William Henry sued for freedom on reaching St. Louis.[23] The steamboat captain confessed judgment in the case.[24] William Hempstead was involved in other dealings with slaves brought to Galena. William Hempstead's father describes his son's travels as taking black servants back and forth between Galena and St. Louis.[25] An enslaved man is listed in his Galena household in 1830. (Was this Perry Bark? Bark lived in his nephew's Galena home later in 1850.)

Nelson Campbell arrived in St. Louis on an earlier boat. He went to Hempstead's store in advance to arrange the transfer. When Hempstead mentioned the possibility that Eliza could sue for freedom, Campbell replied that he had done this before and had always gotten slaves to go with him. This is when he disclosed to Hempstead, perhaps in bragging, that he had been intimate with Eliza before and that she would surely accompany him. When the steamboat carrying Eliza arrived in St. Louis, Hempstead directed Eliza to go to his store in the city. Nelson Campbell was waiting there to receive her. Once at the store, Hempstead told her that Nelson Campbell had bought her from the man regarded as her common-law husband. The legal documents reported that the girl appeared "much dissatisfied" with the news.[26] (Ironically, Nelson claimed in his court papers that Eliza was satisfied being sold, a fact belied by the freedom suit that followed immediately thereafter.)

On April 29, 1835, Nelson Campbell[27] arrived at Hempstead's St. Louis store[28] expecting to receive her. When Eliza was purportedly "transferred" to Nelson Campbell, she responded by suing him for her freedom, the same day asking for $700 in damages.[29]

By Christmas, the case was decided in Eliza's favor without a jury trial.[30] Nelson Campbell did not bother to mount much of a defense. He directed his attention to getting his money back instead. Although Eliza won the suit, she was awarded only 1 cent in damages for her mistreatment. She had not actually ever been put to work as a slave by Campbell, and by this date, that was the legal measure of damages awarded to a successful freedom litigant.

It appears that Eliza Tyler never returned to Galena. She remained instead in St. Louis, presumably near the family she had come to visit. Why would she seek to return to the free state in the wake of being betrayed by someone she believed to be her husband? She registered for her Free Negro Bond as a washerwoman that year. Five years later, Eliza Tyler was still listed in the city census in her own right as the head of her own household of one person.[31] Her neighbors were a small collection of free persons of color living outside the city in St. Louis township.[32] She was not involved in any further lawsuits.

Eliza had spent only a single winter in Galena. She returned to St. Louis deceived but empowered to assert her freedom based upon having lived in a free state. In that, her status had improved. Though she secured her freedom, she never got a chance to confront the man who had betrayed her so deeply. She had been sold by him from safety in the "free" north to a buyer who intended to sell her in the deep south, most likely for prostitution. His deception is almost unimaginable. Because Perry Bark lived outside the jurisdiction, he could not even be called to St. Louis, had there been a suit against him for her injury. In a free state, Eliza's sale had been discussed with two other Galena men.[33] It had been brokered by George Campbell in Galena and facilitated by William Hempstead in St. Louis. Yet none of these men had thought to tell her of the deception that was planned. Galena hardly seems to have been a place of freedom. The drama of the betrayal loomed behind the courtroom scene, but in court, Eliza's defendant simply folded.

Nelson Campbell sued Perry Bark, Hempstead, George Campbell (and their business partners) for the return of Eliza's purchase money. He alleged that he was the victim of a conspiracy to defraud him.[34] Was the slave buyer duped? Perry Bark, Campbell, and Hempstead had deceitfully set up Eliza Tyler, to be sure, but did they also set up her buyer? Probably not. Hempstead and Bark probably believed that the scheme would work. They had taken all the precautions to see it through. Hempstead's past behavior suggests that he was unscrupulous about buying and selling slaves in free territory; he had done so before. Thus, he did not seem to mind setting up Eliza, but as a merchant with commercial standing in the valley, he probably regarded Nelson Campbell as an equal, involved in a deal with some risk. He probably did not intend to cheat him.

As for Perry Bark, he remained with the mercantile partners in one or another of their households for another twenty years until his death. When a man named McMaster went into partnership with Edward Hempstead, he described a black man as "Commodore Perry" who did odd jobs arround the house. Perry Bark is identified by his full name in the 1850 census, living in Edward Hempstead's house.[35] He is never known to have married thereafter. His betrayal of Eliza seems unforgivable, but as he continued to live in Galena, it did not seem to have cost him. Townspeople may have believed the story that Eliza believed when she left: that she had set off to visit relatives, and simply never returned. Yet the legend of William Hempstead that surfaces in post–Civil War accounts was as the savior of Swansey Adams in his kidnapping by the Duncans.[36] It is not clear that this story was anything but pure fabrication. William Hempstead, trader of slaves in free territory, managed his reputation much as Judge Henry Vanderburgh—the man who had deceived and betrayed Peter McNelly and Queen—managed his. Slave trading in the lands of the free Northwest Territory seems to have gone on by persons cloaked in respectability.

Hester Williams's Redemption

By contrast, the tensions of Hester Williams's intimacy with the man who had owned her and his subsequent betrayal were dramatically present in Hester's suit for her freedom, even though her defendant never entered the courtroom to face her. She sued the man who had owned her, fathered her first child, and once given them the papers necessary for their freedom, before changing his mind and selling them to slave traders.

Hester was raised in the plantation slave society of North Carolina, a context more typical of the strictures of southern enslavement. Hester came from the same county and even the very same family of slaves owners as Harriet Jacobs, author of the well-known book, *Incidents in the Life of a Slave Girl*.[37] Hester's life with the Norcoms in Edenton, North Carolina, and her treatment by her master must have been very similar to the life described in Harriet Jacobs's biography. But whereas Harriet succeeded in avoiding sex with her master, James Norcom, Hester could not avoid sex with Norcom's nephew, who was her master.

The focus of this St. Louis redemption song is dramatically different than others in the collection. After Hester's master gave her freedom papers, allowed her to leave his control and live in freedom in St. Louis for four years, he reconsidered, had her taken captive, and attempted to sell her and *his own child* south into enslavement again.

Hester's life began in the Norcom family, as the daughter of either a household slave or a plantation slave. The wealthy Norcom family owned houses in town and farms in the surrounding countryside where slaves could be assigned as needed. Thus, she and Harriet Jacobs must have known each other growing up. Hester was only three years old when 12 year old Harriet Jacobs came to the Norcoms as inherited property. Yet, for the next decade, from 1825 to 1835, they must have shared many of the common experiences of the 80 Norcom slaves.[38]

It is interesting that this sensational redemption song came from the same family as the most famous slave narrative documenting sexual predation of slave women by their white masters. One might even imagine that in a family in which the family patriarch, like James Norcom, engaged in flagrant sexual predation that similarly predatory behavior would be engaged in by its younger men. Harriet described James Norcom as whispering foul things in her ear and "daily violating the most sacred commandments of nature," until she turned from him with "disgust and hatred."[39]

Whether or not Hester knew of Harriet's desperate and elaborate attempts to avoid Dr. Norcom's repeated sexual advances, she certainly knew of Harriet's disappearance in 1835. When the Norcoms discovered that Harriet was missing, their extensive efforts to recapture her were well-known in the community. They believed that she had escaped north and actively tried to find her. They advertised for her as a runaway and searched the surrounding region. In fact, she went into hiding in the secret attic space of the home of her free grandmother for seven anxious years before finding the appropriate time to make the break for the north.[40] Such news of an "escape" would be followed with interest by all the slaves in the same family, if not the whole town. So thirteen-year-old Hester must have noted Harriet's disappearance.

Hester probably did not meet the master who would betray her until he returned to Edenton from his career as a military officer in 1832. The man who would assume such a dominating influence on her life, Frederick Norcom lived something of a charmed life as a young man. The family was sufficiently well connected that he was selected one of North Carolina's designated few sent to

West Point. Only two cadets could be enrolled from each state, and only with the selection and support of their congressmen. His West Point graduation meant that this privileged son not only had the connections to get in, he had a career and a social network upon graduation. He received favorable assignments during the seven years he remained an officer in the army. Rather than being sent to the frontier, where army officers experienced isolation and material deprivation, he was assigned to eastern posts where life was relatively easy and the social life of an officer was rewarding. He spent much of his military career stationed at the army post on Governor's Island outside New York City.[41] By the time that he resigned from the army, he had married a southern belle from his home town. (Like his siblings, the Norcoms married Beasleys.)[42]

Hester probably saw him first when he returned to Edenton, bought a house in town, and took up law. There, he was lucky as well. He fell into an easy vacancy for the North Carolina legislature, and he continued to practice law there for several more years.[43]

Frederick and Mrs. Norcom started their family which would expand to eight children over the next twenty years. In the mid-1830s, he left Edenton, moving his household to Vicksburg, Mississippi, where he expected to become rich. It is likely that he took along then eighteen-year-old Hester and her mother, Charity as two of the five slaves that he held in Vicksburg.[44]

Norcom described the prospects in letters home to Edenton. He enthusiastically encouraged one friend to join him in Vicksburg, writing that he knew more than fifty uneducated men who "five years since could not get credit for a pair of shoes, now worth 100,000 to a million of dollars—I have seen a great number who came here rich, and [are] now immensely rich."[45]

Norcom wrote another letter to the Edenton newspaper chastising naysayers for spreading rumors that Vicksburg's banks were failing. To demonstrate the region's financial stability, Norcom bragged specifically about the high prices at which negroes were sold at the court sales.[46] Nonetheless, Norcom too got caught up in a failing bank, and eventually left his law practice in Vicksburg and the state after spending seven years there.[47]

After Norcom left Mississippi, it appears that he split his time between New York and St. Louis. Hester bore his child, Priscilla in 1845 in Missouri, according to the census.[48] Norcom had little public presence in St. Louis, however. He was not listed in city directories for the time, which was customary for a man of substance and an attorney. Nor is he listed as counsel in any case before the state's high court, though he had done a fair amount of appellate practice in Vicksburg. His only presence in town is evident from his purchase of a key piece of real estate in the city's business district and his litigation about that property.[49] Norcom's large family returned to New York City where his oldest sons went to college. According to the 1850 census, in addition to his wife and several children, his family configuration in New York included two black persons, a woman and a boy, who were originally from North Carolina. Neither of these black servants had a last name. He also had two Irish women as household servants, in keeping with the increasingly fashionable practice of replacing black domestics with Irish domestics.[50]

By 1850, Hester had experienced a series of intense personal experiences that culminated in her living free and independently in St. Louis with her three children and her mother. Two years after her child with Norcom was born, Hester had married a Mr. Williams, with whom she had another two children. Several life-changing events affected Hester in 1849, in no discernible order. Hester had sufficiently separated from Norcom's control that he said that he had freed her in New York in January 1849.[51] Hester became pregnant again by her husband, and she was falsely arrested as a runaway, but released with the aid of Norcom's sending a piece of paper attesting to her freedom.[52] By the 1850 St. Louis census, taken on August 29, she was listed as the head of her own household. Her five-year-old daughter Priscilla was designated in the census as M, for mulatto. Her three-year-old daughter Mary Ella and her seven-month-old son Edward, born in January, were designated as B, for black. An elderly woman, presumably her mother Charity Norcum [sic], age fifty, also lived with them.[53]

There is no Mr. Williams in the household. It is unclear where her husband was: whether he was away working on the river, like many free Black men, or dead; he would die by 1853. (With her youngest child still an infant, her husband was alive in 1849.) Hester and her mother's means of support were unclear. Neither was identified as a washerwoman, the occupation of most free black women.

Hester should have been quite confident in her freedom. Hester still had in her possession the note signed by her master in New York City less than a year earlier. The note said, "This is to certify that [negroe] woman Hester [sic] & children... are free, and have all the rights to go where they please, that other coloured people have—They were set free by me in January last. Signed F. Norcom."[54] Why did Norcom free her? Mrs. Norcom may have resented her presence if she knew the paternity of Hester's child. Or Hester may not have fit into Norcom's newly established New York household as well as the Irish servants. It is from New York that Norcom had written the note attesting to Hester's freedom.

Then three years later, in 1853, almost 4 years to the day that Hester received her freedom paper, Frederick Norcom appeared in St. Louis. He sent for her and she went to see him. Did she have reason to be suspicious? Hester did not importune men, as Leah Charleville did. Hester was a church member in good standing. By this time, Hester's husband was dead.

When Hester visited Norcom, he asked her to show him the note that documented her freedom, and taking it from her, he tore it up. He had sold her to slave traders, Blakey and McAffee. Two days later, the slave traders seized her family and "with force and violence pulled and dragged them" from the public house where they resided, pulled them into the public street, and forced them along several streets, to their negro jail."[55] McAffee held as many as twenty-five enslaved persons at a time in his crowded negro jail.[56]

Within the week, Hester sued for freedom with the help of Jordan Early. Reverend Early, a free black man, was an itinerant preacher for one of the African churches and he owned an ice cream parlor and fruit store. Jordan Early had emancipated his wife, purchased their oldest son, who had been born when she was enslaved and the reunited family now had several additions.[57] He was a believer in family re-unification and since his eldest son was now 18, he was in the process of manumitting him at the time of the lawsuit. (He waited until his son was eighteen years old, because manumitting younger slaves required the owner to post an expensive bond).[58] He agreed to help as next friend for Hester's children.

Once Norcom had sold Hester to slave traders and Hester filed suit, he left things up to his attorney. The same attorney represented Norcom in both his real estate claim and his claim to retain Hester and her children.[59] Norcom's attorney filed many pre-trial motions, all of which had the effect of delaying trial for several terms. In one motion, defendants had the nerve to request that the court deliver Hester to Norcom or his agent "to be *dealt with as his slaves.*" Norcom appears to have been absent from the state during these tactical maneuvers by his attorney. It seems that he watched the proceedings from the distance in New York City. At one point, Hester's attorney sent to New York seeking his testimony.[60] During the years of Hester's lawsuit, Norcom was more concerned with his other lawsuit over a choice piece of real estate on the St. Louis wharf. The suit over the land on Front Street was appealed four times.[61]

There is no indication at all where Hester and the children spent the next three years. The case file is thin. An interesting variety of witnesses were summoned on Hester's behalf for the trial scheduled on April 17, 1856; only some showed up. The group included three local attorneys, the Episcopal bishop, a steamboat pilot, and the other major slave dealer in town.[62] Why were these men called as witnesses? What could they contribute to the suit? Without depositions, it is impossible to know. Why so many lawyers? Were they colleagues of Norcom, or did they know New York law and the legal significance of her piece of paper. Had the steamboat pilot employed Hester's husband, who was now deceased, or had Hester been a passenger on his boat?

The white Episcopal bishop discreetly "could not be found" by the sheriff, so he did not testify. He may have been Norcom's minister; Norcom's family was staunchly Episcopal and both men were from North Carolina. Both the Bishop's summons, and Reverend Early's involvement in the case imply that Hester was a respectable church member.

At trial, the judge redeemed Hester's and her daughters' claims to freedom. (Hester's baby son Edward was no longer mentioned.) Hester heard the ringing words that all freedom litigants waited to hear: she and her children were adjudged to be "liberated and entirely set free from said defendants and all persons whatsoever, if any, claiming under them." Frederick Norcom did not appeal this lawsuit.[63]

Hester never took out a free negro bond after the verdict, so she probably took the children and left the state. Where could she go? She was widowed, but she had her children, and she was free. Perhaps she went to New York City. There are several Hester Williams in the next decades' censuses but one stands out, because within the household there is a "Mary E. Williams," the age of Mary Ella, whose birthplace stands out on the page: it is "Missouri."[64] Why not return to New York? Harriet Jacobs was writing letters to a New York newspaper at the time.

Sex between master and his slave intensified other grievances, and as Harriet Jacobs' narrative illustrated it could be the grievance itself. These two freedom suits demonstrate that enhanced betrayal of being sold by the same master who could command intimacy.

CHAPTER 11

Yours Truly, Lucy A. Delaney

[A]lthough we are each but atoms...we assist in making the grand total
of all history.
—Lucy Delaney, "From the Darkness Cometh the Light"

Lucy's memoir is the only existing first-person account of a freedom suit. In fact, Lucy Delaney describes two freedom suits, occurring separately: her own, and that of her mother. Both lawsuits can be examined from the dual perspective of Lucy's narration and the court documents. By this bifocular perspective a more multi-dimensional understanding comes into view: what the court documents recorded and how the lawsuit was remembered as an experience.

Lucy wrote her a memoir a half-century after her lawsuit, remembering her own experience and the stories told by her mother. She dedicated her post Civil War memoir to "The Grand Army of the Republic."[1] She addressed two audiences: "[t]hose who were with me in the days of slavery" and "[t]hose of you who have never suffered as we have,...and therefore accept with interest and sympathy [these] passages of life...."[2]

Although it is tempting to simply reproduce her redemption song in her own words, that is unnecessary: her short book is widely available. Lucy's prose is engaging, impassioned, and somewhat flowery. The focus here is interpreting what Lucy's memoir adds as context to the many other redemption songs. We can expect the text to accurately reflect her emotional timbre and feelings about the experience of redeeming her freedom. The differing statements of fact pose a question. Do we listen to the memoir in order to understand the legal records, or do we use the legal records to interpret Lucy's memoir?[3]

We cannot expect her memory to be a perfect recounting of events fifty years earlier from the far side of the Civil War which changed so much. Lucy had no access to the court records. Moreover, Lucy's account of her mother's life and lawsuit is even further removed from Lucy's own experience. Lucy was not there, and she would have learned this song from her mother.

Lucy Ann Delaney etching from the frontispiece of her book published in 1891. She was over 60 at the time.

But what is interesting is not the divergence of story from court record but *how* Lucy's two stories depart from the legal records. Her memoir is a song of redemption which has been consciously shaped and perfected into a song of its own. The rough edges of the actual circumstances, as revealed by the case files, have been polished by memory in her account. With two documents, subjective narrative and objective court record, about two lawsuits, the result is a sometimes corroborating and sometimes diverging complexity. This provides its own harmony and dissonance.[4] All the texts, narrative and case files, provide cues and clues for reading legal affidavits from the freedom seeker's perspective. The two accounts side by side strike an interesting chord.

Lucy's account of her trial maps fairly well onto the written record. Thus, there is no reason to doubt those details that she supplements about her experience. Her emotions provide the best evidence about how it felt to be a freedom seeker during a high-risk lawsuit. To that end, I have included two long, first-person passages in Lucy's words. The first passage details what triggered the lawsuit, and the second, her experience of trial. Where the narrative departs from court records is in items that she omits. Perhaps those items were insignificant to her as she composed her memoir. Perhaps, over the course of time, she had forgotten them.

Polly, Lucy's mother, claimed freedom by residence under the principle established in Winny's case. In subjectively recounting her mother's claim, the memoir departs substantially from the court record. Either Lucy misconstrued what she heard or what she was told differed significantly from what was revealed by the judicial record. Her narration of her mother's life is coherent and plausible, much as a song hangs together. But it simply does not track the facts detailed in the case file. This song, inspired by her mother and sung by Lucy, is much more fabricated and embellished in its stylization.

If anything, Lucy presented a more heroic and seemingly more deserving claim for her mother's freedom *as a violation of law* than was necessary for her mother to succeed. Under the rule, it was legally sufficient to demonstrate that Polly had resided in a free state, brought there by her master. Lucy describes Polly's carefree childhood, lived in an ideal free state, before she was cruelly kidnapped. Both the nature of Polly's time in Illinois and the dramatic kidnapping are contradicted by the testimony. The drama is heightened perhaps by her imagined sense of the *legal* injustice of what happened to her mother. In places, Lucy insists at least as strenuously that "the law" wasn't followed in her mother's situation as she rails against the law's injustice authorizing slavery for thousands who had no legal basis to claim freedom in the courts. In this tension, one sees the dilemma of composing a redemption song in the constraint of subordinates speaking the words necessary for redemption. Those bringing freedom suits could not effectively argue that slavery was an immoral law if they wished to succeed. Ultimately, freedom seekers utilizing the freedom-by-residence rule could never challenge slave law directly. Instead, to free themselves, they had to illuminate the exception that made their circumstance different from the thousands of others enslaved.

Other scholars reading Lucy's narrative have concluded that it resists slavery on every level.[5] I draw the opposite conclusion. I find it more surprising how extensively it buys into legal language and legality, even when that very law reinforces the horrible and unjust institution of slavery. That law only worked for Lucy and Polly because it recognized an exception: residence in free territory. Even in this post–Civil War account of a slave-era legal process, the narrator makes every effort to suggest not only that eggregiously unfair things happened because slavery was unfair, but also that her mother was particularly deserving of sympathy because of things that happened that were illegal under the recognized law. That is, rather than simply strike a chord of righteousness against the very legality of enslavement, Lucy argues that the laws were not complied with. Yet her claim, that the laws were not followed in her mother's situation, is really a fabrication when compared to the court record.

Secondly, Lucy's narration of her mother's childhood in particular is much more romanticized than the eyewitnesses' accounts. Perhaps mothers seem to have charmed origins in their daughter's eyes. By Lucy's narrative, Polly's life follows the stylized script of a fictionalized fall from grace, only to be redeemed later by going to court to receive her rightful status. In parallel, Lucy similarly describes her own childhood as happy—an ignorant bliss within an intact nuclear family on Berry's plantation, a happiness that is similarly broken when her father is sold away. Lucy claims that his sale, the first event that destroyed her happiness, was illegal and against the wishes of benevolent masters. But it was not. Both her mother's removal to Missouri from Illinois and her father's sale south were fully legal and consonant with their master's volition. Both were normal practices of the horrendous institution.

The divergence in Lucy's narration of her mother's life may be the result of her mother's intention. Polly may have intentionally masked her true feelings from her daughter, as Lucy said her mother often did from the world at large.[6] Polly may have told her daughter a different redemption song than she provided in her court affidavit in order to protect or inspire her. Lucy admits to believing everything her mother told her with childlike innocence.[7] Different renditions of the same basic facts could foster different survival mechanisms in a child's mind. Consider then the divergence as possibly based upon a mother's desire to infuse her daughter with a strong set of beliefs as a means to foster survival.

So how do the songs sound? Lucy did not begin her account with the circumstances of her mother's birth. She makes no mention of a grandmother, aunts, or uncles. She traced her mother's childhood only as far back as a family in Illinois, as she wrote about the joint household of Mr. Woods and Mr. Posey.[8] Lucy recounts "peace and happiness" for her mother, a little Negro girl living with Mrs. Posey, for five years.[9] Both Woods and Posey later gave depositions on Polly's behalf in her lawsuit.[10]

The depositions indicate that Polly's existence in Illinois was much bleaker. The witnesses described Polly's treatment as that of a slave.[11] Polly was small, but no young child when her master Joseph Crockett brought her to Illinois. She was fourteen or fifteen. Although small (described as "a slip of a girl"), she was already considered an adult.[12] Crockett and his wife came from a region near the Kentucky-Tennessee border, bringing Polly and livestock to Madison County, Illinois. He had sold his Kentucky sawmill, and he was seeking a new home in Illinois or to move on to Missouri. Rather than the five pleasant years Lucy romanticized, the Crocketts stayed only the one brutal winter of 1817–1818.[13]

The elderly, one-armed Crockett was a drinking man from Wayne County, Kentucky.[14] The sawmill might explain the loss of his arm, as well as his decision to move on. Once the Crockett household arrived in Illinois, he rented teenaged Polly out to different households, including the Woods and the Poseys, to be their servant.[15] Polly was never really out of her owner's control, however, since Crockett lived in a cabin on the same property with the other families. All three families had been friends back in Kentucky, so their arrangements were informal. In exchange for offering Polly's labor to the other two families during the winter, Crockett could use a cabin for the winter and be supplied with corn for his cattle.

The Illinois-based witnesses knew Crockett well enough to know that Polly was born to a slave in the Beatty family about 1803. Crockett bought her when she was old enough to leave her mother.[16]

Like Elijah Mitchell before him, the migrating master was indecisive about whether to stay in Illinois or move farther west. The witnesses recalled old Mr. Crockett's indecision over the winter of 1817–1818 about whether he would remain in Madison County.

More important to Polly, Crockett seems to have waffled about what to do with her as well. He knew that he needed to indenture her, to retain her as a bound servant, if she remained in Illinois. But he did not indenture her. To indenture her would declare a limit to her bondage and a date in the future when she would be free. Crockett was not sure when he wanted to give her freedom. He said that he intended to free her when he and his wife died. One person recalled him saying that she "was kinder to him than his own children."[17] It is possible that Polly heard him express these benevolent sentiments and from her vulnerable perspective took him at his word. Crockett was, after all, a drinking man, and what he said while drinking may have been more lugubrious and generous than what he was willing to deliver when sober.[18]

The winter of 1817 grew very cold, one of the coldest on record, and Polly had inadequate clothing for the temperatures. As a result, one condition of her assignment to the Poseys was that they provide her with a "frock."[19] Polly may have regarded this as a kindness, but it was actually a key part of Crockett's deal with the Poseys so that Crockett did not need to clothe her himself. The portrait that emerges from the three witnesses is of a teenage Polly, who was treated as roughly as any slave, shivering during the cold winter and in need of a frock, and owned by a hard-drinking old man, who had bought her as a child, brought her from Kentucky to Illinois, benefited from trading her to his friends in Illinois, and sent her on to the slave state of Missouri. Not exactly the stuff of romantic origins.

Lucy portrays Polly's departure from Illinois as a mass kidnapping that wrested her from tranquility to a buyer in Missouri.[20] Although leaving Illinois might have felt to Polly like a kidnapping, the witnesses explained that it was actually organized by Crockett and carried out by Crockett's son, who suggested that Polly be taken out of Illinois every ninety days and brought back for service. In the end, Crockett told his son to take Polly to Missouri for good. He and his wife followed later in the spring.[21] Thus, Polly was never kidnapped by strangers. She simply was taken to Missouri with her master's consent by her master's son, after which the master followed.

The kidnapping element enhances the sense of injustice. It implies violence and illegality, but such actions were unnecessary to winning Polly's legal case. By Illinois law, the simple fact that Polly resided in Illinois for longer than the ninety days permitted for travelers in transit before registering indentures, rendered her free, whether she was later kidnapped or not. Lucy's account of kidnapping is expanded to include not one, but "four victims" who were "securely bound and gagged."[22] Instead, the witnesses say that old Mr. Crockett's son left for Missouri on pack horses. Placed upon a horse, much as Queen had been when taken from Vanderburghs, would have sufficiently controlled her mobility. Yet it would have been very cumbersome to transport Polly on a pack horse if she were bound or gagged.[23]

The kidnapping story sharply contrasts with the bucolic, peaceful existence of a stable five-year stay with the Poseys. Again, was this an embellishment added by Lucy for her audience, or something Polly told her daughter?[24]

In Missouri, Polly was purchased by a farmer who, when overtaken by business reverses, sold everything, including Polly, at auction.[25] Lucy describes the scene, in which her mother is singled out at auction as a treasure.

> Major Taylor Berry, a wealthy gentleman...had travelled a long distance [from Columbia, Missouri] for the purpose of purchasing a servant girl for his wife. As was the custom, all the negroes were brought out and placed in a line, so that the buyers could examine their good points at leisure. Major Berry was immediately attracted by the bright and alert appearance of Polly, and at once negotiated with the trader...and started for home to present his wife with this flesh and blood commodity, which money could so easily procure in our vaunted land of freedom. Mrs. Fanny Berry was highly pleased with Polly's manner and appearance, and concluded to make a seamstress of her. Major Berry had a mulatto servant, who was as handsome as an Apollo, and when he and Polly met each other, day after day, the natural result followed, and in a short time, with [their masters' full consent, they] were married. Two children were the fruit of this marriage, my sister Nancy and myself....[26]

Lucy could not have known these details, but she certainly knew the custom of public slave sales in St. Louis. At public sales those persons to be sold were prompted to look lively. She accentuates her parents' attractiveness: Polly's appearance that attracted Major Berry's attention and subsequently pleased his wife, and her father's handsomeness. Lucy never disclosed her father's name in the memoir. In enslavement, his name was mutable at the whim of his owner; yet Lucy met him after the slave time and still did not disclose his name. Perhaps his name had changed with his masters.

It appears that as a child Lucy never knew that she was enslaved. This protective shielding of children is a practice described in other slave narratives, too.[27] "How well I remember those happy days! Slavery had no horror then for me, as I played about the place, with the same joyful freedom as the little white children. With mother, father and sister, a pleasant home and surroundings, what happier child than I!"[28]

She describes an incident involving her master: "Major Berry became involved in a quarrel with some gentleman, and a duel was resorted to, to settle the difficulty and avenge some fancied insult." This duel was notorious in Missouri. Lucy continued, "The major arranged his affairs and made his will, leaving his negroes to his wife during her lifetime and at her death they were to be free; this was his expressed wish." Although Berry, like most men approaching a duel, did draw up a will in anticipation of the prospect of death, his will makes no mention of freeing slaves.[29] (The intention to emancipate Polly upon death of a master corroborates with the witnesses describing Crockett, but Crockett never acted upon such a thought.)

Lucy describes her father loyally accompanying Mr. Berry to the fateful duel, almost as if he was the duelist's second, a role in which a black servant would never have served. Her father attended to his master's dying breath and carried him—the good man, who would have freed him—back to his family.

In frontier societies, widows frequently remarried, so Major Berry's widow married Robert Wash, an eminent lawyer, and later a judge of the Missouri Supreme Court. (Wash presided over freedom suits in the Duncans' cases, and was sued by one of his own slaves as well.)[30] The family moved to the "Wash" mansion.[31] After the mistress's death, the troubles began. Judge Wash decided to sell Lucy's father south, an act that Lucy believed was contrary to Master Berry's will.[32] "Judge Wash tore my father from his wife and children and sold him 'way down South!' Slavery! cursed slavery! what crimes has it invoked! and, oh! what retribution has a righteous God visited upon these traders in human flesh!"[33]

At the mistress's death, ownership of Lucy, her mother, and sister appear to have devolved upon Master Berry's two daughters. As the daughters came of age and married, Lucy, Polly, and Nancy went into their households. Lucy tells of her mother's plans and "solemn vow that her children should not continue in slavery all their lives.... [S]he never spared an opportunity to impress it upon us, that we must get our freedom whenever the chance offered."[34]

Lucy's sister got a chance to escape when Mistress Mary married Mr. H. S. Cox, of Philadelphia and they traveled east on their honeymoon, taking Nancy along as waiting maid. As Lucy describes it, "So mother instructed my sister not to return with Mr. and Mrs. Cox, but to run away, as soon as the chance offered, to Canada."[35] And so she did. During the visit to Niagara Falls, Lucy's sister fled across the border. Lucy describes her mother's elation upon learning the news:

"[O]utwardly she pretended to be vexed and angry. Oh! the impenetrable mask of these poor black creatures! how much emotion have they hidden from their tormentors! I . . . remember how wildly mother showed her joy at Nancy's escape when we were alone together. She would dance, clap her hands, and, waving them above her head, would indulge in one of those weird negro melodies, which so charm. . . ."[36]

Lucy was twelve years old, and together she and her mother often discussed how to escape. "No schemes were too wild for us to consider! Mother was especially restless. . . . She did not dare to talk it over with anyone for fear that they would sell her further down the river, so I was her only confidant. Mother was always planning and getting ready to go, and while the fire was burning brightly, it but needed a little more provocation to add to the flames."[37] That provocation for each of their freedom suits would arise in the form of an argument with their mistresses. "Mrs. Cox commenced housekeeping on a grand . . . scale [and] . . . entertained lavishly. My mother cared for the laundry, and . . . I was compelled to go live with Mrs. Cox to mind the baby."[38]

One day, Polly and her mistress had words. Mrs. Cox admonished her, threatening to sell her down river for her behavior in putting on "white airs." Polly put on the bold front "that 'she didn't care'. . . . This so infuriated Mr. Cox that he said, 'How dare a negro say what she liked or what she did not like; and he would show her what he should do.' So, on the following day, he took my mother to an auction-room on Main Street and sold her to the highest bidder, for 550 dollars. Oh! God! the pity of it! . . . [S]old away from her child, to satisfy the anger of a peevish mistress!"[39] Polly was sold to Joseph Magehan, a house builder.[40]

Lucy continues, "My mother returned to the house to get her few belongings, and straining me to her breast, begged me to be a good girl, that she was going to run away, and would buy me as soon as she could. . . . I believed it most fondly, and when I heard that she had actually made her escape, . . . my heart gave an exultant throb and cried, 'God is good!' "[41]

Lucy claimed that Polly ran away, but there is no evidence that she ever did. Lucy explains that slave catchers caught Polly in Chicago and that hundreds of people gathered to resist her return to slavery.[42] This doesn't seem to ring true to public sentiment of 1839. Fifteen years later, after the Fugitive Slave Law was passed, such public outcries responded to the capture of runaway slaves on free soil, but such was not likely in Chicago in 1839. Polly mentions no such incident in her affidavit. Instead, Polly states something seeming to contradict running away: that with her master's permission, she was assigned as a chambermaid to a steamboat that traveled up Illinois rivers.[43] Had Polly made a break for freedom, it would have been much easier to reach Chicago from Peoria than from St. Louis, as Lucy claimed, "navigating by the North Star." Stories of runaway slaves were present in various literatures by the time Lucy wrote her memoir. But the court record and the other documents do not corroborate Lucy's claim that Polly made an escape.

Whatever the circumstances of Polly's absence in Illinois, Lucy explained her mother's return as occasioned by concern for Lucy, whom she had left behind: "[F]earing that Mr. Cox would wreak his vengeance upon me, my mother finally gave herself up to her captors, and returned to St. Louis. And so the mothers of Israel have been ever slain through their deepest affections!"[44]

Polly sued for her freedom.[45] Polly alleged the necessary formal recitation: that on September, 30, 1839, she was "assaulted" by Joseph Magehan.[46] During the pendency of her suit, she was hired out to Elijah Hayden,[47] a schoolmaster from Alton, Illinois.[48] This means that Polly probably lived at his Spruce Street residence during the entire pendency of her lawsuit. Hayden was a liberal reformer. He became a St. Louis School Board member and advocated establishing schools for girls as well as boys. Hayden continued to be supportive of both Lucy and her mother even after the lawsuit. He later posted the substantial bond necessary for each of them to remain in the city as free Blacks in 1846.[49]

Depositions in Polly's cases were taken just across the Mississippi River in Madison County, Illinois, in summer of 1840 at the Woods' house, where Mr. and Mrs. Woods and Jubilee Posey testified.[50] Polly accompanied her lawyer across the Mississippi River, to be present for the witnesses' depositions. It seems that her assigned lawyer was replaced by the seasoned G. A. Bird, who handled the Tituses and Duncans' freedom suits, and occasionally took his clients out of state to find the necessary witnesses.[51]

In the meanwhile, [the other Berry daughter, Martha] had married Mr. Mitchell and taken me to live with her. I had never been taught to work, as playing with the babies had been my sole occupation; therefore, when Mrs. Mitchell commanded me to do the weekly washing and ironing, I had no...idea how it was to be done....But I made the effort to do what she required, and my failure would have been amusing had it not been so appalling....

[T]he Mississippi water was even muddier than now....After soaking and boiling the clothes in its earthy depths, for a couple of days, in vain attempt to get them clean, and rinsing through several waters, I found the clothes were getting darker and darker, until they nearly approximated my own color.

In my despair, I frantically rushed to my mother and sobbed out my troubles....So in the morning, before the white people had arisen, a friend of my mother came to the house and washed out the clothes [but they had been ruined]. [Mrs. Mitchell was furious] scolding vigorously, saying over and over again, "Lucy...you are a lazy, good-for-nothing [n——]!" I was angry at being called a [n——], and replied, "You don't know nothing, yourself, about it, and you expect a poor ignorant girl to know more than you do yourself; if you had any feeling you would get somebody to teach me...."

She then gave me a wrapper [a sleeping gown] to do up, and told me if I ruined that as I did the other clothes, she would whip me severely. I answered, "You have no business to whip me. I don't belong to you." My mother had so often told me that she was a free woman and that I should not die a slave, I always had a feeling of independence, which would invariably crop out in these encounters....; and when I thus spoke, saucily...she opened her eyes in angry amazement and cried:

"You *do* belong to me, for my papa left you to me in his will, when you were a baby, and you ought to be ashamed of yourself to talk so...."[52]

Leaving a slave girl to each daughter comports with a standard inheritance practice in white slaveholding families in the region.

Lucy took the gown, washed it, and ruined it in the process.

But I could not help it, as heaven is my witness. I was entirely and hopelessly ignorant! But of course my mistress [said] that I did it on purpose to provoke her.... She was bound to carry out her threat of whipping me. I rebelled... and would not permit her to strike me; she used shovel, tongs and broomstick in vain, as I disarmed her as fast as she picked up each weapon. Infuriated..., Mrs. Mitchell declared she would [have her husband] punish me. When her husband returned home, she immediately entered a list of complaints against me.... I was in the shadow of the doorway as [she] raved, while Mr. Mitchell listened patiently. [She] appeal[ed] to him to whip me with the strength that a man alone could possess.

Then he declared, "Martha, this thing of cutting up and slashing servants is something I... positively will not do."

"Mr. Mitchell, I will not have that saucy baggage around this house, for if she finds you won't whip her, there will be no living with her, so you shall just sell her, and I insist upon it."

"Well, Martha," he answered, "I found the girl with you when we were married, and as you claim her as yours,... I will make arrangements for selling her at once."

I distinctly overheard all that was said, and was just as determined not to be sold as I was not to be whipped. My mother's lawyer had told her to caution me never [leave] the city,...so I was quite settled as to my course....

[Several days later] I was not surprised to be ordered by Mr. Mitchell to pack up my clothes and get ready to go down the river, for I was to be sold that morning, and leave, on the steamboat Alex Scott, at 3 o'clock in the afternoon.

"Can't I go see my mother, first?" I asked.

"No," he replied, not very gently, "there is no time for that, you can see her when you come back. So hurry up and get ready...!" How I did hate him! To hear him talk as if I were going to take a pleasure trip, when he knew that if he sold me South, I would never see my dear mother again. However, I hastily ran upstairs and packed my trunk, but my mother's injunction, "never to go out of the city," was ever present in my mind....

[Mr. Mitchell's office was] in the dwelling house, and I could hear him giving orders to his clerk, as I ran lightly down the stairs, out of the front door to the street, and with fleet foot, I skimmed the road which led to my mother's door, and, reaching it, stood trembling...with terror and fatigue. [Polly Wash would have lived at Elijah Hayden's house at the time, by virtue of still being hired out to him.]

I could not gain admittance, as my mother was away to work and the door was locked. A white woman, living next door, and who was always friendly to mother, told me that she would not return until night. I clasped my hands in despair and cried, "Oh! the white people have sold me, and I had to run away to keep from being sent down the river. This white lady, whose name I am sorry I cannot remember, sympathized with me, as she knew my mother's story and had written many letters for her, so she offered me the key of her house, which, fortunately, fitted my mother's door, and I was soon inside, cowering with fear in the darkness, magnifying every noise and every passing wind.... Late at night mother returned,...and after getting supper, she took me to a friend's house for concealment, until the next day....[53]

On the morning of the 8th of September, 1842, my mother sued Mr. D. D. Mitchell for the possession of her child, Lucy Ann Berry. My mother, accompanied by the sheriff, took me from my hiding-place and conveyed me to the jail...and there met Mr. Mitchell, with Mr. H. S. Cox, his brother in-law.[54]

Judge Bryan Mullanphy read the law to Mr. Mitchell, which stated that if Mr. Mitchell took me [home], he must give bond and security to the amount of two thousand dollars....Mr. Mitchell...demanded that I should be put in jail.

"Why do you want to put that poor young girl in jail?" demanded my lawyer. "Because," he retorted, "her mother or some of her crew might run her off, just to make me pay the two thousand dollars; and I would like to see her lawyer, or any other man, in jail, that would take up a d—— n—— case like that."

"You need not think, Mr. Mitchell," calmly replied Mr. Murdock, "because my client is colored that she has no rights, and can be cheated out of her freedom. She is just as free as you are, and the Court will so decide it, as you will see."

However, I was put in a cell, under lock and key, and there remained for seventeen long and dreary months, listening to the…foreign echoes from the street, Faint sounds of revel, traffic, conflict keen.…" My only crime was seeking for that freedom which was my birthright!"[55]

Winter was hard on Lucy at the jail. Polly went to court as winter set in the first year and plead that Lucy was "suffering from a severe cold occasioned from a deficiency of clothing and the dampness of the room [where] she was confined."[56] Polly said that without her frequent visits, Lucy's "sufferings would have been incalculable," and "that death would have been the consequences of such cruelty.…"[57] The court ordered the jailer to inquire into her condition as to lodging and clothing and report back.[58]

What Lucy did not mention is that her mother's case was still in litigation when circumstances at the Mitchell household forced her to flee and triggered her litigation. Polly was permitted to sue for her daughter's freedom on September 8, 1842, before she herself had been declared free.[59] This too is a legal anomaly. How was Polly, who was still enslaved, able to sue as next friend for her daughter? The purpose of the "next friend" structure was to put a responsible, independent, free person, able to make legally binding decisions, in as a plaintiff when the under age party was unable to consent to legal matters for herself. Polly, still technically enslaved, was allowed to sue for her daughter's freedom.

Compared to Polly, though, suing for her freedom technically should not have been Lucy's legal "next friend." Lucy had the misfortune to be incarcerated for a very long time. This different treatment may reflect the very real difference in their respective skill levels. An order to hire Lucy out was issued later, but given that she had no skills to justify her keep, not even as a laundress, it does not appear that anyone was willing to hire her. Polly, on the other hand, was a trained seamstress who could earn her hire. Because Polly's higher skill level allowed her be hired out, she was freer to come and go, to travel to Illinois to find witnesses, and to attend to Lucy's suit as well. Polly was adjudged free, while Lucy was still in jail, and thereafter sued for and was awarded her accrued wages. (When Lucy was later declared free, the jailer sued everyone, seeking to get someone to pay the bill for her keep.)[60]

Lucy's mother sought out Edward Bates to plead Lucy's case, and he consented. Bates was just as willing to represent slave owners against freedom suits: he had defended James and Coleman Duncan many times. Bates was a well-established lawyer and statesman in St. Louis at the time, who would go on to become even more prominent as President Lincoln's attorney general. Why did Bates take the case? Lucy herself wondered why such a "distinguished statesman would take up the case of an obscure negro girl."[61] In this instance, Bates may have accepted the case as a handoff from Frances B. Murdoch, who had filed Lucy's petition.[62] Or did he do it to oppose the step-daughters of another important member of the bar, Judge Wash? Was there animosity between them? Bates actually called Judge Wash to the stand as an adverse witness for his slave girl client.

> On the 7th of February, 1844, the suit for my freedom began. A bright, sunny day, a day which the happy and care-free would drink in with a keen sense of enjoyment. But my heart was full of bitterness; I could see only gloom which seemed to deepen and gather closer to me as I neared the courtroom. The jailer's sister-in-law, Mrs. Lacy, spoke to me of submission and patience; but I could not feel anything but rebellion against my lot. I could not see one gleam of brightness in my future, as I was hurried on to hear my fate decided.[63]

Central to the issue of Lucy's freedom was Polly's residence in Illinois. Among the witnesses were Judge Wash, an overseer from his farm, and the carpenter, Joseph Magehan, whom Polly sued.[64] There were also affidavits from Illinois from Posey and the Woods.

> After the evidence from both sides was all in, Mr. Mitchell's lawyer... commenced to plead. For one hour, he talked so bitterly against me and against my being in possession of my liberty that I was trembling...for I certainly thought everybody must believe him; indeed I almost believed the dreadful things he said, myself, and as I listened I closed my eyes with sickening dread, for I could just see myself floating down the river, and my heart-throbs seemed to be the throbs of the mighty engine which propelled me from my mother and freedom forever! Oh! what a relief it was to me when he finally finished his harangue and resumed his seat! As I never heard anyone plead before, I was very much alarmed, although I knew in my heart that every word he uttered was a lie! Yet, how was I to make people believe?...

Judge Bates arose, and his soulful eloquence and earnest pleading made such an impression on my sore heart, I listened with renewed hope. I felt the black storm clouds of doubt and despair were fading away, and that I was drifting into the safe harbor of the realms of truth....Judge Bates chained his hearers with the graphic history of my mother's life, from the time she played on Illinois banks, through her trials in slavery, her separation from her husband, her efforts to become free, her voluntary return to slavery for the sake of her child, Lucy, and her subsequent efforts in securing her own freedom. [C]oncluding, he said:

"Gentlemen of the jury, I am a slave-holder myself, but, thanks to the Almighty God, I am above the base principle of holding anybody a slave that has as good right to her freedom as this girl has been proven to have; she was free before she was born; her mother was free,...and no free woman can give birth to a slave child, as it is in direct violation of the laws of God and man!...[H]ere I rest this case, as I would not want any better evidence for one of my own children. The testimony of Judge Wash is alone sufficient to substantiate the claim of Polly Crockett Berry to the defendant as being her own child."

The case was then submitted to the jury, about 8 o'clock in the evening, and I was returned to the jail and locked in the cell which I had occupied for seventeen months, filled with the most intense anguish....[The sheriff] told me to be in readiness at nine o'clock on the following morning to accompany him back to court to hear the verdict. My mother was not at the trial. She had lingered many days about the jail expecting my case would be called, and finally when called to trial [she] was not present to sustain me....All night long I suffered agonies of fright, the suspense was something awful...I felt so hopeless and alone!...

On the morning of my return to Court...I was so overcome with fright and emotion,—with the alternating feelings of despair and hope—that I could not stand still long enough to dress myself...Mrs. Lacy gladly assisted me...[P]romptly at nine o'clock, the sheriff called and escorted me to the courthouse.

On our way thither, Judge Bates overtook us...on horseback. He tipped his hat to me as politely as if I were the finest lady in the land, and cried out, "Good morning Miss Lucy, I suppose you had pleasant dreams last night!" He seemed so bright and smiling that I was imbued with renewed hope; and when he addressed the sheriff with "Good morning Sir. I don't suppose the jury was out twenty minutes were they?" and the sheriff replied "oh! no, sir," my heart gave a leap, for I was sure that my fate was decided for weal or woe.

I watched the judge until he turned the corner and desiring to be relieved of suspense from my pent-up anxiety, I eagerly asked the sheriff if I were free, but he gruffly answered that "he didn't know." I was sure he did know, but was too mean to tell me. How could he have been so flinty....

At last the courthouse was reached and I had taken my seat in such a condition of helpless terror that I could not tell one person from another....My long confinement, burdened with harrowing anxiety, the sleepless night I had just spent...had brought me to an indescribable condition. I felt dazed, as if I were no longer myself. I seemed to be another person—an onlooker—and in my heart dwelt a pity for the poor, lonely girl, with down-cast face, sitting on the bench apart from anyone else in that noisy room.

At the sound of a gentle voice, I gathered courage to look upward, and caught the kindly gleam of Judge Bates' eyes, as he bent his gaze upon me and smilingly said, "I will have you discharged in a few minutes, Miss Lucy!"

Some other business occupied the attention of the Court, and when I had begun to think they had forgotten all about me, Judge Bates arose and said calmly, "Your Honor, I desire to have this girl, Lucy A. Berry, discharged before going into any other business."

Judge Mullanphy answered "Certainly!" Then the verdict was called for and rendered, and the jurymen resumed their places. Mr. Mitchell's lawyer jumped up and exclaimed:

"Your Honor, my client demands that this girl be remanded to jail. He does not consider that the case has had a fair trial...."

Judge Bates was on his feet in a second and cried: "For shame! is it not enough that this girl has been deprived of her liberty for a year and a half, that you must still pursue her after a fair and impartial trial before a jury, in which it was clearly proven and decided that she had every right to freedom? I demand that she be set at liberty at once!"

"I agree with Judge Bates," responded Judge Mullanphy, "and the girl may go!"[65]

The audience had responded favorably to Lucy's redemption song. Lucy was free at last. Exultation!

Oh! the overflowing thankfulness of my grateful heart at that moment....I could have kissed the feet of my deliverers, but I was too full to express my thanks, but with a voice trembling with tears I tried to thank Judge Bates for all his kindness.

As soon as possible, I returned to the jail to bid them all good-bye and thank them for their good treatment of me while under their care.... As soon as Polly heard of the result, she hurried to meet me, and hand in hand we gazed into each other's eyes and saw the light of freedom there, and we felt in our hearts that we could with one accord cry out: "Glory to God in the highest, and peace and good will towards men."[66]

After Lucy's release, after her redemption, her life seemed to begin again with the normal passages of living free. The last chapter of Lucy's book is one of family reunification. "After the trial was over... [my mother's] next thought reverted to sister Nancy, who had been gone so long.'" Together, Polly working as a laundress, and Lucy as a seamstress, a skill she had learned while jailed, earned enough money for Polly to visit Nancy in Canada. "[I]t was easy to procure all the work we could do, and command our own prices. [M]other and I expended the utmost care in our respective callings, and were well rewarded for our efforts." After visiting Toronto, Polly Wash returned to St. Louis. Polly stayed with Lucy until her death "surrounded by many friends, both black and white, who recognized and appreciated her."[67]

Lucy married, had children, was widowed when her first husband died in a steamboat explosion, and later remarried.

Our children were born free and died free! Their childhood and my maternity were never shadowed with a thought of separation....

I frequently thought of father, and wondered if he were alive or dead; and at the time of the great exodus of negroes from the South, a few years ago, a large number arrived in St. Louis.... I learned that my father had always lived on the same plantation, fifteen miles from Vicksburg. I wrote to my father and begged him to come and see me and make his home with me; sent him the money,... and when he finally reached St. Louis, it was with great joy that I received him. Old, grizzled and gray, time had dealt hardly with him.... [i]nstead of a man bearing his years with upright vigor, he was made prematurely old by the accumulation of troubles. My sister Nancy came from Canada, and we had a most joyful reunion, and only the absence of our mother left a vacuum.... Father could not be persuaded to stay with us, when he found his wife dead; he longed to get back to his old associations of forty-five years standing, he felt like a stranger in a strange land, and taking pity on him, I urged him no more, but let him go....[68]

From Ohio, in the 1890s, Lucy completed her redemption song.

CHAPTER 12

The Slaves of Milton Duty

In 1836, a middle-aged widower named Milton Duty sat down to write a will on his plantation in Warren County, in Mississippi's cotton-growing region.[1] He intended to free some thirty of his slaves. What prompted the wealthy slave owner to this generosity is unknown. He later explained that he had made all his own money, with the help of one of his slaves, and he felt that he had the right to dispose of it as he saw fit. He did not owe his success to any of his family members.

Milton Duty was meticulous in writing out the details of his bequest. After providing that all his debts be paid, he wrote: "I direct, that all my Negroes...consisting so far as I recollect of the following," after which he listed almost thirty names, in no apparent order.[2] Should he have omitted anyone, he added, "Likewise: the various others...." He continued, "[I]n case it should not be necessary to sell to meet the payment of my debts and all other charges and apprentices that may belong to me at the day of my death, to be manumitted—to that they be sent out of this state into the state of Missouri of the United States as...shall be deemed most suitable for their condition."[3]

He was quite clear about his intention and even went so far as to identify those persons who should be sold first, if necessary, and whom he wanted to administer this unusually generous bequest. Noticeably, he omitted his siblings from the list.

What motivated the middle-aged man to free his many slaves rather than sell them or leave them to his relatives is unclear. He made careful provision to not defraud his creditors, to sell all his other items of personal property, horses, livestock, and so forth first to satisfy his creditors. Yet he was not an abolitionist in an unqualified sense. He did specify individuals from the list of enslaved people who should be sold first to satisfy his creditors, if that were financially necessary, and even the two individuals they shoud be sold to, but that they too should be freed if the debts were paid. Milton Duty did not seem to have any immediate family. He had been married once, though there was no evidence that his wife still lived, or that he had children. In the prime of his life, Milton Duty cannot have contemplated his immediate demise, so the will does not appear to be the desperate move of someone preparing to meet his maker. The desire to free so many slaves was both unusual and expensive. Masters occasionally freed one or two loyal slaves in their wills, but freeing this many was exceedingly rare, at least in Mississippi or St. Louis. Moreover, masters who freed slaves usually did so selectively, often identifying those who were approaching their final years and no longer able to work efficiently. The slaves that Milton Duty intended to free were young, strong, and able to work for a living, and, as such, both able to take care of themselves by earning money and similarly worth thousands of dollars if kept as slaves.

Something changed his mind about staying on in Mississippi. Perhaps his relatives became aware of his intentions and attempted to influence him against freeing his slaves. Perhaps this idea of emancipating his black servants was not well received by the friends he had selected to carry it out.[4] Or, more likely, he may have been informed that in Mississippi a will emancipating slaves could never be effected without a special act of the legislature. The likelihood that the Mississippi legislature would grant the slaves' freedom posthumous to their master's desire may have seemed a political impossibility.[5] Even in writing his will he reflected his knowledge that some western areas, like Illinois, might be more suitable for the emancipation of his slaves than others.

He may have learned subsequently that Illinois had taken actions to prevent masters from emancipating their slaves there. In fact, the 1819 Act Concerning Negroes and Mulattoes, section 3 "prohibits any person from bringing any slave into this State for the purpose of emancipating such slave, making it a condition for those who do so, to give bond in the penal sum of one thousand dollars, condition that such slave shall not become a county charge; neglecting so to do, subjected the offender to a fine of $200 for each one so emancipated." The act was amended in 1833, eliminating the penal provision, it but continued to require the $1,000 payment per person.[6]

In any case, he decided to move upriver to St. Louis,[7] bringing the majority of his large group of slaves to prepare them for a free life after his death.[8] He intended to see them on their way to freedom himself because, according to later testimony, he told them repeatedly of his desire to build them cabins in the town of Soulard, south of the city, so they would have their own homes once they were free. Missouri was one of the few states where an owner could emancipate slaves and the freed people could remain to enjoy their freedom. Most southern states required that manumitted slaves leave the state, or be expelled therefrom entirely, and several northern states were already raising barriers to Blacks and mulattoes attempting to enter their jurisdiction. Milton Duty sold his plantations and farm equipment, and even a few slaves whom he did not want to remove from Mississippi, and moved to St. Louis.

Milton Duty settled in a modest house that he rented near the southern end of town. He lived in a very plain, economical, and unimpressive manner. He dressed plainly and boarded himself at very small expense.[9] His personal possessions indicated a man who was comfortable with wealth but not unduly concerned about displaying it. He owned quite an extensive wardrobe, as well as several guns of different description, good bed linen, a spy glass, and a two-volume set of Homer's *Iliad*. His neighbors considered him truthful and correct.

Once master and slaves were settled in St. Louis, the routine of life was established. Duty went into an emerging business of selling salt pork, buying barrels of pork in St. Louis and shipping them down to Vicksburg for sale through business associates there. The thirty slaves were set to earning money by renting themselves out on a day-to-day basis to whoever would hire them. This daily experience became a school for moving the slaves from dependence to autonomy and self-reliance. These slaves, whose lives previously had been limited to the confines of a plantation, were now able to choose their own masters as it suited them, for a day or a week, provided that they bring the money back after they earned it.

Managing the finances of so many slaves presented its own logistical problems. The bondspeople turned their money over to their master when he was in St. Louis, and when he was away on business, they turned it over to Preston, an older bondsmen who was left in charge. Preston, in turn, delivered it to shopkeeper David Coons, for safekeeping. Turning the cash over to a shopkeeper for safekeeping was a customary practice in the west. David Coons ran a local merchandizing firm and he frequently engaged in joint endeavors with Duty, their master. From David Coons's general store, the bondspeople could acquire groceries and items like clothing and other items that they might need while the master was away. Preston looked after these matters.

Apparently through this method of selling their own labor, some of the slaves were able to accumulate some money of their own. The man named Jesse took up work as a drayman and after a while was able to afford to buy his own horse and wagon. The slaves seemed to be well aware that they would eventually be freed upon their master's death, that he planned to build cabins for them in Soulard, and that their current situation was preparing them for that independence.

Although Preston stayed behind to manage the slave community while the master was away, Preston's brother Braxton traveled with Milton Duty when on business. One slave man, Jordan (or Gordon), was sufficiently impatient for freedom upon arrival in St. Louis that he ran away soon after the entourage arrived. He headed out for Illinois, the place that his master had initially designated as their destination, at least in his will. An ad appeared in the St. Louis newspapers in the summer of 1837 requesting the runaway's return: "Gordon ran away age 28 dark complexion, very polite in his manners, weight 160 pds, thick lips, full eyes, little roman nose, quick spoken, bushy hair, five ft 8 or 9."

Jordan got as far as Boone County, Illinois, where he was apprehended by a man who collected a reward for bringing him back.[10] Illinois in 1837, Jordan learned, was not necessarily a sanctuary for runaways. After his attempt to flee, Jordan took up a relationship with one of Duty's women slaves, and with wife and eventually children, Jordan became a stable mainstay of the group for the next three decades.

These thirty-some slaves of Milton Duty should have been the lucky ones to have an owner sincerely intent upon freeing them. Moreover, they had relocated to a state where free status was possible, they were learning the skills of self-maintenance in a market that paid for their daily labor, and they had the promise of cabins of their own someday by a master considered by his neighbors as truthful and correct. Despite the strength of their master's intention, however, freeing slaves wasn't simply a matter of releasing them. In order to legally manumit the group of slaves in Missouri, Duty had to go to court and establish that these slaves were sufficiently independent to be able to care for themselves, that they would not fall upon the state's resources or become beggars or thieves. To secure such a claim during his lifetime, in Missouri as in Illinois, he needed to post $1,000 bond for those most unlikely to be able to care for themselves, any elderly bondsperson and any slave child under age seven. Duty's plan of freeing them upon his death avoided the need to post bond: his plan was simply to manumit them when he died through the disposition of his will. Duty spoke about his plans freely in front of the slaves as well as his St. Louis neighbors.

Duty was congenial and became socially friendly with his neighbors. In St. Louis, he had several business associates as well, principally sort of a venture partnership with David Coons. David Coons worked together with his son, George W. Coons.

Within a year of settling in St. Louis, Milton Duty died.

One hot summer evening, a few weeks after returning from a trip south, he was feeling indisposed. He took a cold drink of water, struggled to the front porch of his house to get air, and collapsed. His slave man Preston, who managed most of his domestic affairs in town, ran to call the near neighbors, who came immediately and stayed as he lay dying. Preston then ran to the Coons household, his master's business partner, to notify him. David was not at home, but his adult son George W. and one of the store clerks were awoken and went quickly to the dying man's house.

At the house, the neighbors had moved the body from the porch to his bed and surrounded him, preparing him for burial. When George Coons and his fellow clerk arrived, they seemed less concerned about the dead or unconscious Milton Duty than about his worldly effects. Minutes after they arrived, the care and custody of his two trunks of clothing and papers, which were to complicate the question of whether the slaves could ever be freed, were delivered over to George W. Coons, son of the master's business associate.

George W. directed Preston to bring his master's trunks from the bedroom. One contained clothing, the other, papers. As the neighbors attended to the body for burial, these two businessmen hurriedly went through Duty's papers, tearing up some, leaving the pieces on the floor, and taking custody of the rest. A grieving neighbor remonstrated with the young men for rifling through the dead man's trunks so quickly and callously, showing so little respect, before the body was even cold. Before a shroud could be acquired for the body, George Coons and the other clerk had removed both trunks from the house.

Thus began a curious odyssey as the slaves of Milton Duty proceeded through the courts of St. Louis, attempting to redeem their freedom under their dead master's will. The written will clearly provided that they should be freed once the debts were paid, but Duty's sudden death made the sum of his debts uncertain. The precipitous removal of Duty's business records complicated the question yet further. At dispute was the amount of his debt and the nature of the papers in the missing trunk. The trunk's contents taken away by George W. Coons were the best evidence of that amount. The slaves, led by Preston, believed that the trunk held the master's cash and his cancelled debts. If the papers disappeared, the cancelled claims of debt could be fraudulently reclaimed again against the estate.

As inventoried, the fate of these twenty-six persons was to be determined by the will. They ranged in age from "Old Mary," who at thirty-four years old was not really that old, to young children. There were more men than women, and all the men were of working age between thirteen and thirty years old. In the years that followed, more babies would be born into the group and several children would die before the probate was finally finished.

The first inventory listed the twenty-six slaves of Milton Duty in order of declining age, from Old Mary to two-year-old Mary Jane. Mary, Preston, Braxton, Nat, Beverly, Jesse, Jordan, Madison, Malinda and her sons: Howard and James, Seany and her children: Lewis and Margaret, Clarissa and her son Beverly, Caroline and her daughter Lucy Ellen, Nelly, Lucy, Lydia, Henderson, and Harry. Of the eight women, four had young children, and four of childbearing age did not have children.[11] Four children were under ten years old. The members of the group were not necessarily related. The older slaves said they had been purchased by Milton Duty rather than inherited, and they composed several distinct families. Preston and Braxton, both in their mid-thirties, were brothers, and two children, six-year-old Jack and four-year-old "Little Mary," were identified as Braxton's children. The children's mother was not identified among the group. She may have been a slave belonging to a neighbor in Mississippi, or she may have died. It would have been somewhat unusual for these children to remain with their fathers—in fact, in their father's master's ownership—given the general rule of matrilineality: that the status of children followed the mothers. Nevertheless, Jack and Little Mary were clearly identified as Braxton's children, with no mother identified.[12]

Under the terms of the written will, the decedent indicated that every slave whom the estate could afford to free was entitled to freedom, once the debts were paid, but three slaves stood within the master's special circle of attachment. Duty specified that they be entitled to privileges and sizeable amounts of money in addition to freedom. Old Mary was to receive any cash remaining in his estate, to a maximum of $1,000. Whether Old Mary was a sister, a lover, or simply a trustworthy servant cannot be said, but her ownership by Duty was of fairly recent origin because he had purchased her only three years earlier. She was too old to be his daughter, and she had no identifiable children. (Old Mary was only "old" in the sense of being distinguished from the girl called Little Mary.)

Preston and his brother Braxton were named to split any remaining cash over the $1,000 amount given to Old Mary. Preston was also to receive his master's gold watch and chain as well as his entire suit of clothes. The dead master's extensive tailored wardrobe befitted a former plantation owner. Included were a number of overcoats in different colors, half a dozen pairs of pants, including some of cashmere, assorted vests tailored to different fashionable styles, jackets called roundabouts, and linen shirts. The master told one of his neighbors that he intended for Preston to actually wear the gold watch and chain, and his clothing too. In an era when clothing was expensive and highly valued by the middle class and lower class alike, this bequest set Preston in good stead. As Mark Twain would later say, "Clothing makes the man." Preston appears to have been the man whom Duty indicated had most helped him make his fortune.

In addition to the rich material inheritance, the will provided that these three persons in particular should be accorded the special privilege of staying on in Warren County, Mississippi, if they so chose. They could stay among their relations if they wished to, instead of removing to a free state. The will said little more that revealed kinship relations among the slaves.

At the probate, the St. Louis court was prepared to appoint a local man as administrator of the estate. This was not an unusual occurrence, given that no one whom Milton Duty named lived in the state. Volunteering for the task of executor was George W. Coons, the only son of Milton Duty's financial partner and the young man who removed the dead man's trunks precipitously after searching them so intently on the summer night of his death. George signed the appropriate papers and he was promptly appointed the estate's executor.

George lost little time in appraising the estate's assets. As a first order of business, he had the slaves appraised, and their combined worth was determined to be the significant sum of $6,750. As administrator, he was allowed to retain possession of the slaves and the trunks during the probate and to charge the estate a fee for his services as well.

The will, which was so generous in attempting to manumit Duty's slaves, neglected to leave anything to his several brothers and sisters. It was not that Duty had broken with them. Duty's young nephew lived with him in St. Louis in order to attend school, and was there when his uncle died. This act of preferring his slaves' freedom to his relatives' financial benefit required some sort of explanation. A neighbor with whom he had shared his plans testified to Duty's thinking: "Duty stated that he himself and one of his slaves had worked hard for what he had, and that no one should be benefitted by it and that he would set all of them free at the time of his death and that he had made a will to that effect."[13] By being passed over, Duty's siblings were prepared to challenge the will for the next several decades if necessary, as potential heirs to a significant inheritance, almost entirely in the form of human property.

Though neglecting to provide for his sisters and brothers, Duty did mention one brother-in-law by name. Ironically, this man had served as his plantation overseer. In the will, Milton Duty left him $500 (half the amount he left to Old Mary) and explained the bequest as a commendation for his services at one of his plantations "during the breakout." The intriguing wording suggests one of two possibilities: that there had been an uprising at one of his plantations, quelled by his overseer brother-in-law, or, more likely, that there had been an outbreak of cholera or smallpox that the man had helped with.

As the legal process played out, Duty's heirs were not the only antagonists to the idea of emancipating the estate's slaves. Over the coming decade, Duty's creditors and a series of men appointed to execute the will would contest the terms of the will as well as the slaves' claim to freedom in order to assert their own interests in the estate.

After the master's death and the official appraisal, it was fully a year before the slaves were hired out in what would become an annual summertime ritual. In the dog days of August 1839, the executor retained an auctioneering firm to hire each of them out on the limestone courthouse steps to serve their highest bidder for a year. The slaves of Milton Duty, who had previously lived together in his rented house and arranged for their own hiring, were to be separated from one another and assigned by the auctioneer to temporary masters for one-year terms. They would be turned over to new temporary masters, subject to their commands and control, and required to look to them for the necessities of life.

In the annual auction sequence that followed year in and year out, only mothers and their small children were allowed to remain together, grouped as a unit in the hire to the same master. Later, as greater attachments formed among some of the men and women, the executor and the auctioneers considered it insurance

Painting of Last Slave Sale at the St. Louis Courthouse steps. The Last Slave Sale painted by Tho mas Satterwhite in 1867 was set on the steps of the St. Louis Courthouse. Slaves like the slaves of Milton Duty were auctioned here every year while they waited for the judge to rule on their suits for freedom. Missouri History Museum, St. Louis

against their running away to hire them out as couples. Thus, after a few years, Jordan and Caroline were routinely hired to the same person, and by the mid-1850s it was clear from the records that Caroline's babies were Jordan's children as well.

The range of bidders showing up at auctions demonstrated the variety of work to be done by hirelings in the bustling frontier city. The bidders were not necessarily major slave owners. Truly wealthy slave owners could afford to buy their own slaves, train them to better level of service, and demand the perquisites of long-term ownership, including the right to the slaves' children. Those men who rented temporary help tended to be less wealthy, but in need of a sufficient amount of labor for the coming year to rent a slave for that long, rather than for the shorter time periods that the Duty slaves had once negotiated for themselves.

In terms of the standard hiring agreement, the employer was obligated to feed, clothe, and house the slave. To make sure that slaves were returned on time the following year, the bidder was required to post a bond, although as often as not the bond was simply the good word of a friend, someone who would stand in as financial security if the slave became injured or ran away before the return date. Though the slaves' basic needs were specified in the rental agreement, there was little incentive for the employer to treat a temporary slave as well as one's own slaves. Hired slaves could be risked by being sent to perform the most dangerous of tasks, given the worst diet, and provided with minimal shelter and clothing to protect them from the elements. These hireling slaves were often more ill-treated because the employer knew that there was no point in investing in the health, care, skills, or maintenance of a slave who was at his disposal for only a year.

In the port city of St. Louis, the hirers were often river men looking for boat hands for the steamboats. Captain James Lafferty hired Henderson for $7 a month on July 15, 1843. An undertaker hired Braxton on July 15, 1842, and again on July 15, 1847.[14] The slaves who were rented out to work on the river risked being injured aboard ship in this era of frequently exploding steamboats, or their owners risked that slaves would take advantage of being in a distant port and slip away from custody.

Others were hired by commission merchants. Thomas B. Dutcher hired the same man, Nat. Even the Coons' firm's other clerk, Hugh Gallagher, who later became a partner in the merchandising firm, purchased several years of slaves' work lives.[15] Some dealers who traded in slaves, men called "Negro traders," or "soul traders," rented different members of the group, presumably to continue to hire them out on a daily basis. Some of the bondspeople were bid off by the auctioneers themselves. This probably indicated that the auctioneers could not get the price they sought and thought they could do better selling the individual's work for shorter time periods.[16] In each successive year for the several decades that the estate remained open, the estate administrator hired an auctioneer to bid the bondspeople off one by one, for a year's worth of service, from the courthouse steps.

The rental price ranged from $1.12 per month for Little Mary's services to $7–8 a month for strong, capable adult men like Henderson and Preston. The rental price roughly reflected the inventoried market values of each slave. Five-year-old Little Mary was the least valued at $150 on the slave market. Children were first hired at age seven, at a very minimal wage that increased with time and maturity. Over the periods of annual hiring, the relative values of the slaves changed according to a regular pattern. Young men in their twenties increased in value: Nat's hire rate of $6.50, when he was twenty, more than doubled a few years later. Men in their mid-thirties could commensurately see their value decline, perhaps as age, excessive labor, or extended ill treatment took its toll on their bodies.

Women's rates seemed most variable, presumably due to health, pregnancy, or illness. Pregnancy obviously took its toll on the servant women's bodies and their work efforts. They could be expected to be hampered in their work efforts by their pregnancy, perhaps require some medical care during the birth, and certainly be distracted by the need to attend to their newborns thereafter.

Ironically, some bidders at the annual auctions of Duty slaves were slave owners who had recently lost their own slaves to freedom suits. Mrs. Bascom hired Lydia for a year, just after her own servant Caroline had established her freedom by suit. Robert Duncan hired Samuel after he and his brothers had lost several of their slaves to successful freedom suits. Samuel did not survive the year with Robert Duncan. According to Duncan, first Samuel was lazy, then Samuel went away, and finally Samuel died. The disappointed master called Samuel "worthless." One wonders what treatment he had endured before he died.

The adult women were placed in particularly precarious conditions. Within that first year of hiring, one of Malinda's children died, and the executor had to pay for the little one's burial, and Sena became pregnant, rendering her sick and her service less valuable. This cycle of pregnancy—births as well as infant funerals—became the pattern of existence for the seven women of childbearing age during the limbo of their existence as assets of an unsettled estate. Sadly, the many hirings lists are interspersed with bills for doctors, coffins, and funerals. Only Old Mary seemed to escape the debilitating cycle of pregnancies. Milton Duty's brother, Gaius, attended at least one of the auctions as well and once bought the services of Old Mary.[17]

In 1841, after the Duty slaves filed suit, the records provide a dual dimension to their legal profiles. The probate court was charged with maintaining them as assets of the estate and answering to the creditors and potential heirs, while the circuit court proceeded with their freedom claims. In the circuit court, they were their own agents: plaintiffs, complainants, and subjects of their lives, represented by attorneys; whereas in the probate court, they were merely assets of the estate, subject to custody and management. The estate's administrator, George Coons, was the pivotal person in both litigation streams. In the probate court, the heirs and creditors looked to Coons to dispose of the slave property most profitably; whereas in the circuit court, he was the defendant who impeded the Duty servants' freedom.

Almost as soon as he was appointed executor, George began to pay money out to the creditors' claims. One of the first claims he allowed was the hefty $3,000 claim by his father. Self-interest seemed to be the motivating rule in administering estates, and he was no different.

The threat of permanent sales seemed to trigger the Duty slaves' freedom suits. On September 7, 1841, George Coons sought an order from the probate court permitting him to sell the slaves permanently in order to pay off the other creditors. He proposed a full and final sale, not the temporary annual auction of the services until all the matters could be resolved. This sale proposed to give full title to any of the persons put up at auction. The probate court judge granted what seemed to be a routine request, and the slaves were advertised to be sold from the courthouse steps on October 12 of that year.

Faced with an imminent sale that would dash any hopes they had of attaining freedom by waiting patiently for the disposal of the estate, all of Milton Duty's remaining slaves sought an immediate injunction in the court of chancery. Attorney Ferdinand Risque, who had recently hired a few Duty slaves himself at the recent annual hiring in July and had successfully taken slaves' freedom cases before,[18] drafted an extraordinary request. Not only did he seek to enjoin the final sale, in a ten-page-long filing, but he laid out the basis for challenging the entire probate proceeding.

The petition recounted the fact that read as a whole, the slaves were legatees of the will, not merely assets under it. Old Mary, Preston, and Braxton were actually entitled to money under the will. They stood as heirs, not merely assets. Jesse was entitled to the return of his horse and dray. But most important, it stated that the will intended to give freedom to every slave who could be liberated after the debts were paid.

The petition recited in detail the events on the night of Milton Duty's death as well as the pertinent events of his business during the months before he died. In particular, by seizing the trunks before anyone else could examine them or see their contents, the slaves accused George Coons of preparing to commit an extensive fraud upon the estate. In combination with and for the benefit of his father, David Coons, the slaves alleged that George W. not only sought immediately to become the estate's administrator but also processed his father's hefty claim first. This particular payment, the slaves maintained, was fraudulent because Duty had already paid it off before his death.

The complaint tallied what the slaves believed were Milton Duty's assets and outstanding debts at his death and argued that since the other assets exceeded the debts, no slave should be sold at all. Instead, each and every one was entitled to liberty. The slaves accused George of destroying the completed receipt of the IOUs from the trunks so that they could be submitted again under the probate. As executor, George Coons, they said, had not honored the will; he had not sought assets that might have been collected in Vicksburg to reduce debts owed to the estate. He had allowed the submission of shaky claims like his father's, and he had even personally bought up claims from other creditors at a discount so that eventually he could claim them in full against the estate by liquidating the slaves. In Ferdinand Risque's elegantly drafted petition, every conceivable facet of conflict of interest and self-dealing by the Coons family was delineated and analyzed.

On the very day that the advertised sale was scheduled, the circuit court judge, sitting as a judge in equity, issued an order to stay the permanent sale of the slaves of Milton Duty. The last-minute injunction blocked the sale.

The logic and argument of the plaintiffs' brief was impeccable. The attorney included extensive affidavits that had been taken much earlier, so he clearly was well prepared for his clients' freedom suit. The slaves of Milton Duty wanted to see proof of the debts before they were paid out. They wanted debts to be proved by actual ledgers, written receipts, and written IOUs, not simply the word of the local white merchant creditors. They wanted a commissioner appointed to oversee George Coon's administration, particularly given his self-interest. He was in the best position to be rewarded for self-dealing if he allowed claims he purchased to be paid out of the estate. They even sought to see that they as slaves were hired out more routinely so that additional moneys could be collected to ensure that they all got their freedom. They seemed willing to work harder to pay off their master's debts in order that all would attain their freedom.

The brothers, Preston and Braxton, in their thirties, were leaders in this litigation effort, and they sought special permission to work alongside the attorneys in gathering the necessary information to establish that there was indeed sufficient money to pay all the debts. Since Preston had collected the slaves' daily wages while their master was away and turned them over to David Coons for safekeeping, he had some idea how much he had turned over to the man. Since Braxton had traveled with the master on his pork-sales business trips to Vicksburg, he knew Duty's Mississippi contacts, he knew that Duty was owed money in Mississippi, and he knew that Duty had received large sums of cash on his last trip south. He had seen him counting the cash on the steamboat home.

Initially, executor George Coons resisted even the service of process. When the sheriff found him in town to deliver the summons or read him the petition, George W. refused to hear it. Eventually, however, he had to deal with the freedom suits filed in circuit court that had now enjoined the probate court's pending sale by hiring an attorney and filing a response. Naturally, he charged off the additional lawyer's expenses to the estate. His response conceded enough facts to show a substantial conflict of interest, however one looked at it, but he basically denied any wrongdoing.

From then on, the lawyers for both sides dug in and fought the case tooth and nail. Every claim and every answer was challenged as vague, nonresponsive, or indefinite. Every motion that could be made to advance or deny the lawsuit was made. Unlike litigation by southern gentlemen steeped in mutual *noblesse oblige*, these lawyers pulled out all the procedural stops to fight on every front possible. The fight pitted the twenty-some black slaves of Milton Duty against an equal number of white creditors, heirs, and even executors. The executors could run out the clock, if need be, while collecting fees as the clock ran. Each year that the adult slaves aged, more babies were born into the uncertain legal status, and gradually more litigants perished.

The inquiry delved ever more deeply into Duty's financial matters. Most of his associates knew about the will and his intention to free his slaves. At issue first were the contents of the trunks: whether cash or satisfied notes had been taken away from the house that night. Were those papers that were torn up and discarded evidence of completed transactions that Coons sought to destroy, or merely empty envelopes, as he claimed?

On Duty's last trip to Vicksburg, he had expected to collect a large amount of money, roughly $3,000, in order to fully pay off the debt he owed to Coons. Did he do so? Braxton had seen him counting a large sum aboard ship. Several of Duty's white business associates verified Braxton's observations. To rebuff the allegations, Coons told a different story about the money: that the thousands in cash that he received from Duty upon his return did not cancel the debt, but instead that Duty was acting simply as a courier to cash some of his father's own notes against the Mississippi bank for other issued currency. Hence, Coons claimed that the $3,000 was his all the time and Duty still owed the debt besides.

George Coons, carrying the ball for the creditors, maintained that Duty's debts were extensive. Duty had suffered a financial setback when a keelboat, loaded with pork he was shipping south, sunk in the St. Louis harbor. Interestingly, the pork had been retrieved from the muddy Mississippi River bottom, and even resalted and repacked in new barrels for further sale and human consumption. Whether Duty was able to sell the refurbished pork in Vicksburg, however, was not clear. What was demonstrated, though, was that during the national financial depression of 1837, some of his Vicksburg business associates had gone under, so if the $3,000 debt had not already been collected in total, that it probably never could be in the future.

Within the first couple months of suit, several witnesses, who could have cleared up some of the ambiguities, died. David Coons, whose large debt was disputed, died before he could be examined as a witness. At the slaves' request that business ledgers be produced, his son, George, executor of the Duty estate, and Coons's wife, the executor of her husband's estate, blithely reported that Coons never kept any ledger books; he kept it all in his head. So none could be produced. The mystery of the amount of debt depended upon who was to be believed.

While the case was in Judge Mullanphy's court and under the able management of attorney Ferdinand Risque, things seemed to look bright for the slaves. The slaves' attorney traveled downriver to take testimony from Vicksburg witnesses about Duty's financial affairs, in particular about the large sum of cash he had carried back on his last trip. At first, Risque personally advanced the money to hire just one slave from the estate, presumably to allow her the autonomy to earn her own wages. The next year he bid for the services of six of his clients.[19]

In Vicksburg, Risque learned that another executor had been appointed by the Mississippi courts and had begun collecting some of the smaller debts owed to Duty by the local Vicksburg people. Now there were two probate proceedings simultaneously eating up the assets of the Duty estate, two administrators competing in the debt collections as well as looking out for their own fees.

The slaves' temporary success seemed to wane when Judge Mullanphy stepped down from the bench in 1844. Inexplicably, months later, the bright and devoted Ferdinand Risque, who had pursued the case assiduously, gave up his practice in St. Louis, left his cases in charge of a younger associate, and moved out of state to the nation's capital.

In their legal limbo, several persons, neither free nor slave but always temporary hirelings, seemed to age before their time. Older women's ages varied most rapidly. Sometimes their recorded ages in annual inventories leaped five years in a single year. Others died, presumably from their poor living conditions and rough treatment. The gradual demise of some highlights both the morbidity and the mortality of their situations. Meanwhile, the executor's administrative fees kept running up larger debts to be charged against the estate. The costs of auctioneering and warehousing the people, from time to time in one of the local slave pens or the jail, were charged back, to be fully paid as debts before the slaves could be freed. While the slaves of Milton Duty waited for the debts to be settled, so that some could be freed, the costs of their enslavement as custodial care were charged back against the debt that held them in limbo.

Sam, a mature man among the group, was assessed at a high value initially, and he brought a reasonably substantial price when first auctioned for hire. But Sam resisted working for his hirer and eventually caused his employer to protest to the executor that the thirty-year-old bondsman was "entirely worthless," and he no longer wished to have Sam in his service. Significantly, there was no claim that Sam was ill and no doctor's bill charged back against the estate. It appears that Sam refused to work for his newly assigned master, to the extent that the man became fed up with Sam and allowed him to leave for a time. Within a year, the estate mysteriously listed Sam, only thirty years old and initially appraised as strong and healthy, as dead.

Five-year-old Howard must already have embraced the idea of his freedom. Initially, he remained with his mother Malinda. A boy so young could not be hired for profit independently, so he followed her to her work designation. Girls that age, like Little Mary, were expected to polish silver, fetch wood, and help tend the fires, but boys were trouble. At the age of seven, Howard was old enough to draw a wage for the first time and be hired out independently. He hid when auction time came, and he could not be found. Someone had to be sent after him, an errand that, of course, generated a fee against the estate. When he was later found, he refused to stay with the individual who hired his mother this time, and it was arranged for him to stay instead with another white master, to whom the boy seemed to be attached, and from whom it was expected he would not run away. At age seven, Howard was forcing the estate to accommodate his wishes.[20]

As the chancery court case headed by Preston and Braxton lost steam without its vigilant attorney, another member of the group filed suit in St. Louis Circuit

Court under the freedom statute. Twenty-seven-year-old Nat took the lead plaintiff's role this time in suing for freedom. Preston and Braxton's discouragement was replaced by Nat's determination to see the several identical cases through to freedom. Nat had seen his hiring price rise from $6.50 a month to $14 as he matured. He was ready for freedom. He too argued in the litigation that there was enough money to satisfy all the creditors without selling any of the slaves, and hence he and the others should be deemed free according to the terms and spirit of Duty's will. He too accused the executor of squandering the estate's assets by three means: (1) discounting debts that should have been collected from white men, (2) collusively running up costs against the estate, and (3) permitting bad claims to be cashed out. Now it seemed that the very freedom litigation was running up additional debts to be charged ultimately against the value of the slaves and their prospect of freedom.

The defense identified the distinct battlefields in the war over the legal boundaries governing suits of slaves. Coons also argued that the very idea of a "Negro" swearing to an affidavit against a white defendant was unseemly. This argument lost because the statute explicitly provided for the process. Later he argued that the will executed in Mississippi was not a legal document under Missouri law.

With Nat sitting in the courtroom watching the proceedings, several witnesses were called on his behalf to attest to his dead master's sincerity in wishing to free his slaves. The two attorneys fought over the admission of every witness, every piece of evidence, and the jury instructions. In the end, Judge Krum favored the defendant in instructing the jury. The judge refused the plaintiffs' requests. When the jury returned its verdict, not surprisingly, they followed the court's clear direction and found against Nat on January 28, 1846, years after the death of Milton Duty.

Nat appealed to the Missouri Supreme Court on the same basis—that he should be liberated immediately as there were sufficient funds in the estate to satisfy all the legitimate creditors without leveraging the value of the slaves. He argued that Judge Krum's ruling was wrong—that the will itself automatically effected his emancipation as well as that of his fellow bondspeople. The high court ruled against the Duty slaves' greatest hope that their emancipation was not automatically effected. Instead, the court chose the rule that the payment of the creditors was a condition precedent to emancipation, so the slaves were not yet freed by the will. Furthermore, the court held that Duty's will, which was executed in the state of Mississippi under Mississippi law, did not necessarily meet Missouri's requirements for executing valid wills. The state high court ruled that if one makes his will while a citizen of another state, and afterward becomes a citizen of Missouri, where he dies, his will is invalid, unless executed according to the laws of Missouri. The case was remanded to see whether the will met the Missouri law technicalities.[21]

Having lost both the trial and the appeal to the state's high court, Nat no longer had reason to believe in the courts. He patiently worked for his hirer on the riverboats for the next two auction seasons. When he was no longer the focus of the litigation, however, he took the occasion to run away from the steamboat in another port. He came away cleanly. Back in St. Louis, the estate hired a law firm to sue the employer for the loss of Nat as an asset of the estate.[22] Madison, also hired out to work a steamboat, successfully escaped as well.[23] Braxton, Preston's brother and father of two children in the group, was hired out to a riverboat pilot and is said to have died in a steamboat accident on the river in 1848.[24]

Several of the women simply disappeared. Whether they perished in child-birth, from disease, or accident is not known. They seem to have exited with considerably less notice and fanfare than the men. Although the first inventory listed thirty persons, by summer 1847, only twenty-six were advertised as up for auction; this net change of four persons included the death of six persons and two new babies born to the estate. By 1850, the corpus of the estate, as it is called at law, was reduced to sixteen bodies.

Of Milton Duty's thirty slaves, only Jesse the drayman succeeded in attaining his freedom through the courts, in an unlikely and indirect fashion. Since Jesse had owned his own horse and dray, he sought return of the property and money he claimed as his own that had been seized by the executor. George Coons simply did not appear when the case was called, and Jesse's attorney, moving quickly to take advantage of the opportunity, entered a default judgment against him. This time the court gave full advantage to Jesse. Jesse was not only entitled to his horse, dray, and money, he was deemed to be free because of the executor's failure to show up in court.[25]

Realizing his error, George Coons immediately sought a warrant asking the sheriff to round Jesse up and take jail him. Jesse's attorney next brought a habeas corpus action against the jailer requiring that the newly freed man be brought into court. The lawyer then confronted the jailer with the *fait accomplit* that Jesse had already been awarded his liberty by the default judgment.[26] After 1845, Jesse was no longer listed as an asset of the estate. The next year, a thirty-three-year-old free black man, Jesse, with no last name, was licensed in St. Louis as a drayman.

Jesse's surprising release must have inspired the other Duty slaves to hold out hope, but the default judgment trick did not work a second time. Ironically, the only Duty slave to be freed did so by bootstrapping freedom onto his claim to a horse and wagon. Preston also had a potential claim to a property, but he had not owned the wardrobe before his master's death as Jesse had owned his horse. Preston saw his claim to the master's wardrobe be auctioned off piece by piece. It's uncertain whatever became of the $150 gold watch and chain; it might have been in the trunks.

After Nat and Madison ran off, it was obvious that others might attempt to escape also. So in 1850, the executor planned to take certain slaves out of the city, to more rural areas of Missouri, where the social controls imposed upon slaves were more stringent and escape more difficult. Jordan, Henderson, Little Mary, and Ellen were taken by steamboat up the Missouri River, to the town ironically called Liberty, to be hired out for the year.[27] The four were escorted by a white man who charged for his services, and they were issued new shoes, leather brogans, for the journey. It was unlikely that they would find shoes in the countryside.

The exceptionally rough treatment of repeated hirings had taken its toll on the vitality of those who remained. Even the heirs realized that their collective value as top-rate servants had declined. The heirs now acted to cut short the prolonged litigation by asking that most slaves be sold and they take custody of only the few remaining healthy persons.[28] In the thirteenth year of litigation, 1849, the heirs sent instructions: "[U]nder the peculiar circumstances in which said slaves have been placed since the death of their late Master Milton Duty, their modes of life and other considerations have lessened their value so much so that we do not wish to own them any longer, and hence we desire [them sold]." Three of the youngest slaves were set apart as sufficiently undamaged to be retained by the Duty family. Harrison, Harry, and Margaret,[29] who had grown from childhood into adulthood in St. Louis in the shadow of the lawsuit, were sent back to an antebellum Vicksburg, a place that they hardly could have remembered. These three young persons still had work lives before them and were considered pliable enough to submit to continued service in slavery in Mississippi.

Preston and Seany were sold in St. Louis. Preston had the relative stability to be repeatedly hired by the same man, Dr. Lilliburn Perry. Now Dr Perry purchased him outright.[30] Seany, under the name Nicene, had the better fortune of being purchased to be freed. She married a free man of color, Henry Clark, during her time in bondage rental. Nicene was purchased by one of the Blow brothers, who had hired her for a year. Blow then gave her her freedom.[31] Ellen, too, was sold in 1851 but continued to join the suits for freedom.

When the heirs indicated their willingness to sell, it was in fact the newly appointed executor who bought out their interest in the remaining slaves. Thomas Harney, an attorney with no prior connection to the estate, entered the lawsuit as administrator and purchased the heirs' remaining interest. He was backed in security by one of the city's more notorious slave traders: Reuben Bartlett.[32]

In the last days of the probate, which had run up bills for more than two decades, it was left to two estate administrators to fight among themselves over who among them would receive the residue ownership of the human property still held in the estate. Their fate made its fifth trip to the Missouri high court over the issue of whether the former administrator's authority had been appropriately terminated before the new one was appointed.[33] Again, these legal fees were charged back to the estate by the prevailing administrator. The key issue, that there was sufficient value in the estate to effect his dead master's desire to free his slaves, was ultimately resolved by spending the estate down to the point that not a single slave was ever freed under Duty's will. Creditors, heirs, and ultimately even administrators found the funds within the very value of the slaves to fight one another until there was nothing left in the estate but the slaves, whose very managing, spent out, had cost them their freedom.[34]

The cabins that had been promised in Soulard were never built. Several members of the group remained together. The census for 1860 listed the following constellation of people living in the same house in the Third Ward of St. Louis: "Gordon Gentry, age 50, store porter, b. Va., Caroline age 38 b. Ky; Louisa age 11, b. Mo; Mary age 4, b. Mo; Humphrey & Elizabeth Ware, Henry & Celia (sic) Clark. Julia Bark age 40 b. Va; Lucy Frazier age 60 b. Va." None of the former bondspeople are known to have taken the last name Duty on their eventual emancipation after a civil war.

CHAPTER 13

Canadienne Rose

As the founders of the city, the Chouteau family occupied the pre-eminent position in St. Louis for more than a century.[1] First as fur traders, indian agents, hosts of traveling dignitaries, and later as real estate developers, commercial agents, steamship owners, and merchants, they continued to grow in wealth and stature. They had established almost monopolistic control of the fur trade in the United States through their company, the American Fur Company.

To sue the Chouteaus was to take on the most formidable family in the city's history. To sue them for freedom pitted David against an angry vengeful Goliath. The Scypion family's lawsuits had demonstrated the degree of sustained coordinated resistance that the Chouteaus could mount. But the Scypions were not the only slaves who had sued the Chouteaus and their extended clan. The Chouteaus litigated slave freedom suits almost continuously from the time Missouri courts were organized until the very end. Resisting slave freedom suits was a Chouteau family avocation and tradition.

By 1840, the Chouteau family had been sued by at least eight enslaved mothers, their children, and a few adult men as well.[2] There were the three Scypion sisters, and their children, numbering close to ten, who had prevailed. There were two more slave women with the same names as two of the Scypion sisters. Francois Lagrange, alias Isidore, and an enslaved family that the Chouteaus had purchased from Manuel Lisa sued. As did Aspasia and Sally. And then there were additional slave litigants who had sued other members of the extended family. Pelagie sued cousin Cabanne. Elizabeth, Virginia, and Victoire sued the Menards. Occasionally, these litigants had been frustrated by happenstance and by Chouteau family resistance. Slave petitioners were defeated when they could not match the Chouteaus' persistence and outwit their tactics. Canadienne Rose's family was one of the last slave families to sue the Chouteaus, and their cases survived even the *Dred Scott* decision.

The *Dred Scott* case was the ultimate litigation, both locally and nationally. Although the Chouteaus had never owned Dred Scott, the Chouteaus played a significant role in continuing the appeal when the case was almost dropped.

The named defendant, John F. A. Sanford had continued the fight for the sake of the Chouteaus.[3] But even after *Dred Scott* concluded, when there was no longer any basis of freedom by residence, Rose's family's case continued as almost an anticlimax, still fought aggressively by the Chouteaus, raising a new issue: were there slaves in Canada?

The redemption song of Rose's children was more like an opera than a song. It has so many parts, each with its own staging, and so many different rising and falling crescendos that it cannot be recounted as a straight-line melody. It began with one litigant, Pierre, but later added two brothers, a sister and her children, and a housemate. Each had a solo at some point. The stories of origin that they tell are all the same; yet given Chouteau resistance, their consistently repeated story didn't bring them freedom very easily or quickly. Like Wagner's *Ring* trilogy, or the Slaves of Milton Duty, this particular opera with a French Canadian inflection lasted twenty-one years, until the very outbreak of the Civil War. Rose's children finally at long last were declared free in 1861, just as the fighting began. Fort Sumner was fired upon, signaling the start of the Civil War.

The audiences in this extended performance were juries. Four different juries were impaneled over the two decades of litigation. There is little consistency in their verdicts, but then the bases on which were asked to decide changed from the convening of one jury to the next. The jury composition necessarily changed with the city population from which the jurors were drawn, yet the jurors were always all white and all male. Because the song was sung for the benefit of the jury, the jury instructions made up a large component of the legal case files of these five litigants.[4]

The composer of this particular opera was the Missouri Supreme Court, an entity that modified the rules twice. Scoring the dispute differently, it altered the rules about what was relevant for the litigants to present, sending them back to reconvene a new trial again and again, and yet again.

The chorus of witnesses is a set of aging Francophone inhabitants of St. Louis county, all of whom at some time in their lives had traveled the great length of the circle from Montreal through the Great Lakes to St. Louis and sometimes back again. The average age of these witnesses was over sixty when they were summoned for the first trial. As they aged, over the course of successive trials, each of which required them to sing the same song of Rose's life, their memories dimmed and their voices grew weaker and weaker. None survived to the final trial in 1861, fully seventy years after the events of Rose's life about which they had been called to testify, but their testimony was reduced to depositions by then that could be read to the final jury. Hearsay was sometimes permitted as evidence to add some supplemental notes.

The judges, who occupied the bench in succession and conducted the trials, played rather minor roles in this drama. The lawyers assumed somewhat more important roles in influencing the adversarial drama. The Chouteaus as slaveholders were consistently defended by the same firm, Spalding and Tiffany, a conventional law partnership that litigated squarely within the city's slaveholding norms. By contrast, the slave petitioners had changing sets of lawyers. Different lawyers took their turns in earnestly pressing their clients' cases. Wilson Primm filed the first case, but he soon gave up representation. Another lawyer, David H. Hall (who also represented Dred and Harriet Scott at the same time) died before the final resolution of any of the case strings of appeals. Henry Cobb took up the final chapter, combining the cases on behalf of Rose's remaining children. This opera was not the lifework of any of these lawyers, however, as it was to become for Rose's children.

As for the litigants, Gabriel Chouteau played the heavy through the entire twenty-one-year span. Gabriel began his role as his mother's executor, and he grew old in the role. He became more harshly defined in these cases as he aged, much as two previous generations of aging Chouteau men had done in their generation's slave redemption songs. Just as his father had once had his slaves whipped for talking freedom, and his cousin got the sheriff to round up the Scypions for sale, Gabriel turned for muscle to the new business in town, commercial traders, who dealt in slaves, buying and selling them for profit, and generally "man-handling" enslaved persons. These slave traders assisted him in attempting to pressure Rose's children into submission.

Rose's children pressed consistently to redeem their freedom, but, faced by adversity, Pierre wore out, sitting in jail for a prolonged period of time and finally losing his mind. Michel acted out, chafing at the owners to whom he was sold. Louis sat in jail in the litigation's second stage, taking his older brother's place by not giving in, even during long months of continuous incarceration. Adrien Paschal eventually ran away from backcountry Missouri, where he had been sent and sold in order to control him. And Charlotte remained in place and, with her children, held out to the final victory, twenty-one years after her older brother first filed suit.

By 1840, the Chouteau stem family had expanded to several households, though it remained dominated by the two patriarchs, stepbrothers Auguste and Pierre Sr. Since the city's founding, the Chouteaus had produced two generations of large families. Marriages between cousins, and brothers marrying sisters, had created an entire clan of tightly related, wealthy Francophones with nationally far-reaching investments.[5] The Prattes, Sarpys, Pauls, Gratiots, Bertholds, Papins, and Cabannes were family names that had become entwined as kin with the Chouteau family and entwined as partners in the Chouteau family businesses.[6] All made their homes within blocks of one another in St. Louis, and all adhered strongly to old French colonial and Catholic traditions. It only made sense that their slaves' lives in these closely connected households would be entwined as well.

August Chouteau had deterred his slaves from discussing claims to freedom by beating them even before Pierre, son of Rose, was born.[7] Pierre Chouteau Sr. had sent slaves away when they became too independent, and Pierre Chouteau Jr. conspired to kidnap one set of slave petitioners and smuggle them by steamboat with the cooperation of other family members.[8] Chouteau's co-conspirator was another old French trader, Francois (or Frances) Menard, his business partner and in-law on the Illinois side of the river. Menard retained many slaves at his home in Illinois. Menard was as involved in quashing slave independence as the Chouteaus were. When the Chouteaus found slaves to be troublemakers, they sent them to him. Menard family members also ran Chouteau family slaves to New Orleans from time to time for sale.[9] Some of Menard's slaves had sued him in St. Louis.[10] One Menard had been involved in selling John Merry.

Rose's children had known no other home than the slave quarters behind Auguste Chouteau's big house. They were born and had grown up in his service. Rose was a cook brought from Canada. She had cooked for voyageurs at different fur trade posts along the great circle of voyageurs. She had worked in Montreal, Mackinac, and Prairie du Chien (in present-day Wisconsin) before being brought to St. Louis and eventually sold to Auguste Chouteau. Trained in Montreal, she probably remained a cook in the big house, where there were always numerous Chouteaus and often visitors to feed. There is an eyewitness description of such a cook at one of the large French mansions at the time, unnamed, but quite likely the Chouteau household. "In the kitchen a kingdom apart, ruled in majesty less only than that of her mistress, the aged negro cook. At her frown her junior satellites quailed, and at her bidding they came and went with a fervor.... Under her benevolent despotism the young girls helped in the kitchen and became themselves cooks in due time."[11] She probably prepared special foods, like cherry bounce, pralines, and gumbo soup with the batterie de cuisine for Sundays, feast days, and other distinctively French celebrations like New Years, which drew the entire family together and reaffirmed their connectedness.[12] Rose had two children when she arrived and four more children were born to Rose while she lived and worked within Auguste Chouteau's impressive household in St. Louis, an enclave ringed by stone walls comprising an entire city block at the city's very center.

Revered as the city founder, Auguste Chouteau was even more venerated than the miller Joseph Tayon.[13] At age thirteen, he helped select the site with his step-father by marking the nearby trees. Auguste was the son of Laclede's common-law wife and Laclede's most trusted friend. Although Auguste had spent his youth advancing the Laclede trading franchise by venturing up the rivers to engage with the tribes, the same stone house had been his home and the family business office since it was built in the 1770s.[14] Returning to St. Louis, Auguste Chouteau became a respected syndic in the village and turned his attention to real estate.[15] So rich in land, he even donated the site for the courthouse and the jail.[16] When Laclede died, he acquired ownership of Tayon's mill; in time, he passed it on to his son, Gabriel Chouteau, who would become the nemesis of Rose's children.

The legendary big house was so central to the town that it was literally ground zero, the base point for the survey of all city lots.[17] Once the street had been called "Rue Royale," but when the streets were renamed in the American fashion, it became Main Street. The elegant stone house, constructed in the French style, with a broad porch supported by pillars, was surrounded by an expansive yard, gardens, and then a very high, thick wall that encompassed the entire city block.[18] The massive wall, initially constructed to protect against Indian attack, enclosed a space where Chouteau traditions were shielded from view and maintained from Yankee influence. The house was elegantly furnished, with a library remarkable for its time. The black walnut floors were polished to a high sheen. It was said that the Chouteau's servants spent hours every morning on their knees, with brushes and wax, keeping them polished. Within the stone-walled enclave, behind the mansion, there were slave cabins, also built of stone, where Rose bore four of her six children. Growing up there, Pierre would know intimately all seven of the master's children, who became the city's next generation of important and wealthy residents.

He would know the family's many slaves even more intimately, by sharing tasks, meals, and even sleeping mattresses with them. The Chouteaus owned over 100 slaves; Auguste Chouteau was the town's largest slave owner.[19] All the Chouteau slaves spoke French, as their master wished, as they had grown up and been instructed. Pierre was ten when the slave Charles was sent from the house to be sold because he was troublesome and a bad influence on the others. Pierre did not necessarily know the Scypions as well (they litigated against Auguste's brother), but it is likely that he knew them. Slaves could be assigned among the houses as needed. Pierre certainly knew those from Auguste's household who sued.

Pierre was twenty-two when his master, Auguste, died in 1829. The fates of his forty-eight slaves were sorted out by family claim and sale, as the estate divided ownership of the slaves. (Since several adult sons still lived in the big house, owning some slaves of their own, the forty-eight to be distributed in the estate did not include every slave living in the yard.) Most distributed slaves were sold to family members as Francophone masters purchased Francophone slaves.[20] Rose, Pierre's mother, at sixty-one years of age, was still living at the time of sale. Yet, she was by no means the eldest; there were others estimated at over 100 years old.[21] Rose's six adult children, Toussant, Benoist, Pierre, Louis, Michel, and Charlotte, and were distributed by sale. The widow, Marie-Therese Cerre took her share by electing to keep Rose, Pierre, Benoist, and Charlotte, among others.[22] Twenty-one-year-old Charlotte had already proven herself fertile by bearing a child, a capability that rendered her more valuable, and hence a slave to be kept in the family.

Rose's son Toussant was sold out of the family, to a merchant who did book-keeping for the Chouteaus, and there his story seems to end.[23] Michel was sold to a cousin, Gabriel Paul, who had married Chouteau's sister. Louis was sold to son Gabriel, who inherited his father's gristmill. Pierre was sold to son Edward, who was exactly his same age, for $600. In the distribution, Rose's two sons Louis and Pierre remained with their family at the compound, for their owners remained in the big house. For another ten years, Pierre worked for the big house.[24]

Auguste's estate carefully detailed the lineage of each slave child by assigning their mother's name as a last name. Hence, Pierre, son of Rose, was identified as Pierre Rose. Charlotte was listed as Charlotte Rose and Louis, Louis Rose.[25] This matrilineal nomenclature differed from the way that St. Louis slaves were identified in the streets. Within the family enclave, maternity was of greater interest because ownership was obvious. With frequent use of the same Christian names, identifying slave children *by their mothers* allowed the household to tell them apart. In the larger world of the streets, identification of a slave's *ownership* was key. Outside, Rose's Pierre was known as Pierre Chouteau. Thus, Pierre, the slave shared the same first and last name as two other prominent, living, white members of the master's family.

Of the forty-eight slaves grouped in connection to their mothers. Rose's was the largest family with six children. Zabetta had five, Clarice, Catiche, and Catherine each had three, and Odile had two. There were three children identified as the children of Pelagie, but there was no Pelagie in the group. The remaining household slaves seemed to lack kinship ties.

Although the sale dispatched some slaves to other households, life remained much as it always had been for Rose's children. Auguste's widow, Marie-Therese Cerre Chouteau remained in the mansion. Some of her adult children and their wives lived under her roof.[26] In 1840, when Pierre filed suit, there were still eleven white family members residing in the mansion, and twenty-six slaves in the slave cabins, more than two slaves for every white family member.

Pierre was thirty-three years old when he filed suit. He had never lived on free soil. He had lived in the same place, the mansion at the center of St. Louis, his entire life. He must have known that slaves often won freedom because their mothers had lived east of the Mississippi River in free territory, and expected that he too could win on this basis. The slave Rachel had won a suit previously based, in part, on her residence exactly at Prairie du Chien.[27] Rose too had lived east of the Mississippi in Prairie du Chien. Moreover, Rose had lived in Michili-mackinac (present-day Michigan), also in the Northwest Territory. Many of the witnesses in Pierre's first trial were called to establish just that.

Together, the witnesses assembled the remembered facts of Rose's life. Unlike most St. Louis slaves, who came from the east by way of the Ohio River, Rose came from the north. She traveled the entire distance—approximately 2300 miles—from Montreal by canoe, up through the chain of Great Lakes through Lake Michigan to Green Bay, up the Fox River, and then by portage over to the Wisconsin River, and then down the Mississippi. French fur traders traveling this route by canoe were not only early venturers into Indian territory,[28] they also brought enslaved Africans into the Northwest Territory by way of the Great Lakes.

Rose was born a slave in Montreal in 1768. The fur trader John Stork took her from Montreal to Mackinaw and then to Prairie du Chien. She remained in service to his family at the cabin in the tiny fur trading post at the site where the Wisconsin River met the Mississippi until his death in 1794.[29] Another Canadian trader acquired Rose from Stork's estate and brought her to St. Louis, where he sold her to the curate of the St. Louis parish.[30] Three years later, the curate sold her once again, to Auguste Chouteau, where she remained for the next forty years.[31]

Although Rose was identified in the court papers as a "negress," her son, Pierre, was identified as mulatto.[32] Pierre was Rose's third son and he, rather than his older brothers, took the lead among his siblings in suing for freedom. In November 1840, Pierre filed suit for his freedom, as the child of a mother free by residence. Parenthetically, his identification as a mulatto raises the question whether he was suing his own kin. He was born after Rose came to the enclave. Was his father one of the men of the tight-knit Chouteau family?

It seems that other litigants' success showed Pierre that it was possible to be adjudged free. Sally had recently succeeded, and the same attorney who won her suit, also filed suit for Pierre. Pierre's first lawyer, Wilson Primm was a multi-talented St. Louis native. Primm's mother was a member of the Francophone Catholic community, yet Primm had equally mastered the English language as well as Anglo-American law. Primm was also the cathedral's active choir director, where he had organized a black male chorus.[33] Primm was no reformer; but he may have seen Pierre's situation as simply entitlement, given other cases he had observed at court.[34] Primm left off his representation, however, soon after.[35]

In leading the fight for freedom in the courts, Pierre acted alone for some time. His younger siblings waited cautiously for two years until Pierre had demonstrated some success before they too filed suit. In this, Pierre was atypical of instigators in family lawsuits. Most family-linked lawsuits were filed almost concurrently, like Winny's. And the great majority were initiated by women, either by mothers or older sisters, yet Rose never sued. What prompted Pierre? And why did he begin when he did, at thirty-one years old? His petition contained no allegation of a trigger, no sense of alarm warning that the time for suit was now. He does not allege being targeted for harsh treatment or by threatened sale south to New Orleans. Nor was there any pending disruption to his home. Owned by Edward, who still resided in the family mansion, Pierre could have expected to stay there, as did his master Edward, for the rest of his life.

Only two incidents in the time span immediately preceding Pierre's filing could have contributed to the timing. Madame Chouteau took the unusual step of freeing Pierre's older brother. Benoist, son of Rose; it was one of very few slaves that the Chouteaus ever manumitted. Who knows what circumstances permitted him this rare privilege? There is some indication that he remained on in the household even after his manumission. The 1840 census records list a single unnamed, free black man in the household. Who but Benoist would have been welcome there as a free black man? The Chouteaus hosted outsiders as guests, but they would not have invited in a free black man. Yet, the rest of Benoist's enslaved family still lived there.[36] Perhaps Pierre was jealous, or his older brother's good fortune impressed upon the thirty-year-old Pierre that he, too, deserved freedom. Or did he simply observe other slaves' litigation success and decide that this was his time for a better life? Sally had grown up in the big house as well, an orphan; her black parents had been promised by their masters that she be freed when she came of age. Sally had sued household member Henry Chouteau, and won.[37] Such a victory could encourage other housemates to consider their circumstances. It's also possible that Pierre was attached to Sally and wished to leave with her.

Pierre filed first against the widow in November 1840. But she died before the case had advanced beyond the pleadings two years later.[38] With the death of his defendant, Pierre's suit was dismissed, and so he needed to refile against her son, Gabriel, the estate administrator.[39] Pierre would spend the rest of his life litigating against this man.

Pierre's trial called forth witnesses, old fur trade participants, people originally from Canada who lived nearby on the surrounding farms. Some depositions were taken in St. Charles, and other witnesses were summoned into St. Louis from the rural county.[40] Most testified that, yes, they had seen Rose as a young woman at Prairie du Chien, others had seen her cooking for voyageurs in Michilimackinac, a stopover for those in transit, and a few had even known her as a girl in Montreal. There was no dispute about identity: yes, that was the same woman Rose, and yes, this was Pierre, her son, who most knew had lived at the Chouteau mansion since he was a child. One witness sought by the Chouteaus was Francois Menard, their close friend and Illinois' largest slave holder. Francois Menard did not know Rose or Pierre. He set himself up as an authority on the law of slavery in Canada.[41]

By February 1844, a jury ruled in Pierre's favor. The court declared "That *Plaintiff be liberated and entirely set free* from the...Defendant and from all persons claiming by through or under him..." Pierre heard these words declaring he had won, and that pronouncement might have kept him going in the lean years to come. He would hear those words only once.

Things looked promising. So siblings Charlotte, Louis, and Michel filed suit. As did a housemate of theirs, young Adrien Paschall, who grew up with them and had been sold in the recent auction.[42] The lawsuits seemed to be coordinated.[43] These litigants approached the same justice of the peace on different days of the same week. They were assigned a different lawyer than Pierre had.[44] Ultimately, attorney Henry Cobb would pursue three of the siblings' claims, while another law firm partnership, Hall and Field, pursued Pierre's claim.[45] (This A. P. Field was the same man who had invaded Lydia's home and kidnapped her children. However, his partner, young attorney David N. Hall, probably did most of the actual work for freedom cases that the firm was involved in.[46]) Pierre, Louis, and Charlotte and her children sued Gabriel Chouteau, while Michel, who had been sold to Gabriel Paul in the earlier estate division, sued him. Adrien Paschal, also sold to Gabriel Paul, sued him on the basis that he had been sent to Illinois to work.

It took Gabriel Chouteau some time to sell and distribute his mother's slaves. He auctioned some. He advertised the sale of some, and still others were sold privately without advertisement. By filing suit, Pierre was spared this auction. Charlotte already had three babies; her oldest son, Antoine, at sixteen was sold separately to Henry Chouteau. Charlotte and her younger children were bid off to another Chouteau cousin Kenneth Mackenzie, in May. When Charlotte filed suit later that year, Mackenzie reacted immediately by canceling the sale.

> Dear Sir.
> Being informed that the Negro woman and children bid off by me at the Court House on Monday last claim that they are free, and that a suit has been instituted for the purpose of obtaining their freedom, I have to inform you, that I decline to pay for, or receive them, because at the time of Sale I understood that there was no dispute regarding the title to them as Slaves.[47]

This cannot have been welcome news to Gabriel Chouteau. Given the multiplier effect—the success of one sibling often translated into success for the entire family—Gabriel had reason to worry that he might lose all of Rose's children to freedom suits. Or at least, he would not be able to sell them off to other buyers in the prospect of litigation.

In his youth, Gabriel Chouteau had followed the family tradition by spending his youth engaged in the family fur trade on the Missouri River. Now approaching his fifties, he remained in St. Louis. Instead of setting up either a residence or a trading house for himself, he lived in the family mansion unmarried, ran the gristmill built at the outflow of Chouteau's pond, and engaged in real estate, as had his father.[48] Before his mother's death, Gabriel's slaves were all men, presumably men who worked at the mill. The death of one of his slaves near the mill pond brought Gabriel under suspicion of murder. The inquest later cleared him of the charge without ever explaining the circumstances. Again as in John Merry's, this death was declared a visitation of God.[49] Once, the mill pond that Tayon had dammed had also been a good source of water for the growing city, a place of recreation and doing laundry. With the city rapidly growing around it, however, Chouteau's pond had become increasingly polluted and considered a nuisance. The city began to take legal action against Gabriel and the nuisance.[50] With the development of other mills, the historic mill no longer held the city monopoly. Yet, Gabriel was an active member of the Millers' Association of the town.

Faced with Rose's children's attempts to gain freedom, Gabriel fought back. The Chouteau family had been under repeated pressure by numerous slave litigants, and they always fought back. And now, with Pierre, even slaves who had come to them from Canada were claiming freedom. Gabriel became the designated Chouteau to litigate zealously.[51] He pursued appeal in this set of cases at every opportunity to squash the possibility that the several children of Canadienne Rose be declared free.

In 1844, Gabriel Chouteau appealed the jury verdict, arguing that Rose had never really lived in free territory at all. His legal argument mixed history, geography, and sovereignty. He argued that when Rose lived at Prairie du Chien, before the War of 1812, the British controlled that area and slavery was then tolerated by Britain throughout its colonies.[52] Prairie du Chien was clearly within the spatial boundaries, north and west of the Ohio River and east of the Mississippi, yet it was unclear how far north U.S. sovereignty extended with the British occupying some of that area before 1812. The British controlled the area, but was its sovereignty uncontested by the Americans? The Northwest Territory had no clear northern boundary until the War of 1812.[53] The Americans had not yet extended their westward reach, though the idea of Manifest Destiny made that extension a foregone conclusion for many Americans by the time of Pierre's lawsuit. This was a gutsy argument to make in 1843 at a point when American territory extended up the Mississippi to its origin, and national expansion was considered inevitable.

Yet surprisingly, the ingenious argument that would have raised eyebrows in the nation's capital prevailed at the Missouri Supreme Court. The court regarded Prairie du Chien as under British sovereignty, not just British occupation, when Rose lived there in the 1790s, so that it was not free soil. Rose was not free by reason of the Northwest Ordinance of 1787.

This ruling became the discordant note of collapsing dreams for Rose's children. Rose left Prairie du Chien in 1795. Had she been able to stay beyond the time of British retreat, her children certainly would have been free. Had she retreated with the British residents, she would have been free as soon as slavery ended in Canada. But as it was, slavery was abolished in the Northwest

Territory on August 7, 1787, before she left Prairie du Chien, though before the United States decisively controlled that area of the upper Mississippi's east bank as part of the Northwest Territory. Had the court considered that the Northwest Territory's reach extended to Prairie du Chien at the time of its enactment, Rose would have been free. The problem was that Rose's masters had moved her before the question of sovereignty was settled. Yet neither of those contesting sovereigns legally recognized slavery any longer in that region. Slavery was abolished in British Canada, after she had left the place. Thus, Rose never really resided in free territory. Political geography really did determine destiny.

The high court countermanded Pierre's victory and ordered the case retried. Like understudies tied to the lead soloist, the lawsuits of Pierre's siblings followed the same fate. By now, Charlotte had four children and the fates of all of them rode on the outcome.[54]

That did not mean that Pierre had no legal argument, but it did mean that the standard argument based on the Northwest Ordinance that had been successful so often before would not work for them. The argument had to be made that Montreal or the wilderness territories where Rose resided were not *legally* slave territories even then. The argument had to be made that Rose's enslavement was extralegal under British Colonial Canadian law, an argument that was a bit of a stretch.[55] There was not a lot of Canadian law to go on, and whatever existed was difficult to ascertain in St. Louis, unless one turned again to the old French Canadians. This time they were asked not only about Rose's life, but also about whether slavery had been legal in those northern areas when they lived there.

This setback must have been disappointing. Pierre's victory was countermanded. Some siblings had just filed suit. Michel had acted up. He was said to have conducted himself as utterly worthless and unmanageable since filing suit. He resisted even more strongly after his old master, Gabriel Paul, died and his son succeeded him. Michel's owners feared that he would flee their control, so they requested that he be hired out or jailed.[56]

Charlotte's trial was next, scheduled to take place just a few months after the Missouri Supreme Court ruled. Again, the facts of Rose's life were undisputed, but was her enslavement legal in the northern lands at the time? The same witnesses and additional Canadian emigrants, eleven in all, were called to address that question at Charlotte's trial.[57]

This was the second time the old French Canadians were called in to the courthouse, and this time they elaborated upon what they had witnessed, on Blacks and slavery generally in Montreal and in the fur trading outposts. The case took on a parochial tone of ethnology, exploring Canadian customs in dealing with their black servants, customs, they emphasized, that differed considerably from slavery in St. Louis. Pierre Cerre testified that his father took seven or eight slaves to Montreal from St. Louis. Blacks were viewed as curiosities there.

Seventy-three-year-old Michel Marli said he couldn't remember too much about his trip to Canada when he was eleven. He had never heard of any other Blacks at Prairie du Chien, but he knew someone, "a slave of St. George who was free, a voyageur, a mulatto." He didn't think Prairie du Chien was occupied by the British then. He hadn't seen any British troops there when he saw Rose. Mr. Dufraine said that he saw some Blacks in Canada: "Can't tell whether they were bound or free, but they seemed to go where they pleased never heard of slavery existing then in Canada." Pierre LaRiviere said that he was a servant himself while in Canada. (Presumably he had been indentured.) He went around the town and didn't see anything that he thought was slavery, although he had known some free black voyageurs. Michel Fontaine claimed that he had traveled the whole of Canada and had never seen or heard of slavery there. Antoine Smith testified that he never saw a Negro sold in Canada. He had seen black persons there but could not tell their condition. They were "employed in the house as domestic servants, had seen them in other homes than three, unwilling to swear they were slaves, always thought they were from their acting, don't know whether any the rights to sell them."[58]

The testimony raised the larger issue: what were the criteria by which a person was recognized as a slave anyway? Madame Tisson testified that she had made clothing for slaves in Montreal. The clothing for Canadian slaves was quite distinctive. The slaves of different households were distinguished by the colors of their clothing. She heard two masters say "they were their property, don't know of there [sic] being paid, they were well treated & clothed & worked only at their matters, never saw the masters whip the slaves, never knew them whipped in Canada. They took same care of them as if they were white."[59]

The testimony took several days, but at the end, the jury ruled against Charlotte. Her attorney quickly appealed. Charlotte's case would press on for years.

With the opening of May term 1847, *Pierre v. Gabriel Chouteau* was next, finally ready for retrial. Pierre had gotten a favorable verdict once before, so there was some hope. During the intervening five years of litigation, he had spent a lot of time in jail. Prolonged confinement was taking its toll on him. The delays in Pierre's case were typical of the obstacles that litigants faced (Lucy had been jailed seventeen months too), but in Pierre's case, the even longer duration intensified the ill effects of incarceration on him.

Pierre was represented by the same idealistic young New England lawyer named David N. Hall, who then represented Dred and Harriet Scott. Hall responded to Pierre's defeat by taking the extraordinarily ambitious step of sending to Montreal for depositions from officials about Canadian law. Although Hall was resourceful in research, he wasn't confident of his trial skills. In this, the second act of Pierre's case, Hall asked Edward Bates, the eminent lawyer who had represented Lucy at trial, to assist him.

The judge was new to the bench. In Bates' own diary, Bates remarked that Judge Hamilton erred in Pierre's trial. "[B]eing in his first official week, [the judge] was particularly green, in giving and refusing instructions."[60] Pierre called the Canadians again. Seventy-eight-year-old Madame Tisson expanded upon servant dress in Montreal. "Of two British officers who had servants, their servants wore uniform cloths also to distinguish the families. The cloths of one family were faced with red and the other with yellow." She described Canadian slaves as liveried servants dressed to display their owner's status, rather than lowly menial servants subjected to the roughest material existence. She claimed that although Rose was never sold in Canada, she had been traded by her master, for a horse. (At another time Rose's value was paid for in deerskins.)[61] Did that make Rose less of a slave, having been bartered rather than having been sold? None of these transaction appeared to have involved her consent. St. Louis slaves were routinely sold by auction outside the courtroom on the very courthouse steps.

After three days of trial, Pierre's case went to the jury. After three more days, the jury returned to say they could not reach a decision—they were hopelessly, irreconcilably split on the matter. The novice judge, conducting his first jury trial, didn't quite know how to respond. So he dismissed them and ordered Pierre back to the sheriff's custody to be hired out.[62] Pierre's hopes must have been raised, only to fall again.

This jury deadlock delayed the case further. Hall took his conscientious representation of Pierre one step further by personally paying for Pierre's hire,[63] presumably to keep him from languishing longer in jail.

By 1849, the cases of Pierre's three siblings had been consolidated. Since the issues were identical, all would be resolved by the first case resolved.[64] By 1849, it seemed from the testimony that Rose was dead.[65] Eighteen hundred forty nine was a calamitous year in St. Louis. A cholera outbreak killed a large percentage of the city's population and a massive fire burned the docks, all of the steamboats in port, and sixteen city blocks of warehouses and buildings.[66] Rose may have succumbed to cholera.

In January, 1850, Dred and Harriet Scott were declared free, after their own four-year ordeal in the courts. The principle for their release, the Northwest Ordinance and the Missouri Compromise line, still had traction for most litigants, though it had been held inapplicable to Rose's children. Thus, the later ruling in *Dred Scott*, reversing freedom by residence, Could not affect Pierre's claims, either positively or negatively.

With the death of his young lawyer later in 1850, Pierre lost his release time from jail and he was also left without a lawyer while awaiting his third trial. Pierre had spent the longest time in jail, because no one wanted to hire him. He had been hired out for a while, but he acted so strangely that his master no longer wanted responsibility for him. So Pierre's hirer returned him to the sheriff, willing to pay his board in jail rather than be responsible for having the rattled man in his household.⁶⁷

Pierre had become a permanent resident of the cell reserved for men of color. The 1850 census for the Third Ward listed "Pierre Chauteau [*sic*] 35, M, M—Prisoner—born in MO—'suing freedom.'"⁶⁸ The jail housed more than a dozen inmates at a time and saw a lot of turnover. But Pierre remained as a constant in the basement cell designated for black men. Black inmates were segregated from whites, and the men apart from the women. The three-story jail had thirty-six cells on opposite sides of a central atrium. A noisy clamor filled the place, and through their barred cell doors, the inmates could shout at one another, and waste their lives away.

As Pierre still sat in jail, running up a bill for his keep, even the sheriff petitioned the court to be relieved of his care and custody. In a changeover of sheriffs, the new man was reluctant to take custody of him. Judge Hamilton tried to find him a home at the county farm. The jailer disclosed that he believed Pierre was of unsound mind and that he had been insane for at least the last ten months that he'd spent in jail.⁶⁹ Since the jail also held the insane, it is where Pierre remained. Pierre continued to languish there, his sanity sorely stretched by almost a decade of incarceration.⁷⁰ The jailer did not want him, nor did the county farm. There was some thought to return him to Gabriel Chouteau, the very man from whom he sought his independence, just so someone else would be responsible for his food, clothing, and shelter.

One night thereafter, Gabriel invited the commercial slave trader Reuben Bartlett to join him in a covert raid on the jail to seize Pierre. While he was locked in his jail cell, the two men jumped him and whipped him violently. But they were unable to remove him that night. The beating was likely a retaliation unleashed for Gabriel's aggravation at the sum of freedom claims brought by his slaves. Pierre was so badly hurt in the attack in the dark that he couldn't tell the sheriff exactly who whipped him, whether it was Gabriel or his jailer. He'd lain suffering and disoriented in the cell all weekend, only to be found beaten and confused on Monday morning. Although Pierre's whipping was discovered on Monday morning, and one would have expected the jailer to have taken more care, somehow Bartlett and Gabriel Chouteau were able to remove him from the jail and conceal him somewhere in the city. When Pierre's newly assigned attorney went to see him that Tuesday, the jailer feigned denying him admittance, knowing fully that Pierre was gone. Pierre's lawyer had to ask the court to find his client.⁷¹

Reuben Bartlett was on a mission. The same month he kidnapped another freedom litigant, George Johnson, also removing him from jail and concealing him somewhere with the intent of selling him out of state.⁷² Bartlett and his accomplice carried Johnson south to Carondelet, before they were intercepted and prevented from smuggling the man out of the state. Bartlett was suspected of attempting to kidnap and remove Charlotte as well. Charlotte and her four children were found to be housed in his slave yard after her attorney went searching for her whereabouts.[73] Charlotte's family had also been taken from the county jail by Bartlett.

How did it all end for Pierre? The court eventually dismissed Pierre's case for failure to prosecute, because at one point no one appeared when the case was called. Pierre's assigned attorney had asked a fellow attorney to stand in for him while he was away, and the friend had left the case slip. The lawyer who represented Pierre's siblings, in cases that were still very active, tried to get Pierre's case reinstated. The motion should have been granted; such errors frequently occurred and usually were reinstated. But this time Judge Hamilton refused. He simply ordered Pierre released from jail. Could a person recognized as mentally incompetent maintain a suit for freedom? Pierre was simply released to the streets, perhaps to be picked up by someone who would help him or, far worse, prey upon him as Gabriel Chouteau had done. The last documented entry for Pierre was in late 1852,[74] then he disappeared.

By 1850, Gabriel Chouteau was still a bachelor, still ran the mill, and still engaged in real estate, but he no longer lived at the family home. The old Chouteau mansion had been torn down to make way for progress, and the siblings adopted the new trend of the rich to build new homes for themselves. A free black French woman ran Gabriel's household, and he had nine slaves.[75] Gabriel was still regarded as a harsh master. He was not above using public officers to whip his slaves and sell them downriver to New Orleans.[76]

In 1852, after the Missouri Supreme Court reversed its rule of freedom by residence in the *Dred Scott* debacle, Charlotte and her younger brothers still pressed on.[77] In fact, they litigated through the entire decade.

For a month in May of 1856, it appeared that Charlotte and her children might still win. The sheriff was ordered to summon eighteen good and lawful men out of whom to impanel a jury for Thursday, May 23.[78] When the day of trial came and the judge was informed that Charlotte and her four children were being held in jail, he ordered them to be released so they could attend the trial.[79] The trial took three days.[80] On May 30, the jury reached their verdict in favor of Charlotte and against Gabriel Chouteau. "Plaintiff be liberated and entirely set free…." Gabriel Chouteau appealed, of course.[81]

The *Dred Scott* decision by the U.S. Supreme Court, signaling the end of most freedom suits, seemed to re-energize Gabriel Chouteau. After all, his family had reason to regard it as a victory. They had urged John F. A. Sanford, to keep up the fight.

On June 1, 1857, another slave trader B.F. Lynch acquired an interest in Louis. Did he hire him from the sheriff? Did Gabriel make a deal with him? B. F. Lynch regularly sold slaves downriver to New Orleans. It appears that Lynch intended to do so with Louis. Lynch refused to put up the sizeable hiring bond that the sheriff required as security against Louis's disappearance. Attorney Cobb went to court warning that Louis was in danger of being removed from the jurisdiction. The Sheriff removed Louis from Lynch's slave pen, thus sparing him from being sent downriver. But the result was that Louis was ordered to remain in jail for his own safekeeping. No one provided the sizeable bond for his release. Just as his brother Pierre had before him, Louis sat in jail for more than three years not because Louis couldn't do work, but because a large bond was required lest he be kidnapped. It was not until January 1861 that there was an attempt to hire Louis out again. This time, the jail keeper came to court asking to be paid for keeping Louis for 918 days.[82] Louis's attorneys requested that the bond be reduced; no one would hire him at such a high bond. As his attorney said, Louis was "confined in a dungeon without having committed any offense, and has simply presented his petition for his freedom."[83]

Thus continued the ebb and flow of jury verdicts and appeals in Charlotte's litigation. The case went to trial almost every two years during the 1850s. Each time that the jury awarded the win to either Charlotte or Chouteau, the loser appealed, and each time the Missouri Supreme Court reversed, ordering a new trial. Charlotte's case rocked like a metronome winding down, resetting the equilibrium in more minute units with every appeal.

Charlotte's four trials and their outcomes

1. Chouteau won at trial, Charlotte appealed. Missouri Supreme Court reversed and remanded in 1847 (Charlotte wins), Charlotte v. Chouteau, 11 Mo. 193 (1847). Basis, not an issue of law, that was settled in Pierre's appeal; only issue is whether jury instructions followed legal principles.

2. Chouteau won at trial in 1853; Charlotte appealed. Missouri Supreme Court reversed and remanded in 1855 (Charlotte wins) Charlotte v. Chouteau, 21 Mo. 690 (1855).

3. Charlotte won at trial; Chouteau appeals. Missouri Supreme Court reverses in 1857 (Chouteau wins), and cause remanded Charlotte v. Chouteau, 25 Mo. 465 (1857)

4. Charlotte won at trial in 1859; Chouteau appeals. Missouri Supreme Court affirms Charlotte's freedom in 1862 giving Charlotte and her children the final victory in the lengthy litigation, Charlotte v. Chouteau, 33 Mo. 194 (1862).

At one point, Gabriel Chouteau sought to move the trial to another county, claiming that he could not get a fair jury in St. Louis. The case stayed where it was.[84]

The issues on appeal became more arcane, mostly disagreements about jury instructions and the interpretation of foreign custom as foreign law. Had Canada ever legally recognized slavery or not? As the issues narrowed, the possible scope of application to other litigants shrank to zero. At the same time, the numbers of Missouri slaves from Canada, or who could trace their mothers back to Canada, was a group that had all but died out.

Only in 1862, a year after the Civil War had begun, did the Missouri Supreme Court affirm Charlotte's final victory.[85] The guns had begun to fire. Charlotte and her brothers and children were finally determined to be free. Rose was not legally enslaved in Canada.

Gabriel Chouteau, however, was a slaveholder to the bitter end. Chouteau knew that the Emancipation Proclamation did not apply to slaveholders who remained loyal to the Union. So when one of Gabriel Chouteau's slaves ran away from his harsh master to help cook at the Union prison kitchen, Chouteau placed a demand on the Provost Marshall to return his man explaining that he had only run away because he feared a beating. Chouteau claimed he should be able to recover his human property. "I am as loyal a man as you can find. There is no 'Secesh' [sic] about me," meaning secessionist.[86] Only secessionists were forfeiting their slaves in Missouri with the Union orders. The Civil War did not free the slaves of the Chouteau family. Only the Thirteenth Amendment of the U.S. Constitution, abolishing slavery, would separate Gabriel Chouteau from his slaves.

CHAPTER 14

The Final Chapter

Our book of songs is coming to a close. There are just two more things to do—synthesize the stories and reveal the end, which you already knew, Dred and Harriet Scott's redemption song, the song that ended the possibilities for songs of redemption. It silenced the chorus. Its concluding notes sounded by the U.S. Supreme Court were that black men had no rights that white men were required to respect.[1]

The twelve stories contained here were selected from 300 filed lawsuits, involving 239 litigants and thirty-eight family groups litigated over more than three decades. This battery of intact judicial records gives us a sufficiently large corpus of evidence to observe variations in the petitioners' circumstances and to draw some conclusions.[2] These cases present larger issues of judicial handling of the rights for subordinate populations and why and when subservient individuals seek help from the courts. What happens when the law protects the rights of persons who otherwise are extremely vulnerable? What is the tensile strength of the rule of law in protecting the rights of the weak?

Contemplating Survivable Exit from Enslavement

One would think that a slave's desire for freedom would be so overwhelming that slaves would file suit as soon as humanly possible in order to exit the circumstance of slavery immediately and live free. Yet the lessons from these cases suggest that survival is a much more significant objective in influencing human behavior than attaining freedom. And for subordinated and vulnerable persons in particular, the exit from slavery must be survivable.

To rail as Patrick Henry did, "Give me liberty or give me death," is an empty boast reserved for those who are already condemned to death. The fictional protagonist in *Uncle Tom's Cabin* who claimed he would rather "die than be held in slavery" is speaking hyperbole.[3] Even the writer Solomon Northup recounts in his biography believing that slaves would fight their way out of slavery before he was caught up by kidnappers and experienced being enslaved.[4] Then he too described how he needed to submit himself to the enslaving forces in order to survive.

Slavery may be social death, as Orlando Patterson says,[5] but it is not actual death. In death there is no future, no second chance; death is the end of possibility. Under slavery, masters may change, conditions may change, locations may change, even sovereigns may change, and harsh circumstances may require endurance, but slavery is not the end of possibility. Nor is it the end of hope. The cases demonstrated time after time that in some circumstances, people find it reasonable to endure continued enslavement as a means of survival and family preservation rather than to risk uncertain survival as a means to freedom.

This is particularly true when the path to freedom requires the bravery of challenging one's master and the perseverance to endure those extra burdens imposed on slave litigants while awaiting judgment. This act of resistance to power cannot be done anonymously.[6] Once the suit has been filed, the petitioner is exposed. There is nowhere to hide. And there are few secure places to wait.

The Gender Effect: Men Run, Women Sue

Most St. Louis freedom suits were initiated by women. Filing suit preserved the status quo; it stayed the masters' ability to sell the litigant downriver, as Eliza Tyler's case demonstrated dramatically. Filing suit kept mothers and children together. Women frequently invoked as their reason for suit that a sale was threatened which would separate them from their children.

Mothers were central to many cases because the rule of matrilineality created a multiplier effect for children and grandchildren. There was a larger potential of expanding the victory when a woman established her freedom than when a man did. When the mother won, all of her children could prevail. The children's suits would follow relatively easily, falling like dominos from the mother's success. Lucy was able to use depositions gathered in her mother's suit as evidence in her own. This rule, freedom by virtue of a free mother, never altered during the entire run of cases. Edward Bates's ultimate emphatic argument in Lucy's case was that "no free woman can give birth to a slave child, as it is in direct violation of the laws of God and man!"[7] Nonetheless, even the children of free mothers (whether black or white) could be involuntarily indentured by the state until they reached adulthood if their parents were unable to provide for them. Does that explain Brunetta and Archibald's placement with the minister? Their mother was obviously independent of any master; was she deemed unable to provide for them? Guardianship registers in which children were involuntarily apprenticed have not been found in St. Louis for this time.

Men could run. They could risk depending on their own wits, physical stamina, and speed. Men's chances of successfully escaping were better, particularly if they traveled alone. Slave masters understood this by encouraging slave men to form attachments with slave women in order to discourage them from escaping. Attachment to their children made escape less possible for mothers than others.[8] Providing a stable environment and source of food, shelter, and clothing for their children deterred mothers from fleeing slavery. Running with children was doomed to fail, but leaving them behind rendered them vulnerable to precarious circumstances and weighed heavily on their mothers. To break away cleanly also meant choosing permanent exile from all the rest of one's family, even those family members who were free. Those who successfully escaped to Canada could never come back.[9] Escape closed the doors on those family members who were left behind.

Every Freedom Suit Needed a Trigger to Change the Balance of Risk

It but needed a little more provocation to add to the flames.
—Lucy Delaney, "From the Darkness Cometh the Light or Struggles for Freedom."

Freedom suits were not undertaken casually, because the personal costs of the lawsuit and the risks of failure were too high. There was no anonymity if one filed suit. The petitioner's identity was exposed, as well as their desire for freedom. which may well have been masked before. Even expressing the desire for freedom was likely to bring sanction or at least tighter constraints. After kidnapped Solomon Northup was impressed into slavery, he was told to speak no more of freedom, or he would be whipped severely.[10] Slave litigants Vincent Duncan and Polly Wash intentionally masked their desire to free themselves from their masters before filing suit.[11] The lawsuit was dangerous because it challenged the very legitimacy of one's master's claim to continued submission.

Because slave survival and slave family networks were precarious, being able to remain in place had some value to enslaved persons who knew that they could later sue for freedom. Polly Wash chose her timing carefully, first for herself, and then for her daughter.[12] Slave family networks were precariously dependent upon the master's choices, the master's ups and downs, and the master's death. Periods of stability and relative domestic tranquility were savored because numerous unexpected factors could upend a slave's life for the worse. "With mother, father and sister, a pleasant home and surroundings, what happier child than I!" Lucy writes of the tranquil days when her family was still intact.[13]

The freedom suits ritually recited the formal claim of assault, a necessary element to the lawsuit, yet these allegations were often legal fictions. The most common date selected in the pleading was January 1 of the year of the suit (or the first day of the previous month). That disproportionate number of beatings cannot have occurred on New Year's Day. Just as the date recited appears to be fictitious, so too, the recitation that a beating occurred at all may have been a legal fiction. Nelson Camphell could not have beaten Eliza Tyler because he had not yet taken full custody of her. Many, many of the petitions hark so closely to the same words in describing the "assault" on the person's freedom as to suggest that these words were part of the template of pleading used by lawyers and court clerks. Thus, alleging a beating did not necessarily explain the decision to sue; it functioned simply as a necessary formality to gain access to the court.[14]

This does not imply that none of the suits were triggered by beatings. There are ample cases with gruesome and brutal details.[15] It suggests, however, that it is more reasonable to infer an actual physical assault only in those circumstances where the petition includes some unique specific detail because a formal recitation was necessary.

Sometimes the lawsuit was triggered by verbal or emotional fireworks between master and slave. Poor work performance or insubordination could anger the master, escalating the conflict until the slave fled or filed suit. The cases present a range of typical triggers: seizure by creditors; death of the master of a stable household; a household disbanding; sale to a slave trader; threat of being sent south; threats that children were scheduled to be removed. These circumstances, when intense enough, were sufficiently disrupting to the slave's life to trigger a lawsuit for freedom.

The courtroom drama was certainly a site of dramatic tension, particularly and disproportionately for the petitioner. Lucy describes her anxiety as almost paralyzing.[16] But the tension in the courtroom was not due to direct verbal confrontation between servant and master on the witness stand. None of the petitioners ever testified on the witness stand, nor did the defendants, who were their masters. At the time, the rules of competency for witnesses precluded parties with a direct interest in the case from testifying because their testimony would be deemed legally incompetent as self-interested.[17] All the witnesses brought to the stand were observers to the events, rather than parties to the lawsuit. The most authentic statement that the slave plaintiff made was the petition, signed by the "X." That is where the plaintiff could most fully tell of acts of forced subordination by the master that often were done under the cloak of private settings.

The most intense, direct confrontations between master and slave occurred in private settings, offstage, in the circumstances leading up to the lawsuit. These confrontations often occurred in secluded places. Peter and Queen were lured away. Both Polly's and Lucy's most direct confrontations with their respective mistresses were heated exchanges in the privacy of each mistress's household. Yet in court, the parties spoke through their attorneys. Neither petitioner nor defendant could take the stand to continue the argument because the evidentiary rules forbade it. Similarly, in another example, Hester Williams's most intense conflicts with her former master occurred in private. He deceived and lured her into bringing her freedom papers to his hotel room. There he tore up the note, attempting to revoke her freedom. Frederick Norcom did not confront Hester in public; he never even attended the trial.[18]

If Norcum's actions are typical of slave owners, then defendants were likely to be absent from the courtroom during the trial because they simply had what they considered more important business to attend to. Or, as gentlemen, they may have seen it as beneath them to actually attend a trial that their former slave had pressed upon them. Lucy does not mention D.D. Mitchell being present in court during the trial, only during the first hearing when bond was set. On the other hand, the scrappy Coleman Duncan seemed to enjoy staring down his opponents and intimidating those who would bear witness against him.[19] If his behavior was more typical, the servant and master would endure a silent, hostile confrontation of glances and stares.

The courtroom dynamic was probably typified by Lucy's trial. The lawyers argued, and the petitioning slave was the only party present in the courtroom, released from the jail or from temporary hiring, to watch the trial unfold and her fate be determined.[20]

How Did a Slave Petitioner Survive During Litigation?

A perennial problem was what to do with the slave during the pendency of the lawsuit. Slave owners feared that if slaves were allowed to go at large during this time, they may try escape.[21] Slave petitioners recognized the irony that they were subjected to much more stringent captivity, being jailed, while attempting to prove their right to independence and freedom than they were subject to before they challenged their enslavement. Lucy stayed seventeen months in jail; Pierre and his brother Louis remained jailed for more than three years each. Although none were accused or suspected of any crime, slaves litigating their freedom were constrained like convicts and housed with them.

The state, for its interest, was concerned that slave masters would steal away their slaves if they did not post bond.[22] So sometimes slaves who could have supported themselves were jailed for their own safety. Even though the jail conditions were poor, so primitive as to be almost intolerable, jailing a slave litigant incurred costs that someone would be asked to pay—costs for the jailer, the sheriff, or ultimately whoever lost the lawsuit.

Everyone has to work for their supper, even while suing for freedom. So the practice developed of hiring the petitioner out to the highest bidder who agreed to post bond. From these unpleasant options, the St. Louis court created a netherworld between the two juridical boundaries, potential freedom and past enslavement. That netherworld, a limbo, was cobbled together from the possibilities of jail, hiring out, the practice of posting bond, and return to their master with the admonition that they should not be treated more severely as a result of filing suit. Someone had to feed and shelter petitioners if they had no means to provide for themselves. The answer most often was jail, at least for some duration.

The practice that evolved was to first offer to return the petitioners to their master, who could work the individual and feed them, if the master posted bail to ensure their security. If the master did not post bail, the petitioners were jailed, to prevent their escape *and* for their own security. In instances in which masters had attempted kidnap, the jail was where petitioners would be safely kept. This led to further contradictions: Lydia Titus's kidnapped family was jailed for their safekeeping together with their kidnappers, who were held on kidnapping charges. Imagine captives and capturers, victims and predators, confined in the same jail.

Hiring out to third-party bidders could produce either the roughest treatment of all or the greatest liberty.[23] The court heard petitions from Lucy's mother that Lucy was so poorly treated in jail that she would have perished without her mother's help. But, because Lucy's mother herself was hired out to a benevolent hirer, she was able to go about more freely during her freedom suit and even to help Lucy.

Several petitioners died while hired out to the highest bidder. There was little incentive for any of the temporary custodians of the freedom litigant to provide adequate food or clothing. For example, Tempe complained that her master would not provide her with adequate clothing because he expected to lose her by the lawsuit. Harry worked in the brickyard without sufficient clothing as the record states "to cover his nakedness."[24] Hirers of slaves were supposed to provide clothing as part of the bargain, but they sometimes neglected to do so because clothing was such an expensive item at the time,[25] and there was little check on whether they did.

In many circumstances, simply enduring the lawsuit was sufficiently difficult that petitioners appear to have accepted accommodation rather than total vindication. At least ten cases end with the entry that petitioner "will not further prosecute."[26] When a child's related case is dismissed, because the mother has just lost her freedom suit, the entry is understandable.[27] Yet in other cases, the plaintiff simply defaulted, either through attorney neglect or litigant fatigue. The judges were usually lenient in allowing the plaintiff to reopen the case and set aside the default judgment, when they failed to appear.[28] (Except in Pierre's case: the legal system could do nothing for disoriented Pierre.)

The Chouteaus as Repeat Players and other Slave Master Strategies

It must be recognized how significant one family, the Chouteaus, were as repeat players in the St. Louis freedom suits, from the very beginning to the bitter end.[29] Some repeat players come out ahead by selectively choosing the cases that they decide to appeal, but this was not the Chouteau strategy; they approached these cases with a full court press. Hundreds of pages of legal documents were devoted to the extended Chouteau family's efforts in resisting slave claims to freedom, more than even the Duncans. From Native American enslavement to slaves brought west along the Ohio, to the children of Rose from Canada, the Chouteaus resisted at trial and pursued appeals. Even Dred and Harriet Scott, neither of whom had ever been owned by the Chouteaus or their relatives, encountered Chouteau resistance when Widow Emerson's inheritance fell to her brother to manage and her brother had married into the Chouteau family. The Scotts may never have fully understood the extent to which the Chouteaus were ultimately their true adversaries.

Some masters tried to evade the lawsuit. Masters could resist passively by dodging service of process. Defendants like James Duncan left the county so as not to be found in the sheriff's bailiwick when the sheriff came calling.

Faced with the possibility of evasion of service of process, one petitioner actually set up a fake defendant. After Eliza's slave master slyly slipped her grasp by maintaining his residence outside the state, Eliza found another St. Louis resident to set up as her putative master in order to file suit.[30] That trick almost worked, though it lured her original master back into the state to protest the setup. One wonders whether Vincent, who had tricked his masters so often before, attempted a similar move when he sued his previous housemate, Jerry Duncan.

Although the statute anticipated retaliation by masters, and attempted to forbid it, several slaves complained that retaliation did occur. Tempe claimed that her master for "a considerable time past subjected her to very harsh, and cruel treatment [she believes] on account of her suit...he has frequently abused and beaten her (and particularly on yesterday) for no other cause [than her present suit] her duties as a servant are rendered much more hard than that of other servants in the family, and that she is seldom spoken to [except] with ill humor and abusive language."[31] Mary claimed that she had received "much other bad treatment and abuse" while she was confined in "negro yards" after her suit.[32] Several masters were caught attempting to smuggle their slaves out of the jurisdiction of the courts. Some got away with it. Quelling a lawsuit by kidnapping the petitioner must have appeared to be a viable option for defendants since it occured with some regularity.[33] Kidnapping seemed to require three persons to overpower a resistant captive.[34] It was begun, quietly and covertly, by segregating the individual from others, in the way that Queen was induced to leave the household. Only in a secluded setting would the kidnapped person discover what was happening, and then there was no one to overhear.

Lawyers

From the pattern of representation, it appears that good lawyers stepped up to help the least well-off in energetic waves. For a time, just after statehood, the McGirk brothers, Isaac and Matthias, advanced freedom suits for Winny's family and the Scypions'. Later on the high court, Matthias McGirk wrote the definitive decision declaring that John Merry was free. For almost a decade, Gustavus Bird advanced freedom suits, winning notable victories for the Duncans, the Tituses and Polly Wash. Participating with him, sometimes in partnership, and sometimes alone, were younger men, Ferdinand Risque and Frances B. Murdoch. The critical mass of these three men zealously representing slave clients led to the greatest burst of successes in the 1830s. Ferdinand Risque's advocacy for the slaves of Milton Duty was exemplary. Then, within a few years, their energies dissipated. Both Risque and Murdoch left town, and Gustavus Bird died.[35] D. H. Hall appeared ready to step up to pursue these claims conscientiously, but he perished in what appears to have been depression and opium before having brought any of his suits to victory.[36] Roswell Field saw to Dred and Harriet Scott after other lawyers had departed,[37] and Henry Cobb saw Rose's children through. But although good lawyers seemed to succeed in these bursts of zealous advocacy, petitioners who didn't catch a wave of good and conscientious lawyers were more likely to fail. George Strother's string of routinely assigned cases resulted more often in the petitioner withdrawing his or her motion, rather than going to trial. There is not much evidence that he ever interviewed witnesses in preparation for any of the cases that he was assigned.

Part of the problem was that lawyers, who were uncompensated, didn't necessarily commit to the case. In other instances, lawyers did the opposite: demonstrated blatant opportunism. The slave woman Rebecca paid her lawyer Harris Sproat $50 for his services in seeking her freedom, but Sproat neglected her case, and it was dismissed because he failed to show up when the case was called.[38] Other lawyers attempted to get fees or services from their clients in return.[39] Gustavus Bird won Lydia's children their freedom, but she lost the farm when he pursued collection of the bill. Other lawyers attempted to get services from their clients in exchange for representation. Even the lawyer opposing Dred Scott saw some advantage in asking Dred to surrender his lawsuit, and come work for him for a promise of freedom sometime later.[40]

Juries and the Rule of Law

The data suggest that juries cannot be trusted as much as judges to uphold the law when the law designed to protect the weak runs counter to social norms. Of ninety-one jury trials held between 1819 and 1851, half the litigants won and half lost. Forty-six petitioners won, but given the fact that the jury award for a mother dictated a win for the child, juries sided with petitioner only thirty-eight times. Thus juries ruled for the petitioners less often. Ten of the jury deliberations resulted in hung juries, almost ten per cent.[41] One poor litigant, Martha Ann, experienced three hung juries before the fourth trial dispensed with the jury and the judge proceeded to rule in her favor.[42] This example was telling. Instead, petitioners succeeded far more often when the parties waived the right to a jury and the case was decided by the judge.

Close cases produced split outcomes when they were tried twice, and random outcomes when not appealed. Milly's two trips to the Missouri Supreme Court produced almost dramatically inconsistent decisions. She lost one and won the next on similar arguments to the very same bench. In close cases, plaintiffs and defendants seemed to take turns scoring wins and losses, as in the case of Rose's children in their suits against Gabriel Chouteau.[43]

The remarkable truth about these cases is that the rule of law held. For three decades, slaves were able to succeed in St. Louis courts, despite the odds.[44] There was some public grumbling about freedom suits. One anonymous writer posted an editorial acknowledging that freedom suits were right, rational, and humane, but complaining that

> "the liberty has become abused, at least in St. Louis, by the ruthless encouragement of those who left-handedly profit by such suits.... Tom wants his freedom, and sallies in quest of legal advice; he states his case, and right or wrong, is flattered to proceed. Pleased with his prospects, he brags to Dick, who after a little scratching of the bump of his reminiscences, takes a notion he has a right to freedom too. Then the hope spreads through the black community. Fired with untried hope, Dick flies to Ned.... Ned catches flame and communicates it to Big Bill--Big Bill to little Jim, and little Jim to everything that wears wool.... [The slave soon] grumbles at his master's commands, neglects his duties, and takes his chastisement with the sullen insolence of one who thinks he shall shortly be able to set the white man at defiance."[45]

Yet even this writer, though critical of the practice and racist, acknowledged that these suits were right, rational, and humane.

Losing masters harbored grudges, acted in retaliation, when they could, and vented their disappointment in secondary law suits. Yet they never mustered the legislative power to overturn the statute enabling slaves to sue for freedom. And the suits never ended until they did so in full collapse, in two judicial reversals in *Dred Scott v. Sandford.* Then, the collapse of freedom suits was attended with the collapse of legal comity between the states and whatever remaining political balance had existed between free and slave states.

The Details of Slave Litigants' Lives

Slaves inhabit their master's agendas during enslavement. From the legal record as from other sources, detail about masters is much more extensive than about slaves. The masters' lives often seem more vibrant and interesting than the slaves' constrained accounts of their own. The subject and subjective quality of their lives was overtaken by their existences as objects, and as objects that belonged to someone else with a subjective life. As slaves, petitioners are described by witnesses in passive voice as having the characteristics of objects. They are sold, moved, transported, sent, and inherited. They do not sell, move, send, or inherit. They are stolen, even "stampeded," by third parties.[46] Even to suggest that a person was "kidnapped," rather than "stolen," imbues that person with the subjectivity of a life rather than simply an existence. Slaves are not kidnapped in the legal sense. Kidnapping implies interfering with the liberty of someone who has a right to liberty. Instead, when captured and moved, they are "stolen" from their owner. So it is interesting that when Peter complained about Queen's kidnapping, it was called "man-stealing."

Often the ultimate outcome in each case can be revealed only by examining what became of the petitioner thereafter. Some petitioners were manumitted immediately or within a relatively short time after the concluding chapter in the courts. Some registered as free Blacks, enrolling for Free Negro Bonds months or years later without any explanation of their transition from slavery to freedom, given that their freedom suits were unsuccessful. Some are later found still within their masters' estates. Some are advertised as runaways, and some simply disappeared without a trace. These combined results communicate a powerful insight, however. Pushing a case through to full vindication may have been a luxury for some subordinated litigants. Subordinated peoples are often required to settle for accommodation, something less than full vindication of their legal rights. They settle by virtue of their subordination, and by virtue of the unsatisfactory legal means necessary to achieve vindication. Still, for dozens of litigants, the St. Louis courts declared that they, who had never lived in freedom and independence before, be fully free from their claimant, and anyone claiming thereunder.[47]

Slaves on the Frontier

These accounts also change our common, shared story of origin as a nation. The majority of cases are based on freedom by residence. The numbers of enslaved persons traversing through and residing in free territory indicates rather strongly that the antebellum frontier, even north and west of the Ohio River, was not as free from slavery as the law decreed. Ira Berlin has identified four great migrations in African American history.[48] This coerced migration to what was then considered the far west, was not as great in number as the transatlantic passage, but it should be recognized as a counterpoint to those who migrated westward voluntarily. The numbers of domestic slaves who were put to work in lands north and west of the Ohio River belies the belief that slavery could not exist there because those lands were unsuitable for plantation production. Domestic slavery was a useful social practice to persons who migrated westward and settled even in lands that had freezing winters.[49] Many early Midwestern pioneers brought slaves with them.

The cases also demonstrate that the wilderness is not a site of freedom, in part because of the absence of courts equipped to protect the rights of the vulnerable. Frontier communities were at least as likely to be subject to the power of petty oligarchs willing to exploit others, like Vanderburgh and Dubois in Vincennes, as they were to be law-abiding with regard to a law that restricted their interests. A Galena witness to Eliza Tyler's residence in that free state remarked that she could establish her freedom if she could get to a court. When eventually courts and judges were introduced to protect the weak from these predations of the strong, judges ruling on their behalf were sometimes forced to leave the vicinity.

In addition, the wilderness is a site where survival can be sorely tested. In a period of adversity, Peter described feeling most hopeless when he was left tied up and exposed to the elements. Though the American frontier has repeatedly been valorized as a destination for heroic, rugged individualists, in actuality, arranging the necessary food, clothing, and shelter to survive in the lands north and west of the Ohio River required the cooperation of a social or trading network. It was almost impossible to survive solo—and even harder if one needed to support a family of dependents.

Native American peoples inhabiting wilderness lands did so by means of their social networks. Runaway slaves were not necessarily welcomed into their social networks, as Peter's story demonstrates. Hence, the idea of fleeing slavery by running to the wilderness is not a strategy of survivable exit for anything but the very short term. Even on the edge of the wilds, as far as possible from the trappings of oppressive slavery laws and entrenched institutional practices, Indians captured Peter and Queen and traded them back to the settlement.

This account runs contrary to decades of American frontier mythology that has valorized the frontier as a promised land, free from oppressive social structures, such as servitude.

Dred and Harriet Scott, the End of Redemption Songs, and the Beginnings of Civil War

Without knowing about these redemption songs, without awareness of the hundreds of cases that preceded their lawsuit, a reader could regard the Scotts' catastrophic loss as inevitable. After all, who would expect that a slave could win freedom in a slave state before a jury of all white men? But, as this book demonstrates, many did, and the Scotts should have won their lawsuits easily. The law was on their side. The freedom by residence rule was well established and had produced success for dozens of slave litigants before in the St. Louis courts alone. Several free Blacks who had taken advantage of the law lived in St. Louis as their neighbors. And the Scotts had the necessary witnesses.

When Dred and Harriet Scott filed their lawsuit in 1846, they were married and had children. They sued six years after settling in St. Louis. They remained a couple, despite having experienced some time of separation. Dred had just returned from Texas, from the Army of Observation, where he served as an officer's body servant. He approached his mistress, offering to buy his freedom, but she refused. The Scotts' eldest daughter had just turned seven, the age at which masters often opted to set children to work, the first step that enslaved children took on a lifelong path of coerced labor.

The Scotts had all the legal elements necessary to win their case without difficulty, given what was already the accepted law in Missouri. Dred had resided in a free state, Illinois, and at Fort Snelling, north of the border that marked the Missouri Compromise. Harriet had also resided at Fort Snelling, and her master had relinquished her, giving her in marriage to Dred. Her marriage and her master's departure seemed to signal the intent to manumit her in circumstances in which any more formal manumission was impossible, and, given their extended residence on free lands, probably unnecessary.

The Scotts had witnesses, and when they filed suit they had the luck of a good lawyer to assist them. Both the Scotts had lived in St. Louis long enough to know how to survive there. They had figured out how they would earn their livings. Harriet would take in laundry, of course, as most black women did. And Dred would find something to do. He was sociable, had traveled with educated military men, and could do something.

Dred and Harriet's profile matched that of other slaves who had redeemed their freedom by serving military officers in the Northwest: Rachel had lived at

Fort Snelling and Fort Crawford, and had won her freedom; and Courtney had lived at another fort at Green Bay on Lake Michigan.[50] Like others, both Dred and Harriet had been brought to the unsettled wilds of the Northwest to provide domestic service where it was difficult to find servants.

To a certain extent, however, the Scotts were the last of their kind: African American slaves taken to free northern lands to serve their masters in an environment where good servants were impossible to find. The labor force for this work was changing. Irish immigrants had come west in great numbers seeking work. Irish men were the army's new enlistees, and Irish women became the new model of domestic servant. Officers entitled to subsidies for their servant allowance were increasingly turning to Irish serving women, rather than seeking slaves, to accompany them. Irish women were replacing black women as maids in well-to-do households in St. Louis as well.[51]

Moreover, the periphery had shifted. The westward migration ran into a new boundary, the dry plains and prairies. After states had been carved out of almost the entire remaining vestiges of land of the Northwest Territory, westward settlement had run up against what was referred to as the "Great American Desert." Without water, settlement patterns in the Great Plains proceeded much differently from the gradual expansion west that was possible through the valleys and woodlands of the Northwest Territory. Thus, the continual and gradual movement west by persons walking and taking flat boats for short distances from the Wabash River to the valley of the Mississippi did not continue as before. The numbers of new freedom suits filed in St. Louis had even started to slow down in the late 1840s.

So what explained the result in the *Dred Scott* case, and indeed, the end of all redemption songs? On the local level, the Scotts were singularly unlucky due to random circumstances that taken together delayed the ordinary processing of their case. At one point, the defendant's representation faltered, and it seemed the Scotts might win. Hugh Garland, who represented Mrs. Emerson, passed the case on to a junior lawyer as a case likely to lose.[52] Mrs. Emerson might have given up the appeal. But that junior lawyer brought an intense zeal to the effort. The Scotts faced additional obstacles. Their legal representation changed four times, as effective lawyers died or moved away. The Scotts lost one trial when they were assigned an unprepared attorney at the last moment. David N. Hall, who had zealously represented Pierre by even sending to Canada for evidence and hiring his clients out so that they need not wait in jail, had the misfortune to lose his young wife and newborn to the ravages of childbirth. Subsequently, David N. Hall seemed to self-destruct on opium.[53]

Natural disasters delayed the Scotts' case as well. While they awaited trial, two unusually extreme calamities descended on the city. Litigation slowed to a standstill the entire year of 1849. An enormous fire swept up all of the many steamboats at the docks and spread to the town, hollowing out the town center. Even before the fire, the year 1849 was plagued by the greatest outbreak of cholera that the city had ever seen. Had the case been tried that year, it is likely that the Scotts would have secured a victory. The larger forces had not yet come into play to stage the reversal of fortune.[54] But with the cholera outbreak, it was difficult to even convene a jury.[55]

As the case was delayed, larger political forces beyond the litigants' control were mounting in the national conflict between slave and free legal and political regimes. The Fugitive Slave Act was passed and enforced for the first time. St. Louis became ever more attuned to the mounting conflict because the telegraph hastened communication reaching it from the East. Whereas once St. Louis stood at the end of the settled world—several flat boat or steamboat journeys, from the news at the nation's political center—the telegraph brought the town the alarming news of emerging abolitionist sentiment with lightning speed.[56] The debates over expanding slavery in the west intensified and took a different path after the Missouri Compromise was waived to allow local option decisionmaking about slavery in the igniting state of Kansas to the west.

The Scotts won their jury trial in 1850. They heard the precious words, and yet they could expect an appeal. Before the appeal could occur, however, the composition of judges on the Missouri Supreme Court changed. A rule change to elect judges rather than appoint them put in place the three-judge panel that ruled against the Scotts, by a vote of two to one. The rather lackadaisical representation of the defendant's attorney, Hugh Garland, was replaced by a young, firebrand attorney and political newspaper editor, Lyman D. Norris, who mounted an inflammatory attack on the very rule of freedom by residence. The Missouri Supreme Court borrowed Norris's rhetoric in writing the decision. And, by a margin of one, it reversed its own rule of freedom by residence. This rule had liberated more than 100 litigants in St. Louis alone.[57]

The tensile strength of a rule that protected the least well-off, a class of persons without sympathy or resources, had broken on the state level. The rule had been time-tested before. Juries that failed to find for the plaintiff were reversed by the Missouri Supreme Court in decisions shoring up the jury instructions on remand. In some cases, like Milly's and the Scypions', this happened repeatedly until the case produced a win for the plaintiff. This time, however, the Missouri Supreme Court did not affirm the judgment in favor of freedom. It reversed its own precedent that dated back to statehood. In this the Scotts were unlucky again. If the Missouri Supreme Court wished to reverse thirty years of precedent, the most prudential decision would have been to apply the new rule prospectively only, leaving the jury verdict intact. Instead, the court invalidated the jury decision. There was no possibility of remand because the court had vaporized the basis for the suit.

At this point, the Scotts' only option was to attempt once again to buy their freedom or sue in federal court. Their putative owner, Mrs. Emerson, had moved to Massachusetts and married again, another doctor, but this time, a doctor who ran for Congress on the Free Soil ticket. The Scotts' new attorney filed suit against Mrs. Emerson-Chaffee's brother-in-law, John F. A. Sanford.[58]

Once again, the Scotts had bad luck. The case could have easily floundered and ended there by the defendant's default. After all, the new defendant lived in New York. He had fallen into the role only by virtue of his administration of his father's estate, but he had no real personal interest in these particular slaves or their value. And he probably had never even met them. He managed the worldwide American Fur Company empire. The only value in the family as a saleable commodity was Harriet and the Scotts' two daughters. But the man to whom the defense fell, John F. A. Sanford, was the devoted son-in-law of Pierre Chouteau Jr.

Sanford did it for the Chouteaus. Years later, when Mrs. Emerson-Chaffee was asked why the suit did not simply die for lack of response, she replied that Sanford pursued it because the Chouteaus wanted it pursued.[59] It was relatively easy for Sanford to defend: Sanford had a litigation team in place in St. Louis, and he had the agent who had handled his father's slaves in place to monitor the Scotts.

Freedom cases of subordinates often resulted in some accommodation, such as allowing the slave to buy himself after some length of service. Why didn't this one? According to Mrs. Emerson-Chaffee, the case would have settled, but the Chouteaus were angry at the escape of some of their slaves, and persuaded John F.A. Sanford to pursue it. "This was the … Chonteau [sic] family, into which John Sandford [sic] had married.… [T]he family was so angry over the matter that its members persuaded Sandford [sic] to fight out the Scott case till the last. Accordingly, Sandford [sic] took up the matter on his own account… and carried it on."[60]

By the time that the Scotts' suit reached the U.S. Supreme Court, they were but a small speck of dust caught up in a very large windstorm. The appellate lawyers were conscious of acting out a larger drama on a much larger national stage than the lawsuit on which it was based. The facts stipulated by both sets of attorneys misstated many of the details of the family's lived experience. But no one except the family may have cared about that.

The Scotts lost their bid for freedom. The U.S. Supreme Court did so much more damage than simply reverse the rule of freedom by residence. The Supreme Court rendered a ruling that slammed the door on all African Americans seeking to establish rights, both slaves and free Blacks. The opinion collapsed these freedom suits by stating that these people, vulnerable in so many ways, had no rights at all. The rule of law, justice, and comity between the states collapsed by denying them the capacity to be citizens, or persons with any rights that white men were obligated to respect. Without rights, without concomitant obligations, there would be no protection needed from the law. The courts need not hear from them.

And so, the series of redemption songs ends as it began, with a case opposed by the Chouteau family, fifty years after Auguste Chouteau, inquiring about the Scypions, ordered his Indian slaves beaten for talking freedom. The Chouteaus

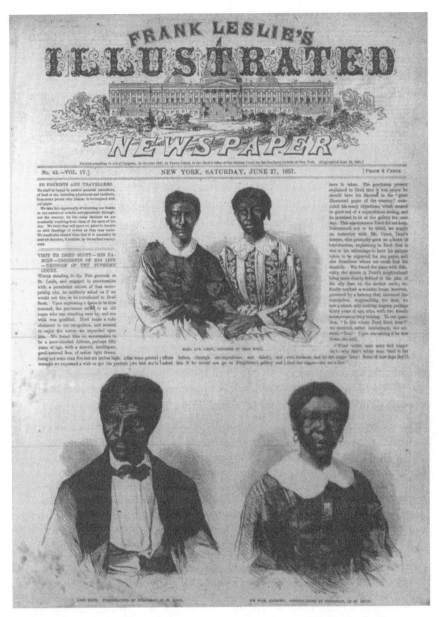

The Supreme Court decision became so well-known nationally that the leading periodical, *Frank Leslie's Illustrated* had daguerrotypes made of the Scott family, which were then reproduced on its front page. Frank Leslie's Illustrated.

had opposed more freedom suits than any other family. Now they won the rule that silenced the suits that had annoyed them so.

Sanford triumphed, though he had gone mad, was confined to a sanitarium, and may never have even realized his victory, if he ever really cared.

The decision led to the embarrassment of Mrs. Emerson-Chaffee and Calvin Chaffee, her new husband, seated in Congress as a Free Soil Republican from Massachusetts. The national press discovered that the most famous slave in America was owned by a Massachusetts congressman. Ownership was hastily transferred to someone residing in Missouri. (Only a Missouri resident could legally manumit a slave in Missouri). So the son of one of Dred's former owners filed the papers manumitting the Scotts before the same judge who had twice presided over their trials and heard their redemption song.

The remarkable Missouri statute was not repealed thereafter. It still offered to appoint attorneys and contained the refrain: "Plaintiff be liberated and entirely set free." Eventually, even Charlotte and the grandchildren of Canadienne Rose heard these words.[61] But the words were heard in court far less often after the *Dred Scott* decision. Without the rule of freedom by residence, slaves who had resided on free soil no longer had a case. Instead, the liberating statute was repurposed, in line with other Southern state statutes. It corrected mistaken status. In some circumstances, it was available to slaves promised manumission in their master's last will and testament. But for the Milton Duty slaves, the litigation itself created the debts in the futile cycle by which they continued to be held in slavery to work to pay for those debts.

The twin decisions in the *Dred Scott* case, one by the Missouri State Supreme Court in 1852, and the other, at the U.S. Supreme Court in 1857, ended the legal rule of freedom by residence for Missouri slaves. The U.S. Supreme Court's decision in *Dred Scott* meant that freedom by residence ended in other slave states as well.[62]

The nation's migratory pattern was also changing. Travelers continued to migrate west in great numbers, but without stopping over or residing on the northern free shore.

In the decade immediately before *Dred Scott* was decided, more litigants utilizing the rule of freedom by residence had done so by being sent from their St. Louis masters across the river to do work on the Illinois side. In Illinois, hired labor was available only at a premium. These cases describe the work that the enslaved person did. For example, Louis Scott was sent to Illinois to repair stills purchased from a St. Louis merchant. Charles was sent by the priests to repair a roof on an Illinois nunnery. Slave women were sent to Illinois to care for the sick or taken along when their mistresses went visiting.[64]

Transit sites always seem to be loci of litigation. They are the emergency rooms for travelers in legal distress. They are the courts that the weak will turn to for protection. The St. Louis court was still at a transit point in westward travel, even with the introduction of railroads, but the material circumstances that had created so many lawsuits had altered with time.

NOTES

These endnotes and more supplemental material about the people and laws in this book can be found at: http://blogs.law.uiowa.edu/vandervelde/redemptionsongs

Preface

1. For a complete list of appellate cases at Missouri Supreme Court, see the bibliography.
2. *Rachel, a woman of color, v. Walker, William,* 82, CC case no. 351 (1834); *Rachel v. Walker,* CC case no. 351 (1836).
3. Kenneth Clarence Kaufman, *Dred Scott's Advocate: A Biography of Roswell M. Field* (1996).
4. This took place in 1997 before laptop computers were common, so data processing was set apart in a facility that could keep the mainframe air-conditioned.
5. *Rachel v. Walker,* CC case no. 351 (1836).
6. *Deposition of John, a man of color, Rachel v. William Walker,* CC case no. 82 (1834); *Rachel v. Walker,* 4 Mo. 351 (1836).
7. See, e.g., Thomas Cobb, *An Inquiry into the Law of Negro Slavery in the United States of America.* And the many works that have relied on him.
8. In fact, Robert Moore had found Mel Conley and her shoebox before I did. Robert Moore, "A Ray of Hope, Extinguished: St. Louis Slave Suits for Freedom," *Gateway Heritage* 14 (Winter 1993–1994).
9. Each time I ended the day, a shower and fresh clothes were in order. No one had told me that archival work was so dirty.
10. William Wells Brown's autobiography features the slave trader William Walker. William Wells Brown, *From Fugitive Slave to Free Man.*
11. *Gabriel v. Andrew Christy and Mary Coons, executors of estate of David Coons,* CC case no. 324 (1846).
12. See, e.g., *Nelson Kerr v. Mathew Kerr,* CC case no. 104 (1834).

Chapter 1 A Metaphor for the Voices of the Subordinate Buried in History

1. Harriet Jacobs gave false names in telling her life story, a story which was authenticated more than a century later. Yellin, *Harriet Jacobs: A Life.* Other works listening for slave voices include Genovese, *Roll, Jordan, Roll*; Litwack, *Been in the Storm So Long*; VanderVelde, *Mrs. Dred Scott: A Life on Slavery's Frontier* (2009); Gross, *What Blood Won't Tell.*
2. See chapter 9.
3. See chapter 8.
4. VanderVelde, *Mrs. Dred Scott,* 267–319.

5. White, "Subordination, Rhetorical Survival Skills." Catharine MacKinnon and C. Gilligan, *In a Different Voice* "MacKinnon's objection that we cannot know what women's values are, since at present women are victims, poses epistemological and cognitive problems not easily resolved." O'Donovan, "Engendering Justice," 139. The feminine, MacKinnon argues, is defined by a patriarchal culture: "For women to affirm difference, when difference means dominance, as it does with gender, means to affirm the qualities and characteristics of powerlessness.... [W]hen you are powerless, you don't just speak differently. A lot you don't speak." MacKinnon, *Feminism Unmodified*, 39. "Take your foot off our necks, then we will hear in what tongue women speak," Ibid. at 45. See generally, Spivak, "Can the Subaltern Speak?"

    On the authenticity of slave narratives, see Yellin, *Harriet Jacobs: A Life*, and Eric Gardner, "You Have No Business."

6. See generally James C. Scott, *Weapons of the Weak*.

7. By comparison, Proquest yields 166 documents under the search string "slaves and slavery, lawsuits, and petitions to southern county courts." The 166 are divided geographically: 51 from St. Louis; 48 from Louisiana, of which are from Orleans Parrish; 19 from Jefferson County, Kentucky; 7 from the District of Columbia; 4 from Fayette County, Kentucky; and 4 from Jones County, Georgia. Loren Schweninger's remarkable database, the Digital Library on American Slavery, provides many more documents under the search string "freedom suits," but a small percentage of them are actual lawsuits brought by slaves; many more are petitions to legislatures often brought by slave owners.

8. *Dred Scott v. Sandford*, 60 U.S. 393 (1857).

    Slave voice is not present in cases like *Prigg v. Pennsylvania*, 41 U.S. 539 (1842), because the case is the criminal prosecution of the slave master. The enslaved person is not even a party to the lawsuit.

9. See, for example, Vincent C. Hopkins, *Dred Scott's Case*, v–vii.

10. VanderVelde, *Mrs. Dred Scott*, 11–12. Recognizing Harriet as a primary party in interest provides a better understanding of the motivations and interests at stake in this lawsuit, specifically the right to claim the Scotts' daughters as slaves or to see them free.

11. Johnson, *Soul by Soul*, 12.

12. Eliza Tyler did not delay even a day. *Eliza Tyler v. Nelson Campbell*, CC case no. 35 (1835).

13. The Latin phrase, *Partus sequitur ventrem* was the name of the legal doctrine that the slave status of a child was determined by the mother's status. Finkelman, "Crime of Color," 2085. Goodell, *The American Slave Code*, 27. Hurd, *The Law of Freedom and Bondage*, 211.

14. Developed in VanderVelde, *Mrs. Dred Scott*, 230–231. Frazier, *Runaway and Freed Missouri Slaves*, 93.

15. VanderVelde, *Mrs. Dred Scott*, 395 n. 76; Frazier, *Runaway and Freed Missouri Slaves*, 93.

16. See list of cases in the bibliography. See list of freedom suits dismissed for failure to prosecute in chapter 14, n. 26.

17. For example, *Leah v. Mitchell*, CC case no. 68 (1832) was dismissed by Leah herself acting voluntarily, presumably because she had reached some accommodation with her putative master.

18. Freedom suits appealed to the Missouri Supreme Court include: *Winny v. Whitesides aka Prewitt*, 1 Mo. 473 (1824); *LaGrange aka Isidore v. Chouteau*, 2 Mo. 20 (1828); *Hay v. Dunky*, 3 Mo. 588 (1834); *Meechum v. Judy aka Julia Logan, a woman of color*, 4 Mo. 361 (1836); *Paca v. Dutton*, 4 Mo. 371 (1836); *Randolph v. Alsey, a colored person*, 8 Mo. 656 (1844); *Gabriel Chouteau v. Pierre*, 9 Mo. 3 (1845); *Charlotte v. Chouteau I*, 2 Mo. 465 (1847); *Scott v. Emerson*, 15 Mo. 576 (1852); *Charlotte v. Chouteau II*, 21 Mo. 590 (1855); *Charlotte v. Chouteau III*, 25 Mo. 465 (1857); *Mary Charlotte v. Gabriel S. Chouteau IV*, 33 Mo. 194 (1862).

19. The Missouri statute titled "Freedom: An Act to Enable Persons held in Slavery to Sue for their Freedom" was enacted January 27, 1835. Before 1835, some damage awards exceeded $100. Afterward, even a trespass case resulted in the award of a single penny.

20. These figures are based upon probate inventories of some St. Louis estates during this period. See, for example, Trexler's use of probate data to determine slave value. Trexler, *Slavery in Missouri*.

21. For example, when Winny successfully sued Samuel Donner for freedom, a secondary suit occurred between Donner and Jennings Beckwith. *Samuel Danner* [*sic*] *v. Jenings* [*sic*] *Beckwith* CC case no. 1446 (1818); *Jennings Beckwith v. Samuel Donner, aka, Danner,* Chancery court case no. 5625 (1819); *Winny v. Samuel Donner,* CC case no. 70 (1820). When Eliza Tyler established her freedom against Nelson Campbell, Campbell subsequently sued Perry Bark, William Hempstead, and others, from whom Campbell had purchased Eliza. See chapter 10.

22. For accounts of the rule's development in eastern states, see Ablavsky, "Making Indians 'White,'" 1494–1517; Gillmer, "Suing for Freedom," 601.

23. Ariela Gross and others have demonstrated that the degree of blackness and racial performance was part of the freedom suits concerning mistaken identity in southern states' suits. Gross, *What Blood Won't Tell*; Gillmer, "Suing for Freedom." This issue was not raised in the St. Louis freedom suits. Degree of blackness and racial performance did arise in suits involving the privileges of free persons of color in St. Louis. See Vandervelde, *Mrs. Dred Scott*, 245, 302.

24. *Winny v. Samuel Donner,* CC case no. 70 (1820); *Gabriel v. Andrew Christy, executor; Mary Coons, executrix,* CC case no. 324 (Nov. 1846); *Jane McCray v. William Hopkins, et al.,* CC case no. 162 (1845). The fourth litigant, John Merry, alleged that he had an agreement to purchase his liberty, but in the end he prevailed on his residence in free territory. See chapter 6.

   A remarkably large number of slaves were able to purchase their freedom without legal controversy. This suggests that agreements between slaves and their masters to self-purchase did not generate very many freedom cases, unlike in some more notable instances in the South.

25. Christopher Phillips describes conversions from slavery for life to slavery for a term of years as a sort of partial manumission to a state of "quasi-freedom." Phillips, *Freedom's Port*, 30–56.

26. Andrew Fede describes this as the process in many southern states. Fede, *Roadblocks to Freedom*, 139–143.

27. The Revised Code of the Laws of Virginia, "An Act providing for the Re-publication of the Laws of this Commonwealth," passed March 12, 1819.

28. See chapter 5.

29. For an excellent account, see Jones, "Time, Space, and Jurisdiction."

30. Missouri statute outlawing anyone advocating abolition. 1837 Missouri Statute, "An Act to Prohibit the Publication, Circulation, or Promulgation of the Abolition Doctrines."

31. See, for example, Attorney Edward Bates, who represented both slave plaintiffs like Lucy Delaney, and slave owners like the Duncans, owned slaves himself.

32. Delaney, "From the Darkness," 42.

33. Keir Nash identified these three issues as follows: first, the "comparative exploitativeness" of U.S. and Latin American slavery; second, the debate over the "repressible conflict vs. the irrepressible conflict" in the Civil War's origins; and third, the shift from legal formalism to legal instrumentalism during the period from Yorktown to the early nineteenth-century and back to formalism before the end of that century. Nash, "Reason of Slavery," 12–13.

   Finkelman, *Imperfect Union*, demonstrates that increasing lapses of judicial interstate comity were contributing causes of the Civil War.

   Typical of this sort of scholarship is the question, were punishments of slaves more severe than punishments of sailors, or than punishments of convicted criminals? Attempting to evaluate different slave states to produce a linear array from most humane to most inhumane by criteria of issue recognition, Keir Nash came up with several issues upon which state supreme courts can be ranked as either pro- or antislavery. The odd thing about this rating system is that there is no understanding of the role that path dependence plays in reaching a particular result. There is no assessment of which of the fifteen issues is more or less important than others to human survival or flourishing or group organization. Tennessee, which by Nash's ranking scores best on humane issues in slavery, appears to have been no nearer to abolishing the institution at the beginning of the Civil War than Virginia, which scores much lower. Nash, *Radical Interpretations*, 302–309; Nash, *Reason of Slavery*; Nash, "Fairness and Formalism" 76–81.

34. Mclaurin's work was an exception for its focus on the trial phase in a murder case. See Mclaurin, *Celia, a Slave*.

35. Schafer, *Becoming Free*. More recently, Jason Gillmer focused upon freedom suits in Gillmer, "Suing for Freedom." Ariela Gross mentions freedom suits in *What Blood Won't Tell*, 1–75.

36. Higginbotham and Higginbotham, "Yearning to Breathe Free"; Higginbotham and Kopytoff, "Property First, Humanity Second." Professor Taunya Banks called our attention to Elizabeth Keys' freedom suit in her article, "Dangerous Woman."

37. Russell drew upon Catterall's five-volume compendium, but he never provided the list of cases identified as freedom cases, nor the grounds on which he claimed that the slaves won their freedom. There is no definitive list of final judgments. Russell, "American Slave Discontent," 418–419.

    One of the few sources of published jury verdicts is Cranch's reports of the District of Columbia for 1801–1841. Because Cranch was both judge and reporter of that bench, he frequently included information on jury verdicts.

38. Russell, "American Slave Discontent," 418–419. Quoted again in Konig, "Long Road," 59 n. 86. Appellate lawsuits do not reliably reveal numbers about whether the litigating slave received freedom, because many of them result in remand rather than outright judgments of freedom. So, it is actually impossible to derive accurate data about freedom outcomes from appellate sources alone.

    Other scholars included discussions of freedom suits as one component of other discussions of courts, slaves, race, and ideology. Keir Nash examined "suits for freedom" as one component in an analysis of judicial attitudes in appellate opinions. Nash, "Reason of Slavery," 98–104. Nash deploys suits for freedom together with manumission cases as evidence of differences of judicial attitudes toward race and slavery. Ibid. See also Nash, "Fairness and Formalism." Andrew Fede discusses freedom suits in one chapter of his excellent work on manumission in the South. Fede, *Roadblocks to Freedom*, 1–34.

39. See, for example, Tushnet, *American Law of Slavery*.

40. Marion Russell, for example, relied on Catterall in reaching his 57 percent estimate.

41. But see Schafer, *Becoming Free*, and Loren Schweninger's database, Digital Library on American Slavery.

42. Some began as suits of foreclosure by creditors upon their debtors' slaves. These lawsuits sometimes led to freedom suits when black servants, who creditors attempted to levy upon, could prove in a freedom suit that they were free rather than property of the creditors' debtor. See, for example, *Catharine; Felix; William; Minta, persons of color v. Thomas Hundley; D. Pattison; William Russell*, CC case no. 20 (1843). Most of the 300 did not originate that way, however.

43. Missouri had distinctive regions, like the Missouri Valley, that were economically organized like the southern states. That region even acquired the name "Little Dixie" for its plantation culture. See generally Hurt, *Agriculture and Slavery*.

44. During the Civil War, Missouri engaged in a prolonged state of conflict about whether or not to secede.

45. Contemporary newspapers and books that described St. Louis inevitably stressed its "westernness," even in their choices of names. See, for example, Edwards and Hopewell's 1860 publication about St. Louis titled *Edwards's Great West and Her Commercial Metropolis*. Newspapers included "The Western Banner," "Westliche Post," and "Anzeiger Des Westens."

46. Letter of Judge Stuart to the Secretary of State (Feb. 13, 1813) reprinted in Illinois Territorial Papers, 299.

47. There was no direct path of communication or transport to St. Louis from core southern states like the Carolinas, Georgia, and Alabama.

48. Frederick Jackson Turner, *Significance of the Frontier*. Jackson has been extensively criticized for his optimistic portrayal of frontier communities as egalitarian. See Aron, *American Confluence* exploring these critiques.

49. Gitlin, et al., *Frontier Cities*, 197–198.

50. Banner, *Legal Systems in Conflict*, 85–100.

51. *Somerset v. Stewart* (1772) 98 ER 499. *The Slave, Grace* (1827) 2 Hag Adm 94, 166 ER 179, 2 State Trials NS 273.

52. Nor was it a place of commodities exchange like some cities in the South. See, generally, Scharf, *History of St. Louis*, describing the city's economic base before 1840.

53. It could just as well have become the provisioner of slaves to the west at a crucial time in American history, and, in fact, it seems to have played that market role for military personnel stationed at western forts. See, e.g., *Rachel v. William Walker*, CC case no. 82 (1834). See also VanderVelde, *Mrs. Dred Scott*, 24, n. 13.

54. In New Orleans, petitioners basing freedom claims upon residence on free soil were more frequently slaves who had travelled to France than slaves who had travelled through the Northwest Territory. Schafer, *Becoming Free*, 15–16.

55. But surprisingly, slaves who moved between Maryland, Virginia, and the District of Columbia, all jurisdictions recognizing slavery, could sometimes claim freedom based upon that transfer. See Cranch Circuit Court cases from the District of Columbia. Freedom suits were generated by Maryland and District of Columbia statutes barring the introduction or "importation" of slaves from other states. See, e.g., *Negro Sylvia v. Coryell*, 1 Cranch C.C.32 (1801) and *Negro William Foster v. Simmons*, (1806). I thank Professor Will Thomas for introducing me to the cases in the Cranch reports.

56. Once Missouri concluded that they had too many slaves, they looked to recolonization not farther west, but to Africa. Later, St. Louis editorials urged southerners to keep their slaves home and stop sending them to Missouri.

57. See chapter 12, The Slaves of Milton Duty. St. Louis was also the site of a few other large-scale manumissions, but *Preston, et al. v. George W. Coons*, CC case file 674 (November 1841), was the only case that generated a freedom suit generated by a large scale manumission.

58. Berlin and Morgan, *Cultivation and Culture*, 77.

59. Buchanan, *Black Life on the Mississippi*, 3–18.

60. VanderVelde, *Mrs. Dred Scott*, 179, 196.

61. See chapter 12. On Milton Duty's last fateful steamboat voyage, he carried bank notes issued by one state that he wished to convert into another state's currency.

62. Banner, *Legal Systems in Conflict*, 96.

63. See, for example, Genovese, *Roll, Jordan, Roll*.

64. Aron, *American Confluence*, 106–147 "The State of Missouri shifted from *being* a frontier to *having* frontier." Ibid, xxi. (emphases in original.); Arenson, *Great Heart*, 28–29; Gitlin et al., *Frontier Cities*, 162.

65. See Salafia, *Slavery's Borderland*.

66. This has been recognized since William Blackstone's *Commentaries*. "[C]ourts of justice are instituted in every civilized society, in order to protect the weak from insults of the stronger, by expounding and enforcing those laws, by which rights are defined and wrongs prohibited." Blackstone, *Commentaries on the Laws of England*, Book III, 2.

67. Nor is the tensile strength of law tested when law simply organizes political pressures. The functional usefulness of the organizing principle encourages compliance rather than invites opposition. Rules that require one to file certain papers rather than others, or, for example, to drive on the right side of the road rather than the left, invite no organized opposition.

68. Bowditch, *Rendition of Anthony Burns*; Jackson and McDonald, *Finding Freedom*; Baker, *Rescue of Joshua Glover*; Cover, *Justice Accused*; Houston, "Another Nullification Crisis."

69. Similarly "corrective," many Maryland slaves sought to advance freedom claims by tying their ancestry to a white, indentured servant grandmother or great grandmother. Whitman, *Price of Freedom*, 63. Fede, *Roadblocks to Freedom*.

70. Only two cases are clearly of that type: *Elsa Hicks v. Patrick T. McSherry*, CC case no. 121 (1847), and *Jane McCray v. William R. Hopkins, et al.*, CC case no. 162 (1845). (When the plaintiff failed to appear and defaulted, the defendants permitted it to be reinstated with the language: "Suit is amicable in its character." CCRB, Feb 21, 1849.) It is also possible that the suit between two putative brothers, *Vincent v. Jerry, a free person of color*, CC case no. 14 (1829), was an amicable suit.

71. Legislative efforts to limit the number of free Blacks in St. Louis can be seen in the law requiring free Blacks to register and be licensed to reside in St. Louis.

72. Blackstone's *Commentaries*, Book 3, chapter 1.

73. *Winny v. Phebe Whitsides,* CC case file no. 190 (1821); *Winny v. Whitesides alias Prewitt,* 1 Mo. 472 (1824).
74. All cases in this book were litigated in St. Louis with the exception of Peter McNelly's case, the earliest case based on the Northwest Ordinance, which is addressed in chapter 1.
75. See generally Catterall, *Judicial Cases.*
76. Ibid.
77. *Laws of the Territory of Louisiana, Chapter 35, Freedom:* "An Act to enable Persons held in Slavery, to Sue for their Freedom" (June 27, 1807), section 4.
78. *Dred Scott v. Sandford,* 60 U.S. 393 (1857).
79. Ibid. VanderVelde, *Mrs. Dred Scott,* 305–319.
80. The first statute establishing the procedure for freedom suits for the Missouri Territory was titled "An Act to enable Persons held in Slavery, to Sue for their Freedom" (June 27, 1807).

Chapter 2 Peter's Dual Redemption

1. Philbrick, "Law, Courts, and Litigation," 14–15 (discussing Vanderburgh's involvement but not giving the year or the petitioner's name).
2. Dunn, *Indiana: A Redemption,* 454; Dunn, *Indiana and Indianans,* 47; Esarey, *History of Indiana.*
3. Finkelman, *Imperfect Union,* 17.
4. Francis S. Philbrick's introduction to *Laws of the Illinois Territory*; Philbrick, *Laws of the Indiana Territory.* For dates of appointment, see *Territorial Papers of the United States,* vol. 7.
5. Finkelman, *An Imperfect Union,* 85 n. 53, noting that Philbrick attributed the case to Judge Symmes.
6. Gaskell, "Illinois Legal Research."
7. Letters and telephone calls between Lea VanderVelde, reference librarian John Bergstrom, and the Indiana State Archives, Indiana Historical Society, Regional Office of National Archives, Indiana Supreme Court.
8. For example, in the 1880's it was very popular to publish county histories in Illinois. In most of these accounts only the earliest French importation of slaves was mentioned, and almost all of the men who had resided in the county were described as anti-slavery men. In addition, the concept of slavery was mentioned more often than the actual practice within the state's borders. See, e.g., *Counties of Cumberland, Jasper, and Richland, Illinois,* Chicago: F.A. Battey & Co. 1884.
9. *The Case of Mary Clark, A Woman of Colour,* 1 Blackf. 122, 125–26 (Ind. 1821).
10. *Peter McNelly v. Henry Vanderburgh* (Vincennes 1794).
11. The finding aid states, "Little is known of the manner in which English acquired his manuscripts." "Guide to the William H. English Collection 1762–1895," http://www.lib.uchicago.edu/e/scrc/findingaids/view.php?eadid=ICU.SPCL.ENGLISH. Another website states that William H. English was a member of the House of Representatives from 1852 to 1860 and the Democratic party's candidate for the vice presidency in 1880. Before his death in 1896, he had written *The Conquest of the Northwest & the Life of George R. Clark,* and his unpublished manuscript, which traces the history of Indiana to approximately the year 1800.
12. This partial manuscript resides in the collection in its original manual typewriter and pencil-marked form. William H. English Collection 1762–1895, University of Chicago Library http://bmrcsurvey.uchicago.edu/collections/1506.
13. I found the William H. English Collection through reading the footnotes of a wonderful compendium of information by Dexter, *Bondage in Egypt.* I was looking for clues for the next earliest case, one involving William Henry Harrison and Simon VanOsdal, which I knew to be the first case *after* 1800. Although I had copies of the freedom case against VanOsdal from Indiana, William H. English had taken some of the documents of that litigation into his papers as well, and Darrell Dexter had found them and cited them in his book about Illinois slavery. Dexter also deserves the credit for first discovering the cases of *Peter McNelly v. Vanderburgh* in the William English Collection. Dexter, *Bondage in Egypt,* 142–44, 164. When I read Dexter's footnotes, I could not get to the University of Chicago library soon enough.

14. William H. English Collection.

15. I thank the late Robert Fogel, University of Chicago Professor Emeritus, and his team for finding this document.

16. White, "Subordination."

17. Revolutionary War Pension file of Peter Mcanelly [*sic*], Indiana Number 13923.

18. Ibid. He "was marched to Richmond under the chief orders of Gen'l Wilson, when the british [*sic*] under Cornwallis he believes, had possession of Manchester [t]hat after some time the said Regiment under Col'l [*sic*] White was ordered from Richmond to York."

19. Peter McNelly was then in Captain Johnson's unit, according to his pension file.

20. I have been unable to definitively locate records of an Anthony Thompson who would have owned or at least claimed Peter.

21. The Indiana Territory was created by act of Congress, May 7, 1800.

22. Chief Justice Marshall would later say "in occupancy" of the region. *Johnson v. M'Intosh*, 21 U.S. (8 Wheat.) 543 (1823).

23. Indiana historical sources document Indian raids on settlements. See, for example, entries in the messages and letters of William Henry Harrison, Indiana Historical Collections Governors' Messages and Letters, vol. 1, 1800–1811 (1922).

24. Deposition of Peter McNelly given before Judge George Turner, Knox County, Territory of the United States Northwest of the Ohio, June 7, 1794, William H. English Collection, Special Collections Research Center, University of Chicago Library.

25. Revolutionary War pension petition of Peter McNelly.

26. Even with the man's name, Peter Smith, it has been impossible to identify this individual.

27. This was first fort to be called Fort Knox, rather than the now more famous Fort Knox. This fort is usually referred to by local historians as Fort Knox I. It was located at the present-day intersection of First and Buntin Streets in Vincennes. During the relative peace with both the British and the Indians from 1787 to 1803, Fort Knox was the westernmost American military outpost.

28. Deposition of Henry Vanderburgh, September 30,1794.

29. Taylor, *Biographical Annals of Ohio*, 136.

30. Deposition of Peter McNelly, June 7, 1794.

31. Burnet, *Notes*.

32. Monks, et al., *Courts and Lawyers of Indiana*.

33. Deposition of Peter McNelly, June 7, 1794.

34. Dubois carried a slave of Buntin from Vincennes to Kaskaskia for reassignment or sale. *Judy v. John Berry Meachum*, CC case no. 11 (1835). He also took messages from the Detroit fur trader John Askin to his lawyer at Vincennes for legal proceedings. John Askin Collection, Burton Library, University of Michigan.

35. Deposition of Joseph Baird, June 30, 1794.

36. Ibid.

37. Each was to receive 45 livres a piece, equal at Vincennes to $11.25. Dubois arranged to pay two of those assistants, and Baird was to pay the other one.

38. LaMotte was also an Indian interpreter employed by the United States.

39. Deposition of Peter McNelly, June 7, 1794.

40. Deposition of Joseph Baird, June 30, 1794.

41. Ibid.

42. Deposition of Toussaint Dubois, August 11, 1794.

43. Deposition of Peter McNelly, June 7, 1794.

44. Ibid.

45. Deposition of Joseph Baird, June 30, 1794.

46. Deposition of Peter McNelly, June 7, 1794.

47. Ibid.

48. The man who took Queen was identified as Richard Levins of Kentucky, a constable for Jefferson County. Deposition of Joseph Baird, June 30, 1794.

49. Ibid.

50. Original notes of Judge Turner, William H. English Collection.
51. Letter from Judge Turner to Governor St. Clair, Vincennes, June 14, 1794. St. Clair, *St. Clair Papers*, vol. 2, 325.
52. Ibid.
53. Ibid., 325–326.
54. Deposition of Joseph Baird, June 30, 1794.
55. Deposition of Joseph LaMotte, no date available.
56. Ibid.
57. Toussaint Dubois later transported the enslaved woman, Judy from Indiana to Illinois. She later sued for freedom in St. Louis. *Judy v. Barry Meachum*, CC case no. 11 (1835).
58. Judge Turner to Governor St. Clair. Vincennes [*sic*], June 14, 1794. St. Clair, *St. Clair Papers*, vol. 2, 325–26.
59. Fehrenbacher, *Slaveholding Republic*, 256–57.
60. Letter of Governor St. Clair to Judge Turner, Dec. 14, 1794. St. Clair, *St. Clair Papers*, vol. 2, 331.
61. Argument of Barthelemi Tardiveau to Governor St. Clair, June 30, 1789.
62. "[W]hereas, on the other hand, had the Constitution the effect to liberate those persons who were slaves by the former laws, as no compensation is provided to their owners, it would be an act of the Government arbitrarily depriving a part of the people of a part of their property— an attempt that has not been made and would not be submitted to, and is not to be drawn from the mere construction of words." Letter from Governor St. Clair to Judge Turner, Dec. 14, 1794. St. Clair, *St. Clair Papers*, vol. 2, 331.
63. Ibid.
64. Ibid., 331–332.
65. Barthelemi Tardiveau to Arthur St. Clair, June 30, 1789. Alvord, *Kaskaskia Records*, 488, 493, 503–509.
    Memorial by Barthelemi Tardiveau, July 8, 1788. "Many of the inhabitants of these districts have Slaves, and Some have no other property but Slaves. If they wish to preserve their property, they must transport themselves to the Spanish Side of the Mississippi; but if they do, they shall lose the lands granted them by Congress. One law tells them: leave the country, or ye shall forfeit your negroes: the other Saith; Stay in the country, or your lands shall be taken from you."
66. *Turner v. Prior.* "The threats which you are pleased to menace me with I heartily despise as well as the author who pened [*sic*] them and the people you talk of can exist nowhere but in your own distemperence brain." Letter of Abner Prior to Judge Turner, in the William H. English Collection.
67. Deposition of Stephen Ashby, June 8, 1794.
68. Sheriff's return, case file of *Peter McNelly v. Henry Vanderburgh*.
69. St. Clair's biographer, William Henry Smith, is quite critical of Judge Turner: "Previously court had met both in Cahokia and Kaskaskia, Judge Turner, who was arrogant and dictatorial in the extreme, succeeded, both at Post Vincennes and Kaskaskia, in putting every body by the ears, and necessitated the active interference of the Governor to quiet the storm. He proposed having Henry Vanderburgh, judge of probate and justice, impeached for some informality in the administration of office; and in the Mississippi country he removed William St. Clair, clerk of the court of St. Clair county, for presuming to keep the records of the court at Cahokia instead of Kaskaskia. The Governor, in order to accommodate the inhabitants, had provided that the courts should be held at stated periods, at three different places, and the clerk of the court, in the same spirit, kept the books of record at Cahokia, where they were accessible to the greatest number of landowners. But Judge Turner, without authority, directed that Kaskaskia should be the only county seat, and, without waiting for an explanation, in the most arbitrary manner, commanded the clerk to produce the books, within twelve hours, at that place. He also, without authority, appointed a Mr. Jones assistant clerk, and placed the books in his possession." St. Clair, *St. Clair Papers*, vol. 2, 346, 372.
70. 5 *Annals of Cong.* 1338 (1796). See also Davis, *Judge George Turner*.
71. Peter claimed that he remained in Knox County, Indiana, for the rest of his life and that he joined the Cumberland Presbyterian Church. Deposition of Peter McNelly in Revolutionary War Pension application. Peter sued a man for debt in Vincennes records, *Peter McNelly*

v. Samuel Gregory, seeking to recover $100 in damages. McNelly claimed that he was owed $50 for certain services he had performed for Gregory. The case was eventually dismissed.

72. The 1840 U.S. Federal Census, for Knox Country, Indiana lists Peter McNelly and an un-named Black woman. Both are between the ages of 55 and 99 years old.

73. Indiana counties were named after both Vanderburgh and Dubois. Each county history in-cludes an account of their namesakes as heroes of the War of 1812 and the battles against Tecumseh. See Elliott, *History of Evansville*; Wilson, *History of Dubois County*.

Chapter 3 The Three Daughters of Marie Scypion

1. Freedom: An Act to enable Persons held in Slavery to Sue for their Freedom (January 27, 1835).

2. Ibid. at § 12: "If the plaintiff be a negro or mulatto, he is required to prove his right to freedom."

3. There is only one instance of a slave purporting to sign her own name (see discussion of Milly in Chapter 7).

4. Sailing from France, Philip Francois Renault in 1719 brought 200 mechanics, miners, and laborers to the New World. Stopping at the island of San Domingo, he secured 500 Negro slaves to work in the mines. They were the first slaves in Illinois. McDonough, et al., *Combined History*. Descendants of these slaves trafficked from San Domingo continued to populate Prairie du Rocher for generations. Brown, *History as They Lived It*.

5. Foley, "Slave Freedom Suits," 2.

6. *Marguerite v. Chouteau*, 3 Mo. 540 (1834).

7. Fort Chartres was located near the village of Prairie du Rocher in Illinois. See generally Brown, *History as They Lived It*.

8. Foley, "Slave Freedom Suits," 3.

9. See Kinnaird, *Spain in the Mississippi Valley*, 172–79.

10. One of Pierre Chouteau's prime witnesses claimed that Marie Scypion's father had been of Indian heritage, and her mother an African, a distinction that would have rendered Marie Scy-pion and her children slaves. Deposition of Jacques Chauvin (Lucas trial notes 1806), William Foley, "Slave Freedom Suits," 10.

11. There were other reasons for the departure as well. Laclede, who had been given an exclusive franchise to trade with the Indians, encouraged the French colonists there to join him across the river, and the British were threatening to occupy the east bank of the Mississippi. William Foley, *The Genesis of Missouri*.

12. Technically, Tayon sold the gristmill to Laclede, who was the Chouteau family patriarch. The mill then passed from Laclede to stepson Auguste Chouteau, and then to his son Gabriel. Houck, *History of Missouri*, vol. 2, 28–29.

    Old Joseph Taillon, who lived on Main and Market Streets, had eight children. Being cho-sen one of the village syndics attested to his popularity and standing. The spelling of the fam-ily name was changed from Taillon to Tayon. Tayon's son Charles, a lieutenant in the militia company, became the first commandant at St. Charles. Stevens, *St. Louis: The Fourth City*, vol. 2, 666. See also Houck, *History of Missouri*, vol. 2, 9 n. 23.

13. Stevens, *St. Louis: The Fourth City*, vol. 1, 406.

14. See chapter 13.

15. VanderVelde, *Mrs. Dred Scott*, 296 n. 44; *New York Times*, December 22, 1895.

16. "All inhabitants and residents of this province are informed that the wise and just laws of His Majesty very expressly forbid any subject of any quality or condition whatsoever to make any Indian a slave or to possess any such, under any pretext whatever, even though there be an open war against that Indian's nation. In consequence whereof, all subjects of His Majesty, and even all transients, are expressly forbidden to acquire, purchase, or take over any Indian slave, beginning from the day of publication of this order. The present owners of the aforesaid slaves are also informed that they shall be unable to part with those they now have in any manner whatsoever, except to give them back their liberty, until receipt of orders from His Majesty." *Spain in the Mississippi Valley*, American Historical Association, *Annual Report*, vol. II, 125–26, edited by Kinnaird.

17. Brown, *History as They Lived It*, 51.
18. There were 339 Creole families (American-born people of French or Spanish descent), along with 33 free blacks and 274 Native American and African slaves. The full list of declared Indian slaves can be found in Kinnaird, *Spain in the Mississippi Valley*, 172–79.
19. By 1772, the total population of St. Louis was 497, of whom almost half, 198, were slaves. Ekberg, *Stealing Indian Women*, 61. See also account of Joseph Tayon, resident, on July 18, 1770, American Historical Association, *Annual Report*, vol. II; Kinnaird, *Spain in the Mississippi Valley*, "The Revolutionary Period, 1765–1781"; Scharf, *History of Saint Louis City*.
20. The breakdown is as follows: 681 whites, 55 mulattoes, 6 free Negroes, and 268 slaves. From the 1799 Census of De Lassus, available in American Historical Association, *Annual Report*, vol. II; Kinnaird, *Spain in the Mississippi Valley*.
21. With the destruction of many of the original case files of the Scypion sisters' litigation, the best existing documentation can be found in the Missouri Supreme Court Database, where the depositions, documents and testimony were transcribed on appeal.

    Unfortunately, William Foley and I have been informed that the documentation in the Jefferson County Courts, the venue to which the St. Louis cases were transferred, was destroyed. Professor Foley was the last person to read the original material before it was destroyed.
22. Foley, "Slave Freedom Suits."
23. Tayon's family tree is documented in Beckwith, *Creoles of St. Louis*.
24. It was customary to assign a slave child to work at the age of eight and common to assign the child away to a new household to learn the tasks of work. Between ages seven and eight, a slave child moved from nursery status to assume small work tasks. This young worker could then be separated from his or her mother, given away, or sold. Neal, *Unburdened by Conscience*, 123.
25. Helene and Marie-Louise Tayon served as godmothers in the baptisms of several Indian servant children according to papers in the Drouin collection.
26. Early U.S. French Catholic Church Records, Drouin Collection. Marie Scypion's descendants appeared in the church registry by name, age, and relation, due to these mistresses' efforts. By comparison, Chouteau family slaves were often only referred to coldly by status and gender, without even a name of their own.
27. Little's Administrator v. Chauvin, 1 Mo. 626 (1826).
28. Ibid.
29. Pelagie Kiersereau, the daughter of Marie-Josephe Tayon Kiersereau, was raised by her grandparents, the Tayons, after her parents died, Beckwith, *Creoles of St. Louis*. She married Pierre Chouteau, bore him four children and then died.

    Like his brother, Auguste Chouteau, Pierre Chouteau had an elegant domicile. "He, too, occupied a whole square with his mansion, bounded on the east by Main street, ... the whole square being enclosed with high solid stone walls and having port-holes, in like manner as his brother's." Stevens, *St. Louis" The Fourth City*, vol. 1, 88.
30. Although the tie of affection linking Joseph Tayon to his granddaughter was stronger because she had grown up in his household, she too was now dead. See note 29.
31. Helene Chevalier was much younger than her husband. He received a land grant from the French crown for service in warfare, but by the time he had married Helene, he was well on in years. After he died, Helene moved her household from her husband's land near the city of St. Louis to the town of St. Charles, slightly upriver from St. Louis, where her brother Charles Tayon retained considerable authority. In 1804, Veuve (or Widow) Chevalier as she was called still owned part of block 86 of the city of St. Louis. Scharf, *The History of St. Louis*, vol. 1, 148.

    The town of St. Charles at this time had fewer than 100 families, according to Houck.

    The division of M. Chevalier's estate was determined according to the prenuptial marriage contract that the betrothed couple's parents had entered into twenty years earlier. The Chevalier marriage had been sealed with a 1774 marriage contract. The contract was made between Louis Chevalier, (sometimes spelled Chevallier,) merchant voyager, son of Louis Chevallier and Mary Reaume, and Helene Michel Tayon; daughter of Joseph Michel Tayon and Marie-Louise Bosset of St. Louis.

32. San Luis de Ilineuses, December 22, 1780. Louis Chevalier's entry is "Luis Chavalie; 32; Canada; Habitant," Louis Houck, *The Spanish Regime in Missouri*, vol. 1, 185 (1909).

    Louis Chevalier, who came from Cahokia, was "well versed in the language of the Indians," and for his services in this expedition the governor of Louisiana was ordered by the King to bestow on him an appropriate "gratification," which meant a grant of land. Houck, *The Spanish Regime in Missouri*, vol. 1, 191 n. 36.

    As governor of the territory, Charles was sometimes referred to under the Spanish title of "Don Carlos Tayon." Charles and her late husband were close friends, before her marriage. They served together in the army, and both received recognition from the Spanish governors. Louis Chevalier was designated godfather for Charles's son. Houck, *History of Missouri*, vol. 2, 42–43.

33. Foley, "Slave Freedom Suits," 6.

34. According to baptismal records, "Early U.S. French Catholic Church Records (Drouin Collection), 1695–1954. In Piernas's original survey conducted for Governor O'Reilly in 1770, Dame Chouteau declared that she owned two Indian slaves: Therese and Manon. Kinnaird, *Spain in the Mississippi Valley*, 173.

35. Foley, "Slave Freedom Suits," 6; Foley, *Genesis of Missouri*, 118.

36. Foley, *Genesis of Missouri*, 188.

37. Houck, *History of Missouri*, vol. 2, 199. "Appeals were not common and those who made them could have no other object in view than the reversal of erroneous judgments."

38. Joseph Tayon died in 1807 at the age of 92.

39. Foley, "Slave Freedom Suits," 17 (citing depositions of Auguste Chouteau and Bernard Pratte).

40. This is a Native American–African American variation on a theme developed by Ariela Gross. Gross, *What Blood Won't Tell*, 13, 44, 88, 100, 106, 163, 297 (discussing racial performance in order to determine the predominant racial category for an enslaved person).

41. *Black's Law Dictionary* (9th ed., 2009), 778, defines habeas corpus as follows: "A writ employed to bring a person before a court, most frequently to ensure that the person's imprisonment or detention is not illegal (habeas corpus ad subjiciendum)."

42. *Marguerite v. Chouteau* (II), 3 Mo. 540 (1834).

43. Foley, "Slave Freedom Suits," cites *U.S. v. Chevalier* and *U.S. v. Chauvin*, October 30, 1805. Celeste and Catiche were released in habeas corpus proceedings.

44. *U.S. v. Francois Tayon*, Nov. 5, 1805.

45. Deed of Joseph Tayon to Pierre Chouteau, Joseph Tayon Sr. Sale of Slaves to Pierre Chouteau Sr. This document is in the Chouteau Collection at the Missouri History Museum's Archives. Original is in French. Translation by C. David Rice.

46. Foley, "Slave Freedom Suits," 10.

47. See definition of habeas corpus in note 41. A similar circumstance of habeas corpus as a revolving door occurred in St. Louis when two courts disputed whether an individual should be held in jail or released. Vander Velde, *Mrs. Dred Scott*, 266.

48. In those several big auctions, most buyers of French-speaking slaves, whether at closed sale or public sale, were other members of the extended Chouteau family. At the deaths of Auguste Chouteau and later his widow Therese Cerre Chouteau, large numbers of slaves were sold to someone in the extended family. See, for example, the probate file of Auguste Chouteau (1829), and that of his wife, Marie-Therese Cerre Chouteau (1842), both in St. Louis Probate Court files, on the web at http://www.sos.mo.gov/archives/mojudicial/stl_history.asp.

49. Joseph Tayon's son Charles had served in the army under the Spanish with Louis Chevalier. Don Louis Chevalier, as he was referred to by the Spanish, was a lieutenant, and Don Carlos Tallon, his sublieutenant. Letter of Fernando D. Leyba to Senior Don Bernardo de Galvez, July 15, 1779, in American Historical Association, *Annual Report*, vol. II, Kinnaird, ed. *Spain in the Mississippi Valley*, 247–48. Don Luis Chevalier was deemed "a person versed in the languages of the Indians" by Francois Cruzat in his letter to Senor Don Esteban Miro. He and Don Carlos Tayon engaged in an expedition together and were commended for actions. Ibid., 431. Letter of August 6, 1781.

50. Account of the sales in 1806 is reproduced at several places in the subsequent litigation.

51. Celeste's son Paul, initially sold to Pierre Chouteau, was later sold to Francois Tayon (who had once been given Marguerite). Celeste's daughter Sophie went to J. P. Cabanne (a Chouteau uncle by marriage), and her son Antoine to another Chouteau uncle, Sylvester Labaddie. Sylvester Labaddie married another Chouteau daughter.

52. Deposition of Madame Chauvin in transcript of *Marguerite v. Chouteau*, Missouri Supreme Court Database.

53. In 1811, Madame Chevalier sued Jean P. Cabanne in St. Louis court for replevin of Celeste. In 1813, Cabanne sued her brother Charles Tayon in foreclosure of a mortgage on Helene Chevalier's several slaves. In 1816, Helene Chevalier sued Pierre Chouteau for replevin of Celeste's oldest boy, Paul. In 1821, she sued Sylvester Labadie for attachment, presumably of a slave. In 1822, she sued the administrator of John Little's estate for replevin of Sophie and sought $1,000 in damages. She had the venue changed from St. Louis to her home of St. Charles for this case. In March 1822, a jury in St. Charles awarded Mme Chevalier $450 for the replevin of Sophia. Jury verdict. In *Helen Chevalier v. William Rector, administrator*, St. Charles Circuit Court Case Files—Civil, Box 31, Folder 36. Spreadsheet of St. Louis cases, case no. 1869, July 1811. In St. Charles County Circuit Court spreadsheet, case no. 12-28, case no. 30-26, and case no. 31-36. Given the condition of the records, this list of lawsuits may not be comprehensive. There may have been more.

54. The church records list: "Andre, Negre a Mad Chevalier, July 5, 1809, baptized Andre, son of William and Sophie, Negress of Md Chevalier, b. June 7, 1809. Godfather: Pascal Negre, and Godmother Marie, Mulatress." Andre was buried a week later July 12, 1829. Early U.S. French Catholic Church Records (Drouin Collection), 1695–1954, available at Ancestry.com.

55. The agreement between McGirk and Chevalier, Aug. 28, 1816. Copy contained in *McGirk v. Chauvin, administrator of Chevalier*, St. Louis Circuit Court case file 7416. There was no known Clarisse in the family chain. This may have been a misspelling of Celeste.

56. The 1821 city directory lists: Chouteau, Peter, sen., 124 North Main, above north E; Chouteau, Peter, Jr., fur merchant, 11 and dh 111 North Main; Chouteau, Auguste P., Indian trader, 94 North Main; Papin, Laforce, Indian Trader, 90 North Main, above north D; Labadie, Sylvester, north of the Brewery, which was also located on North Main.

57. *McGirk v. Chauvin*, administrator of Chevalier, 3 Mo. 237 (1833). Celeste's family, assessed at $1,500, comprised the majority of Helene Chevalier's $1,581 estate. Probate of Helene Chevalier's estate, inventory, July 31, 1823. Her probate is filed under "Chevallier" in the St. Louis Probate Court records.

58. Ibid.

59. Not only had Spain transferred its interest back to France in March 1804, the area was officially transferred to U.S. territory under the Louisiana Purchase. In 1821, Missouri entered the Union as a state under the Missouri Compromise.

60. The lineup was Celeste and her children, Auguste, Paul, Antoine, and Sophie, and Sophie's two children Edward and William versus the estate of Madame Chevalier. Catiche, (sometimes spelled Cartiche) Helen, Joseph, Julie, and Carmelite, and Carmelite's daughter Marie sued Pierre Chouteau, as did Marguerite and her four children, Antoine, Baptiste, Michael, and Francois. Cited as File 274, Jefferson Court Records, in Foley, "Slave Freedom Suits," 15 n. 54. *Celeste and her children & grandchildren v. Lefrenier J. Chauvin, adm. of H. Chevalier, dec.*, May 17, 1825, 466.

 Isaac C. McGirk presented one petition on behalf of Celeste and her children and grandchildren seeking to sue the administrator of Helen Chevalier's estate and he presented a similar petition for Cartiche alias Catherine, Julie, Joseph and Helen seeking to sue Pierre Chouteau. CCRB May 15, 1826. Several pleas were filed in the month of August 1825. *Baptiste, Michel, Antoine, Mary, Carmelite, Marguerite, Francois v. Pierre Chouteau*, Aug. 4, 1825, p. 199. *Edward v. Lefrenier Chauvin & others*, Aug. 5, 1825, p. 199. *William, Antoine, Celeste, Auguste, Paul, Sophia v. Lefreneir [sic] Chauvin, adm.*, Aug. 5, 1825, p. 200.

61. *Catiche alias Catherine, Julie, Joseph and Helen v. Pierre Chouteau, Sr.*, May 15, 1826, St. Louis Court Records; *Marguerite v. Chouteau*, 2 No. 71 (1828).

62. *Marguerite v. Chouteau,* (I) 2 Mo. 71 (1828) and *Marguerite v. Chouteau* (II), 3 Mo. 540 (1834).
63. *Catiche and Others v. The Circuit Court of St. Louis County,* 1 Mo. 608 (1826).
64. *McGirk v. Chauvin, Adm'r of Chevalier,* 3 Mo. 236 (1833).
65. *William v. Lefrenier Chauvin, Administrator; Charles Tayon; Pierre Chouteau, Sr., et al.,* Spreadsheet of St. Charles cases, case no. 39-12. Edward did not sue until seven years later. *Edward v. Administrator of Helene Chevalier,* CC case no. 46–33.
66. *Francois v. Pierre Chouteau Sr.,* St. Charles County case no. 42-22. *Michel v. Pierre Chouteau Sr.,* St. Charles County case no. 42–23.
67. Foley, "Slave Freedom Suits," 20.
68. As a result, two completely different enslaved persons, both named Celeste, sued the extended Chouteau family. In addition, two completely different persons, both named Marguerite, and two different Catiches or Catherines, sued the Chouteaus at roughly the same time. This second Celeste was the daughter of Judy who was brought from Vincennes. This Celeste had a sister Aspisa and children, Lewis and Andrew. This different Marguerite had a child named Marie on whose behalf she sued Auguste Chouteau in 1821. *Marie, a free mulatto girl, by next friend and mother, Marguerite v. Auguste Chouteau,* CC, case no. 205 (1821). There was also a different woman named Catiche similarly suing the Chouteaus: Theotiste aka Catiche lawsuits. *Theotiste v. Chouteau, Pierre, Jr.,* CC case no. 6 (1827); *State of Missouri v. Walker, John K. (jailor of St. Louis); Chouteau, Pierre; Pratt, Bernard; Amelin, Alexis,* CC case no. unavailable (March 1826). *Catiche, Helen, and Julie, persons of color v. Pierre Choteau,* May 25, 1826, p. 357. This Catiche's identity is distinguishable by telling a story of being born in Prairie du Rocher in 1782, sold to Barbeau, then to Manual Lisa, then sold from Manuel Lisa's estate to Chouteau. This Catiche has children: Julie, Joseph, and Helen.
69. Of Marie Scypion's grandchildren, Celeste's children were Antoine, Paul, and Sophie; and Sophie's children were Auguste and Edward; Catiche's children were Carmelite and a baby boy; and Marguerite's children were Antoine, Francois, Baptiste, Michel, and possibly Elizabethe.
70. Similarly differentiating the suits are different bases for claiming freedom. The two Celestes, the two Catiches, and the two Marguerites recite different chains of title. Marie Scypion's daughters sued based upon Indian ancestry, while the other Celeste, Marguerite, and Catiche based their suits on residence in Illinois. *Celeste v. LaForce Papin,* CC case no. 41 (1837); *Celeste v. Alexander Papin,* CC case no. 335 (1839); *Celeste, a minor, by and through her next friend, Judy v. William Sullivan,* CC case no. 42 (1837); *Theotiste alias Catiche v. Pierre Chouteau,* CC case no. 6 (1827).
71. Catiche petitioned the Jefferson County Court on November 22, 1828.
72. Foley, "Slave Freedom Suits."
73. *McGirk v. Chauvin, Adm'r of Chevalier,* 3 Mo. 236 (1833).
74. Although the Boone County records appear to be unavailable these facts are attested to in the suit of *McGirk v. Chauvin,* filed in St. Louis Circuit Court. Case number 143, case file 7416, St. Louis Circuit Court case files. The case transcript is available on-line in the Missouri Supreme Court Database.
75. According to the CCRB, McGirk gave notice of intent to sue Chevalier's estate on Sept. 15, 1830. Suit was filed in St. Louis Circuit Court in July 1831, *Matthias McGirk v. Lefrenier J. Chauvin,* suit for damages concerning ownership of Paul. St. Louis Circuit Court Case Index.
76. *McGirk v. Chauvin, Adm'r of Chevalier,* 3 Mo. 236 (1833).
77. *Marguerite v. Chouteau* (II), 3 Mo. 540 (1834).
78. Probate of Helene Tayon Chevalier, January 30, 1836. St. Louis Probate records. 00604 1823 C 27463, June 12, 1839.
79. Ibid.
80. Ibid. Dr. Millington's receipt contains such items as: "Extracting tooth for Boy;" "Powders and Cathartics (Neg Baby)." "Bleeding Neg Girl & Pills Neg Boy." "Calomiel [*sic*] and Castor Oil for boy and girls."
81. 1840 U.S. Census for St. Louis Township. Celeste Chevalier cannot be located in the 1850 census. The free black woman, named Celestine LaCompte, who is found there, is Judy LaCompte's

daughter and the petitioner in a different freedom suit: *Celeste v. Alexander Papin*, CC case no. 335 (1839), and previously *Celeste v. Laforce Papin*, CC case no. 41 (January 1837).

82. Contrary to my reading of the materials, Professor William Foley, who studied the cases most thoroughly before this account, concluded that Marguerite and Catiche survived, but Celeste died, citing the Jefferson County Circuit Court Records, which no longer exist. Shirley Christian relies on the Foley article. Christian, *Before Lewis and Clark*. None of Marie Scypion's children show up in the Free Negro Bonds, but because they were deemed Indian slaves rather than Negro slaves, they were not required to register.

83. He is mentioned consistently as a household servant in both the 1837 estate of her husband and her 1852 estate. Probate of Jacques Chauvin (1837) Inventory assesses Francois as about twenty-four years old. Probate of Marie-Louise Chauvin (1852) St. Louis Probate Files.

84. A child named Francois is included in the 1825 lawsuit of the Marguerite and Catiche families against Pierre Chouteau. Lefrenier Chauvin's 1846 probate contains five slaves, but none of the ages or names match up with the grandchildren of Marie Scypion. The Probate of LeFrenier Chauvin contains the following slaves: "Ned 50 yrs; Ann 28 yrs; Henry 8 yrs; Benjamin 5 yrs; Robert 2 yrs."

85. *Peggy Perryman v. Joseph Philibert*, CC case no. 255 (1848); *Nancy v. Enoch Steen*, CC case no. 4 (1848).

Chapter 4 Winny and Her Children

1. See Cotter, "The Somerset Case"; Oldham, "New Light on Mansfield."

2. The hypothesis framed by Frederick J. Turner maintained for decades that American identity was crafted by this movement of pioneers. Turner, "Significance of the Frontier."

3. Whiteside's station or Whiteside station was described as a family fort, five miles north of Waterloo. Smith, *A History of Southern Illinois*, 509. "The oldest permanently settled place in what is now Columbia precinct was Whiteside station. [A war between Indians and settlers] began in 1786, and continued till 1795.... The Whitesides and their early connections were born and raised on the frontiers of North Carolina...and immigrated to Kentucky." McDonough et al., *Combined History*, 449. In 1793, a band of emigrants from Kentucky, including the Whiteside family, settled there. Davidson and Stuvé, *History of Illinois*, 223. "Joel, Thomas, and another Whiteside man were killed between 1793 and 1794." Ibid., 224.

4. *Combined History of Randolph, Monroe and Perry Counties*, 75–82.

5. It is difficult to identify this John Whiteside in the Whiteside genealogy book, which contains so many family members named John. See generally www.whitesideancestry.org.

6. Governor O'Reilly, Decree Concerning Indian Slaves, Dec. 7, 1769. Houck, *Spanish Regime*, vol. I. 249–50.

7. The village was later called "Owen's Station" after Robert Owens received a grant from the Spanish governor to establish a village there. Robert Owens was still very much alive and in charge as the village syndicate when the Whitesides settled there.

8. Florissant and Owen's Station. This village was described as follows: "near the Missouri River, only about three or four miles from St. Ferdinand, was laid out, by permission of the lieutenant governor, Trudeau, by Robert Owens, who had been a resident of the country since 1789, and where, in 1793, Francois Honore and others had first formed a station to protect themselves against the Indians." Houck, *History of St. Louis*, vol. 1, 77.

9. Digest of the Laws of Louisiana, appendix 4. Steven Hempstead also had a farm in the general area. The nature of his family life is recorded in his diary. Hempstead, "I at Home."

10. Notes to Steven Hempstead, "I, at Home." See also Houck, *History of St. Louis*, vol. 2, 59–72, footnote to chapter on Marais des Liards. "Juan Wedsay dit John Whitesides (1799), his widow Phebe Wallace." Ibid., 78.

11. The western proscription against slavery north and west of the 36°30' latitude was called the Missouri Compromise. Congress adopted the Missouri Compromise in 1821, at the same time that Missouri entered the union as a slave state.

12. See generally, Houck, *A History of Missouri.*

13. John Whitset/Whiteside's probate had only three folders. The 1803 inventory then lists only one Negro woman and two Negro boys. It names his widow "Feeby Whitesides."

   Ten years later, in 1813, Phebe Whiteside Pruitt delivered the following list of persons to John Richardson and John Howdeshell, trustees for the heirs and representatives of "John Whitsides."

   "One Negro woman and her 6 children named Jerry, Daniel, Jane, Nancy, Lydia, and Sally. 5 head of horses young and old, 6 cows and calves, 2 oxen, 3 steers, 3 heiffers, [*sic*] 50 hogs of all descriptions running at large, 2 beds and bedsteads and furniture with all household and kitchen Furniture and Farming utensils," May 25, 1813. Phebe relinquished all her claims except that necessary to support herself to the heirs as determined under Spanish law at the time of John Whiteside's death.

14. Fields or Fielding Pruitt is said to have married Whitesides' widow, although no marriage record can be found. There is a marriage record to a different woman, Hanna Hull, in the area about the same time. Illinois marriage records for St. Clair County, in August 22, 1808.

   The 1820 U.S. Census lists Fields Pruitt in Powers Township, Bond County, Illinois.

15. Service of process on Phoebe Whitesides (Feb. 9, 1819) was done at the home of William Musick, Bonhomme Township. *Winny v. Phebe Pruitt*, CC Case no. 190 (1821).

16. The deed's language is curious, noting that because John Whitesides died in 1803, the same year as the Louisiana Purchase and Lewis and Clark's journey west, the estate should be divided according to the Spanish law of the area at the time. John Whitset/Whiteside probate.

17. "A negroe woman named Winn & a child named Hannah appraised to $450. A boy named Jeremiah, $400; A boy named Daniel, $350; One Girl named Jean $300; One girl named Nancy $300; One named Lide $250; One named Sarah $200."

   Inventory completed on May 27, 1814, in the Probate of John Whiteside Jr., filed in 1820.

   Phebe Pruitt died before the end of April 1823. Probate of Phebe Pruitt [*sic*], case no. 00594.

   Thomas Whitsetts/Whitesides estate administered by David Musick. Thomas Whitesides/Whitsetts Probate, case no. 00309, 1818. Additional entries include the following:

   "Public sale March 22, 1827. 86 acres in Marais des Liardes belonging to his father."

   "Administrator received $72 from Louis Martin for hire of negro Jerry. Dec 7, 1825."

   "Mar 2, 1825, money for hire of farm and $62 for hire of negro boy in 1823."

18. The files for the cases of Winny and her children are quite jumbled. Some are in the state archives and some are at the Missouri Historical Society. The transcripts remain in the appeals to the Missouri Supreme Court. The earliest items date from 1818. Affidavit of Francis Colliard dated (June 8, 1818) in *Winny v. Phebe Pruitt.*

19. The precise dates are uncertain. The two brothers and their mother Phebe died between 1818 and 1823. Phoebe was still alive to be sued in 1818 when the first suit was filed, but she had legally relinquished her interest to her sons; Son Thomas was dead by the time of the suit. Phebe died before April 1823, Thomas died sometime before 1818, and John sometime in 1820. John Whiteside Probate, St. Louis Probate Court 1820. His wife had married Michael Sandford by October 1821. Ibid.

20. See, for example, description of Harriet Scott's decision to sue in VanderVelde, *Mrs. Dred Scott,* 229–32.

21. In 1821, Jenny sued Robert Musick, whom she then worked for. *Jenny v. Robert Musick*, CC case no. 194 (1821). Jerry sued Charles Hatton.

22. Blackstone, *Commentaries*, Book 1, chapter 15.

23. "Phebe in argument with then deponent [Francis Collard] that Winney could not be free in as much as she was under age when brought away." *Winny v. Phebe Pruitt*, deposition of Frances Collard, signed June 8, 1818.

24. Who was Frances Collard? She may have been James Piggott's widow who married Jacob Collard and moved from Illinois to St. Louis in 1803. *History of St. Clair Country, Illinois,* 301.

25. *Jerry v. Charles Hatton*, CC case no. 16 (1826); *Jenny v. Robert Musick*, CC case no. 17 (1826). Jane aka Jean aka Jenny must have been transferred to Ephraim Musick.
26. Service of process on Phoebe Whitesides, Feb. 9, 1819. *Winny v. Phebe Pruitt*.
27. The most thorough account of the first trial appears in the transcript of *Winny v. Whiteside*, on appeal. Missouri Supreme Court Database.
28. *Winny v. Phebe Whitsides (Alias Pruitt)*, CC case no. 190 (1821). Judge Matthias McGirk wrote the opinion.
29. Pettibone originally defended Phebe Whiteside Pruitt in the several suits, which may explain how he came to have an interest in the litigants.
30. Record book of the Missouri Supreme Court, Nov. 8, 1824, "Whitesides v. Winney, a woman of Colour, Judge Pettibone being interested was not on the bench. And now at this day came the parties aforesaid by their respective attorneys aforesaid and the court now here being sufficiently advised ... consider that the judgment ... by the Circuit Court rendered be in all things affirmed and stand in full force and effect."
31. *Nancy v. Voteau*, CC case no. 143 (1821), p. 6.
32. See Chapter 3.
33. *Winny v. Whitesides alias Prewitt*, 1 Mo. 472 (1824).
34. The U.S. Constitution permitted that persons held to service in another state be returned. U. S. Constitution. Article. IV, section 2.
35. Scott, *Degrees of Freedom*, 28; Scott, "Explaining Abolition"; de la Fuente, "Slaves and the Creation."
36. Emphasis added. *Winny v. Whitesides alias Prewitt*, 1 Mo. 472 (1824). "In our opinion, the measure of damages is the worth of the defendant's labor; and any ill treatment during the time of the defendant being held in slavery might have been given in evidence in aggravation of damages."
37. *Nancy v. Isaac Voteau*, CC case no. 193 (1821).
38. Inventory Appraisement of Personal Estate of Rufus Pettibone Deceased with slaves in possession. Oct 25, 1825. St. Charles, Missouri, Probate File. Lindey is probably Winny's daughter, Liddy or Lydia.
39. The 1830 census lists two households headed by free women of color located adjacent to each other. The match fits.
40. Winny of the Whiteside family should not be confused with either Winny Cottle, from the Cottle family, or Winny Beckwith, who sued for her freedom in *Winny v. Samuel Donner*, CC case no. 20 (1820). Winny Beckwith was previously held by Jennings Beckwith.
41. The 1840–41 city directory lists a "Minney Whitesides, col'd washerwoman," living at "2nd & Hazel." The 1860 census lists a woman of color named Minney White.

    The registry of free black persons licensed to remain in Missouri lists the following, all registered in June 1842: "Matilda, age 29, 5′ 4″, washer; Wright, Jane, age 30, 5′ 3½″, chambermaid; Winny, age 60, 5′ 4″, washer." Jenny, Winny's daughter, was sometimes called "Jane".
42. There are two different John Whiteside probates: one for John Whiteside, the father, in 1803, which did not close for at least ten years; and another for John Whiteside, the son, in 1820. St. Louis Probate Court Files.

    The 1803 probate inventory contained the following: "One negro woman and her six children: Jerry, Daniel, Jane, Nancy, Lydia, Sally."

    The 1820 probate inventory of John Whiteside mentioned "Winn," and daughter Hannah; then Jeremiah [must be Jerry] came into the possession of Charles Hatton, who married Thomas Whiteside's widow, Sally.

    Daniel, Jean [Jane, must have become Jinny] was sold to Ephraim Musick in 1814. When she established her freedom, Musick sued the sellers on the warranty to get his money back.

    Nancy came into the possession of Isaac Voteau. Lide [this must be Lydia] came into possession of John Butler. Sarah came into possession of Michael Hatton, who had married one of the Whiteside daughter-in-laws.

43. Death Register: "Winney Fleming, 20 Aug 1865 St Louis Mo Calvary 2nd Bet Almond & Poplar."

"Winnie, 11 Jan 1865 St Louis Mo Wesleyan St Louis."

44. *Jarot v. Jarot*, 2 Gilman 1 (Ill., 1845).

45. In 1835, The Missouri legislature amended "An Act to enable Persons held in Slavery to Sue for their Freedom" to provide that "the plaintiff shall not recover any damages." Ibid., section 14, approved January 27, 1835.

Chapter 5 The Kidnap of Lydia's Children

1. Many of the persons in this chapter were illiterate, both the primary actors and the witnesses. Thus, it is almost impossible to designate a single official name for many. In addition, nicknames were frequently used in depositions and even on sheriffs' summons. For ease of reading, I have used more consistent spelling, rather than reflect all the variations in spelling in the written records. Because there is often no single, correct official name in this society, I have not used the convention "[*sic*]" where spellings diverge.

   Lydia is referred to as "Lyd," "Lydie," and "Lydia." Bob is sometimes spelled "Bobb." Mitchell is sometimes spelled "Mitchell" and other times, "Mitchel." Jinsey" is "Jinsy," "Jinny," and "Jenny." Lydia's husband, Nathan, is sometimes referred to as "Nace," or "Nance." Elijah is often "Elisha." Badgely's name is spelled with great variation, "Badgely," "Badgeley," and "Badgley" in the case files. Even Alexander Pope Field sometimes has his name spelled "Fields."

2. In May, Mitchell rented some land from George Valentine for a term of two years. Ichabod Badgely's deposition in Mahala's case. *Mahala v. Martin Mitchell*, CC case no. 6 (1832). Harrisonville is across the river from Herculaneum, Missouri.

3. An Act concerning the Introduction of Negroes and Mulattoes into This Territory, passed 17th September, 1807. Rev. Code of 1807, vol. 2, 467, by the Territory of Indiana.

4. Deposition of Ichabod Badgely in *Mahala v. Martin Mitchell*, CC case no. 6 (1832).

5. In context of a conversation with Badgeley, Mitchell's words, "she was mother to my children" does not seem to imply that her children were Mitchells.

6. There was also a claim made in the jury instructions about a freedom suit in 1825, but that cannot be validated in the Randolph, St. Clair, or Madison County Records.

7. Rufus Easton represented the defendant; Edward Hempstead, the plaintiffs.

8. February 3, 1809.

9. Judith Gaskell, "Illinois Legal Research," chapter 14.

   In 1809, Congress divided the Indiana Territory, and the western part became the territory of Illinois. The appointed governor of this new territory was Ninian Edwards; the three appointed judges were Alexander Stuart, Obadiah Jones, and Jesse Burgess Thomas. These men determined that most of the laws of the former Indiana Territory were still in force in Illinois. They proceeded to enact new laws, including one to reorganize and simplify the court system. The first session of the new court was held in Kaskaskia in June 1809.

   Moreover, unlike Virginia or Missouri, there was no favorable state statute in Illinois to appoint an attorney for petitioning slaves. Illinois had taken its laws from Indiana Territory, and Indiana Territory from Pennsylvania. Pennsylvania, in the course of gradual manumission, had not felt the need to respond to abolitionists' "threats" by enacting a statute to permit suits for freedom and to assign attorneys to petitioning slaves.

10. Deposition of Ichabod Badgely.

11. Signed Griggs & John Grovenor.

12. *Robert Patton v. Jinsey Mitchell*, Randolph County Court files, Chester, Illinois.

13. A note of July 15, 1808.

14. John Rector was one of the famous Rector brothers. He had practiced law briefly in Vincennes before moving west to Kaskaskia. After a short time in Kaskaskia, he moved on again, although it is unclear where or when. One of his brothers, William Rector, became the Surveyor of Lands; another was active in Arkansas. It is said that one John Rector was killed by Indians.

Rector is not known to have owned other slaves, or to have stayed in the area long, though his several brothers did.

15. The Randolph County indenture for Hess, age eight, describes Hess as removed from Kentucky, Sept. 19, 1809.

16. There is no evidence of Hess having been sold after the indenture.

17. Arthur Morgan, foreman of the jury, presented the verdict. "We the jury find that the Def [*sic*] is guilty—that the plaintiff is free, and assess his damages as twenty five cents."

18. Witnesses called by Jinsey Mitchell included John Sulvin and William Winn. Prospective witnesses Daniel Winn, Franny Taylor, Patsey Weas[f]ley, Charles Moore were not in the vicinity. George Acheson. Witnesses called on behalf of Bob and Lydie were: Elizabeth Gibbons, George Valentine, Elijah Talbot, Abraham Clark, John Everett, William McGalughlin, Robert L. Eidd, and James W. Roberts. [Elih]u Mather, Wm Clark, & Savannah, wife of Abraham Clark." *Bob & Lydia v. Jincey Mitchell*, capias (1810), St. Clair County Court, case no. 1754.

19. Ichabod Badgley deposition in Mahala's case. "Deponent recollects that there was a suit and as deponent understood was a suit brought by said Wench for her freedom."

20. Deponent Badgely claimed that when Mitchell arrived in Illinois, he had a Negro man named Bob who he hired out to a man named John Byron. Bob worked for 3 days making sugar troughs for Byron. Badgley deposition.

21. Joseph and Benjamin Ogle were in the area as early as 1788. Nebelsick, *History of Belleville*, 9.
    "Where the road from the Bellefontaine to Cahokia descended the bluff, settlements were made by the Ogles and Biggs in the year 1790. The Ogle family brought a considerable tract of land under cultivation in the bottom adjoining the bluff.... After a few years this settlement was abandoned entirely." McDonough et al., *Combined History*, 77.

22. Lydia married another man, Nathan Titus.

23. Randolph County Marriage Records indicate that on Oct. 14, 1813, Jinsey Mitchell married Michael Masterson. Michael Masterson appears to have been married before. Masterson, Michael married Nolin, Sarah according to St. Clair marriage records. Michael Masterson was a constable for Mitchie township in the second decade of the 1800s. McDonough et al., *Combined History*, 130.

24. *Matilda v. Isaac VanBibber* (April 1815), St. Charles County case files, Box 14, Folder 14.

25. *VanBibber v. William Christy*, CC case no. 1670 (1818).

26. The Bureau of Land Management Government Land Office records show four original purchases by the Titus brothers in St. Clair County. Nathan Titus's land was listed as "NW 20 02N 08W 3" December 21, 1816." Brother Samuel purchased land nearby a month later, in 1817, and a second parcel later that year. www.glorecords.blm/gov/.

27. In the 1818 Illinois census, the family of ten free persons of color was listed under the name "Nan Titus, a black."

28. "Deponent knows that said Wench was married to a coloured man in Illinois about deponent believes 20 years ago and upwards named Nace Titus, and that she has had several children by him." Affidavit of Ichabod Badgeley.

29. Probate of Nathan Titus's estate (1822), St. Clair County Courthouse.

30. Ibid.

31. *Lydia Titus and others v. William Degraffinreind, Daniel Winn, and Elisha Mitchell* (August 1825), St. Clair County Court, case no. 3317.
    According to the Bureau of Land Management records there was an Elisha Mitchell who took out a land claim in Macoupin, Illinois. It is not clear if this is the same man. The name Degraffinreind cannot be found in the history of Madison County, Illinois, though there are families of that name found in Kentucky. Daniel Winn, a Monroe County resident, lived on a farm below Ivy Landing, a site which was later washed away by the river. Between 1826 and 1831, he and his wife were prime witnesses in a prosecution against a woman for infanticide. The infant's body was found near their house. McDonough et al., *Combined History*, 140.

32. In the 1830 U.S. census for St. Louis, Lavina Titus is listed on the first page of the upper ward, next to another free woman of color, Nancy, and Nancy's child. The white head of household

preceding her is John C. Swan, who was a steamboat pilot. Others on the block were Rene and Gabriel Paul, both of whom had married daughters of Auguste Chouteau.

33. She was taken before Richard Welsh, according to the affidavit in *Vina v. Martin Mitchell* (1832). According to the affidavit "[S]he has been a servant of the city of St. Louis where she now resides since 1827."

34. In December 1831, "Martin Mitchell was not found in county." Sheriff's return.

35. Mahala was not abducted with the rest of the family, but rather was arrested separately in St. Louis. She was seized under the accusation made by Martin Mitchell that she was a runaway, and confined to the St. Louis jail. Martin Mitchell pretended to be acting as attorney-in-fact for the executor of her mother's owner's estate.

36. Körner, *Memoirs*, vol. 1, 335. Pierce, *Field Genealogy*, vol. 2, 1123: "[A] fine voice, that he could modulate almost at will, [such that] his power and influence over jurors were almost unlimited."

37. *History of Madison County*, 184.

38. Governor Edwards must have sent Field a letter admonishing him. Field responded with a letter a short time later, stating: "Our Courts have commenced, and I am necessarily compelled to attend to them. However, if I can I will go to Vandalia and remain there a few days, and return to our Court, which commences on the 18th of October. You say that my continuance in office depends upon my future attention to business." Letter of A.P. Field, Sept. 34, 1830, contained in the letter books of Governor Ninian Edwards.

39. He would continue in this office for the rest of the decade. He attempted to stay on, even after attempts to remove him.

40. Nathan Cole was one of the first local butchers to go into meat packing, packing salted beef in barrels for shipment by river. He settled in St Louis in 1821. He "foresaw that eventually St Louis must become the source of supply of salt meats for Orleans and other cities. He was the first to embark in the business." Barns et al., *Commonwealth of Missouri*, 683. See also McDonough, *Combined History* (discussing Nathan Cole's business in St. Louis), 286. Nathan Cole listed as having livestock in 1821 St. Louis tax records.

   1830 U.S. census: Nathan Cole, St. Louis City. Nathan Cole purchased land first in St. Clair County in 1834 from his residence in St. Louis and thereafter in Randolph County in the years 1836–1839.

41. Affidavit of Nathan Cole, *Matilda v. Mitchell*, CC case no. 55 (1832).

42. One affidavit states: "Personally appears Nathan Cole makes oath that he believes the facts in the…petition…are true and further that Alexander P. Fields, Elijah Mitchel and others arrested…Nathan yesterday claiming him as a slave and that last night they took said Nathan away from St. Louis and that they will remove him out of the State.…Habeas Corpus."

43. Affidavit of Sheriff George Hammond, Esq., May 30, 1832. Similarly, in response to the request for habeas corpus, G. Hammond stated, "I have the body of Sam before said court on the 26th instant at Jefferson County, Missouri. A Warrant was executed against Martin Mitchel and H.C. Russel, the said Michel calls his name Henry G. Mitchel said Michel and Russel was [*sic*] arrested by virtue of a warrant for kidnapping on the day aforesaid and Sam was put in the Jail of Said County where he has been kept and detained for safekeeping and for no other cause," May 30, 1832. Hillsborough was the Jefferson County seat and the site of the County jail.

44. See, for example, Sheriff's notation for Matilda.

45. The sheriff's writ stated, "Nathan taken out of possession of Mr. H.C. Russell and Henry G. Mitchell which Russell and Mitchell was arrested in the county of Jefferson on the 26th May on a warrant of kidnapping." See also habeas corpus writ addressed to George Hammond, Esq., to produce Michael, May 30, 1832. "Geo Hammond states I have the body of the within named Michael before said court on the 26th instant taken out of the possession of Henry G. Michel and H.C. Russel on a warrant for kidnappings [t]he said Mitchel was arrested by the name of Martin Mitchel & the said Michael was part and has been detained in the Jail of Jefferson County for safekeeping and for no other cause. May 30, 1832."

46. Henry C. Russell was served with process on May 28, 1832, in St. Louis. Thereafter, he could be not found. (A man named Henry A. H. Russell lived in St. Charles and was involved in two

court matters there, but the clarity of distinctive middle initials suggests that it was not the same man.)

47. Mahala's petition expressed the concern that the captors intended to take her to Kentucky to be disposed in her mother's former master's estate. Matilda similarly alleged fear of removal. *Mahala v. Martin Mitchell* CC case no. 6 (1832); *Matilda v. Elijah Mitchell,* CC case no. 55 (1832).

48. The Kentucky legislature mentioned Henry G. Mitchell of Warren County in two acts passed for his benefit as the owner of a water grist mill on Big Barren River. In 1834, "Chap. 391.—An Act to Improve the Navigation of Barren River," approved February 13, 1834; and in 1851, "Chapter 654. An Act for the Benefit of Henry G. Mitchell and John Mitchell," approved March 24, 1851.

49. The 1830 U.S. census lists Henry G. Mitchell in Warren County, Kentucky, with a household consisting of a white nuclear family with four boys, and a young slave woman. Martin Mitchell was also listed in Warren, Kentucky. His household consists of a larger white family, and five slaves. There were several other Mitchell households in Warren, Kentucky, as well. There was also a "Mitchell, Martin, b. 1812 in Illinois; age 20 1832."

50. Deponents simply said he was from Kentucky.
     "In Dec 1808 Elisha Mitchell deceased was removing negroes from…Kentucky to the Territory of Missouri…" Affidavits of Solomon Shank, Daniel Winn, & William Everett.

51. On May 30, 1833. Statement of Bird & Strother for plaintiffs and S. W. Foreman for defendants.

52. The sheriff ordered to take possession of Michael and hire him out from time to time with $600 security, May 30, 1832.

53. Depositions taken at William Everett's house in Monroe County, Illinois (July 1, 1832, and July 23, 1832, and July 31, 1832). Other depositions were sought at Joshua Scott's house in Madison County, Illinois.

54. Ichabod Badgely deposition filed in Mahala's case.

55. May 3, 1833. George Swagert and Christopher Holdeman, also called as witnesses, could not be found. "George Swaggert" was likely the same St. Clair County man whose name appears with different spellings in the St. Clair County Court files from 1819 to 1835.

56. Stephen W. Foreman filed the defendant's answer on July 26, 1832. Foreman had been a witness in the impeachment of Judge James H. Peck and he was alleged to have headed a gang of counterfeiters in 1835. He presented his license to practice law in Gasconnade County, Missouri in 1821. Conard, *Encyclopedia of History of Missouri.*

57. Jury instruction marshalling the evidence in the case. *Marianne v. Elijah Mitchell and Alexander J. Fields* [*sic*], CC case no. 51 (1832). Mary Ann's name is sometimes spelled Marianne, as it is on the case file, and other times Mary Ann as it is in the Circuit Court Record Book.

58. "About 13 years since she obtained her right to freedom by a judgment of the court under Missouri territory that from that time to this she has resided in the state of Illinois and all…considered [her] a free woman" until May 22, 1832, when she was taken by force. *Matilda v. Henry G. Mitchell and Henry Russell,* CC case no. 55 (1832).

59. Madison County Probate Court, Probate of Nathan Titus. Inventory and sale of items (1822).
     There is a free Black man named William Clark living in St Clair, Illinois in 1830 according to the census. His family is comprised of three persons, himself, a man between 24 and 35, a woman of the same age and a boy under 10 years old. It is possible that Matilda was William Clark's spouse and that this represents their oldest son. A man of color named "William Clark, 6 ft tall, scar near corner of left eye; free born in Virginia in 1794," had free papers issued to him on November 13, 1819, in Madison County. Illinois Servitude and Emancipation Records.

60. The 1850s census for St. Clair County, Illinois has the following entry, which is probably Matilda and Michael.
     "Wilda Clark 40 FB b. S.C." followed by "Michael Clark 17 MB b. St. C."

Although "b. S.C." could be born in South Carolina, the more likely interpretation is that it was shorthand for the very county in which the census was being recorded. "S.C." for St. Clair County. "Wilda" is probably a misspelling of Matilda.

Ten years later the 1860 census lists:

"Matilda Clark T 2 R 10, St Clair, IL 59 1800 North Carolina Female Black

Michael Clark T 2 R 10, St Clair, IL 25 1834 Illinois Male Black," along with more members of Michael Clark's family.

The neighboring household lists a Levina: "Levina Thompson T 2 R 10, St Clair, IL 50 1809 North Carolina Female Black."

It is impossible to be certain of this identification, presumably of Lydia's children. All three names are fairly common. But the constellation of the names seems to heighten the likelihood that these may be Lydia's children.

61. A young man about the right age named Michael Clark, son of Matilda Clark, is registered as a free Negro in Illinois. Illinois Servitude and Emancipation Records. February 17, 1855.

62. 1850 U.S. census for St. Clair County, Illinois contains the entry: "Anson Clark 21 M B Laborer b. Ill American Bottom, St Clair County, Illinois."

63. St. Louis CCRB, May 3, 1833.

64. Jury verdict in case of *Mary Ann v. A.P. Fields* [*sic*] *and Elijah Mitchell*, recorded May 3, 1833 CCRB.

65. *Gustavus A. Bird v. Lydia Titus*, CC case no. 8170 (1833).

66. Ibid. Bird first sued Lydia in St. Louis. With that judgment from the Missouri court, he crossed the river to execute his judgment against her property in St. Clair County, Illinois. *G. Bird v. Lydie Titus*, St. Clair County Court, case no. 3746 and 7660 (September 1834).

67. *Lavinia Titus v. Jerry Duncan*, CC case no. 8288 (1833).

68. See chapter 8.

69. *G. Bird v. Lydie Titus* [Debt]. St. Clair County Court, case no. 3746 and 7660. (September 1834).

70. When St. Louis required free persons of color to register, two women, Matilda Clark, age thirty-five, and Levina Titus, age twenty-nine, registered themselves. Matilda Clark was listed as a washerwoman in the 1838 St. Louis city directory.

71. February 17, 1855. Illinois Servitude and Emancipation Records.

72. *Nathan Cole v. Alexander P. Field*, CC case no. 50 (1832).

73. Cole was in partnership with Samuel Stookey. Stookey deposition in *Nathan Cole v. Alexander P. Field*, CC case no. 50 (1832).

Chapter 6 John Merry, Also Known as Jean Marie: Free Born

1. Fehrenbacher and Mcafee, *Slaveholding Republic*, 257–58.

2. The "French slaves of Illinois" and their descendants continued to be held in Illinois in bondage through a transition period of more than fifty years, which did not finally terminate until 1843 when another slave owned by Jarrot, as John Merry and his wife had been, sued in Illinois for freedom. *Joseph Jarrot, alias Pete, alias Joseph, a colored man v. Julia Jarrot*, 2 Gilman 1, 7 Ill. 1 (1845).

3. See chapter 2, pages 34–36.

4. This succession of sovereign legal regimes raises the same issue as arose west of the Mississippi with a different succession of sovereigns. See chapter 3, pages 40, 46, and 52.

5. Three influential lawyers and statesmen, John Reynolds, Sidney Breese and Adam W. Snyder married women of French ancestry who had acquired "French slaves". Reynolds married a relative of Julien Dubuque, and Snyder married Adelaide Perry. Snyder's biography written by his grandson mentions that Snyder bought slaves "[t]o surmount the difficulties presented by the labor problem, and relieve his wife of the unavoidable drudge of rural housekeeping." He insists that all four slaves were "French Slaves" and that he bought two of them from Judge Reynolds. J. F. Snyder, *Adam W. Snyder*, 62; see also Breese, *Early History*.

6. In a speech to the legislature, John Grammar stated, "Hain't [*sic*] I got as much rights as any Frenchman in this state? Answer me that, Sir?" *The Edwards Papers*, 453.

7. "In 1803 Harrison and the judges, in order to secure some relief for the labor market, passed a law permitting the indenture of servants, which was in fact a disguised form of slavery. So hostile was the opposing faction that it later made this law, or rather a repetition of it, one of the charges against the governor." Alvord, *The Illinois Country*, 423.

8. Reynolds, *My Own Times*, 133.

9. For readings on the Illinois system of indenture, see Zebina Eastman, "Black Code of Illinois;" Dwight Harris, *The History of Negro Servitude in Illinois and of the Slavery Agitation in That State 1719–1864*; Pease, *The Frontier State, 1818–1848*.

10. Deposition of Peggy Pelkie, a woman of color, in *Judy v. Meachum*, CC case no. 40 (1837).

11. Davidson and Stuvi, *History of Illinois*.

12. Dexter, *Bondage in Egypt*, 52.

13. Virginia Act of Cession, March 1, 1784.

14. Letter from Governor St. Clair to Judge Turner, Dec. 14, 1794. St. Clair, *St. Clair Papers*, vol. 2, 331.

15. Susette was indentured under the name of "Lufetta." Quite probably her name is transcribed inaccurately (as a script *S* can be mistaken as an *L* and a small *f* as an *S*). The entry reads:
    "ST. CLAIR County, LUFETTA [*sic*] Jarrot, Nicolas [*sic*], F, M, 17 years indenture, 3-10-1817." http://www.cyberdriveillinois.com/departments/archives/databases/servant.html.

16. A glance at the indenture ledger of Randolph and St. Clair Counties shows masters with Francophone names repeatedly registering bills of sale, but not formal indenture papers.

17. Nicolas Jarrot bought four slaves from Moses Short in 1815 and conveyed two of them to his son-in-law Clayton Tiffin. In the 1818 census, Nicolas Jarrot owned ten slaves, and in the 1820 census, twelve slaves. McDermott, *Old Cahokia*, 184–87.

18. Ibid. "Sale of the Personal Property of the Late Nicholas Jarrot, 13 June 1821." Includes seven persons, including one family, "John Mary [*sic*] and his Wife Suset & Child," valued together at $900. All three were sold to McCracken. The others sold were a 'Yellow Woman Mary, sold to West, A Black Man Francis, sold to William Montgomery, a black Girl Kezzett sold to Abraham Prickett, and someone named Louis sold to James Mason." Ibid.

19. Concerning the effect of the Code Noir, see Banner, *Legal Systems*, 43. "The only aspect of life that continued to be formally regulated by French law was slavery. The Code Noir, published in 1685 to govern slavery in the French colonies, was adapted to French Louisiana in 1724, and became the only French law expressly retained in Louisiana by the Spanish." Ibid.
    Under the Code Noir, black slaves, but not necessarily Indian slaves, had some expectations that if they were sold, they would be sold together as a family unit. Ekberg, *Colonial Ste. Genevieve*, 108. This expectation and rough protection of family integrity does not seem to have carried over into slaveholding practice once the region came under American authority. I have seen no invocations of the Code Noir in upper Louisiana in any of the legal materials after 1803.

20. The spelling of the family name, Pensonneau, varies widely in documents of the era, but there seems to be no mistaking that all of these names refer to the same family. Spellings include Penconneau, Pinconneau, Pinconeau (with and without the cedilla) Pinsoneau, and even Pensino.

21. Susette's oldest child was John Jr., followed by Angelique and Edward. *Susette v. John Reynolds*, CC case no. 9 (July 1828).

22. The Pinconneau brothers, Louis and Etienne, had many slave dealings in St. Clair County, Illinois. There were at least eight different slaves mentioned in deeds and indentures registered in St. Clair. All documents in Illinois indentures online http://www.cyberdriveillinois.com/departments/archives/databases/servant.html.

23. Deposition of John Merry, *John Merry v. Louis Menard and Clayton Tiffin*, CC case no.18 (1826).

24. Leichtle and Carveth, *Crusade against Slavery*, 84 (describing the decisions of Manuel, one of the slaves that Governor Edwards manumitted, along with his wife.)

25. See, for example, *Ann Davis v. James T. Symington* ("said Symington intends her off to some of the southern states then to sell her and make her a slave for life"); *Margaret v. George Brown, William Dallam* ("Dallam by his agents have been…making preparations to carry off your petitioners to the South beyond the reach of assistance where it will be impossible for them to assert their right to freedom"); *Thenia, otherwise called Sarah v. Green Crowder* ("Immediately after the purchase, Mr Crowder carried your petitioner & her Child to the jail of this country, for safe keeping until he should be ready to take them to the southern market. And she is in hourly fear that she & and the child will he hurried from jail, or board a steam boat, & transported to the south, without an opportunity to assert their claim to freedom").

26. Deposition of Julie Bordeau.

27. Section 14 of the Illinois code, enacted in 1819.

28. "Sometime in January 1825, an oral contract was drawn up that Lewis Penconneau (Pensino in the court document) would free John Merry for $450 ($900 in other documents) within three years. Immediately thereafter, John Merry paid him a down payment of $230 in value ($200 plus two horses) and John claimed that Penconneau liberated him. But Penconneau later went to St. Louis, where John Merry had gone seeking work, in order to re-enslave him. He had John Merry jailed. Taken from jail, John Merry was chained and put on a boat to New Orleans to be sold by John G. Stephenson, as agent for Pinconneau; Andrew Sheckony bought him around April 1, 1825." Statement of the case in *John Merry v. Louis Menard and Clayton Tiffin*, CC case no. 18 (1826).

    In the later New Orleans lawsuit, John Merry's purchaser is named as Andre Chexnaider in the lower court filings and Cexnaider on appeal. *John Merry, free man of color v. Andre Cexnaider*, 8 Mart. (N.S.) 699. First Judicial District Court, March 1830, Docket #1877, Eastern District.

29. The 1830 U.S. Census lists Andre Sexnaider living in St. John the Baptist, Louisiana. His household of twenty-four persons contains nine slaves. In 1840, the entry is spelled "Andre Seichneider," still living in Saint John the Baptist, Louisiana; however, with a much smaller family and fewer slaves: six white persons and only two slaves.

30. He was seized by Sullivan Blood and others.

31. Because the Pensonneau brothers lived in Cahokia on the Illinois side of the river, they were capable of moving purported slaves back and forth with ease.

32. Clayton Tiffin married Louise Jarrot on November 10, 1815, in St. Clair County.

33. Clayton Tiffin owned three slaves in St. Clair County, Illinois, in 1818 and 1820. In addition, there was one free person of color residing in his household in Madison County in 1820, according to the Illinois censuses. Dr. Tiffin practiced medicine on both sides of the river, and having settled in St. Louis, continued to own the several slaves brought with him from Illinois. John Merry's checkered title would not have deterred Tiffin from acquiring Merry, since at least two of his own slaves had similar claims to freedom if Merry was declared free.

34. *John Merry v. Clayton Tiffin and Louis Menard*, CC case no. 18 (Nov. 1826) CCRB at 408 (plea filed).

35. The witnesses were Julia Barada, Alexis Amelin, Baptiste Lebrun, Pierre Bennet, Joseph Garnier, John Walker, Sullivan Blood, Joseph Walton. For the defendant, August Trottier and Louis Pinconeau [*sic*] were deposed.

36. VanderVelde, *Mrs. Dred Scott*, 248–250.

37. CCRB, April 3, 1827, p. 512.

38. Virginia Act of Cession, March 1, 1784.

39. *Merry v. Tiffin and Menard*, 1 Mo. 725 (1827).

40. Ibid.

41. Ibid.

42. The Missouri Supreme Court cited few sources other than the Virginia Act of Cession, the Northwest Ordinance, and their prior decision in *Winny v. Whiteside*, 1 Mo. 472 (1824).

43. *Merry v. Tiffin and Menard*, I Mo. 725 (1827).

44. Francois (Francis) Menard and Pierre Menard, who were related to the man selling John Merry to Tiffin, held several slaves in the next county on the Illinois side of the river. Francois held nine, and Pierre, eighteen. They continued to record the children of the first generation of slaves as slaves themselves. 1830 U.S. Census, Randolph, Illinois. It was not until 1845, eighteen years later, that another man, who also had been held by Nicholas Jarrot, challenged the Illinois practice to the Illinois high court. *Jarrot v. Jarrot,* 2 Gilman 1 (Ill. 1845). When the Illinois Supreme Court did hear such a case later, they used the ruling in *Merry v. Tiffin and Menard* to further dismantle the "French slaves" exception in Illinois. *Merry v. Tiffin* is cited in the Illinois case of *Jarrot v. Jarrot,* 2 Gilman 1 (Ill. 1845) (stating mistakenly that Merry lost his trial by jury).

45. *Theoteste v. Chouteau,* 2 Mo. 144 (1829).

46. There are several cases involving slaves claimed by Menard and the Chouteaus. See, for example, *La Grange v. Chouteau,* 2 Mo. 20 (1828).

47. John Merry indictment for keeping a disorderly house. CCRB November 1827.

48. Samuel T. McKinney, a slave trader, was a state's witnesses in the criminal prosecution against John Merry for keeping a disorderly house. Sullivan Blood had seized him in Illinois on Pensonneau's orders.

49. St. Louis CCRB, March 26, 1828. *Susette, a free woman v. John Reynolds,* CC case no. 9 (July 1828).

50. Attorney Joseph Charless Jr. represented John Merry, Suzette, young John, Angelique, and Edmond. Charless practiced law only a short time before switching to the chemical and drug manufacturing business. Joseph Charless Jr. gained recognition later for posting bond in the Dred Scott case. He was married to Charlotte Blow, whose family had once owned Dred Scott. For more on Charless's connection to the Dred Scott case, see VanderVelde, *Mrs. Dred Scott,* 248–49.

51. Complicating the identification is the fact that Merry's wife also had aliases, sometimes going by the name "Judith Bequette," sometimes "Suzette," and sometimes "Suzette Merry." *Susette, a free woman v. John Reynolds,* CC case no. 9 (July 1828).

    "Suzette aka Judith Bequette aka Suzette Merry was born in the Missouri home of Ms. Beauvais, who left her to her grandson Nicholas Jarratt [*sic*]. Suzette was indentured in 1817 to Nicolas Jarrot. She bore a son named John about 1820 in Illinois. Later that year she and her child were sold to Jaratt's son-in-law Robert McCracken at Nicholas Jaratt's [*sic*] sale. McCracken then sold them to Pinconeau." Ibid.

52. Sheriff summons for July 12, 1828. Ibid.

53. Reynolds grew up east of Kaskaskia. Reynolds, *My Own Times,* 45. In the winter of 1814, he established his office in Cahokia. Ibid., 109. Reynolds was a member of the Illinois legislature in 1826 and 1827 and elected as Illinois governor in 1830. Ibid., 192. John Reynolds is listed in the 1830 census as living in St. Clair County, Illinois, and having two slaves in his household, one girl under ten years old and one young woman age ten to twenty-three. John Reynolds himself had "French slaves" in his household, through his wife's "French" connections. Reynolds held two indentured French servant-slaves himself. http://www.cyberdriveillinois.com/departments/archives/databases/servant.html.

54. Sheriff summons return for July 12, 1828. "John Reynolds not found in my county." John Reynolds is a fairly common name but it does not turn up elsewhere in the multiple St. Louis databases currently available, so the John Reynolds living in East St. Louis is the most likely defendant.

55. Indictment of Moses Whiteside and Jacob Judy. St. Louis Criminal Court, case file no. 1158 (1828).

56. *State v. Jacob Judy and Moses Whitesides,* Criminal Court case no. 1158 (November 1828).

    The elder Jacob Judy was a longtime area resident on the Illinois side of the river. He built Judy's Mill for grinding grain in what later became Monroe County. Judy's mill was a short distance east of Whiteside's station. Smith, *A History of Southern Illinois,* 510. (Whiteside's station is where Winny had resided thirty years earlier. See chapter 4.) Jacob Judy's son, Samuel

Judy married into the Whiteside family, and this Jacob Judy was presumably his son. Each of these men had married the other's sister. McDonough, et al. *Combined History.*

57. John Merry's lawyer, Joseph Charless Jr., and John Darby gave testimony in the indictment. *U.S. v. Jacob Judy & Moses Whitesides,* Nov. 1828.

58. *History of Madison County, Illinois,* 76 (1882).

59. John Reynolds himself documents that year as the time when some of his neighbors moved to Peoria. "In April, 1829, Abner Eads, J. Hersey, and some others, left St. Clair County, and located in Peoria. This was the first settlement of this city by the Americans...." Reynolds, *My Own Times,* 150.

60. In July 1828, Moses Whiteside took out a mining permit in Galena. Hansen and Mueller, Galena Mining Permits filed in the Galena Public Library. Vital Statistics of Galena states that Moses Whiteside administered the estate of a friend in Galena on May 8, 1840. Mrs. Whiteside died May 20, 1841.

61. Ibid., 264 (declaring that he first visited Galena in 1829).

62. See this chapter note 15.

63. CCRB, August 10, 1827.

64. *John Merry, free man of color v. Andre Cexnaider,* 8 Mart. (N.S.) 699. First Judicial District Court, March 1830, Docket #1877, Eastern District.

65. "Precisely the same case has been decided by the Supreme Court of the State of Missouri wherein... it was held that plaintiff was under the ordinance, entitled to his freedom. I have no doubt of the correctness of that decision. And accordingly order and decree that the petitioner do recover of the Defendant his freedom with costs." Ibid.

66. *John v. William Campbell,* CC case no. 6 (1832).

67. Ibid.

68. In the 1830 U.S. census, John B. Sarpy's entry is next to that of Dr. Clayton Tiffin. There is no "Margaret" identified with the name Sarpy in the Drouin records of the St. Louis Catholic Church. Nor is there a Margaret Sarpy listed in the family genealogy included in Beckwith, *The Creoles of St. Louis.*

John called the Jarrots and the Tiffins as witnesses. A witness identified as Francis Jarat [*sic*], son of Nicholas Jarrot, testified that "Robert McCracken [married to Hortence Jarrot in 1818] bought them & sold Suset & John to Louis Pensino [*sic*] Senior." *John v. William Campbell,* CC case no. 6 (1832). He also testified that he saw John with William Campbell in Galina in 1830 and told him that John was not "a slave for life." Ibid.

69. *John v. William Campbell,* CC case no. 6 (1832). John, Jr. was set free May 1833.

70. The St. Louis Coroner's inquest, April 9, 1835, indicated that John Merry, a free man of color, died at the house of Joseph Montaigne.

71. U.S. Census for St. Louis, 1840.

Chapter 7 David Shipman

1. Tazewell County was divided off from Peoria County in 1827, just about the time of the events that occurred in this chapter.

2. *Journal of the Illinois State Historical Society (1908–1984),* 122–132.

3. On June 30, 1823, Sampson, a free man of color, published his will, providing that after his wife's death, all his land should pass to David Shipman, son of his former owner. David Shipman also provided an affidavit in the Kentucky case of *Amy (a woman of colour) v. William Smith.* June 19, 1822. 1 Litt. 326, 11 Ky. 326 (1822). Court of Appeals of Kentucky. Deposition taken at Lexington. My attempts to find that affidavit from the Kentucky archives have been unsuccessful.

4. The 1820 census for Shelby County, Kentucky, Population of Shelbyville lists David Shipman's household as: one white male over forty-five and one white female over forty-five and only one male slave under age fourteen. Aug 7, 1820.

5. The factual circumstances described in this chapter are drawn from the several case files: *David, a free mulatto boy v. Stephen Smith*, CC case no. 17 (1827). *Stephen Smith v. Nathan Dillon and John Summers* (July 1827). *Milly v. Stephen Smith*, CC case no. 14 (1827). Stephen Smith also sued white David Shipman on the debt. *Stephen Smith v. David Shipman*, case no. 285 (1829).

6. The two slaves foreclosed upon were Eliza about fifteen years old and Sarah about twenty-seven years old, both as of Oct. 17, 1826.

7. *David Shipman, a free mulatto boy v. Stephen Smith*, CC case no. 17 (1827).

8. It is not certain exactly when his wife rejoined him. She appears to have been with him near Peoria by the 1830 census.

9. CCRB, April 13, 1829, pp. 274–278. It is unusual that these detailed court findings are included in 4 pages of the Circuit Court Record Book.

10. Nathan Dillon's affidavit. *Milly v. Stephen Smith*, CC case no. 14 (1827).

11. These two men, Nathan Dillon and Johnson Summers, were Tazewell county neighbors of the Shipman household. The men were Quakers and as such refused to take an oath. *Milly v. Smith*, CC case no. 14 (1827). *Stephen Smith v. Nathan Dillon and Johnson Summers*, CC case no. 13 (July 1827). Nathan Dillon was a Peoria County Commissioner in 1826–27, the year before Tazewell County was created.

12. Plaintiffs' petition to sue as poor persons, filed May 9, 1827. *Milly v. Stephen Smith, Harry Dick v. Stephen Smith, William, a free negro boy v. Stephen Smith*, and *David Shipman, a free mulatto boy v. Stephen Smith*. *Milly v. Stephen Smith*, CC case nos. 14, 15, 16, and 17. (July 1827).

13. *Stephen Smith v. Nathan Dillon and Johnson Summers*, CC case no. 13 (July 1827).

14. The signatures are on a single petition for all four Plaintiffs contained in the file of *Milly v. Smith*, CC case no. 14 (1827.) None of the four persons resorts to an "X," all signatures appear shaky, and may have been enscribed by one or more persons. Every other attestation in any freedom suit has been an "X" or a sign of the cross. Several of these signatures are displayed on the back cover.

15. Petition of Milly, signed with an "X," on affidavit for appeal, March 31, 1828.

16. *Milly v. Smith*, CC case no. 14 (1827).

17. *Milly v. Smith*, 2 Mo. 36 (1828); *Milly v. Smith*, 2 Mo. 171 (1829).

    Trials in the cases took place on March 31, 1828 (petitioners lost; Stephen Smith was found to be not guilty). CCRB, March 31, 1828. The parties consented to a retrial. CCRB, December 19, 1828. Stephen Smith sued David Shipman on the original debt in March. CCRB, March 31, 1829.

18. CCRB, April 3, 1828, p. 122. Entry states that Milly and her children are now in jail, though the sheriff is ordered to hire her to the highest bidder. *Robert Simpson, Sheriff v. Isaac A. Letcher, & James L. Lyle*, CC case no. 11 (March 1831). Deposition of John Simonds Jr., Sept. 5, 1831.

19. Enslaved men were regularly assigned to Letcher and Bobb's brickyard to earn money for their masters. See, e.g., Eliot, *The Story of Archer Alexander*. The brickyard was a rough place. Cases of fighting by slaves at Letcher's brickyard sometimes led to deaths, inquests, or murder charges. See, for example, Coroner's inquest into death of William, a slave, in the service of Isaac A. Letcher by Sam, also a slave of Letcher. St. Louis case no. 25171 (1836).

20. See, for example, U.S. prosecution of John Bobb for assault on John Riley. 1819 criminal case file 1772. Letcher's leasing of slaves is demonstrated in suits against Isaac A. Letcher for detinue of the Negro man, Sam. St. Louis Civil case index case no. 4622 (1827). *Robert Simpson v. Isaac A. Letcher and James L. Lyle*, for hiring of Harry Dick. St. Louis Civil case index no. 7158 (1831); *Jacob O. Bradshaw v. Isaac A. Letcher*, for recovery of a slave man, Rail. St. Louis Civil case index no. 8171 (1833).

21. Deposition of John Simonds Jr., sheriff, Sept. 5, 1831.

22. *Missouri Republican*, July 6, 1830.

23. *Milly v. Stephen Smith*, 2 Mo. 36 (1828), C 25798, Record 5: 1827–1830, CCRB, p. 109, Mar. 26, 1828, thereafter p. 115.

24. All plaintiffs agreed to be bound by the decision in Milly's case. *Harry Dick v. Stephen Smith*, CC case no. 15 (1827); *David Shipman, a free mulatto boy v. Stephen Smith*, CC case no. 17

(1827). "The parties to this and the two succeeding suits to wit William and David Shipman agree to abide the decision of Milly against the said Stephen Smith provided she prosecuted her appeal at the next term of the Supreme Court. These three cases to be set aside if the judgments be reversed."

25. *Milly v. Smith*, 2 Mo. 36, 39 (1828).
26. Ibid.
27. U.S. Constitution, art. IV, § 2.
28. The judge expressed his own ambivalence, stating, "When the argument in this case was first opened. I felt strongly inclined to doubt the legality of the former opinion of this court delivered when this case was up before. But I feel myself at last constrained to affirm that opinion." *Milly v. Smith*, 2 Mo. 171, 174 (1829).
29. Judge Robert Wash dissent in *Milly v. Smith*, 2 Mo. 171, 176 (1829).
30. CCRB, April 19, 1830 pp. 538–541.
31. *Missouri Republican*, July 6, 1830.
32. 1840 U.S. Census, David Shipman, Tazewell County, Illinois. The household is comprised of one elderly white man, aged seventy to eighty, and a large, free black family of ten people.
33. Harry Dick appears to have changed his name to Harry Green. Harry Green, a black man whose age matches that of Harry Dick, married Maryan Dotson on August 9, 1842, in Jasper County, Illinois. Illinois marriage records, Illinois State Archives website.
34. The 1850 U.S. census lists Charles W. Shipman, age twenty-three, David Shipman, age twenty-four, and Thomas G. L. Shipman, age sixteen.
35. Moses Shipman married Nancy Winslow on December 19, 1844, in Tazewell County. Illinois marriage records, Illinois State Archives website.
36. David Shipman married Elizabeth Ashby (both were identified as "colored") on January 28, 1849, Peoria. Illinois marriage records, Illinois State Archives website.
37. Revolutionary War veteran final pension lists August 11, 1845, as his date of death.
38. Will of David Shipman, a Revolutionary Soldier Buried in Tazewell Co., Ill, Compiled by Mrs. George Spangler, Historian of Peoria Chapter, Daughters of the American Revolution. David Shipman was buried in Antioch Cemetery in Tremont.
39. According to the 1850 U.S. Census, one George Shipman, age thirteen, lived at the inn called the Peoria House, where he presumably was a servant. The inn had another black man who was the cook, and George is listed directly beneath his name. "George W. Shipman, age 13, race: Mulatto, Peoria, Illinois."

 The other George Shipman was aged seventeen and residing in the household of George Washington. "Geo Washington, age 33, Virginia, Black male, Labourer; Abigail Washington, age 28 Penn, Black Female; Albert Washington, age 2; Geo Shipman, age 17, Labourer."
40. David Shipman, Revolutionary War pension request, filed in Tazewell County, Illinois, marked "rejected," p. 14, August 1839. In fact, David Shipman eventually was awarded a pension, although it was delayed because he was presumed dead by the pension office long before he actually died. The presumption was a result of problems finding his address in the postal system.

Chapter 8 The Duncan Brothers: Black and White

1. Robert Duncan's 1842 probate is available in the digitized records of the St. Louis probates. Over the length of time that Robert's estate was probated, each of his brother's deaths are noted: Robert, Coleman, and his common law wife, Sally Adams died in 1842, William across the river in Illinois in 1845, James in 1846, and John in 1848.
2. A man named Jesse Duncan married Anne Pigg on May 1, 1784, Pittsylvania County, Virginia. There was no Mrs. Duncan in Jesse Sr.'s will by 1819, when he died. The will mentions only the children. Jesse Duncan's will can be found in the Hopkins County, Ky. Will Book, vol. 1, p. 313.
3. One slave woman Judy Logan and her son, Green Berry Logan, who sued John Berry Meachum, had been owned by a Benjamin Duncan in Kentucky before being lent out to Indiana. I have not been able to link the two persons named Benjamin Duncan among the dozen Benjamin Duncans residing in Kentucky at the time. *Green Berry Logan v. Berry Meachum*, CC case no. 22 (1836).

4. Witnesses in one Hopkins County law suit said that Metcalf and the Duncans were sometimes intimate, sometimes quarreling, yet combined together as part of the same gang. Transcript of *Bishop v. Duncan*, Hopkins County Case no. 1737 (1829, et seq.)

5. See, for example, Isaac *Metcalf v. John Duncan & Adam Smith*, Book 1, p. 672 (1822) (tearing up property with horses); *James Metcalf v. John Duncan*, Book 1, p. 805 (1823) (suit over a horse trade); *James Duncan v. Isaac Metcalf*, Book 1, p. 875 (1824) (defamation suit; James accused of burning Metcalf's still).

6. *Edward Ridley v. Coleman Duncan, et al.* General Index to Civil Cases, Hopkins County book, p. 1213 (Sept. 1827), and p. 1249 (March 1828).

7. In contrast to his bachelor brothers, William does not appear in these suits at all.

8. *John Duncan v. John Shields, et al.*, 1064 (Mar. 1826). While drunk, John signed away his wages to Blacksmith. General Index to Civil Cases, Hopkins County book. Book 1, p. 1064 (1826). On another occasion, a witness describes John as drinking pretty freely and being a little intoxicated, when John offered to trade Vincent away. Affidavit of Reason Neighswonger, in *Vincent v. James Duncan*, CC case no. 14 (1829).

9. Coleman Duncan said that at one time he had spent $800 of his brother Jesse's money and that he had lost his money at St. Louis. Isaac Metcalf's deposition, April 9, 1833.

10. For Coleman Duncan conducting the interrogation of witnesses, see his questioning of Mayberry Wright and Larkin Bashear in the long, drawn out *Bishop v. Duncan* litigation. See also *Coleman Duncan v. Warren Adams* (June 1832) (over losing at cards), *Coleman Duncan v. Mayberry Wright*. (Sorrel mare swapped for gray horse. Sorrel mare was supposed to be with foal from Topgallant.) General Index to Civil Cases, Hopkins County book, p. 1611. In addition to the sixteen freedom suits brought against the brothers that derived from their inheritance, they were involved in almost another dozen lawsuits in Hopkins County, Kentucky on different matters.

11. *James Duncan v. Isaac Metcalf*, Hopkins County Book 1, p. 875 (1824).

12. Civil Divorce Proceedings of Sally Adams and Calvin Adams, Supreme Court of Missouri (1809). In June 1815, Calvin Adams sued Robert Duncan for assault and the destruction of property. Calvin Adams was prosecuted for assault and battery on his wife Sally. Robert Duncan and his slave, Solomon, were prosecuted for assault and battery on Calvin Adams, July 1815. Missouri Supreme Court Database.

13. See various suits by Calvin Adams in the Missouri Supreme Court database. There is no record of a marriage between Robert Duncan and Sally Adams in the early marriage listings in the area. In town, she charged bills under the name of Mrs. Sally Duncan. Sally Adams probate, 1842, St. Louis probate files.

14. The 1823 St. Louis tax records show Robert Duncan owning $250 worth (a significant amount) of slaves. See also Dowling, "Queer St. Louis Names," *Missouri Republican*, August 4, 1879.

15. Walter Stevens describes the development of the island. "At first it was a sand bar off Market street. The lower end grew until it was above the water level. Bushes appeared. The sand became soil which encouraged vegetable growth. David [*sic*] Adams, a noted hunter on the plains, took up his residence on the island." Stevens, *St. Louis*, 654. Calvin Adams also obtained the ferry license from Frances Piggott Collard in 1803. *History of St. Clair County, Illinois*, 301.

16. Inquest into the suicide of Asa Walker on Duncan's Island (December 4, 1833). Death of a Sam, slave of Milton Duty, in Milton Duty case file. Inquest into death of unknown man died on Duncan's Island, April 18, 1839: "The affair of Major E. T. Langham, for shooting Jas. Adams, on Duncan's Island" *Daily Missouri Republican* (St. Louis), Saturday, May 29, 1841, col. A. Other bodies were found on Duncan's Island: James Brady, July 15, 1839; unknown white boy, July 30, 1840; unknown man, May 25, 1841; Pierre Gunette, July 2, 1841; unknown Negro man, September 16, 1840; another unknown man, May 29, 1842. Foul play was suspected in death of an unknown man found with his throat cut, July 23, 1842. Inquests of the Coroner of St. Louis, 1822–1842.

17. Jonathan's manumission papers identify his mother as Rachel, and brothers, "Winston" and "Kildare." "Winston" is probably "Vincent," a transliteration that is used elsewhere and "Kildare" is likely "Gilbert." Jonathan was manumitted by Robert Duncan July 2, 1823, recorded CCRB book 3, page 260. Historian Robert Moore of the Old Courthouse site of the National Park Service has done impressive work in assembling comprehensive lists of St. Louis manumissions, Free Black licenses, auctions on the Courthouse steps and criminal cases involving African-Americans.

18. Ibid.

19. The 1823 city map shows ten arpents of land carved from the expanses of Auguste Chouteau's property and located at the site of a spring that fed into a creek.

20. Jerry was a fairly common name for slaves in St. Louis. There were two men named Jerry manumitted in St. Louis (one on Nov. 18, 1825, by Edward Tracy, CCRB 4:251; the other on April 6, 1829, by the firm Scott & Rule, CCRB, 5:300), although neither by a Duncan. Since Jerry was known to be a free man by 1828, the earlier manumission seems more likely. Jerry was one of the three slaves to be divided between Robert and his younger brothers. He was probably allotted to Jesse Jr. James Duncan offered a $25 reward for the return of a runaway Negro man in the *Missouri Intelligencer*, just one week before the first man named Jerry was manumitted. November 11, 1825, p. 3, col. 3.

21. The sandbar extended from the foot of Market Street to the mouth of Mill Creek, or La Petite Riviere, and kept on growing by steady accretions until about the year 1829 or 1830.

22. Dowling, "Queer St. Louis Names," *Missouri Republican*, August 4, 1879.

23. "He lived near the bridge which crossed Hill creek, on Second street." Ibid.

24. Ibid.

25. For example, on November 26, 1814, the newspaper, *Missouri Gazette* contained an article on the subject of Robert Duncan, "Resident of St. Louis warning against hauling wood from his land." http://shs.umsystem.edu/newspaper.shtml.

26. A black man named Jerry Klinger lived in the community. He may have been related to Fanny. Jonathan was a member of the Methodist church from the year of his manumission until about 1848. Transcript of *Farrar v. Finley*, CC case no. 51 Chancery (1848.)

27. Jonathan Duncan & wife, Fannie conveyed property to Orland Fish, filed 10-9-1834; to Pierre Gernon, 3-11-1834; to Abner S. Ross, 12-18-1835; to Jobe P. Doan, et al., filed 10-17-1839; to Wyllys King, filed 10-17-1839 1 & 2 631; and to David B. Hill, 1-16-1840. All of these transfers are entries in the St. Louis Registry of Deeds.

    Fanny, sometimes spelled Fannie, is not named in Jonathan Duncan's later transfer filed 3-20-1841, though she is again in the transfer to Thos. Shields filed 8-28-1848 T-4. The last entry suggests a trust: "Duncan, Jonathan to Tr. of Fanny, his wife" filed 8-28-1848 V-4 296 166.

28. St. Louis directories are available for 1840, 1842, 1847, 1850, and 1854, and Jonathan Duncan is usually listed, living on North 4th Street in the early years, and later at the corner of Morgan and 7th Street.

29. Criminal case 1159, Nov. 1828 Conspiracy *State of Missouri v. Barney Moore; Lewis Pilcher; Warren & James Adams,* (To defraud, betting on card game "Spanish or Santa Fe") June 1835. This criminal case for gambling involved the men that Coleman played cards with. When Coleman was cheated at cards, he later sued them.

30. Shadrach by Coleman Duncan of Hopkins County, Kentucky, CCRB, book no. 5, p. 18, Feb. 10, 1828. Shadrach's wife and children are identified in Shadrach Duncan's probate file, 1851.

31. The Northwest Ordinance, art. VI, 1787.

32. From 1807 to August 26, 1818, the rent to the United States from the salines was 158,394 bushels and $28,165.25. The government demanded 10 percent of the salt produced as rent. Myers, "History of the Gallatin County Salines."

33. This practice of using slaves in Illinois salt production was noted by the Illinois Supreme Court in *Joseph Jarrot v. Julia Jarrot*, 7 Ill. 1 (1845) at 29.

34. John Funkhouser census had ten persons as "slaves or servants" in the 1818 census. In 1820, "Funkhowser, [*sic*] Robert R.," had in his household 2 free people of color and 23 slaves or servants.
35. Funkhauser statement regarding slave Vincent in *Vincent v. James Duncan*, CC case no. 14 (July 1829).
36. "That Robert Duncan came as the agent of said James and Coleman for the purpose of hiring [Vincent to Letcher] and assumed [Vincent] to be of bad character and they wished to hire him to a man who would keep a tight reign over him." *Vincent v. James Duncan*, testimony of Isaac A. Letcher, Aug. 16, 1830.

   The 1842 city directory listed "Isaac Fletcher, [*sic*] brick maker." The slave man Archer Alexander was also hired out to Letcher and Bobbs' brickyard. Eliot, *The Story of Archer Alexander*.
37. *Vincent, a free person of color v. Jerry, a free person of color*, CC case no. 14 (July 1829).
38. *Lavinia Titus v. Jerry Duncan*, replevin action for horse, CC case no. 8288 (1833).
39. Jerry's daughter was suspected of neglecting a white child in her care, a crime whose investigation later led to reveal Jerry's thefts. "Theft, and Attempt to Murder," *Missouri Republican*, July 29, 1841.
40. Vincent did not file suit against Jerry immediately upon being hired to him. Rather, he sued him halfway into the yearlong term. Jerry Duncan had leased Vincent for one year of labor from Sept 17, 1828, to Sept 17, 1829.
41. *Vincent v. Jerry Duncan*, CC case no. 14 (April 22, 1829).
42. Bird swore Vincent was detained in possession of James Duncan who intends to send him to New Orleans. Request for habeas corpus. *Vincent v. James Duncan*, CC case no. 110 (Nov. 7, 1829).
43. Affidavit of sheriff David E. Cuyler. *Vincent v. James Duncan*, CC case no 110 (Nov. 1829).
44. Ibid.
45. *Jesse Duncan, administrator v. William Wilson* (March 1830), General Index to Civil Cases, Hopkins County book, p. 1397, mortgage of slave woman Clarisse; *James Duncan, administrator v. William Wilson* (Sept. 1830), General Index to Civil Cases, Hopkins County book, p. 1590, regarding slave woman Clarisse.
46. *James Bishop v. James Duncan*, (Sept. 1829) General Index to Civil Cases, Hopkins County book, p. 1372. Isaac Metcalf testified: "James Duncan had bought this boy on his way from Missouri & that James brought him here to stay on till he got big enough to work & James intended to take them back to Missouri." Ibid.
47. Joe died before any affidavits were taken in his case. *Joe v. James Duncan*, CC case no. 47 (1830). The affidavits generally provide a considerable amount of the physical description of the slaves as means of identification. When asked to describe Ralph, Lowry Hay testified: "I have but an indistinct recollection of the man, but believe him to be about Forty years of age & of middle stature, I can't recollect any other particulars by which to describe him." *Ralph v. James & Coleman Duncan*, CC case no. 35 (1830.)
48. James is said to have transported Swansey to Galena in September 1828. There was also a digger's permit for Robert Duncan, June 1825. Swansey was said to have worked for Captain Comstock.

   "There is now living in Galena a venerable old colored man, Swanzy Adams, born a slave, in Virginia, in April, 1796, who moved to Kentucky, and thence, in April, 1827, to Fever River, as the slave of James A. Duncan, on the old steamer 'Shamrock.' His master 'hired him' to Captain Comstock, for whom he worked as a miner. He subsequently bought himself for $1,500 (although he quaintly says, 'good boys like me could be bought in Kentucky for $350'), and discovered a lead on Sunday that paid it, but he was compelled to serve 5 years longer as a slave, and was once kidnapped and taken to St. Louis. 'Old Swanzy,' as he is familiarly called, is the sole survivor of the slaves held under the Black Laws of Illinois, then in force, but which have long since been swept from her statute books. It is pleasant to add that, by hard labor, industry and economy, since he owned himself, 'Swanzy' has secured a comfortable home and competence against want in his declining years." *History of Jo Daviess County*, 257.
49. On July 13, 1829, probate papers were granted in Kentucky to James Duncan for his brother Jesse's estate. Hopkins County probate records, Hopkins County, Kentucky.

50. All case information is to be found in Jo Daviess County CCRB, Books 1829–32.

51. Raphael must have been Ralph. Jo Daviess County CCRB, p. 28: "Raphael (a man of color) v. James Duncan: This cause is dismissed at plaintiff's costs."

   Jo Daviess County CCRB, p. 39: "*Swansey v. James Duncan*, Tues May 11, 1830 Galena." In this case James Duncan came into court and filed his disclaimer and affidavit of himself and Coleman Duncan to the allegations of the complainant's Bill and moved the court to dissolve the injunction and dismiss the bill which motion is sustained and the injunction ordered to be dissolved and the Bill dismissed accordingly to the said *James Duncan having announced* [*sic*] *all claim to the services of the said Swansey as a slave or servant*" (emphasis added).

   Jo Daviess County CCRB, p. 39: "*Raphael v. James Duncan* Injunction dismissed."

   Jo Daviess County CCRB, p. 47: May 12, 1830: "*Swansey, JOSEPH a man of color v. James Duncan*." In both places where Swansey is written, it looks like "Joseph" is written over it.

   Jo Daviess County CCRB, May 18, 1830, p. 103: "*Swancey v. James Duncan*, Assault. dismissed. *Gilbert v. James Duncan*, Same order. *Joseph v. James Duncan*, Same order. p. 105 *Gilbert v. James Duncan*, dismissed."

52. See chapter 10.

53. Jo Daviess County CCRB, p. 39.

54. Jo Daviess County CCRB, p. 194: "Fall 1830 *People of the State of Illinois vs. James Duncan*: Indictment." Jo Daviess County CCRB, p. 284: "Nov. 13, 1830 *The People vs. James Duncan*: Kidnapping." Then no court was in session for several months followed by a standard entry of continuance in April 1831. Jo Daviess County CCRB, p. 285: "April 11, 1831 continuance and alias capias. *People vs James Duncan*: Indictment for Kidnapping. On motion of the atty for the people this case is ordered to be taken from the docket and further it is ordered that the same shall be reinstated on docket at any subsequent time on motion of the prosecuting attorney." One inference is that James Duncan had left town, prosecutors would not pursue him, but they would be ready if he returned.

55. The only difference is that Raphael now sued as Ralph. In subsequent proceedings, he asserted a last name: "Gordon."

56. The Galena records themselves show a confusion over Joe and Swansey. In places where one name is written, it has been crossed out and the other name is written over it, until the parchment smudges "Joe" and "Swansey" together. Either the clerk wasn't sure which name to use in the document, or he lost count confusing the two men.

57. The St. Clair County clerk of court annotated their individual cases to reflect on their personal appearance and bearing. Gilbert was described as "colored," Swansey as "free nig," and Joe was referred to in the simple, more pejorative form of "Negro." Although all three black men had parallel paperwork, the clerk distinguished each slightly by these descriptions.

   Gilbert v. Coleman Duncan, St. Clair County CC case no. 3534 (1831); *Joe v. Coleman Duncan*, St. Clair County CC case no. 3541(1831); *Swansey v. Coleman Duncan*, St. Clair County CC case no. 3547 (1831).

58. James advertised for Ralph's arrest as a runaway. *Missouri Republican*, June 19, 1830.

59. *Jonathan Duncan v. James Duncan, Coleman Duncan, and Wahrendorf*, CC case no. 304 (1831).

60. Gilbert was expected to earn the purchase money by his own labor, and the purchase price was to be spread out over three installments. When the second payment came due, Coleman Duncan sued Jonathan for the rest of the money. *Coleman Duncan (use of Gilbert) v. Jonathan Duncan*, CC case no. 7431 (1831).

61. The dispute was over whether Jonathan Duncan owed Coleman Duncan the purchase price for Gilbert, who became a free man either before or after contract for sale. By the terms of contract, Jonathan had not paid second payment. April 30, 1832.

62. Swanston was emancipated by Shadrach Duncan (May 4, 1832) CCRB, Book 6, page 317.

   "Duncan, Shadrach, drayman, 103 s 3rd" was listed in 1837–1838 St. Louis city directory.

63. Jo Daviess County CCRB, p. 368, between Aug. 22, 1831, and Sept. 3, 1831: "*People v. Swansey man of color*: To keep peace: On motion of States atty the defendant is discharged from his recognizance to keep the peace."

64. See this chapter, notes 92–96.

65. Joe, or Joseph, was bequeathed to Coleman, which may indicate why Coleman took the lead in smuggling him out of St. Louis.

66. *Vincent v. Duncan*, 2 Mo. 214 (1830); *Ralph v. Duncan*, 3 Mo. 194 (1833); *Gordon v. Duncan*, 3 Mo. 385 (1834).

67. The law required that the judge admonish the defendant that the petitioner should have access to his attorney, ("An Act to Enable Persons held in Slavery to Sue for their Freedom". January 27, 1835) but it did not say anything about the attorney taking the petitioner out of state.

68. Timothy Guard, another of the saline lessees who held many slaves, was deposed.

69. Illinois census, 1820, lists Robert R. Funkhouser with twenty-three slaves in his household.

70. Vincent worked at the Illinois salt mines as early as 1817 and as late as 1825. A man named Hume worked with Vincent as a woodchopper. Hume chopped wood and Vincent tended the furnace for about two years. Hume saw Vincent almost daily. Hume believed that Vincent was in Illinois the entire time. Another man testified that Vincent told him that he had rented furnaces and carried on business himself before 1825. Transcripts in *Vincent v. Duncan*.

71. John Steele had also served as a witness to a free black woman's will on November 9, 1831. It was unusual for a free black person to make a will at this time in St. Louis, but Esther had been granted a tract of valuable land several decades earlier and she wrote a will to leave her land to her children. Winch, *Clamorgans of St. Louis*, 59.

     Originally Steele's newspaper, *The Free Press*, had consisted of a set of advertisements, but more recent to the period under discussion, Steele had begun to carry articles about slavery. Steele would later go off to Arkansas, run a newspaper in Helena, and be awarded the lucrative contract to publish the region's first set of laws.

72. Deposition of Lawson Robertson, Nov. 15, 1831, *Ralph v. James and Coleman Duncan*.

73. Timothy Fisk, a Baptist preacher, testified favorably about John Steele. "When John Steele first came in my neighborhood he commenced teaching an English school near my house ... I never knew anything against him, but always thought him to be a man of truth and honesty and I believe he bore that name in our settlement and should think his Oath good in a Court of Justice and should believe him myself." Deposition of Timothy Fisk, Nov. 29, 1833. One former student said that Steele's character was good. It was the character of one of his detractors, John Robertson, that was bad. Deposition of Abner Martin Jr. (date unknown).

     Ambrose Gordon testified that the last he had heard, Steele was in St. Louis editing a paper called the *Free Press*. His wife, Polly Downy, and their three children were at her father's place. "[H]e trifled about him for some time and went off and left his wife and little children. I would not credit him where oath. He attempted to make a living here by preaching but could not succeed, then he tried the plan of horse racing and upon that quit the county." Deposition of George Clark, Aug. 20, 1833.

74. Deposition of John B. Laffoon, *Ralph v. James and Coleman Duncan*, CC case no. 35 (1833).

75. *Ralph v. Duncan*, 3 Mo. 194 (1833). "This assent may be inferred from circumstances."

76. Jo Daviess CCRB, April 18, 1835.

77. *Gordon v. Duncan*, 3 Mo. 385 (1834).

78. *Mary Ann aka Julia v. Robert Duncan*, CC case no. 63 (1835). *Julia v. Robert Duncan and Sally Adams*, CC case no. 141 (1836).

79. Milly was in the Galena and Dubuque region from August 15, 1834 to June 1835.

80. Tristram Polk was the plaintiff's attorney in both cases. A second defendant named in the case was John C. Smith. Ann's petition was also filed by "T. Polk."

81. Both suits were filed against James Duncan in St. Clair County, Illinois, Oct. 17, 1835. The jackets of the case filings provided descriptive distinctions between Ann and her mother. The jackets read *Ann (free nig) v. James Duncan et al.*, case no. 3822 (Feb. 1836), and *Milly (colored lady) v. James Duncan et al.*, case no. 3837 (Feb. 1836).

82. *Milly v. James Duncan*, CC case no. 63 (1835). H. R. Gamble was appointed as Milly's attorney. Another attorney in the firm, Tristram Polk appears to have done much of the work.

83. The Galena directory of 1854 lists last name first, "Milly, Ann, (col) laundress, h near Dodge." Among her boarders was "Shelly, John, (col) on river, bds Ann Milly." Galena city directory 1854, pp. 106 and 116.

84. *Alsey v. William Randolph*, CC case no. 305 (1841). Deposition of James Duncan, Dec. 29, 1841.

85. Vincent Duncan, Free Negro Bond, 1835. Vincent is listed as living at "225 8th, b. Wash & Carr, upstairs."

86. Coroner's inquests. "Vincent Duncan (colored age 80), cause of death: debility and old age case number 169, February 10, 1859."

87. "Theft, and Attempt to Murder," *Missouri Republican*, July 29, 1841.

88. Shadrach Duncan probate, St. Louis probate files (1851). *Shadrach Duncan v. Chancey Lewis & Richmond J. Curle*, (Jan. 7, 1842), (Suit over a 20 year old slave named Edmund, owned by Shadrach Duncan.)

89. Jonathan was a Methodist, had been a church leader and an "exhorter" in the African Methodist church. He bought the first log cabin as a place to hold worship in 1822 the same year that he was manumitted. He remained attached to the church through the 1850s. But by the time of the law suit between the church's black trustees and its white trustees in 1850, he was no longer a member. Transcript of *Farrar v, Finney* 21 Mo. 569 (1855).

    Jonathan Duncan put up security of several $1,000 bonds for five persons to obtain their free Negro licenses in December 1846: George W. Johnson, a minister of the gospel; Lewis Chavers and for Eliza Chavers; and James and Julia Anderson. Jonathan Duncan always had a co-bondsmen in these transactions. St. Louis Freedom bonds are available at digital.wustl.edu/legalencodingproject/.

90. *Missouri Republican*, March 28, 1846 (advertising sale of Sarah). There was another slave girl in the household who sued under two different names: Julia, also known as Mary Ann. *Mary Ann v. Robert Duncan*, CC case no. 46 (1834); *Julia also known as Mary Ann v. Robert Duncan and Sally Adams*, CC case no. 141 (1836).

91. Mary Duncan Metcalf emancipated 23 year old mulatto girl Eliza Ann, CCRB December 17, 1852.

92. On May 22, 1848, there are two conveyances to Shadrach Duncan, one from Robert Duncan's estate and one from the heirs of William Duncan. On April 2, 1852, there are four conveyances to Shadrach Duncan from James Duncan and James Duncan's heirs, John Duncan's heirs, Robert Duncan's heirs, and William Duncan's heirs respectively. On Dec. 17, 1852, the same day that Mary Duncan Metcalf freed Eliza Ann, there is a sale of all remaining property of John Duncan's estate, the last surviving brother, to Jonathan Duncan. St. Louis Recorder's Office.

93. No slave named Swansey or Swanston is listed in Jesse Duncan Sr.'s will, though like Gilbert, he may have been the other unnamed slave man bequeathed to James.

    Swansey Adams is listed with two different birth sites in different censuses. The U.S. Census for 1860 says that he was born in Virginia, while the U.S. Census for 1850 claims that he was born in Kentucky.

94. "Swanzey Adams" was identified as a "(col) water drayman Bench near Green" in the Galena city directory, 1854. Swansy Adams married Margaret Menard, March 28, 1845, marriage certificate for Jo Daviess County, listed in Illinois marriage records, Illinois State Archives website. Both are identified as "colored."

95. The account also says that he worked at the levy, weighing lead for transport in 1828. There is no corroboration for this.

96. Gary Henry, "Galena, Illinois During the Lead Mine Era," M. A. dissertation, 1976, Eastern Illinois University. The 1830 U.S. census entry for William Hempstead of Galena, Illinois lists one male slave living in his household.

97. For more about William Hempstead's character, see chapter 10.

98. Although William Hempstead had a slave in St. Louis, he is not associated with any acts of manumission in the St. Louis Court record books or the Jo Daviess CCRB, for Jo Daviess County, Illinois.

99. Drumm, "Robert E. Lee," 157.

Chapter 9 Leah Charleville

1. *Leah v. Arthur Mitchell*, Brown County, Ohio, referred to in Leah's later cases; *Leah v. Arthur Mitchell*, CC case no. 68 (1832); *Brunetta Barnes v. John Berry Meachum*, CC case nos. 40, 121, 123 (1840); *Archibald Barnes v. John Berry Meachum*, CC case nos. 41, 120 (1840).

2. House of Jesse Grant, in Georgetown, Brown County, Ohio. This account is from Jesse Grant's affidavit in *Brunetta Barnes v. John Berry Meachum*, CC case no. 121 (1840).

3. Ibid. Jesse Grant moved to Clement County, Ohio, by 1840. Peter Grant died in Maysville, Kentucky.

4. See Census entries for Arthur Mitchell, 1820 and 1830.

   Ellsberry, *Marriage Records* demonstrates that Arthur Mitchell married Nancy Daulton on November 29, 1809. Mitchell was originally from Pittsburgh, though his wife was from Virginia. There is no good information on how Mitchell acquired Leah. It's possible that Mitchell had bought Leah in Kentucky, but slightly more likely that she came from the bride's family when they were married in Kentucky and Leah was only seven.

5. The 1810 Maysville, Kentucky, census lists three Mitchels: John, a cabinetmaker, George, a boot- and shoemaker, and Arthur, a hatter. The 1820 U.S. census for Maysville lists the Peter Grant family of fifteen, one slave, and John Mitchell, family of seven, no slaves.

6. Even before the enactment of the Fugitive Slave Law, anyone harboring another's slave could be sued for the common law action of enticement, simply for giving the servant of another master a place to sleep.

7. *Leah v. Arthur Mitchell*, CC case no. 68, writ of habeas corpus (1832).

8. Jesse Grant contributed to the *Castigator*, a local antislavery newspaper. McFeely, *Grant*, 12.

9. The 1830 U.S. census lists Arthur Mitchel, St. Louis, Middle Ward, Missouri. His household is comprised of a family of nine, including three slaves: a boy and a girl, both under ten, and a woman between 24 and 36.

10. Leah's petition. *Leah v. Arthur Mitchel*, CC case no. 68 (Sept. 27, 1832).

11. CCRB, July 1883.

12. Other witnesses in the case were Robert King and Betsey Johnson, wife of James Johnson. They received service of process on July 19, 1833. Joseph Powell posted bond with Arthur Mitchel. Attempts to locate these individuals in other records have been unsuccessful.

13. All other entries are in CCRB.

14. When a case like Leah's is discontinued, it is difficult to determine whether it can be considered a victory for the slave or not. Discontinuation does not reveal what the power arrangement is that succeeds the act of litigation. The slave owner may have succeeded in subduing the insolent slave, or the slave owner may have simply backed off from asserting control over the slave. All that can be said for sure is that the active intervention of law did not reorder the power dimension, even if the passive availability of law may have been all that the slave needed to negotiate a circumstance that produced more tolerable living conditions.

15. The 1840 U.S. Census lists Arthur Mitchell in Aberdeen Township, Brown County, Ohio. In 1850, he is still there. Arthur Mitchell is age 64 b. Pa, his wife, Nancy age 63 b. Va, and Margaret Ivory age 12, b. Mo.

    "Arthur Montifore Mitchell born 8 Aug 1786 in Pittsburgh, Pennsylvania died Nov 27, 1868 in Aberdeen, Brown Co., Ohio Arthur Mitchell married Nancy Daulton on 29 Nov 1809 in Mason County, Kentucky." Kentucky Marriages at Ancestry.com.

16. Other black Charlevilles in St. Louis include Louis Charleville. See Billon, *Annals of St. Louis*, vol. 1 (describing that the Charleville name is not a common French name, but in the St. Louis area it is derived from a family, Chauvin dit Charleville). A bill of sale in the St. Clair, Illinois, records lists "Pierre (a metif), sold to Charliville [*sic*], Fras [*sic*]., Bill of Sale, March 3, 1782. If this Pierre was Peter Charleville, he would have been just a boy at the time.

17. The hotel next door was the National Hotel, established in November 1832. *Missouri Republican*, November 13, 1832. The 1840–1841 city directory lists the National Hotel as operated by Stickney and Knight. Inhabitants of hotels were listed in censuses with the hotel owner as head of household. Benjamin Stickney was listed with a population of 158, including 13 slaves, most (9) were young men between 10 and 24. The 1845 city directory lists the National Hotel as operated by "A. & B. J. Vancourt." The 1840 city directory entry for Peter read: "Peter Shalival, [*sic*], colored boatman, 21 S. 3rd."

18. VanderVelde, *Mrs. Dred Scott*, 79–80.

19. The 1840 directory lists two households of residents at her address, 21 S. 3rd Street: Peter Sharlival and Benjamin Hart, a trader to New Orleans.

20. Henderson, Chambers, and Melody, *Trials and Confessions*, 29.
21. The St. Louis city directory of 1838–1839 lists "Meachum J.B. (C) cooper, 11 n 2d, r 108 n 2d."
22. The 1840 U.S. Census lists John B. Meachum as the head of a household that contained sixteen persons. Ten of the household residents were free persons of color, and six were slaves. The slaves were: one young man between ten and twenty-three; two adult men between thirty-six and fifty-four; one young woman between ten and twenty-three; and two adult men between the ages of thirty-six and fifty-four.
23. *Archibald Barnes v. John B. Meachum*, CC case no. 41 (1840); *Brunetta Barnes v. John B. Meachum*, CC case no. 40 (1840).
24. Who was Barnes? There were at least five men named Barnes who married in Mason County, Kentucky, between 1806 and 1822. Mason County, Kentucky Marriage Records, 1804–60 vol. II-VI. Ancestry.com There was a Mrs. Ann Barnes in Mason County, Kentucky, in 1840 with three male slaves between ages of ten and twenty-four. 1840 U.S. Census.
25. Leah could have been their guardian *ad litem*, but having Peter fill the role is consistent with the notion that Peter and Leah were married, and under coverture, a wife's interests were subsumed in his, even her interests in children brought to the marriage.
26. Reverend Meachum included his autobiography with his Address. Meachum, *Address to All the Colored Citizens*. See also, Loren Schweninger, "Prosperous Blacks," 43–44.
27. See, for example, Kennerly papers for December 27, 1837: "B. Meachum preached at funeral of Betsey, Kennerly's slave, and a number of Blacks attended." Kennerly Papers, Missouri Historical Society Collections.
28. Meachum, *Address to All the Colored Citizens*.
29. "This gentleman was very wealthy, and had at one time, two fine steamers plying on the Mississippi, all under the command and management of white men, to whom he trusted altogether.... [A]lthough he could read and write, [he] was not sufficiently qualified and skilled in the arts of business to vie with the crafty whites of the Valley. But before his sons were fitted for business,... his whole property was seized and taken; and as he informed the writer himself, he did not know what for, as he had no debts that he knew of, until these suits were entered." Delany, *Condition, Elevation, Emigration, and Destiny* 151.
30. An Act to Prohibit the Publication, Circulation, or Promulgation of the Abolition Doctrines. Enacted by the Missouri Legislature, Feb. 1, 1837.
31. Petition in *Judy alias Julia Logan v. Berry Meachum, a man of color*, CC case no. 11 (1835).
32. Meachum freed Louisa in 1834; Diana, age thirty, in 1836; and Green, age thirty-three, in 1842. St. Louis Manumission list.
33. *Green Berry Logan, an infant v. John Berry Meachum, a free man of color*, CC case no. 22 (1836); *Judy a/k/a/ Julia Logan v. John Berry Meachum*, CC case no. 40 (1837); *Brunetta Barnes v. John Berry Meachum* CC case no. 40 (1840) and again CC case no. 121; *Archibald Barnes v. John Berry Meachum* CC case no. 41 (1840) and again CC case no. 120; *Judy (also known as Julia Logan) v. John Berry Meachum*, CC case no. 11 (1835) *Meachum v. Judy, alias Julia Logan*, 4 Mo. 361 (1836).
    By the early 1840s his business seemed to be foundering, and several of his suppliers were pursuing him to collect on his debts. See lawsuits in which he was the defendant in the St. Louis Circuit Court case file.
34. *Judy (also known as Julia Logan) v. John Berry Meachum*, CC case no. 11 (1835), and *Judy v. John Berry Meachum*, CC case no. 40 (1837).
35. Despite having lived and worked in Indiana, she had been sold from person to person until she was eventually sold to John Berry Meachum with a warranty. Meachum had allowed her to hire her time, and she had hired herself out in Galena, Illinois, for a month. *Judy (also known as Julia Logan). v. John Berry Meachum*, CC case no. 11 (1835.) *Green Berry Logan v. John Berry Meachum*. The plaintiff prevailed by defendant's default, judge's order, Missouri, April 13, 1836.
36. Meachum made the attenuated argument that since a white man had warranted Judy's title to him, if Louis were allowed to testify, he would in effect be testifying against a white man. The sheriff's summons is addressed to "Louis (a slave)." *Green Berry Logan v. John Berry Meachum*, summary, Dec. 21, 1836. Some of the papers refer to him as a free man of color, but in one he was referred to as a slave. *Judy (also known as Julia Logan) v. John Berry Meachum*, CC case no. 11 (1835). Louis,

under the name Lewis, sued for his own freedom three months later. *Lewis, a man of color v. James Newton and Jacob Cooper,* CC case no. 7 (July 1835).

37. Judy Logan's freedom was registered as affirmed on March 24, 1836, and she was awarded $1. CCRB March 24,1836. *Judy (also known as Julia Logan) v. John Berry Meachum,* CC case no. 11 (1835).

38. Book 8, p. 304. *Meachum v. Judy, alias Julia Logan,* 4 Mo. 361 (1836). This Judy was a large black corpulent woman and the mother of Celeste and Aspisa, and the grandmother of two other children. As a result, by 1835, Judy Lecompte was registered as a free woman in the city of St. Louis. Free Negro Bond for Judy Lecompte, age fifty, five feet three inches, "black corpulent woman."

39. Meachum, *Address to All the Colored Citizens,* 21.

40. *Brunetta Barnes v. John Berry Meachum,* petition, Nov. term, 1840. Although it is possible that Meachum had his own cow to milk, his primary business was barrel making. Meachum's wife worked as a milkmaid. Only a handful of women, all licensed in 1835, listed "milkmaid" as their profession in the Free Negro Bonds: Jonathan's wife, Fanny Duncan b. 1779; Jane Anderson, b. 1794; Mary Meachum, b. 1801; Julie Labadie, b. 1811; Theresa Joyal, b. 1798. Only Jonathan Duncan, a key figure in Chapter 8 of this book, also licensed in 1835, is listed as dairyman by profession.

41. *Brunetta Barnes v. Meachum,* petition by Thos. Gantt, attorney for plaintiff. November 1840.

42. See note 22, this chapter.

43. CCRB Book 11, p. 225. Sept. 5, 1840.

44. *Brunetta Barnes v. John Berry Meachum,* CC case no. 121 and *Archibald Barnes v. John Berry Meachum,* CC case no. 120.

45. Ibid.

46. Peter Grant had drowned in a flood by this time.

47. The 1840 census misspelled Peter's last name, but he was inscribed in the census as "Peter Sharlival, colored boatman, at 21 s. 3rd street." Also listed in the directory as living at the same address was Benjamin Hart, a free man of color. Near Hart's census entry was Felix Franklin, also a free man of color, and D. Martin.

According to the testimony in the confessions, Mary Beaufils also took meals at Leah's. Mary Beaufils was probably the wife of Joseph Beaufils. Mary Louise Grimault married Joseph Beaufils on April 10, 1830, St. Louis Marriage Records, Ancestry.com.

48. The primary narratives are contained in the published pamphlet about the trial and the confessions, *Trials and Confessions.* The 1840 U.S. Census lists Edward Ennis in Ward 3, Baltimore, Maryland, in a household comprised of thirteen free persons of color. If this is the same man, he had only recently moved west.

49. One took off up the Missouri, another went up the Ohio, one headed down the Mississippi, and one crossed over the Illinois side of the river to lay low. Ibid.

50. Blanchard confession in Henderson, Chambers, and Melody, *Trials and Confessions,* 13.

51. Testimony of Edward Ennis. Ibid., 6.

52. Ibid., 59.

53. Ibid., 31.

54. Warrick rented a little shop of his own. Ennis worked for another. Ibid.

55. Ibid., 8.

56. Warrick confession, ibid., 46.

57. Ibid., 31.

58. The gang considered the following targets: J. R. Scott, brick building on Third Street, south of Market; Mr. Goodell's store on Market, next to the museum; a gentleman's lodging over Johnson's Drugstore, Braun and Hollander; the grocery store on Main Street below Walnut; a small fancy dry goods store across the street from Braun and Hollander, Sinclair Tailor; E. & A. Tracy on the wharf on Water Street; Mr. Brant's house; a bank in Illinois; and finally the Collier & Pettus counting house.

59. Ibid., 34.

60. Henderson et al., *Trials and Confessions,* 30.

61. Ibid., 59.

62. The goods he had were stolen from the store of Sinclair Taylor & Co. Ibid., 4.

63. Ibid., 12.
64. The Niles' Weekly Register mentions Leah and Peter Charleville. Niles' Weekly Register 1841 Item notes: v. 60 page 190 (1841) Richard Edwards and Merna Hopewell, *Edwards's Great West* (Edward's Monthly 1860).
65. In 1840, Edward Ennis attempted to get a Free Negro Bond to remain in the city of St. Louis. It is not clear whether he had been living in the city the entire time or only just returned. The court denied his request. July 31, 1840, book 2, p. 333, permissions denied.
66. CCRB, Monday August 22, 1842, p. 326.
67. Brunetta and her two sons registered together for their free Negro licenses on the eve of the Civil War. "Brunetta Thompson, age 35; 5 feet 1 inch. Security: John E. D. Couzins. Occupation: washer $500.00 April 20 1861," CC book 10, p. 321. Sons John Finley, age sixteen, and Edward Finley, age thirteen, are included in her filing: "children of Brunette, included in her bond & license."
68. The 1860 U.S. Census entry for Robert W. Thompson lists him as head of household: Robert W. Thompson, age forty-seven, a cook by profession, born in St. Domingo. Brunette Thompson, age twenty-seven, mulatto, occupation washerwoman; place of birth not listed. Her sons John, age fifteen, and Edward, age nine, are identified as steamboat boys, both born in Missouri. The two youngest children are six-year-old Anna Barnes, and five-year-old Austrey Barnes. Listed among the family is a forty-five-year old woman named Caroline Mosey, also a cook born in Kentucky.
69. Who was Finley? There was a "Finley, Hardin, drayman, 41 Poplar."
70. Edmond Finley was buried at Greenwood Cemetery, January 31, 1877.

Chapter 10   Sex and Servitude in Women Litigants' Cases

1. A. D. Davis, "Private Law of Race and Sex," 221.
2. See, for example, McLaurin, *Celia*.
3. W. W. Brown, *A Fugitive Slave*, 38.
4. By law, The status of a child derived from the status of the mother. See note 13, chapter 1.
5. McLaurin, *Celia*, 96–97.
6. John Mullanphy, in his will stated, "I solemnly declare before God that she is not by daughter." John Mullanphy will, written February 27, 1830, recorded September 11, 1837. St. Louis Probate Court Files.
7. Northup, Twelve Years a Slave, 53, describing Eliza's life.
8. *Tempe v. Risdon H. Price*, CC case no. 181 (1821) and *Laban v. Risdon H. Price*, CC case no. 182 (1821) and *Dred Scott v. Irene Emerson*, CC case no. 1 (1846) and *Harriet Scott v. Irene Emerson*, CC case no. 2 (1846). For an account of Leah, see chapter 9.
9. Tracing the identities of Eliza's early series of masters has been difficult. Several George Taylors resided in St. Louis and Galena, although none of them appear to match up with the key dates in her account. The probate of Phillip Taylor in St. Louis mentions a George Taylor. Another George Taylor came to Galena as a schoolteacher. Eliza's case never went to a jury trial, or else the George Taylor who had been her master would have been called as a witness or deposed. The first time she was sold was to a man named "Cheek." That name is similarly hard to identify.
      The details about Perry Bark can be found in McMaster, *Sixty Years on the upper Mississippi*, 230.
10. Ibid., 4.
11. Dexter, *Bondage in Egypt*. See, generally, Illinois State Archives containing indenture records.
12. Deposition of Michel Byrne, in *Nelson Campbell v. Perry Burke* [sic], *et al.*, CC case no. 6879 (July 1835).
13. Campbell & Morehouse. George Whitaker Campbell first came to Galena in the employ of William Hempstead and then formed a company called Campbell and Morehouse with D. B. Morehouse. *History of Jo Daviess County*.
14. Aug 25, 1834, deed of sale of Eliza from George Taylor to Perry Burke. *Nelson Campbell v. Perry Burke, Hempstead, Beebe, Campbell, Morehouse*, CC case no. 6879 (July 1835). *Eliza Tyler v. Nelson Campbell*, CC case no. 35 (1835).
15. Deposition of Michael Byrne.
16. Eliza Tyler v Nelson Campbell, CC case no. 35 (1835).

17. Deposition of George Campbell in *Nelson Campbell v. Perry Bark, et al.*

18. 1835 Free Negro Bond for Eliza Taylor, St. Louis.

19. Deposition of George Campbell, in *Campbell v. Perry Bark, et al.*

20. April 18, 1835, deed of sale from Perry Burke to Nelson Campbell, *Campbell v. Perry Bark, et al.*

21. Ibid. Campbell's attorney was Charles J. Learned.

22. "In July 1830, William Henry, a thirty-one-year-old black man sued Galena-based Steamboat captain David G. Bates in St. Louis for his freedom. William Henry, born a slave in Virginia was brought to Kaskaskia in 1828. Elijah Inge took plaintiff to live in Galena, where he served Inge until June 1829. He was then sold to William Hempstead, who sold him to steamboat captain David G. Bates to work as a fireman on Defendant's steamboat." *William Henry v. David Bates*, CC case no. 30 (1830).

23. He won his suit within a month, and received one penny in damages instead of the $500 that he had requested.

24. Aug 16, 1830, "guilty. Jmt for Pl. judgment for P by agreement of the parties, William freed Dec. 21, 1846," p. 442.

25. Hempstead, "I at Home," mentions Hempstead siblings comings and goings to the Galena area, including transit of daughter Manual's girl, Rosalie, April 9, 1828.

26. *Nelson Campbell v. Perry Burke and William Hempstead*, CC case no. 6879 (1835).

27. There are several possibilities for Nelson Campbell. This man is probably John Campbell listed in the 1830 U.S. Census for Iberville, Louisiana as owning 46 slaves.

28. The 1836–1837 directory lists William Hempstead and E. H. Beebe as partners of Hempstead and Beebe. William Hempstead and Edward H. Beebe also ran a commission house in Galena. Edward Hempstead Beebe was born July 15, 1809. Hempstead, "I at Home."

29. The law firm was Learned & Hamilton. John F. Darby was assigned as her counsel. Nelson Campbell was represented by Charles J. Learned, the attorney he had consulted before, the man from whom he had received legal assurances before he paid for Eliza.

30. Judgment for plaintiff, registered, book 7, p. 481. December 1, 1835.

31. "Eliza Taylor, 24 years old, born 1811, 5'4' washer woman 1835, very light mulatto woman with freckled face," Free Negro Bond (1835). 1840 U.S. Census, St. Louis: "Eliza Tyler, one free woman of color, age 24–35."

32. Eliza Tyler's neighbors in the county were Moses Hempstead, Haskins Randell, Ross Davis, and Samuel Stokes; there was no one named Tyler, Taylor, or Cheek nearby to indicate a possible family member. Moses Hempstead had been the slave of Stephen, William Hempstead's father. Moses features prominently in Stephen Hempstead's 20 year diary, "I, at Home."

      The 1836–1837 St. Louis city directory lists "Moses Hempstad [*sic*], drayman" as living at 77 N. Third Street. The 1854 directory lists "Hempstead, George, drayman, ns. Spruce, b. 14th & 15th" and "Hempstead, Louise, (c) widow, ns. Spruce, b. 14th & 15th."

33. Terrah B. Farnsworth, Galena, discussed the matter with Nelson Campbell. Frederick Stahl, another experienced merchant-banker, was also consulted.

34. *Nelson Campbell v. Perry Burke, Hempstead, Beebe, Campbell, Morehouse*, CC case no. 6879 (1835). Injunction sought. This case was heard in Chancery.

35. 1850 U.S. Census for Jo Daviess County. See also McMaster, *Sixty Years on the Upper Mississippi*, p. 23.

36. Gary Henry, "Galena, Illinois During the Lead Mine Era," 75 (1976); The African Diaspora Archeology Network Newsletter, Sept. 2008, p. 5.

37. *See* Jacobs, *Incidents in the Life of a Slave Girl* (1861).

38. 1830 U.S. Census for Edenton, North Carolina lists four Norcom households James, John, Joseph, and William, containing 87 slaves altogether.

39. Jacobs, *Incidents*, 148–148. See also Bynum, *Unruly Women*, 38.

40. Jacobs, *Incidents*.

41. Cullum, *Biographical Register*, vol. 1, 358–59.

42. Frederick Norcom married Maria Beasley in 1828 in North Carolina. North Carolina Marriage Bonds, 1741–1868. He resigned from the army, August 13, 1832. Cullum, *Biographical Register*, vol. 1, 358–59.

12. According to the depositions in *Polly Wash v. Joseph M. Magehan*, CC case no. 167 (1839), Polly would have been in her teens in 1817–1818, either 14 or 15 years old based upon her birth in 1803.
13. Depositions in *Polly Wash v. Joseph M. Magehan*.
14. "Crockett and the brother-in-law of deponent, that is, James Wood were both drinking men." Deposition of Naomi Wood.
15. Depositions in *Polly Wash v. Joseph M. Magehan*.
16. A Madison County witness testified that Polly was born at the Beattys'. *Polly Wash v. Joseph M. Magehan*.
17. Ibid.
18. "[H]e was a little addicted to drink." Deposition of Samuel Woods. About Crockett's health, "I say he was failing I mean that he was failing in Constitution as any other drinking man does." Deposition of Naomi Woods.
19. Deposition of Jubilee Posey, "[H]er services were paid for by a frock; the winter was a severe one." "I may have paid him in corn or other things I do not recollect but I know Crockett was paid for her services."
20. Delaney, "From the Darkness," 9–10.
21. Crocket wrote to his son William and son-in-law David Beatty (presumably of the same slave-holding Beatty family from which Polly was bought), asking them to come and take her away to Missouri. Deposition of Naomi Woods.
22. Delaney, "From the Darkness," 9–10.
23. Ibid.
24. Lucy describes her own childhood as blissful ignorance of the slave life to come. Ibid. If Lucy had reflected her own life circumstance back against the life she imagined her mother had had "as a free girl in Illinois," she would have imagined her mother in an age of innocence as well.
25. Thomas Botts was later sought in Polly's lawsuit but could not be found. Sheriff's return, *Polly Wash v. Joseph M. Magehan*.
26. Delaney, "From the Darkness," 10–11.
27. See Harriet Jacobs' account of her childhood, Jacobs, *Incidents in the Life*.
28. Delaney, "From the Darkness," 13.
29. Ibid., 1. Taylor Berry's will can be found in the Howard County Will Book, H371, H374.
30. Delaney, "From the Darkness," 12. Judge Wash was on the Missouri Supreme Court for 21 years, and joined in most freedom-by-residence rulings. See discussion in Frazier, *Runaway and Freed Missouri Slaves*, 55.
31. Delaney, "From the Darkness," 12–13.
32. Taylor Berry's will, Howard County Will Book, H371, H374.
33. Delaney, "From the Darkness," 14.
34. Ibid., 16.
35. Ibid.
36. Ibid., 18–19.
37. Ibid., 19–20.
38. Ibid., 19.
39. Ibid., 21–22.
40. *Polly Wash v. Joseph M. Magehan*, CC case no. 167 (1839). The 1840 city directory lists J.M. Magehan as a house builder who resided on Third Street.
41. Delaney, "From the Darkness," 22. "At this time the Fugitive Slave Law was in full operation, and it was against the law of the whole country to aid and protect an escaped slave; not even a drink of water, for the love of the Master, might be given, and those who dared to do it (and there were many such brave hearts, thank God!) placed their lives in danger." Ibid., 23. The Fugitive Slave Act was not passed until 1850. Polly sued in 1839.
42. "A large reward was offered, the bloodhounds (curse them and curse their masters) were set loose on her trail. In the day time she hid in caves and . . . woods, and in the night time, guided by the wondrous North Star . . . my mother finally reached Chicago, where she was arrested by the negro-catchers. . . . The presence of bloodhounds and 'nigger-catchers' in their midst, created great excitement and scandalized the community. Feeling ran high and hundreds of

people gathered together and declared that mother should not be returned to slavery...." Ibid., 22–23.

Lucy may have collapsed her account of her mother's escape into popularly known fugitive slave trials like Shadrach Minkins and Anthony Burns that occurred a decade later after the Fugitive Slave Act was enacted.

43. See transcript of Polly's petition in note 46, this chapter.

44. Delaney, "From the Darkness," 23.

45. Lucy claimed that Polly employed "a good lawyer." Ibid, 24. In fact, as a poor person, she was assigned one. *Polly v. Magehan*, CC case no. 167 (1839.) Lucy recounts only two sentences about her mother's law suit. "She had ample testimony to prove that she was kidnapped, and it was so fully verified that the jury decided that she was a free woman, and papers were made out accordingly." Delaney, "From the Darkness," 24.

46. Polly's affidavit states the following:

"Sometime in the year of 1820 or 21 she was residing in Wayne County, Ky. in the custody of and as the slave of one Joseph Crockett, that sometime..., when she was 14 years of age she was removed by said Crockett her master and owner...to the state of Illinois and resided under his charge and immediate control at a place about 4 miles from the town of Edwardsville [Illinois] for several weeks during which time she was hired out by her master to different persons, to spin and perform the usual labours and duties incumbent upon a house servant at the rate of $2 a week. That her master regularly received this amount of wages as the remuneration for her services. That afterwards your petitioner was taken up the Missouri river & detained for about five years. That after different sales and trespass she was at last located in the family of one Taylor Berry and there remained twelve or 13 years. During which time after the decease of said Berry, one judge Wash of this county who married the widow of said Berry acted as the agent in hiring out of your petitioner—and about 4 years ago was hired out by said Wash to one Capt. Wayne of the Steamboat Banner as chambermaid and in that capacity of chambermaid made several trips up the Illinois river as afar as Peoria, for wages...of $15 a month and at the time within the jurisdiction of the State of Illinois was detained for at least five weeks. That she was hired by said Wash for the express purpose of running up said river of Illinois and judge Wash received the wages..." *Polly Wash v. Joseph M. Magehan*, CC case no. 167 (1839).

47. St. Louis CCRB, January 20, 1840, p. 87.

48. "Elijah Hayden, School director, ss Spruce w of First" in 1845 directory. E. Hayden was not listed in 1840–1841 directory. "Elijah Haydon [sic], Spruce b 1st & 2nd" in 1842 directory. In the 1840 census he is listed as "Elizah Hayden" [Elijah Hayden]. His household was comprised of one white man between the ages of 70 to 79, a white woman between 50 and 59, a white woman between 20 and 29 and 10 slaves: five children under 10 years old, 4 young slave women between 10 and 23 years old, and an adult slave woman between 36 and 54 years old. Elijah Hayden was the father of seven children. He survived the Civil War, living until 1869. In his will, he asked to be buried next to his wife in Alton, Illinois. Probate of Elijah Hayden, St. Louis probate files.

49. Free Negro Bond for Polly Wash and Lucy Turner. "Polly Wash, 38 years old; 5 feet 4 inches; brown complexion. Security Elijah Hayden. Occupation. Washerwoman, $200.00." September 26, 1843, Book 3, p. 439.

"Lucy A. Turner, 22 years old; 5 feet 3 ½ inches. Security—Elijah Hayden & George Ridenaun. Occupation: washer. $1,000.00." December 23, 1846, Book 4, p. 401.

50. Samuel Wood lived near Troy, Madison County, Illinois.

51. Harris Sprout was originally appointed as Polly's lawyer. Gustavus Bird took over from Sprout. Depositions in Polly's case. G. A. Bird also took his slave client Ralph Gordon out of state to find witnesses. *Ralph Gordon v. Duncan*, CC case no. 35 (1830), case no. 99 (1833). See chapter 8.

52. Delaney, "From the Darkness," 24–26.

53. Ibid., 27–32.

54. The jail was located on Sixth Street, between Chestnut and Market, where the Laclede Hotel later stood.

55. Delaney, "From the Darkness," 33–35. "At the time my mother entered suit for her freedom, she was not instructed to mention her two children, Nancy and Lucy, so the white people took advantage of this flaw, and showed a determination to use every means in their power to prove that I was not her child. This gave my mother an immense amount of trouble, but she had girded up her loins for the fight, and, knowing that she was right, was resolved, by the help of God and a good lawyer, to win my case against all opposition." Ibid., 35.

56. CCRB, December 13, 1842. p. 391.

57. Ibid.

58. Ibid.

59. Eric Gardner, in *Unexpected Places*, similarly plays off the contrast of language between Lucy's narrative, where she says that her mother was suing for her child, and the true next friend styling of the petition. He doesn't raise the further legal complexity of how a slave could stand in as next friend.

    Polly was not the only enslaved mother to stand as next friends for their younger children in their suits. See, for example, *Green Berry Logan v. Berry Meachum*, which was prosecuted by the plaintiff's mother Judy, alias Julia Logan his next friend. CCRB, December 22, 1836, p. 174. Similarly. *Andrew (Andrea)* [*sic*] *by Judy his next friend v. John B. Sarpy*, August 25, 1837, p. 306, and the motion for new trial in the same case, August 25, 1837, p. 308.

60. An example of the controversy over costs is found at CCRB, June 14, 1844. "Lucy Ann Britton v. David D. Mitchell, on the motion of said Defendant by his attorney it is ordered by the Court that the Bill of Costs against said Defendant be retaxed, which is done by striking out of said Bill the item of Jailor's fees for seventy eight dollars."

61. Delaney, "From the Darkness," 36.

62. *Lucy Ann Britton v. David D. Mitchell*, CC case no. 18 (1844.)

63. Delaney, "From the Darkness," 39.

64. Lucy's account transcribes Magehan as "MacKeon." Ibid., 39–40.

65. Ibid. Defendant moved for a new trial at the verdict. CCRB, Feb. 8, 1844, p. 368. Overruled. CCRB, March 1, 1844, p. 411.

    In the end, the jailer attempted to tax D. D. Mitchell for the jailer's fees of $78 for the cost of keeping Lucy. Mitchell's attorney was able to get the jailer's fee waived. CCRB, June 14, 1844. In the final entry for the case, CCRB, June 3, 1845, p. 271, Lucy voluntarily agreed not to prosecute the suit that might have gotten her damages. Given that very few litigants in that decade were receiving more than a penny of damages, Lucy did not forfeit much by this agreement.

66. Delaney, "From the Darkness," 49–50.

67. Ibid., 52–59.

68. Ibid., 58–61. "I became a member of the Methodist Episcopal Church in 1855; was elected President of the first colored society, called the 'Female Union,' which was the first ever organized exclusively for women...." Ibid., 62.

    Lucy Delaney then revealed another objective of her book: to demonstrate how capable her family was in succeeding and taking care of themselves. "[T]his sketch...may settle the problem in your mind, if not in others, 'Can the negro race succeed, proportionately, as well as the whites, if given the same chance and an equal start?'" Ibid., 63–64.

    It is interesting to reflect that this issue was in question in the 1890s when Lucy authored her memoir.

Chapter 12 The Slaves of Milton Duty

1. Waldrep, *Roots of Disorder*, 10; see also Morris, *Becoming Southern*.

2. To wit: "Charity—Nat, Louise, Braxton, Preston, Louisa, Melinda, Howard, Sassy, Clarissa, and Eliza, Susy, Mary, Louisa, Mary, Beverly and Alfred, Ann, Christine (?), Alan, Lesse, Lydia, Molly, Ann Beth, Jordan, Madison, Hendersons, Harry, Charlotty, Harrison." Milton Duty's will.

3. Duty's will, Milton Duty Probate file, St. Louis probate files.

4. Three men named by him as possible executors charged with the task of freeing thirty slaves promptly relinquished their willingness to serve as executor soon after the will was filed.

5. *Nat (of Color) v. G. W. Coons*, 10 Mo. 543 (1847).

6. Illinois Statute "An Act respecting Free Negroes, Mulattoes, Servants and Slaves."

7. March 1837 is said to be the date that Milton Duty moved his slaves to St. Louis, according to *Preston v. Coons*, CC case no. 674 (1841), CC case no. 34 (1844).

8. Those slaves whom he had designated to be sold first were not in the inventory. They probably did not accompany him to St. Louis. Neighbors said he sold some slaves before he left for St. Louis or thereafter.

9. Affidavit of neighbor James Adams, Milton Duty Probate, St. Louis probate files.

10. The man who captured Jordan was named David Early. He submitted a bill to the estate.

11. Malinda, Seany, Clarissa, and Caroline, all had young children.

12. A comparison of inventory names with the names originally listed in his will a few years earlier suggests that some slaves had already been sold.

13. Affidavit of William Adams, Milton Duty Probate, St. Louis probate files.

14. R. M. O'Blennis. Milton Duty Probate, St. Louis probate files.

15. Hugh Gallagher, a clerk in the Coons merchandizing firm, and young Coons' accomplice in removing the dead man's trunk, purchased the time of several slaves: Lucy $2.50 July 15, 1842 and July 15, 1843; Harry $7.50 July 15, 1843; Henderson $11.00 July 16, 1848; and Nat $6.50 July 15, 1842 and July 15, 1843. By 1845 the merchandizing firm was known as Coons and Gallagher.

16. The auctioneering firm of Murdoch and Dickson hired Preston each year from July 15, 1842 until 1848. The last hiring date was July 15, 1847 for one year. They also hired Jordan on July 15, 1847- and again the following two years. They hired Caroline to join Jordan the last two years. Murdock & Dickson, July 16 1848–1849 $5 per mo. hiring July 15 1849.

    Auctioneer R. B. Peck hired Nelly and Little Mary in July 15, 1842. Although Nelly dropped off the auction docket, (she may have died) Peck hired Little Mary the following year again for a lesser price. July 1843, $1.12 per month. Attorney F. W. Risque hired Clarissa on July 15, 1842.

17. July 1849 auction of the slaves of Milton Duty's estate.

18. See, for example, *Andrew, by grandmother and next friend, Judy v. John B. Sarpy*, CC case no. 43 (1837).

19. See note 16.

20. On July 15, 1847, Howard was hired to T. P. Fennell from whom he ran away. It was agreed that he be hired to John F. William to whom he was attached, so that he would not run away. By July 13, 1850 Howard was constrained and boarded in Lynch's slave pen.

21. *Nat (of Color) v. G. W. Coons*, 10 Mo. 543 (1847).

22. *Harney, Adm'r of Duty v. Dutcher & Dutcher*, 15 Mo. 89 (1851).

23. Madison was hired out to Thomas Gray.

24. Braxton was hired out to Edmund Shacklet.

25. *Jesse v. George W. Coons*, CC case no. 32 (1844). Case filed June 3, 1844. Defendant refused to hear writ June 10, 1844. Default ordered and judgment of freedom and costs on March 26, 1845.

26. "Kept in Jail from July 17-July 19, 1845". Milton Duty Probate charged by jailor. *Jesse v. George W. Coons*, CC case file no. 395 (April 1845), habeas corpus. Petitioner discharged from custody in hearing July 19, 1845.

    According to the 1840 Census for St. Louis Township, George W. Coons lived next to David Coons. George W. was listed as having twenty-seven slaves. These individuals are probably the slaves of Milton Duty's estate, over whom he had administrative control.

27. Executor Thomas Harney on September 3 stated, "As I could not hire some of the slaves with any reasonable security for their return in the city of St. Louis, I sent Henderson, Jordan, Mary & Ellen to be hired out in Liberty in the state."

28. All of Milton Duty's heirs were his siblings and their children: brother Gaius Duty, three living sisters, Maria Kirkwood, Lydia Anderson (wife of David W. Anderson), Edwina Anderson (wife of Joel D. Anderson), and sister Nancy Galloway (deceased), leaving six children.

    Warren County Mississippi weddings include these entries: "Duty, Milton married Fortner, Nancy on 24 Feb 1825" and "Anderson, David W. married Duty, Lydia on 24 Nov 1825."

29. Harrison was delivered to Gaius Duty on July 13, 1851. Harry was distributed to Vicksburg by *S. B. Pacific*, July 12, 1851. Margaret was brought back from country to the city and taken to Vicksburg, January 12, 1851. Harrison and Harry were both twenty-six years old. Margaret was eleven.

30. "Sibbon [*sic*] P. Perry, St Louis, St. Louis, Missouri 1840." "Sibbon" was undoubtedly a misspelling of Liliburn Perry.

31. The 1840–1841 city directory lists a "Niceney," a washerwoman living at First between Poplar and Plum.

32. See Pierre's treatment in chapter 13.

33. *Harney v. Scott*, 28 Mo. 333 (1859). The previous trip to the Missouri Supreme Court was in *Harney, Adm'r of Duty, v. Dutcher & Dutcher*, 15 Mo. 89 (1851). *Nat (of Color) v. G. W. Coons*, 10 Mo. 543 (1847).

34. The 1840 U.S. Census lists Geo W. Coons in St. Louis township: His household is comprised of three white persons and 27 slaves. See note 26.

    The 1840 U.S. census lists "David Coons household consists of 9 free white persons and 2 young slave women."

Chapter 13   Canadienne Rose

1. See generally, Gitlin, *The Bourgeois Frontier*; Hyde, *Empires, Nations, and Families*; Foley and Rice, *The First Chouteaus*; Winch, *Clamorgans*; Hoig, *Chouteaus*; entries of Pierre Chouteau Jr. and Auguste Pierre Chouteau in Hafen & Carter, *Mountain Men*; Christian, *Before Lewis and Clark*.

2. The multiple cases filed against the Chouteau family dynasty can be listed in a variety of ways: by chronology, by defendant household, or by slave family.

    Marie, a free mulatto girl (Marie Constant LaLande) v. Auguste Chouteau, CC case no. 205 (1821).

    Pelagie v. Francois Valois, and again later against Jean P. Cabanne, CC case nos. 12 and 9 (1822).

    Aspasia v. Francois Chouteau (son-in-law of Menard) and Pierre Menard, CC case no. 24 (1827), and again in CC case no. 5 (March 1828).

    The Scypions' suits include: *Marguerite v. Pierre, Sr. Chouteau*, CC case no. 26 (July 1825); *Pierre Chouteau, Sr. v. Marguerite*, 12 Pete 507 (1838); *Celeste v. LeFreniere Chauvin, Adm. of Helen Chevalier*.

    Francois Lagrange v. Bernard Pratte; Pierre Chouteau; Bertholemew Berthold; Jean P. Cabanne, CC case no. 29 (1827); *Theotiste v. Pierre, Jr. Chouteau*, CC case no. 6 (1827); *Elizabeth, Virginia, and Victoire v. Francis Menard and Andre Landreville*, CC case nos. 13, 14, and 15 (1827).

    Sally v. Henry Chouteau, CC case no. 101 (1835); *State of Missouri v. Walker, John K. (jailor of St. Louis); Pierre Chouteau; Bernard Pratt; Alexis Amelin*, St. Louis Court criminal index, case no. 1148, for habeas corpus of four slaves who were held on steamboat (March 1826); *Aspisa v. Joseph Rosati and Hardage Lane*, CC case no. 39 (1837); *Celeste v. Alexander Papin*, CC case no. 335; she had previously sued Laforce Papin. Later her children and sisters sued persons that they had been assigned to. *Lewis, a boy of color, by Celeste, his mother v. John Stacker* CC case no. 185 (1839); *Andrew, a boy of color by Celeste, his mother; also by Judy, grandmother v. John B. Sarpy and Peter Sarpy*, CC case no. 43 (1837), 20 (Nov. 1839); *Pelagie v. Francois Valois*, CC case no. 12 (Feb. 1822); *Pelagie v. Jean P. Cabanne*, CC case no. 9 (June 1822).

3. See discussion of *New York Times* interview of Mrs. Emerson Chaffee, in VanderVelde, *Mrs. Dred Scott*, 211.

4. Several pages of suggested jury instructions are included in Charlotte's case file. *Charlotte v. Gabriel Chouteau*, CC case no. 13 (1843). Juries were impaneled for trial on May 24, 1845, May 30, 1846, October 13, 1853, and May 28, 1856.

5. Hyde, *Empires, Nations and Families*, 31–32.

6. Beckwith, *Creoles of St. Louis.*

7. Foley, *Genesis of Missouri,* 118.

8. Francois LaGrange alias Isidore alleged that he was about to be subjected to severity of treatment by Pierre Chouteau, Jr., who he was suing for freedom. CCRB, December 5, 1826, p. 487. See also the state prosecution against Pierre Chouteau and others for attempting to kidnap four other freedom litigants. *State of Missouri v. John K. Walker (jailor of St. Louis); Pierre Chouteau; Bernard Pratt; Alexis Amelin,* St. Louis Court index.

9. Louis Menard took two of Auguste Chouteau's slaves to sale in New Orleans in December 1822; Francoise, age nineteen, and Adelaide, age sixteen, both mulattoes, were sold to Madame Eugenie Delassize, widow of Louis Avart. Missouri Historical Society, http://cdm.sos.mo.gov/u?/CivilWar,9220.

10. Francis Menard had been sued by Mary and her children. *Mary v. Francis Menard and Andre Landreville,* CC case no. 7 (1827). Since Menard resided in Illinois, he was able to remove the cases from the Missouri circuit court to federal court.

11. Papin, *The Village under the Hill,* 24. Papin describes seeing this firsthand. As a Chouteau relative, Auguste Chouteau's house would have been one of those great houses familiar to him.

12. Ibid., 29. See also Kennerly, *Persimmon Hill,* 21–22 (describing the French methods of celebrating New Year's in St. Louis).

13. Scharf, *History of St. Louis,* vol. 1, 66.

14. Auguste Chouteau owned at least four stone houses, stables, warehouses, and other post and beam houses as early as 1804. Ibid., 147.

15. Scharf, *History of St. Louis,* vol. 2, 1025. "Auguste Chouteau...liked to turn over property frequently, 'to realize on it' now and then....Chouteau built, traded, developed industries, turned his money over and over again, and was not afraid of taxes."

16. Ibid., 728, 734. Auguste and his wife Marie Therese Cerre Chouteau executed the deed in September 1823.

17. Ibid., 652. Auguste Chouteau's home had served as the place of hospitality both when explorer William Clark first passed through and when he brought his bride to settle in St. Louis. Kennerly, *Persimmon Hill,* 25.

18. The fortified stone wall was two feet thick and ten feet high. Darby, *Personal Recollections.*

19. Scharf, *History of St. Louis,* 193. Auguste Chouteau owned eight slaves in 1811. Rose's family must have been among them.

20. John Darby reported that as late as 1818, all the city's slaves spoke French. "Madame Chouteau had a splendid mansion, and a large number of servants (slaves), all of whom spoke French." Darby, *Personal Recollections,* 235.

21. Twelve years later, by the widow Chouteau's death, Rose too had died. She was not listed in the estate. Therese Chouteau Probate, St. Louis Probate files.

22. Pierre was born about 1807.

23. Peter Powell died in 1847, but Toussant is not listed in his estate. Peter Powell Probate, St. Louis Probate files.

24. The 1840 census lists twenty-six slaves owned by Cerre Chouteau, which was a shortened form of Marie-Therese Cerre Chouteau. There were also 11 white people and 1 free black man in the household. The single free black man may have been Benoist, Pierre's brother, whom Maria-Therese Cerre Chouteau freed.

25. The forty-eight slaves were grouped by several principal mothers.

    Rose age sixty-one, and her six children: Tousant, thirty-one, sold to Peter Powell; Benoist, thirty-three, retained by widow Marie-Therese Cerre Chouteau; Louis Rose; Michel Rose, twenty-one; Charlotte Rose, twenty-one; Pierre Rose, twenty-seven or twenty-nine. Antoine Charlotte was Rose's grandchild and Charlotte's oldest son.

26. According to Scharf, remaining in the family home was a Chouteau tradition. "Mr. P. Chouteau, Sr., for a few years after his first marriage, continued to live at his mother's house, southwest corner of Main and Chestnut." Scharf, *History of St. Louis,* vol. 1, 182. Auguste's son Henry and his wife and children lived there, as did unmarried adult sons Edward and Gabriel.

27. *Rachel v. William Walker,* CC case no. 82 (Nov. 1834).

28. Jay Gitlin refers to this as the French corridor. Gitlin, *Bourgeois Frontier*.
29. By the time Rose was twenty-five, around 1794, she resided at Michilimackinac and Prairie du Chien in John Stork's cabin home. *Pierre v. Therese Cerre Chouteau*, CC case no. 192 (1840).
30. The Montreal merchant was Andrew Todd. In 1794, the Spanish governor gave Andrew Todd, "a young and robust Irishman," the right to the exclusive trade of the upper Mississippi. "Don Andreas," as he came to be called, appears to have been successful in the undertaking, sending vast stores of goods up from New Orleans and bringing back furs. Jacob Van der Zee, "Fur Trade Operations in the Eastern Iowa Country under the Spanish Regime," 366.

Rose was sold to Pierre Joseph Didier on October 28, 1795. *Pierre v. Therese Cerre Chouteau*, CC case no 192. (1840).
31. Rose was sold to Auguste Chouteau on August 8, 1798. Ibid.
32. 1840 petition. Rose may have been mulatto also. One witness described her as "yellowish, rather than black black." Deposition of Madame Tisson.
33. The St. Louis cathedral was the only church with a choir. Wilson Primm was its principal singer. Stevens, *St. Louis: The Fourth City*, vol. 2, 657.
34. Sally's circumstance differed from Pierre's because she had been placed with the Chouteaus at her parents' death with a promise of her eventual freedom.
35. Breckenridge, "Biographical Sketch of Judge Wilson Primm." Primm's last appearance in Pierre's case was November 22, 1843.
36. It is likely that Benoist was freed by Therese Chouteau. A man named Benoit [*sic*] (age thirty-nine) was freed by a Cerre Chouteau on August 17, 1836. Therese Chouteau's maiden name was Cerre, and after her husband's death, she was often known as Cerre Chouteau. See, e.g., the 1840 U.S. Census entry. Therese Chouteau manumitted only two other slaves, Clarisse and her daughter Lucile. Lucile was manumitted first, and later her mother Clarisse on July 23, 1841.

It is possible that Benoist and Clarisse were a couple. On the other hand, a free man of color known only as Benoist manumitted a mulatto woman named Victoire on July 20, 1841, CCRB p. 373. Were Benoist and Benoit the same man?
37. *Sally v. Henry Chouteau*, CC case no. 101 (1835). Sally was declared free on April 10, 1837. CCRB, p. 223.
38. Among Therese Chouteau's thirteen slaves were Pierre Rose and Charlotte as well as Charlotte's children: Victorine, daughter, b. 1839; Euphrasie, daughter, b. 1841 or 1842; Angela, or Angeline, daughter; Antoine, son, b. 1827 (b. 1826 according to Auguste Chouteau's will); and Pierre Sophia, Frederick, Justine, Francois, Julie, Cornelia, and Peter. Therese Chouteau Probate, St. Louis Probate files.
39. CCRB, August 22, 1842, p. 326.
40. Paschall Cerre, Marianne Tison [sometimes spelled Tisson] and her son Francoise, Antoine Smith, and Dr. Trudeau were summoned for testimony.
41. Deposition of Francois Menard.
42. *Adrian Paschall v. Richard W. Ulrici*, CC case no. 340 (1844).
43. *Louis v. Gabriel Chouteau*, CC case no. 51 (1843); *Michel v. Gabriel Paul*, CC case no. 151 (1844); *Mary Charlotte v. Gabriel S. Chouteau*, CC case no. 13 (1843).
44. Charlotte made out her affidavit before Kretchmar, a justice of the peace. Charlotte was appointed Henry Cobb, as her attorney. He who practiced law with a partner. Louis was assigned Cobb's partner, Duncan, as his attorney. Effectively, both were represented by the same firm.
45. *The Western Journal and Civilian* lasted at least until May 1855. M. Tarver and H. Cobb were its editors and proprietors. Scharf, *History of St. Louis*, vol. 1, 940.
46. See Chapter 5.
47. Letter from Kenneth MacKenzie to Gabriel Chouteau (May 3, 1843), Missouri Historical Society, Slave Papers, Slave Sale Letter.
48. Scharf, *History of St. Louis*, vol. 2, 1232 (describing the Millers' Association organized by Gabriel and others). Gabriel Chouteau was involved in the development of Washington Square, as described by Darby in his memoir, *Personal Reflections*.
49. The Coroner's entry reads: "1837, August 26, Antoine Fetia, a slave, folder 29, no. 37, Gabriel Chouteau, visitation of God, Chouteau's pond." Another slave named Anderson, a slave of

Bernard Finney, was found drowned in Chouteau's pond within a month of Antoine Fetia's death. The coroner deemed that death an accident. Coroner's inquest into Anderson, a slave, case number 25859 (1837). Another black man named Fayette drowned in Chouteau's mill pond in 1839. Coroner's folder 29, no. 36. Additional drownings seemed to occur there regularly.

50. *Missouri Republican,* July 23, 1852.

51. Gabriel Chouteau owed his lawyers, the firm of Spalding and Tiffany, $110, by the time that Josiah Spalding died, as well as a yet undetermined amount for Pierre's suit for freedom. Gabriel would be charged separately as administrator in that litigation. Accounts due in Josiah Spalding Probate, St. Louis Probate Court Files.

52. Slavery was abolished in Canada on August 1, 1834, by the British Parliament's Slavery Aboli- tion Act, an act which extended throughout the British Empire.

53. The War of 1812 set the boundary when the United States pressed north but lost the military effort to overtake all the land north of the Great Lakes. The border was resolved in the Treaty of Ghent 1814.

54. Charlotte had four children, Victorine, Euphrasie, Antoine, and Angela, when she was sold to Kenneth Mackenzie, May 1, 1843. By 1853, she had another infant.

55. *Gabriel S. Chouteau v. Pierre,* 9 Mo. 3 (1845).

56. *Michel Paul v. Adolphe Paul,* CC case no. 143 (1845). "Within the last few days, Michel gave by his actions your petition reasonable grounds for [supposing] that he will from the lines of this state and be out of the jurisdiction."

57. More depositions were taken from Paschal Cerre, Michael Marlé, Dr. Trudeau, Antoine Smith, Marianne Tison, Dufraine, J. B. Lesparance, Precis, Cuigan, Michel Fortan, and Pierre LaRiviere. *Mary Charlotte v. Gabriel S. Chouteau,* CC case no. 13 (1843).

58. Depositions in *Mary Charlotte v. Gabriel S. Chouteau,* CC case no. 13 (1843).

59. Deposition of Madame Tisson.

60. VanderVelde, *Mrs. Dred Scott,* 251, quoting Bates's journal, May 1, 1847, Bates Family Papers.

61. Transcript of sale of Rose from Didier to Auguste Chouteau. *Pierre v. Therese Cerre Chouteau,* CC case no. 192 (1840). The price was six cents fifty piasters in deerskins.

62. Deposition of Madame Tisson. Perhaps Pierre inherited his "mulatto" appearance from his mother, though none of his siblings were identified that way.

63. Hall's estate was charged amounts paid for Dred Scott, as well as Milton Duty slaves. David N. Hall probate, St. Louis Probate Files, group 8 and 53. There does not appear to be a document about Pierre's hire in the probate file.

64. Nov. 25, 1846, filing in *Michel Paul v. Gabriel Paul,* CC case no. 151 (1844). When Michel's defendant died, he had to refile against his administrator. Michel was the only slave man listed in that estate.

65. This is gleaned from discussions of Rose's life in the past tense, as if it had ended, in the wit- nesses' testimony.

66. VanderVelde, *Mrs. Dred Scott,* 269–70.

67. Sheriff's affidavit in *Pierre v. Gabriel Chouteau,* CC case no. 125 (1842).

68. Deposition of Lewis H. Martin and Wm H. Kerrick, February 17, 1849, *Pierre v. Gabriel Chou- teau.* The jailer and deputy jailer stated "that Pierre a man of color has been in said jail for about ten months, that there affiants have seen him almost daily during that time, and have observed his conduct, that in the opinion of these affiants he is at times of unsound mind and insane; and the said Kerrick states that he believes from what he has seen of said Pierre and his conduct, that he believes him to have been insane the whole time of his incarceration; that said Pierre is the same who is now suing for his freedom in the St. Louis Circuit Court."

69. See Dorothea Dix's description of the St. Louis jail in VanderVelde, *Mrs. Dred Scott,* 262–263, and 451n61.

70. Sheriff's affidavit in *Pierre v. Gabriel Chouteau,* CC case no. 125 (1842).

71. Pierre was beaten and removed from the jail by Gabriel Chouteau and Reuben Bartlett some- time between August 21, 1852 and September 13, 1852. "Affidavit of Chas H Mercier that pff was subjected to severity & c, & concealed by deft. Filed Oct 22nd 1852." *Pierre v. Gabriel Chouteau,* CC case no. 125 (1842).

72. *State v. Reuben Bartlett,* indictment September 6, 1852. "That Reuben Bartlett late of Saint Louis County aforesaid on the first day of _____ [*sic*] in the year of our Lord one thousand eight hundred and fifty two at Saint Louis County aforesaid, with force and arms unlawfully

fraudulently and feloniously without lawful authority and forcibly did seize and confine inveigle and kidnap one George Johnson a free man of color then and there feloniously fraudulently and unlawfully and without lawful authority [caused] to be taken and sent out of this state of Missouri...." Samuel Lucas, otherwise called Sterling Lucas, was charged with assisting Bartlett in the crime.

George Johnson had originally sued Henry Moore for freedom, *George Johnson v. Henry Moore*, CC case no. 36 (1852) and he later sued Reuben Bartlett. *George Johnson v. Reuben Bartlett*, CC case no. 281 (1852).

73. *Mary Charlotte v. Gabriel Chouteau*, Sheriff's writ, December 6, 1853. This writ is misfiled, and can be found in the 1843 case file. Several of the many filings in the related case of Rose's children are misfiled. Given the repeated calls of the same witnesses over more than a decade, the misfiling are understandable.

74. Ibid.

75. Gabriel Chouteau may have taken up with either Louisa or Mary Labadie, both free women of color. Both women are listed as living in his home in both 1850 and in 1860. Curiously, young children who had been identified as Robert, Oliver, and Louisa Chouteau in 1850 are identified respectively with the last name "Labadie" in the 1860 census, still living in Gabriel's home. Cyprian Clamorgan describes Gabriel Chouteau's housekeeper, Mary Labadie, in 1860 as a free woman of color working for one of the richest white businessmen in the city. Clamorgan, *Colored Aristocracy*, 88. There is no marriage certificate to be found for Gabriel Chouteau, and no marriage noted in the family genealogy, Beckwith, *Creoles of St. Louis*.

Pierre was listed separately in the jail. 1850 U.S. Census for St. Louis, 2nd Ward.

76. W. Johnson, *River of Dark Dreams*, 139–40.

77. *Charlotte v. Chouteau*, 21 Mo. 590 (1855), and later 25 Mo. 465 (1857).

78. *Mary Charlotte v. Gabriel Chouteau*, May 16, 1856 p. 416.

79. *Mary Charlotte v. Gabriel Chouteau*, Tuesday, May 27, 1856, p. 427. "[T]he Court having been informed by the attorney for the plaintiff that she and her children are now confined in the Jail of this County on motion of plaintiff's attorney it is ordered that the said plaintiff and her children be brought into court to attend the Court during the trial of this cause...."

80. Also *Mary Charlotte v. Gabriel Chouteau*, May 29, 1856, pp. 429–30.

81. *Mary Charlotte v. Gabriel Chouteau*, May 30, 1856, pp. 430–431; *Mary Charlotte v. Gabriel Chouteau*, May 31, 1856, p. 432. Affidavit for appeal filed.

82. "Louis Chouteau, the plaintiff in the above named suit, of Louis Chouteau vs Gabriel S. Chouteau, being duly sworn on his oath says that on the 6th of June 1857 he the plaintiff was committed by the Sheriff of St Louis Court, for safe keeping to the Common jail of said County, where said plaintiff is now kept to prevent him said plaintiff from being removed out of the jurisdiction of this Court...." Bill of jailer for Louis's keep. *Louis v. Gabriel Chouteau*, CC case no. 51 (1843).

83. Motion of Louis's attorneys to reduce bond. Ibid.

84. Motion of Gabriel Chouteau for change of venue. *Charlotte v. Gabriel Chouteau*, CC case no. 13 (1843). These motions were made more than once, occurring in 1855, 1857, and 1859.

85. *Charlotte v. Chouteau*, 33 Mo. 194 (1862).

86. Even after losing this lawsuit, Gabriel Chouteau continued to pursue his slaves to the full. The Union Provost Marshal Records for St. Louis contain a complaint of Gabriel Chouteau that his slave, Thomas Frazier, left him to escape punishment. F1186. March 20, 1863; and another in which Gabriel Chouteau asks for the return of his escaped slave known to be working at the Provost Marshal's prison. F1186. March 24, 1863.

Chapter 14 The Final Chapter

1. Chief Justice Roger Taney decision in *Dred Scott v. Sandford*, 60 U.S. 393, 406 (1857).

2. In addition to the lawsuits for which we have intact records, there is evidence of eleven additional cases in the CCRB for which no records have been found or the records are very incomplete. *Amy v. Nance, Administrator*, filed April 10, 1821; *Seely and George v. William Soublette*,

filed June 15, 1823 and June 20, 1823 respectively; *Letty Fenwick v. Samuel Abbot*, filed October 1823; *Judy and Josiah v. Ephraim Town*, filed August 22, 1825; *Randal v. Owen Riley*, filed August 19, 1831; *Nathaniel alias Nat v. Stephen Ruddell*, filed April 22, 1834; *Thomas Lindsay and John Lindsay v. John Chandler and John James*, filed March 1835; *In the Matter of Toney, alias William Morton—on habeas corpus*, 11 Mo. 661 (July 1848); *Ellen Stevens v. Henry Spence*, filed November 1848; *Anderson Stewart v. John M. Jamison, jailor*, filed 1844; *Henry Lohre v. Gaius Duty*, filed 1852.

In an additional thirteen cases, the records are incomplete because the venue was changed.

Jeffrey v. Robideaux, after a long fight to set aside the verdict, venue finally changed to Jefferson County, August 27, 1836, CCRB, p. 121.

Catiche v. Chouteau, venue changed Dec. 8, 1828.

Agnes v. Menard, case removed to U.S. District Court, Dec. 5, 1835, p. 489.

Paul Auguste Allan, an infant of color, by nxt frd, Benjamin Lawhead v. Bazile Allard, case removed to U.S. District Court for Mo., July 17 1835, p. 410.

Hetty v. Arthur L. Magennis, venue changed to Washington County, April 30, 1836, p. 66.

Sally Melvin and Daniel Wilson v. Robert Cohen, venue changed, July 27, 1837, p. 285.

Celeste v. Laforce Papin, venue changed to St. Charles County, Sept. 12, 1838.

Charles v. Verhagen and Rosati, case transferred to Court of Common Pleas, April 26, 1841, p. 319.

Charles v. Belina Christy, case transferred to Court of Common Pleas, Jan. 6, 1842, p. 204.

Squire Brown v. Charles Anderson, case transferred to Court of Common Pleas. June 18, 1844, p. 131.

Thomas Jefferson v. Hopkins, case transferred to Court of Common Pleas, May 27, 1844, p. 77. "P defaults on Colton/Moulton suit Nov. 30, 1846, p. 390 Common Pleas, March Term 1844 #219."

Rebecca v. James Black, Thos Horine & Geo H.C. Melody, case transferred to Court of Common Pleas requested. May 27, 1844, p. 80.

Chloe Ann v. Franklin Knox, Jan. 26, 1846. "Plff clms she cannot have a fair trial in this ct because she believes the judge is prejudiced against her right to recover. Jan 30, 1846, Field & Murdock moved to set aside nonsuit because requested change of venue. Motion to set aside nonsuit & certify cause to Court of Common Pleas" January 30, 1846, p. 67.

Often additional information essential to understanding these freedom suits is found in other documents, such as runaway ads or probate or criminal case files.

3. For Harriet Beecher Stowe's fictional character, George, the proper response to enslavement was to take the risk and run away. Stowe, *Uncle Tom's Cabin*, Chapter 11.

4. Solomon Northup, *Twelve Years a Slave*, 26.
   "I was too ignorant, perhaps too independent, to conceive how anyone could be content to live in the abject condition of a slave.... [A]nd never once, I am proud to say, did I fail to counsel anyone who came to me, to watch his opportunity and strike for freedom." Ibid.

5. See generally Patterson, *Slavery and Social Death*.

6. See generally Scott, *Weapons of the Weak*.

7. Delaney, "From the Darkness," 42.

8. For example, master Edward Bates expressed complete surprise when a slave mother fled, leaving behind her four children. Yet, her action prompted him to sell the children immediately. He would provide them no care in her absence. Edward Bates's diary, cited in VanderVelde, *Mrs. Dred Scott*, 226, n. 77.

9. Harriet Jacobs described the dilemma of permanent separation posed by the decision to flee to the north in her memoir. She realized that in escaping she was about to leave her North Carolina family forever. Jacobs, *My Life*, 236. Similarly, Polly Wash had to visit her escaped daughter in Canada in order to see her; her daughter could not safely return to St. Louis until after the Civil War.

10. Solomon Northup, *Twelve Years a Slave*, 45–46.

11. Scott, *Weapons of the Weak*, 34.
12. See chapter 13. Lucy claims that her mother had been advised not to file the lawsuits simultaneously. Delaney, "From the Darkness", 23–24. Polly's first lawyer was Harris Sprout, who neglected other slave clients as well. See note 38.
13. Ibid., 13.
14. The degree of false signaling is shown by the fact that an extraordinary number of petitions alleged that the beating took place on the same formulaically chosen date: January 1. Although New Year's Day was a day of revelry in the St. Louis community, that revelry did not include slave beating.
15. For example, Phillis alleged that her master put a rope around her neck "so as to choke her." *Phillis v. Redding Herrin*, CC case no. 51 (1836). In another case, defendant Samuel Abbott acknowledged that he "chastised" Lethy Fenwick, but claimed it was justified because she had behaved badly: "[J]ust before time of assault plaintiff neglected her duty as said servant and in and about Defendant's business behaved & conducted herself in a disorderly, saucy, contemarious [*sic*] & improper manner toward Defendant & contrary to obedience due Plaintiff, resisted and refused to obey the lawful commands of Defendant whereupon...Defendant...did moderately chastise & correct said Plaintiff for her neglect of duty, disobedience & misconduct, & in so doing did necessarily & unavoidably a little beat, bruise & illtreat Plaintiff and imprison her for a space of time as was lawfull for him to do." *Lethe Fenwick v. Abbot, Samuel*, CC case no. 99 (1823).
16. Delaney, "From the Darkness," 47.
17. See generally Fisher, "Jury's Rise." Missouri first permitted parties to testify on their own behalf in civil suits after 1866. Missouri: An Act in Relation to the General Statutes of the State of Missouri, ch. 144, § 1, 1866 Mo. Laws 586, 586.
18. When it was publicly revealed that he was the father of Hester's oldest child, he was absent from the state.
19. See Chapter 8.
20. Delaney, "From the Darkness", 39–43.
21. Statement of D. D. Mitchell in Delaney, "From the Darkness," 34.
22. This concern was addressed in section 4 of the Missouri statute, Freedom: An Act to Enable Persons held in Slavery, to Sue for their Freedom, which provided:
    "If the court or judge is satisfied, at the time of presenting the petition at any time during the pendency of the suit, that the petitioner has been, or is about to be, restrained by any person, of reasonable liberty of attending his counsel on the court, or is about to be removed out of the jurisdiction of the court, or that he has been, or is about to be, subjected to any severity on account of his application for freedom, the court or judge shall cause the petitioners to be brought up by a warrant under the seal of the court or hand of the judge."
    Similar rules were in effect in other jurisdictions, like Washington, D.C., as well. See, for example, *Ex parte Negro Letty*, Cranch C.C. 328 (July term 1806.) which held that a master must post security before the sheriff can release the servant from custody, presumably lest she be stolen away.
23. Zaborney describes hired slaves' opportunities to pressure their owners to accept their preferences in hirers. Zaborney, *Slaves' for Hire*, 82–85. It is unlikely that slaves hired out by sheriffs enjoyed this type of leverage. The directive was to hire the slave to the highest bidder. See also Martin, *Divided Mastery*.
24. *Harry Dick a free negro man v. Stephen Smith*, CC case no. 15 (1827). See also *Tempe, a black woman v. Risdon H. Price*, CC case no. 181 (1821). Tempe complained that her master "refused to supply her with clothing necessary, for comfort and decency, alleging as a reason that he expected soon, to lose, her...."
25. *Lucy Ann Britton v. David D. Mitchell*, CC case no. 18 (1844); *Harry Dick, a free negro man v. Smith*, CC case no. 15 (1827).
26. *Lethy Fenwick v. Samuel Abbot; Betsy Hagan v. Philip Rocheblave; Dorinda v. John Simonds; Molly Rector, a free woman of color, by Louis A. Benoist as next friend v. John Bivens; Elizabeth, Victoire, and Virginia v. Francis Menard and Andre Landreville*, (after their mother, Mary, lost her lawsuit); *Mary v. James Clemens, Sr.; Mary Farnham v. Samuel D. Walker; Matilda Thomas and Missouri*

Littleton v. William Littleton; Thomas Scott v. James Harrison; David McFoy v. William Brown; Joseph Jefferson v. William McCutchen; James McKnight; Caroline Bascom, a free mulatto woman v. John H. Ferguson.

27. See, for example, Mary Johnson's children, Elizabeth, Victoire, and Virginia. Each of their cases ended with the entry that plaintiff would no longer prosecute, soon after Mary Johnson lost her suit. *Mary, a free woman of color v. Francis Menard; Elizabeth, a free girl of color v. Francis Menard; Victoire, a free girl of color v. Francis Menard; Virginia, a free girl of color v. Francis Menard,* CC case numbers 21–24 (1829).

28. *Susan v. Henry Hight.* See, for example, Aspasia, where she defaulted and her case was re-opened later. *Aspasia v. Francois Chouteau and Pierre Menard,* default, December 10, 1827, but case proceeds in 1828.

29. Marc Galanter coined the term "repeat player" as a party engaged in a series of successive lawsuits who has the opportunity to shape legal rules by deciding which cases to appeal and which to settle. Galanter, "Why the 'Haves' Come Out Ahead?"

30. *Elsa Hicks, a mulatto girl v. Patrick T. McSherry,* CC case no. 121 (1847).

31. *Tempe, a black woman v. Risden H. Price,* CC case no. 181 (1821).

32. *Mary and her children, Samuel and Edward v. Launcelot H. Calvert,* CC case no. 2 (1851).

33. Several are detailed in this book: the family of John Merry, the Titus family; the attempt to kidnap Pierre, son of Rose, while he was in jail; the Duncans' multiple attempts to kidnap slaves suing for freedom; Stephen Smith's kidnap of the former Shipman slaves. Others not detailed in this book include: *Randal v. Owen Riley,* Aug. 19, 1830, p. 55. *Malinda and Nelly v. Robert Wilburn,* October 8, 1823. *Cartiche alias Catherine, Julie, Joseph and Helen v. Pierre Chouteau; Francois LaGrange alias Isidore v. Pierre Chouteau, Jr.,* December 5, 1826, p. 487. *Josephine LaCourse v. Edward Mitchell,* December 1, 1835, pp. 481–482. *Daniel Talbot v. James C. Music, Prudence Music & Delford Benton,* Nov. 30, 1839, p. 591. *Charles v. Belina Christy,* March 1, 1841, p. 121; *In the matter of Squire Brown (Squire Brown v. Charles R. Anderson),* January 26, 1844, p. 357; *Adrean (Adrian) Paschall v. Richard W. Ulrici,* March 19, 1844, pp. 435–436; *Chloe Ann Smith v. Franklin Knox,* September 9, 1844, p. 220; *Laura v. Henry B. Belt,* February 26, 1852, p. 421; *In the matter of Henry Lohre Suing for freedom,* February 26, 1852, pp. 421–422.

34. See Dexter, *Bondage in Egypt.*

35. See the discussion of Murdoch's departure in VanderVelde, *Mrs. Dred Scott,* 242–43.

36. Isaac McGirk died in 1830. Matthias McGirk left St. Louis and moved to Montgomery County Missouri in 1827. Ferdinand Risque left St. Louis at the end of 1843. Frances B. Murdoch left in 1846. VanderVelde, *Mrs. Dred Scott,* 243. Gustavus Bird died in 1847. D. H. Hall died in 1850.

37. See generally, Kaufman, *Dred Scott's Advocate.*

38. *Rebecca, a negro woman v. James Black and Thomas Horine & George H. C. Melody,* CC case no. 24 (1843).

39. In Illinois, which provided no statute for the appointment of attorneys, enslaved Lucinda sought the help of Murray McConnel. A contemporary recounted the story:
    "So advised [of her right to freedom in Illinois], Lucinda went to a lawyer, Murray McConnel, one 'Who feared not God and regarded not man.' The fee he demanded was a large one, two years of service in his kitchen without wages. The case was easy: she was free."
    Steiner, "Abolitionists," 218.

40. VanderVelde, *Mrs. Dred Scott,* 292–93.

41. The following cases resulted in hung juries. *Delph v. Stephen Dorris,* December 6, 1837, p. 401; *Celeste & Celestine v. Alexander Papin,* September 1, 1838, p. 247; *Alsey v. William S. Randolph,* January 10, 1842, p. 211. *Louis Scott v. William Burd,* January 18, 1844, p. 339; *Pierre of color v. Gabriel S. Chouteau,* May 4, 1847, p. 575. *Martha Ann of color v. Hiram Cordell,* May 13, 1847, p. 592. All pages noted are in the CCRB.

42. In the case of *Martha Ann v. Hiram Cordell,* hung juries were recorded on January 21, 1846, p. 47, May 7, 1846, p. 280; May 13, 1847, p. 592. She eventually prevailed, December 12, 1849. All references are to the CCRB.

43. Jury decisions in Pierre and Charlotte's cases seemed to alternate wins and losses for the petitioners.

44. There is an alternative hypothesis to explain some positive outcomes for slave petitioners. The victory may not be attributable to the strength of the plaintiff's case as much as to the slave owner's vulnerability before juries. The black minister John Berry Meachum lost five cases, every lawsuit brought against him by slaves that he owned: Brunetta, Archibald, the two Judies, and Judy Logan's child. If St. Louis norms frowned upon Free Blacks owning slaves, as an upset of the racial order, then his position as a slaveholder defending his property claim would be more vulnerable than the white slave owners'. But if, on the other hand, these cases simply followed the rule of law, every slave petitioner who sued him did produce the evidence sufficient to win.

    Brunetta Barnes v. John Berry Meachum, CC case no. 40 (1840); *Archibald Barnes v. John Berry Meachum*, CC case no. 41 (1840); *Archibald Barnes v. John Berry Meachum*, CC case no. 120 (1840); *Brunetta Barnes v. John Berry Meachum*, CC case no. 121 (1840); *Brunetta Barnes v. John Berry Meachum*, CC case no. 123 (1840); *Judy (also known as Julia Logan) v. John Berry Meachum*, CC case no. 11 (1835); *Judy v. John Berry Meachum*, CC case no. 22 (1836); *Green Berry Logan, an infant of color v. John Berry Meachum, a free man of color*, CC case no. 22 (1836).

    Another discrete group that lost more suits than other slave owners were slave traders. This trade was viewed with some disdain in the local community. The fact that slave traders repeatedly turned over their inventory in human beings was a practice that some local slaveholders found most objectionable. Freedom cases against slave traders included *Mary Ann Steel v. William Walker*, CC case no. 97 (1835); *Harriet, an infant v. Samuel T. McKenney*, CC case no. 17 (1833); *Rachel v. William Walker*, CC case no. 82 (1834); *James Henry, a boy of color v. William Walker*, CC case no. 83 (1834); *Hester Williams, Ella Williams, and Priscilla Williams v. A.B. McAfee, Frederick Norcum, Glanville Blakey, William Moore*, CC case no. 119 (1853); *Samuel, infant of color v. Bernard T. Lynch*, CC case no. 29 (1851); *George Johnson v. Reuben Bartlett*, CC case no. 281 (1852).

45. *Missouri Argus*, Jan 20, 1837.

46. Articles in the *Missouri Republican* described episodes in which several slaves escaped together as "slave stampedes." See, for example, *Missouri Republican*, July 16, 1856.

47. The following cases are listed in order of their victories and identified by plaintiff and defendant only *Winny v. Donner*; *Tempe v. Risden Price*; *Laban v. Risden Price*; *Winny v. Whitesides* and her many children; *Marie v. August P. Chouteau*; *John Merry v. Clayton Tiffin and Louis Menard*; *John v. William Campbell*; *Israel v. William Rector and Isaac C. A. Letcher*; *Milly, Harry Dick, David Shipman, and William v. Stephen Smith*; *Aspasia*; *James Singleton v. Alexander Scott and Robert Lewis*; *Matilda v. Philip Rocheblave*; *George Relfe v. Thompson H. Ficklin*; *Vincent, Ralph, Nicholas Jones v. John W. Honey*; *William Henry v. David G. Bates*; *Harriet v. Samuel McKinney*; *Dunky v. Andrew Hay*; Lydia Titus's children in their several suits; Marcelline Vincent and her children; *James Wilkinson v. Aaron Young*; Mary Ann aka Julia; Judy Logan and her son; Judy Lacompte and her children; Josephine Lacourse; Eliza Tyler; Daniel Wilson; *Lewis v. James Newton*; *Ben v. Thomas J. White*; Lewis, Nancy, Phebe, Robert, and William Stubbs; Rebecca; Charles Endicott; Polly Wash and daughter Lucy; Diana Cephas; Leah Charleville and her children; Jonathan; Alsey; Vica and her children; Jinny Jackson and her children; *Mary v. James Dougherty*; *Hannah v. John Pitcher*; Martha Ann; *James v. Hiram Cordell*; Martha Drusella; *Sarah v. William Waddington*; *Gabriel v. Andrew Christy*; Patsy Curd; Mary and her children suing Calvert; and Hester Williams and her children.

48. Professor Ira Berlin identifies the four great migrations as: the transatlantic voyage, from the seaboard to the interior, or black belt, from the rural south to the urban north, and most recently, the global diaspora to American cities. Berlin, *The Making of African America*, 31.

49. See VanderVelde, *Mrs. Dred Scott*, describing Harriet's winters as a servant in what was regarded as the far north, Ibid. 52–61 and the account of Rose's early life as an enslaved servant north of the Great Lakes and in Prairie du Chien, Ibid. 251.

50. *Rachel v. William Walker*, CC case no. 82 (1834); *Courtney v. Samuel Rayburn*, CC case no. 10 (1836).

    Dred's master had been a military doctor rather than an army officer, but the distinction was negligible as far as being stationed at a fort in free territory.

51. VanderVelde, *Mrs. Dred Scott*, 281.
52. Ibid., 274.
53. Ibid., 284.
54. The change in the composition of the Missouri Supreme Court did not occur until October 1851. VanderVelde, *Mrs. Dred Scott*, 285–86.
55. Ibid., 268.
56. Ibid., 280.
57. It should be noted that freedom suits were also brought in Missouri courts outside of St. Louis. St. Charles County entertained several freedom suits, including the one brought by Lydia Titus' daughter, *Matilda v. Isaac VanBibber* (April 1815) St. Charles County case files Box 14, Folder 14. St. Louis's location as a steamboat hub and regional commerce center made it a popular location for these lawsuits.
58. VanderVelde, *Mrs. Dred Scott*, 295.
59. "Famous Dred Scott Case: Mrs. Chaffee, owner of old slave, still living in Springfield," *New York Times*, December 22, 1895.
60. Ibid. This claim seems a bit exaggerated. I have not been able to find reference to that incident in the *Missouri Republican*, where ads for runaways were usually posted. It is more likely the Chouteau family was animated by years of losses in freedom suits. See chapter 13, note 2.
61. See Chapter 13.
62. See, for example, the practices in Louisiana courts after the *Dred Scott* decision. Schafer, *Becoming Free*, 2.
63. Jordan Early is said to have walked the entire way from Virginia to Missouri. Early, *Life and Labors*, 15. Similarly, William Wells Brown recounts making the entire trip west by walking. Brown, *From Fugitive Slave*, 95–110.
64. *Louis Scott v. William Burd*, CC case no. 362 (1841); *Charles v. Peter Verhagen*, CC case no. 203 (1840). Hannah was sent to Boston to travel with the family. *Hannah v. John Pitcher*, CC case no. 16 (1844).

BIBLIOGRAPHY

Abbreviations

Every County Circuit Court had a Circuit record book. CCRB refers to the St. Louis Circuit Court record book unless it is identified with another county, such as the Jo Daviess CCRB or St. Clair CCRB, for the Circuit Court Record Books of Jo Daviess County and St. Clair County respectively.

CCRB = St. Louis Circuit Court Record Book.

CC case files = St. Louis Circuit Court case file number. Office of the City Clerk, City of St. Louis, Missouri.

U.S. Statutes

The Missouri Compromise of 1820 (Missouri Enabling Acts), ch. 22, 3 Stat. 545 (March 6, 1820), U.S. Code.

The Northwest Ordinance of 1787 (passed July 13, 1787), U.S. Code.

State Statutes

ILLINOIS

The Act of 1819, Illinois code, Sections 1-25, Act approved March 30, 1819 (popularly known as An Act Respecting Free Negroes, Mulattoes, Servants, and Slaves, published in The Revised Laws of Illinois, Containing All of a General and Public Nature Passed by the Eighth General Assembly, at Their Session Held at Vandalia, Commencing on the Third Day of December, 1832, and Ending on the Second Day of March, 1833, Vandalia: Greiner & Sherman, 1833, 457.

The Act of January 7, (1829), amending An Act Respecting Free Negroes, etc.

The Criminal Code, approved February 16, 1833. Published in The Revised Laws of Illinois...

An Act to prevent the Immigration of Free Negroes into this State (passed February 12, 1853), A Compilation of the Statutes of the State of Illinois, of a General Nature, in Force January 1, 1856, Collated with Reference to Decisions of the Supreme Court of Said State, and to Prior Laws Relating to the Same Subject Matter., Chicago: Keen & Lee, Booksellers, 1856, 780.

MISSOURI

Missouri Revised Statutes, Ch. 167, Art. II, 1845. "An Act to Enable Persons Held in Slavery, to Sue for Their Freedom" (June 27, 1807), *Laws of a Public and General Nature of the District of Louisiana, of the Territory of Louisiana, of the Territory of Missouri, and of the State of Missouri up to the Year 1824*, Vol. I. Jefferson City, MO: W. Lusk & Son, 1842, 96–97.

Freedom: An Act to Enable Persons Held in Slavery to Sue for Their Freedom. January 27, 1835.

Slaves: An Act concerning Slaves. Approved March 19th, 1835.

Acts of a Public Nature. Abolition: An Act to Prohibit the Publication, Circulation or Promulgation of the Abolition Doctrines. Persons Circulating Abolition Doctrines, How Punished. Approved Feb. 1, 1837.

Slaves: An Act Amendatory of an Act, Entitled, "An Act to Enable Persons Held in Slavery to Sue for Their Freedom." Approved Feb. 11, 1841.

Slaves: An Act Supplementary to an Act, Entitled "An Act concerning Slaves." Approved Feb. 13, 1841.

An Act to Amend "An Act concerning Free Negroes and Mulattoes." Approved March 26, 1845.

Negroes and Mulattoes. An Act Respecting Slaves, Free Negroes and Mulattoes. Approved Feb. 16, 1847.

VIRGINIA

Virginia Act of Cession, March 1, 1784.

1795 Virginia Acts 16 (1795).

An Act to Amend an Act Entitled, "An Act to Reduce into One, the Several Acts concerning Slaves, Free Negroes, and Mulattos, and for Other Purposes." Virginia Acts, Ch. 189, Dec. 25, 1795.

Archival Documents

U.S. Census Records. Census records, 1820, 1830, 1840, 1850, and 1860. A note on Census material for St. Louis, all the territorial censuses for the area have been lost. Missouri became a state in 1821, so the first U.S. census for the state did not occur until 1830.

Illinois Census Returns: 1810, 1818. Springfield, IL: Illinois State Historical Library, 1935.

The Territorial Papers of the United States, Vols. 2–17. Washington, DC: U.S. Government Printing Office, 1934–1975.

Papers and Letters Collections

Bates Family Papers. AMC96-000082. Missouri Historical Society, St. Louis.

Chouteau Family Papers. AMC93-000504. Missouri Historical Society, St. Louis.

Drouin Collection. Early U.S. French Catholic Church Records, 1695–1954. Available at Ancestry.com.

English, William H. Collection, Special Collections Research Center, University of Chicago Library. http://bmrcsurvey.uchicago.edu/collections/1506.

Fur Trade Collection. AMC93-000758. Missouri Historical Society, St. Louis.

Kennerly Family Papers. Missouri Historical Society, St. Louis.

John Askin Collection, Burton Library, University of Michigan.

Litigation Collection, 1773–1901 of the Missouri History Museum Archives.

Napton, William Barclay. William Barclay Napton Papers. AMC93–000025. Missouri Historical Society, St. Louis.

Norris, Lyman Decatur. Letters, Norris Family Papers. Bentley Historical Library, University of Michigan, Ann Arbor.

———. *Notre Dame Archives Perpetual Calendar*. http://archives.nd.edu/calendar/cal1834.htm.

Scott, Dred. Dred Scott Collection. Family Papers, AMC93-000616. Missouri Historical Society, St. Louis.

Taliaferro, Lawrence. Lawrence Taliaferro Papers, 1813–1868. Minnesota Historical Society Manuscript Collection, St. Paul.

Taliaferro, Lawrence. Lawrence Taliaferro Journals. Minnesota Historical Society Manuscript Collection, St. Paul.

Wells, Judge. Letter from Judge Wells. June 6, 1862, Colby College, Waterville, ME.

U.S. Government Records (National Archives)

Arthur J. Stansbury. *Report of the Trial of James H. Peck, Judge of the U.S. District Court for the District of Missouri, before the Senate of the United States on an Impeachment Preferred by the House of Representatives Against Him for High Misdemeanors in Office.* Boston: Hilliard, Gray, 1833.

St. Louis Court Records and Local Records.

Krum, John. *The Revised Ordinances of the City of St. Louis*. St. Louis: Chambers & Knapp, 1850.
———. *The Revised Ordinances of the City of St. Louis*. St. Louis, Chambers & Knapp, 1853.
Free Negro Bonds, Slavery Collection, Missouri Historical Society.
St. Louis Criminal Case Docket Files, on file with author.

Original Court Files, St. Louis

ST. LOUIS FREEDOM SUITS

1814, CC case no. 7: *Tarleton, William, a black man v. Horine, Jacob.*
1818, Oct., CC case no. 111: *Jack, a free man v. Harris, Barnabas.*
1818, CC case no. unavailable: *Arch, a black man v. Harris, Barnabas.*
1819, Aug., CC case no. 20: *Milly, a free woman v. Rose, Mathias.*
1820, Aug., CC case no. 70: *Winny, a woman of color v. Donner, Samuel.*
1821, April, CC case no. 181: *Tempe, a black woman v. Price, Risdon H.*
1821, April, CC case no. 182: *Laban, a black man v. Price, Risdon H.*
1821, April, CC case no. 190: *Winny v. Whitesides, Phebe.*
1821, April, CC case no. 191: *Sarah, a free girl v. Hatton, Michael.*
1821, April, CC case no. 192: *Lydia, a free girl v. Butler, John.*
1821, April, CC case no. 193: *Nancy, a free girl v. Voteau, Isaac.*
1821, April, CC case no. 194: *Jenny, a free girl v. Musick, Robert.*
1821, April, CC case no. 195: *Jerry, a free man of color v. Hatton, Charles.*
1821, April, CC case no. 196: *Daniel, a free man v. Whitesides, John.*
1821, April, CC case no. 197: *Hannah, a free girl of color v. Whitesides, Phebe.*
1821, April, CC case no. 198: *Malinda, a free girl of color v. Whitesides, Phebe.*
1821, April, CC case no. 199: *Lewis, a free boy of color v. Whitesides.*
1821, April, CC case no. 205: *Marie, a free mulatto girl v. Chouteau, Auguste.*
1822, Feb., CC case no. 12: *Pelagie, a woman of color v. Valois, Francois.*
1822, Feb., CC case no. 127: *Susan, a black woman v. Hight, Henry.*
1822, June, CC case no. 9: *Pelagie, a person of color v. Cabanne, Jean P.*
1822, Oct., CC case no. 39: *Jeffrie, a mulatto boy v. Robidoux, Joseph.*
1823, Oct., CC case no. 7: *Malinda, a free person of color v. Wilburn, Robert.*
1823, Oct., CC case no. 8: *Nelly, a free person of color v. Wilburn, Robert.*
1823, Oct., CC case no. 99: *Fenwick, Lethe v. Abbot, Samuel.*
1824, CC case no. unavailable: *State of Missouri v. Young, James, a free man.*
1825, July, CC case no. 11: *Lorinda, a free girl of color v. Pettibone, Rufus; Hatton, Charles; Wingfield, Owen; Voteau, Isaac; Butler, John; Whitset; Sanford.*
1825, July, CC case no. 12: *Winny, a free woman of color v. Pettibone, Rufus; Hatton, Charles; Wingfield, Owen; Voteau, Isaac; Butler, John; Whitset; Sanford.*
1825, July, CC case no. 13: *Malinda, a free girl of color v. Pettibone, Rufus; Hatton, Charles; Wingfield, Owen; Voteau, Isaac; Butler, John; Whitset; Sanford.*
1825, July, CC case no. 14: *Harry, a free boy of color v. Pettibone, Rufus; Hatton, Charles; Wingfield, Owen; Voteau, Isaac; Butler, John; Whitset; Sanford.*
1825, July, CC case no. 15: *Jenny, a free woman of color v. Musick, Ephraim; Hatton, Charles; Wingfield, Owen; Voteau, Isaac; Butler, John; Whitset; Sanford.*
1825, July, CC case no. 16: *Winetta, a free girl of color v. Musick, Ephraim; Hatton, Charles; Wingfield, Owen; Voteau, Isaac; Butler, John; Whitset; Sanford.*
1825, July, CC case no. 26: *Marguerite, a free woman of color v. Chouteau, Pierre, Sr.*
1825, CC case no. unavailable: *Molly, a free woman of color v. Mulliken, Charles; Mulliken, John.*
1826, March, CC case no. 21: *Israel, a free man of color v. Rector, William.*
1826, March, CC case no. 42: *Dorinda, a woman of color v. Simonds, John, Jr.*
1826, July, CC case no. 25: *Jenny, a free girl v. Musick, Robert.*
1826, July, CC case no. 26: *Jerry, a free man v. Hatton, Charles.*

1826, July, CC case no. 77: *Hagan, Betsy v. Rocheblave, Philip.*

1826, Nov., CC case no. 16: *Jerry, a free man v. Hatton, Charles.*

1826, Nov., CC case no. 17: *Jenny, a free girl v. Musick, Robert.*

1826, Nov., CC case no. 18: *Merry, John, a free man of color v. Tiffin, Clayton; Menard, Louis.*

1826, Nov., CC case no. 23: *Jefferson, Joseph v. McCutchen, William; McKnight, James.*

1826, CC case no. unavailable: *State of Missouri v. Walker, John K. (jailor of St Louis); Chouteau, Pierre; Pratt, Bernard; Amelin, Alexis.*

1827, March, CC case no. 29: *LaGrange, Francois, a free man of color v. Pratte, Bernard; Chouteau, Pierre; Berthold, Bertholemew; Cabanne, Jean P.*

1827, July, CC case no. 14: *Milly, a free mulatto woman v. Smith, Stephen.*

1827, July, CC case no. 15: *Dick, Harry, a free negro man v. Smith, Stephen.*

1827, July, CC case no. 16: *William, a free negro boy v. Smith, Stephen.*

1827, July, CC case no. 17: *Shipman, David, a free mulatto boy v. Smith, Stephen.*

1827, July, CC case no. 24: *Aspasia, a woman of color v. Chouteau, Francois.*

1827, Nov., CC case no. 6: *Theotiste, a woman of color v. Chouteau, Pierre, Jr.*

1827, Nov., CC case no. 7: *Mary, a woman of color v. Menard, Francis; Landreville, Andre.*

1827, Nov., CC case no. 13: *Elizabeth, a free girl of color v. Menard, Francis; Landreville, Andre.*

1827, Nov., CC case no. 14: *Virginia, a free girl of color v. Menard, Francis; Landreville, Andre.*

1827, Nov., CC case no. 15: *Victoire, a free girl of color v. Menard, Francis; Landreville, Andre.*

1827, Nov., CC case no. 23: *Singleton, John, a free man of color v. Scott, Alexander; Lewis, Robert.*

1827, Nov., CC case no. 26: *Rector, Molly, a free woman of color v. Bivens, John.*

1828, March, CC case no. 5: *Aspasia, a free woman of color v. Chouteau, Francois; Menard, Pierre.*

1828, March, CC case no. 12: *Peter, a free man of color v. Walton, James.*

1828, Jul., CC case no. 7: *Dolly, a free woman of color v. Young, John.*

1828, Jul., CC case no. 9: *Suzette, a free woman of color v. Reynolds, John.*

1828, Jul., CC case no. 10: *Angelique, a free woman of color v. Reynolds, John.*

1828, Jul., CC case no. 11: *Edmund, a free boy of color v. Reynolds, John.*

1828, Jul., CC case no. 12: *John, a free boy of color v. Reynolds, John.*

1828, Jul., CC case no. 64: *Relfe, George, a man of color v. Ficklin, Thompson H.*

1828, Nov., CC case no. 38: *Matilda, a free girl of color v. Rocheblave, Philip; Rocheblave, Mary Louisa.*

1829, March, CC case no. 21: *Mary, a free woman of color v. Menard, Francis.*

1829, March, CC case no. 22: *Elizabeth, a free girl of color v. Menard, Francis.*

1829, March, CC case no. 23: *Virginia, a free girl of color v. Menard, Francis.*

1829, March, CC case no. 24: *Victoire, a free girl of color v. Menard, Francis.*

1829, March, CC case no. 53: *Simpson, Robert v. Strother, George F.*

1829, July, CC case no. 14: *Vincent, a free person of color v. Jerry, a free person of color.*

1829, July, CC case no. 39: *Milly, a woman of color v. Williams, Wiley.*

1829, July, CC case no. 40: *Peter, a man of color v. Walton, James.*

1829, July, CC case no. 41: *Jones, Nicholas, a free man of color v. Honey, John W.; Gray, John.*

1829, Nov., CC case no. 10: *Ewton, Carey, a free man of color v. Wilder, Benjamin.*

1829, Nov., CC case no. 14: *Whiten, Maria, a free woman of color v. Rucker, Garland.*

1829, Nov., CC case no. 16: *Henry, Patrick, a free boy of color v. Rucker, Garland.*

1829, Nov., CC case no. 110: *Vincent, a man of color v. Duncan, James.*

1830, July, CC case no. 30: *Henry, William, a black man v. Bates, David G.*

1830, July, CC case no. 35: *Ralph, a man of color v. Duncan, Coleman; Duncan, James.*

1830, July, CC case no. 47: *Joe, a black man v. Duncan, Coleman; Duncan, James.*

1831, March, CC case no. 53: *Cary, a man of color v. Wilder, Benjamin.*

1831, March, CC case no. 58: *Matilda, a woman of color v. St Vrain, Charles de.*

1831, March, CC case no. 66: *Julia, a woman of color v. McKenney, Samuel T.*

1831, March, CC case no. 67: *Peter, a man of color v. Walton, James.*

1831, March, CC case no. 304: *Jonathan & Gilbert, free men of color v. Duncan, Coleman; Tracy, Edward; Wahrendorff, Charles.*

1831, July, CC case no. 2: *Richards, Nelly, a woman of color v. Sewel, William.*

1831, July, CC case no. 3: *Jack, a man of color v. Collins, Charles.*

1831, July, CC case no. 12: *Dunky, a colored woman v. Hay, Andrew.*

1831, July, CC case no. 13: *Mariquette v. McKenney, Samuel T.*

1831, July, CC case no. 22: *Jane, woman of color v. Dallam, William.*

1831, Nov., CC case no. 4: *Margaret, a girl of color v. Dallam, William.*

1831, Nov., CC case no. 7: *Sally, a girl of color v. Dallam, William.*

1831, Nov., CC case no. 8: *Henry, a boy of color v. Dallam, William.*

1831, Nov., CC case no. 12: *Anna, a woman of color v. Higginbotham, Thomas.*

1831, Nov., CC case no. 75: *Louisa, a girl of color v. Calvert, Sandford.*

1832, March, CC case no. 1: *Washington, Tenor, a woman of color v. Scott, Henry; Scott, John; Johnson, Jeremiah.*

1832, March, CC case no. 6: *John, a boy of color v. Campbell, William.*

1832, March, CC case no. 9: *Thenia, a woman of color v. Crowder, Green.*

1832, March, CC case no. 10: *Charlotte, a colored girl v. Crowder, Green.*

1832, March, CC case no. 19: *Vina, a woman of color v. Mitchell, Martin.*

1832, March, CC case no. 29: *Duncan, Coleman v. Duncan, Jonathan.*

1832, July, CC case no. 47: *Matilda, a woman of color v. Mitchell, Elijah.*

1832, July, CC case no. 48: *Anson, a boy of color v. Mitchell, Elijah.*

1832, July, CC case no. 48: *Michael, a boy of color v. Mitchell, Elijah.*

1832, July, CC case no. 49: *Sam, a person of color v. Field, Alexander P; Mitchell, Elijah.*

1832, July, CC case no. 50: *Nathan, a person of color v. Field, Alexander P.; Mitchell, Elijah.*

1832, July, CC case no. 51: *Mary Ann, a person of color v. Field, Alexander P.; Mitchell, Elijah.*

1832, July, CC case no. 55: *Matilda, a woman of color v. Mitchell, Henry G.; Russell, Henry.*

1832, July, CC case no. 56: *Michael, a boy of color v. Mitchell, Henry; Russell, Henry.*

1832, July, CC case no. 57: *Anson, a boy of color v. Mitchell, Henry; Russell, Henry.*

1832, Nov., CC case no. 6: *Mahala, a free woman of color v. Mitchell, Martin.*

1832, Nov., CC case no. 7: *Susan, a girl of color v. Parker, Lemon.*

1832, Nov., CC case no. 18: *Washington, Tenor, a woman of color v. Scott, Henry; Emerson, John.*

1832, Nov., CC case no. 27: *Barton, Jack, a man of color v. Glasgow, William; Glasgow, Ross.*

1832, Nov., CC case no. 68: *Leah, a woman of color v. Mitchell, Arthur.*

1833, March, CC case no. 5: *Susan, a woman of color v. Parker, Lemon.*

1833, July, CC case no. 9: *Sarah, a girl of color v. Johnson, Thomas; Johnson, Janus.*

1833, July, CC case no. 17: *Harriet, an infant v. McKenney, Samuel T.; Walker, William; James, Thomas D.*

1833, July, CC case no. 28: *Milly, a woman of color v. Williams, Wiley.*

1833, July, CC case no. 54: *Harriet v. McKenney, Samuel T.*

1833, July, CC case no. 99: *Ralph, a free man of color v. Duncan, Robert; Duncan, James.*

1833, July, CC case no. 102: *Wilkinson, James, a man of color v. Young, Aaron.*

1833, Nov., CC case no. 34: *Mary, a woman of color v. Menard, Francis; Busby, Daniel.*

1833, Nov., CC case no. 49: *Vincent, Adolphe, a boy of color v. Leduc, Marie P.*

1833, Nov., CC case no. 50: *Vincent, Marcelline v. Leduc, Marie P.*

1833, Nov., CC case no. 52: *Vincent, Louise, a woman of color v. Leduc, Marie P.*

1834, July, CC case no. 19: *Henry, a man of color v. Morrisson, William; Swan, John C.*

1834, July, CC case no. 20: *Reuben, a man of color v. Morrisson, William; Swan, John C.*

1834, July, CC case no. 104: *Kerr, Nelson, a free man of color v. Kerr, Mathew.*

1834, July, CC case no. 114: *Dutton, Andrew, a free boy of color v. Paca, John.*

1834, July, CC case no. 115: *Dutton, Abraham, a free boy of color v. Paca, John.*

1834, July, CC case no. 116: *Dutton, Lemmon, a free girl of color v. Paca, John.*

1834, Nov., CC case no. 46: *Mary Ann, an infant of color v. Duncan, Robert.*

1834, Nov., CC case no. 82: *Rachel, a woman of color v. Walker, William.*

1834, Nov., CC case no. 83: *Henry, James, a boy of color v. Walker, William.*

1835, March, CC case no. 11: *Judy (also known as Julia Logan) v. Meachum, John Berry.*

1835, March, CC case no. 43: *Hetty, a woman of color v. Magenis, Arthur L.*

1835, March, CC case no. 67: *Ligon, Nancy, a woman of color v. Ligon, Daniel; Myers, William.*

1835, July, CC case no. 7: *Lewis, a man of color v. Newton, James; Cooper, Jacob.*

1835, July, CC case no. 10: *Wilson, Daniel, a man of color v. Melvin, Edmund.*

1835, July, CC case no. 12: *Melvin, Sally, a woman of color v. Cohen, Robert.*

1835, July, CC case no. 13: *Wilson, Daniel v. Cohen, Robert.*

1835, July, CC case no. 35: *Tyler, Eliza, a woman of color v. Campbell, Nelson.*

1835, July, CC case no. 48: *Farnham, Mary v. Walker, Samuel D.*

1835, July, CC case no. 66: *Johnson, Mary (also known as Bevinue) v. Menard, Michael.*

1835, July, CC case no. 67: *Allard, Paul Auguste, an infant of color v. Allard, Bazil Auguste; Rutgers, Arend.*

1835, July, CC case no. 96: *Steel, Mary Ann v. Skinner, Curtis.*

1835, July, CC case no. 97: *Steel, Mary Ann v. Walker, William.*

1835, July, CC case no. 101: *Sally, a person of color v. Chouteau, Henry.*

1835, Nov., CC case no. 3: *Agnis (also known as Agathe), a woman of color v. Menard, Pierre.*

1835, Nov., CC case no. 11: *Edwards, Michael, a colored lad v. Birdsong, J. J.*

1835, Nov., CC case no. 22: *LaCourse, Josephine, an infant of color v. Mitchell, George.*

1835, Nov., CC case no. 63: *Milly, a woman of color v. Duncan, James.*

1836, March, CC case no. 10: *Courtney, a woman of color v. Rayburn, Samuel.*

1836, March, CC case no. 50: *Ben, a man of color v. White, Thomas J.; Woods, William L.*

1836, July, CC case no. 22: *Logan, Green Berry, an infant of color v. Meachum, John Berry, a free man of color.*

1836, July, CC case no. 141: *Julia (also known as Mary Ann), an infant of color v. Duncan, Robert; Adams, Sally.*

1836, Nov., CC case no. 4: *Delph (also known as Delphy), a mulatress v. Dorris, Stephen.*

1836, Nov., CC case no. 51: *Phillis, a free woman of color v. Herring, Redding B.*

1837, March, CC case no. 39: *Aspasia, a woman of color v. Rosati, Joseph.*

1837, March, CC case no. 40: *Judy, a woman of color v. Meachum, John Berry.*

1837, March, CC case no. 41: *Celeste, a woman of color v. Papin, Laforce.*

1837, March, CC case no. 42: *Celestine, a woman of color v. Papin, Laforce.*

1837, March, CC case no. 43: *Andrew, a boy of color v. Sarpy, John B.*

1837, July, CC case no. 132: *Stubbs, Lewis v. Burd, William.*

1837, July, CC case no. 133: *Stubbs, William v. Burd, William.*

1837, July, CC case no. 263: *Aspasia, a woman of color v. Lane, Hardage.*

1837, Nov., CC case no. 38: *Jack, a man of color v. Link, Absalom.*

1837, Nov., CC case no. 169: *James alias Haskins, James v. Haskins, Charles.*

1837, Nov., CC case no. 521: *Stubbs, Nancy v. Burd, William.*

1837, Nov., CC case no. 522: *Stubbs, Robert v. Burd, William.*

1837, Nov., CC case no. 523: *Stubbs, Phebe v. Burd, William.*

1838, July, CC case no. 237: *Rebecca, a colored girl v. Black, James; Matlock, Louis.*

1838, Nov., CC case no. 501: *Stokes, Samuel, a man of color v. Finney, John; Finney, William.*

1839, March, CC case no. 92: *Talbot, James v. Benton, Delford; Musick, James C.; Musick, Prudence.*

1839, March, CC case no. 515: *Davis, Ann v. Symington, James F.*

1839, July, CC case no. 116: *Endicott, Charles v. Clapp, Benjamin.*

1839, July, CC case no. 185: *Lewis, a boy of color v. Stacker, John.*

1839, July, CC case no. 335: *Celeste, a woman of color v. Papin, Alexander.*

1839, July, CC case no. 347: *Aspasia (also known as Aspisa) v. Lane, Hardage.*

1839, Nov., CC case no. 20: *Andrew, a person of color v. Sarpy, Peter.*

1839, Nov., CC case no. 167: *Wash, Polly v. Magehan, Joseph M.*

1839, Nov., CC case no. 219: *Briscoe, Eliza v. Anderson, William.*

1840, March, CC case no. 3: *Seyton, a woman of color v. Littleton, William.*

1840, July, CC case no. 203: *Charles, a man of color v. Verhagen, Peter.*

1840, July, CC case no. 254: *Cephas, Diana, a woman of color v. Scott, James.*

1840, July, CC case no. 361: *Cephas, Josiah, a colored boy v. Scott, James; McConnell, Mary.*

1840, Nov., CC case no. 40: *Barnes, Brunetta, of color v. Meachum, John Berry.*

1840, Nov., CC case no. 41: *Barnes, Archibald, of color v. Meachum, John Berry.*

1840, Nov., CC case no. 120: *Barnes, Archibald, of color v. Meachum, John Berry.*

1840, Nov., CC case no. 121: *Barnes, Brunetta, of color v. Meachum, John Berry.*

1840, Nov., CC case no. 123: *Barnes, Brunetta, of color v. Meachum, John Berry.*

1840, Nov., CC case no. 192: *Pierre, a mulatto v. Choteau, Therese Cerre.*

1841, March, CC case no. 161: *Tompson, Richard, a man of color v. Blount, James; Baker, Leakin.*

1841, March, CC case no. 162: *Talbot, James v. Benton, Delford; Musick, James C.; Musick, Prudence.*

1841, March, CC case no. 305: *Alsey, a woman of color v. Randolph, William.*

1841, March, CC case no. 343: *Charles, a man of color v. Christy, Belina.*

1841, March, CC case no. 362: *Scott, Louis, a man of color v. Burd, William.*

1841, July, CC case no. 5: *Cephas, Diana, a woman of color v. Scott, Leakin.*

1841, July, CC case no. 119: *Brown, Squire, a man of color v. Anderson, William C.*

1841, Aug., CC case no. 75: *Charles, a man of color v. Verhagen, Peter.*

1841, Nov., CC case no. 30: *Robertson, Mary, a person of color v. Watson, Ringrose D.*

1841, Nov., CC case no. 32: *Jonathan, a man of color v. Brotherton, Marshall; Danah, Joil; Willoughby, Aza.*

1841, Nov., CC case no. 84: *Peter, a man of color v. Richardson, John.*

1841, Nov., CC case no. 674: *Preston; Braxton; Mary; Nat; Beverly, et al v. Coons, George W., Administrator, et al.*

1842, Feb., CC case no. 359: *Charles, a man of color v. Christy, Belina.*

1842, July, CC case no. 23: *Mary, a woman of color v. Dougherty, James alias E. C.; Curle, Richmond.*

1842, July, CC case no. 31: *Vica, a woman of color v. Hobart, Samuel.*

1842, July, CC case no. 32: *Alonzo, Thadeus, a boy of color v. Sparr, John; Hobart, Samuel; Mellody, George.*

1842, July, CC case no. 33: *Gazen, Musa Ben Abel, a boy of color v. Sparr, John; Hobart, Samuel; Mellody, George.*

1842, July, CC case no. 102: *Jackson, Jinny, a woman of color v. Fraser, James O.*

1842, July, CC case no. 103: *Jackson, Henry, a person of color v. Fraser, James O.*

1842, July, CC case no. 104: *Ann Maria, a person of color v. Fraser, James O.*

1842, July, CC case no. 105: *Jackson, Sally (also known as Sarah), a person of color v. Fraser, James O.*

1842, July, CC case no. 106: *Jackson, Margarett, a person of color v. Fraser, James O.*

1842, July, CC case no. 107: *William Henry, a person of color v. Fraser, James O.*

1842, July, CC case no. 108: *Smith, a person of color v. Fraser, James O.*

1842, Nov., CC case no. 125: *Pierre, a mulatto v. Chouteau, Gabriel.*

1843, March, CC case no. 14: *Jefferson, Thomas, a man of color v. Hopkins, Milton W.*

1843, March, CC case no. 24: *Rebecca, a negro woman v. Black, James; Horine, Thomas; Melody, George.*

1843, April, CC case no. 232: *Brown, Squire, a man of color v. Anderson, Charles.*

1843, Nov., CC case no. 13: *Mary Charlotte, a woman of color v. Chouteau, Gabriel.*

1843, Nov., CC case no. 20: *Catharine, Felix; William; Minta, persons of color v. Hundley, Thomas; Pattison, D.; Russell, William.*

1843, Nov., CC case no. 328: *Brown, Squire, a person of color v. Anderson, C. R.; Morris, S.*

1844, April, CC case no. 6: *Samuel, a man of color v. Howdeshell, John.*

1844, April, CC case no. 51: *Chouteau, Louis, a man of color v. Chouteau, Gabriel.*

1844, April, CC case no. 151: *Paul, Michel v. Paul, Gabriel.*

1844, April, CC case no. 340: *Paschall, Adrian, a man of color v. Ulrici, Richard W.*

1844, April, CC case no. 386: *Speaks, Mary Ann v. Jameson, John M.*

1844, April, CC case no. 390: *Stewart, Anderson, a free man of color v. Jameson, John M.*

1844, April, CC case no. 394: *Ann, a woman of color v. Jameson, John M.*

1844, Sept., CC case no. 219: *Jefferson, Thomas, a man of color v. Hopkins, Milton W.*

1844, Nov., CC case no. 8: *James, a person of color v. Cordell, Hiram.*

1844, Nov., CC case no. 9: *Martha Ann, a person of color v. Cordell, Hiram.*

1844, Nov., CC case no. 15: *Celestine, a woman of color v. Dumont, Julia.*

1844, Nov., CC case no. 16: *Hannah, a woman of color v. Pitcher, John.*

1844, Nov., CC case no. 18: *Britton, Lucy Ann v. Mitchell, David D.*

1844, Nov., CC case no. 28: *Hannah, a woman of color v. Pitcher, John.*

1844, Nov., CC case no. 32: *Jesse, a man of color v. Coons, George W., Administrator.*

1844, Nov., CC case no. 34: *Preston, a man of color v. Coons, George W., Administrator.*

1844, Nov., CC case no. 35: *Nat, a person of color v. Coons, George W., Administrator.*

1844, Nov., CC case no. 39: *Ann, a person of color v. Wilson, William; Jamison, John M.*

1844, Nov., CC case no. 120: *Smith, Cloe Ann, a woman of color v. Knox, Franklin.*

1844, Nov., CC case no. 173: *Brown, Jane (also known as Jinny), woman of color v. Sturges, Francis I.*

1844, Nov., CC case no. 174: *Moore, Amy v. Moore, Robert N.*

1844, Nov., CC case no. 213: *Speaks, Mary Ann v. Quissenbury, James; Jameson, John.*

1844, Nov., CC case no. 229: *Brown, Jim v. Head, William.*

1844, Nov., CC case no. 230: *Brown, Mary v. Head, William.*

1844, Nov., CC case no. 231: *Brown, Stephen v. Head, William.*

1844, Nov., CC case no. 252: *Drusella, Martha v. Curle, Richmond L.*

1844, Nov., CC case no. 346: *Mary, a negro woman v. Clemens, James, Jr.*

1845, April, CC case no. 11: *Robinson, Mary, a woman of color v. Watson, Ringrose D.; Corson, Amos.*

1845, April, CC case no. 55: *Hicks, Elsa, a mulatto girl v. Burrell, S; Mitchell, Louis.*

1845, April, CC case no. 143: *Paul, Michel v. Paul, Adolph, Administrator.*

1845, April, CC case no. 187: *Steele, Rachel, a colored woman v. Taylor, Thomas.*

1845, April, CC case no. 395: *Jesse, a man of color v. Coons, George W.*

1845, Nov., CC case no. 24: *Jefferson, Thomas, a man of color v. Colton, George A.; Moulton, Jonathan.*

1845, Nov., CC case no. 81: *Sarah, a colored woman v. Waddingham, William.*

1845, Nov., CC case no. 162: *McCray, Jane, a mulatto woman v. Hopkins, William R.; Miller, William; Oliver, Eliza, et al.*

1845, Nov., CC case no. 220: *Malinda, a woman of color v. Coons, George W., Administrator.*

1846, April, CC case no. 20: *Bascom, Caroline, a free mulatto woman v. Ferguson, John H.*

1846, Nov., CC case no. 1: *Scott, Dred, a man of color v. Emerson, Irene.*

1846, Nov., CC case no. 2: *Scott, Harriet, a woman of color v. Emerson, Irene.*

1846, Nov., CC case no. 28: *Thomas, Matilda, person of color v. Littleton, William.*

1846, Nov., CC case no. 29: *Littleton, Missouri v. Littleton, William.*

1846, Nov., CC case no. 324: *Gabriel, a man of color v. Christy, Andrew, Executor; Coons, Mary, Executrix.*

1847, Nov., CC case no. 121: *Hicks, Elsa, a mulatto girl v. McSherry, Patrick T.*

1848, April, CC case no. 4: *Nancy, a free woman of color v. Steen, Enoch.*

1848, April, CC case no. 37: *Cotton, Jane, a free person of color v. Little, James A.*

1848, Nov., CC case no. 90: *Scott, Thomas, a man of color v. Harrison, James.*

1848, Nov., CC case no. 93: *Taylor, Alfred, a free man of color v. Van Houten, Cornelius; Martin, Lewis; Conway, Samuel.*

1848, Nov., CC case no. 255: *Perryman, Peggy, a woman of color v. Philibert, Joseph.*

1850, April, CC case no. 1: *Curd, Patsy v. Barksdale, William H.*

1850, April, CC case no. 17: *Duty, Harry, of color v. Darby, John F.*

1850, April, CC case no. 18: *Duty, Ellen v. Darby, John F. Administrator.*

1850, April, CC case no. 19: *Duty, Nelly v. Darby, John F., Administrator.*

1850, April, CC case no. 20: *Duty, Jordan v. Darby, John F., Administrator.*

1850, April, CC case no. 21: *Duty, Preston v. Darby, John F., Administrator.*

1850, April, CC case no. 22: *Duty, Lucinda v. Darby, John F., Administrator.*

1850, April, CC case no. 23: *Duty, Caroline v. Darby, John F., Administrator.*

1850, April, CC case no. 24: *Duty, Mary v. Darby, John F., Administrator.*

1850, April, CC case no. 37: *McFoy, David v. Brown, William.*

1851, April, CC case no. 2: *Mary, of color & her children Samuel & Edward v. Calvert, Launcelot H.*

1851, Nov., CC case no. 29: *Samuel, infant of color v. Lynch, Bernard T.*

1852, April, CC case no. 16: *Gabriel, of color v. Wiles, Michael.*

1852, April, CC case no. 22: *Laura, a woman of color v. Belt, Henry.*

1852, April, CC case no. unavailable: *Lohre, Henry, of color Duty, v. Gayns.*

1852, Nov., CC case no. 36: *Johnson, George, a man of color v. Moore, Henry.*

1852, Nov., CC case no. 281: *Johnson, George, a man of color v. Bartlett, Reuben.*

1853, Nov., CC case no. 35: *Kinney, Thornton, a man of color Hatcher, John F.; Bridges, Charles C.*

1853, Nov., CC case no. 119: *Williams, Hester; Williams, Ella; Williams, Priscilla v. McAfee, A. B.; Norcum, Frederick; Blakey, Glanville; Moore, William.*

1854, April, CC case no. 107: *Mount St. Mary's College v. Jameson, Francis B; McCabe, Edmund.*

1854, Nov., CC case no. 253: *In the matter of Slaughter, Samuel, a negro.*

1855, April, CC case no. 96: *Mary, a woman of color v. Bellis, Samuel B.*

1859, Sept., CC case no. 111: *Clinton, Richard, a man of color v. Blackburn, John, Edward, Martha A., Charles A., and Rufus C; Edward Hall, Curator.*

1860, Feb., CC case no. 12: *Louisa Hart, v. Henry N., Administrator.*

1860, Feb., CC case no. 456: *Shaw, Isham v. Evans, Augustus H.*

1860, Feb., CC case no. 457: *Shaw, Julia v. Evans, Augustus H.*

OTHER ST. LOUIS COURT CASES

VanBibber v. William Christy, CC case file no. 1670 (1818).

Samuel Danner v. Jenings Beckwith, CC case file no. 1446 (1818).

Jennings Beckwith v. Samuel Donner, aka Danner, CC case file no.5625 (1819).

Stephen Smith v. Nathan Dillon and John Summers, CC case file no. 13 (July 1827).

State v. Jacob Judy and Moses Whitesides, CC case file no. 1158 (1828).

Stephen Smith v. David Shipman, CC case file no. 285 (1829).

Robert Simpson, Sheriff v. Isaac A. Letcher, & James L. Lyle, CC case file no. 11 (1831).

Coleman Duncan (use of Gilbert) v. Jonathan Duncan, CC case file 7431 (1831).

State v. Barney Moore, Lewis Pilcher, Warren Adams & James Adams, CC case file 1159 (1828).

Coleman Duncan, v. Johnathan Duncan, CC case file no. 29 (1832).

Coleman Duncan v. Warrren Adams (June 1832).

Nelson Campbell v. Perry Burke, Hempstead, Beebe, Campbell, Morehouse, CC case file no. 6879 (1835).

Gustavus A. Bird v. Lydia Titus, CC case file no. 8170 (1833).

Lavinia Titus v. Jerry Duncan, CC case file no 8288 (1833).

St. Louis Probate Court Files. http://www.sos.mo.gov/archives/mojudicial/stl_history.asp.

James Farrar v. John Finney; William Finney, CC case file no. 51 Chancery (1848).

Shadrick(sic) Duncan v. ChanceyLewis & Richmond J. Curle, CC case no. 52 (1852).

OTHER INDIANA COURT CASES

Peter McNelly v. Henry Vanderburgh, William H. English Collection of the University of Chicago Library.

The Case of Mary Clark, a Woman of Colour, 1 Blackf. 122, 125–26 (Ind. 1812).

OTHERS KENTUCKY COURT CASES

General Index to Civil Cases, Hopkins County book, A–K and L–Z, Hopkins County Courthouse.

John Duncan v. John Shields, (Mar. 1826), Hopkins County book, p. 1064.

Coleman Duncan v. Mayberry Wright, (June 1832), Hopkins County book, p. 1611.

Jesse Duncan, adm v. William Wilson (Mar. 1830), Hopkins County book, p. 1397.

James Duncan, admin v. William Wilson (Sept. 1830), Hopkins County book, p. 1590.

James Bishop v. Coleman Duncan (Mar. 1831), p. 1532.

Coleman Duncan v. James Bishop (Sept. 1831), p. 1562.

James Bishop v. James Duncan, et al., (May 1834) p. 1737.

James Bishop v. James Duncan, Hopkins County book, p. 1372. (Sept. 1829) Appealed, *Bishop v. Duncan,* 33 Ky. 15 (1835).

MISSOURI LOCAL RECORDS

Missouri Marriages online at Ancestry.com.

St. Louis Register of Deeds Volumes, St. Louis Registry of Deeds, St. Louis, Missouri.

Civil Divorce Proceedings of Sally Adams and Calvin Adams, Supreme Ct. of Missouri (1809).

Probate of Rufus Pettibone, St. Charles Probate Court Files (1825).

MISSOURI SUPREME COURT CASES

Winny v. Whitesides, 1 Mo. 472 (1824).
Catiche v. The Circuit Court of St. Louis Cnty., 1 Mo. 608 (1826).
Merry v. Tiffin & Menard, 1 Mo. 725 (1827).
Tiffin & Menard v. Merry, 1 Mo. 780 (1827).
LaGrange v. Chouteau, 2 Mo. 20 (1828).
Milly v. Smith (I), 2 Mo. 36 (1828).
Marguerite v. Chouteau (I), 2 Mo. 71 (1828).
Theoteste v. Chouteau, 2 Mo. 144 (1829).
Milly v. Smith (II), 2 Mo. 171 (1829).
Vincent v. Duncan, 2 Mo. 214 (1830).
Jeffrie v. Robideaux, 3 Mo. 33 (1831).
Ralph v. Duncan (I), 3 Mo. 194 (1833).
McGirk v. Chauvin, 3 Mo. 236 (1833).
Chouteau v. Merry, 3 Mo. 254 (1833).
Julia v. McKinney, 3 Mo. 270 (1833).
(Ralph) Gordon v. Duncan (II), 3 Mo. 385 (1834).
Nat v. Ruddle, 3 Mo. 400 (1834).
Marguerite v. Chouteau (II), 3 Mo. 540 (1834).
Hay v. Dunky, 3 Mo. 588 (1834).
Rachael v. Walker, 4 Mo. 351 (1836).
Meechum v. Judy, alias Julia Logan, a woman of color, 4 Mo. 361 (1836).
Paca v. Dutton, 4 Mo. 371 (1836).
Wilson v. Melvin, 4 Mo. 592 (1837).
Randolph v. Alsey, 8 Mo. 656 (1844).
Chouteau v. Pierre, 9 Mo. 3 (1845).
Wash v. Randolph, 9 Mo. 142 (1845).
Nat v. G.W. Coons, 10 Mo. 543 (1847).
Charlotte v. Chouteau (I), 11 Mo. 193 (1847).
Harney, Adm'r of Duty v. Dutcher & Dutcher, 15 Mo. 89 (1851).
Scott v. Emerson, 15 Mo. 576 (1852).
Youse v. Norcum, 12 Mo. 549 (1853).
Norcum v. Gaty, 19 Mo. 65 (1855).
Norcum v. Sheahan, 21 Mo. 25 (1855).
Charlotte v. Chouteau (II), 21 Mo. 590 (1855).
Charlotte v. Chouteau (III), 25 Mo. 465 (1857).
Durham v. Durham, 26 Mo. 507 (1858).
Charlotte v. Chouteau (IV), 33 Mo. 194 (1862).
Harney v. Scott, 28 Mo. 333 (1859).
Joshua v. Purse, 34 Mo. 209 (1863).

Local Records

Circuit Court, St. Louis. St. Louis Circuit Court Clerk's Record Book. In notes as CCRB.
Index to St. Louis Circuit Court Records, 1774–1835. (Produced by Michael Everman, St. Louis
    Local Records Project Director.)

Illinois Records

LOCAL RECORDS: JO DAVIESS COUNTY

Jo Daviess Circuit Court Record Book, at Jo Daviess County Courthouse, In notes as Jo Daviess
    CCRB.
Raphael (a man of color) v. James Duncan, May 11, 1830, Galena, Jo Daviess County.

Swansey v. James Duncan, May 11, 1830, Galena.
Gilbert v. James Duncan, May 11, 1830, Galena.
Joseph v. James Duncan, May 11, 1830, Galena.
The People vs. James Duncan, Jo Daviess County Circuit Court record book, p. 284, Nov. 13, 1830.
People v. Swansey man of color, Jo Daviess County, Illinois, court register, p. 368, date uncertain (between Aug 22, 1831, and Sept 3, 1831).

Local Records: Randolph County

Randolph County Court Files, Register of Deeds, Chester, Illinois
Robert Patton v. Jinsey Mitchell, Randolph County Court files, Register of Deeds, Chester, Illinois.

LOCAL RECORDS: ST. CLAIR COUNTY

St. Clair County Court files, Illinois Regional Archives Depository, Springfield, Illinois
Bob & Lydia v. Jincey Mitchell, case no. 1754.
Lydia Titus and others v. William Degraffinreind, Daniel Winn, and Elisha Mitchell, case no. 3317.
Simon Vanowsdal v. Lydia Titus, case no. 3252 (March 1825).
Gilbert (Colored) v. Coleman Duncan et al., case no. 3534 (April 1831).
Joseph v. Coleman Duncan, case no. 3541 (April 1831).
Swansey (free negro) v. Coleman Duncan, et al., case no. 3547 (April 1831).
Ann (free negro) v. James Duncan, et al., case no. 3822 (Feb. 1836).
Milly (colored lady) v. James Duncan, et al., case no. 3837 (Feb. 1836).
Gustavus Bird v. Lydie Titus, case no. 7660 (Sept. 1834).

St. Clair County Probate Files, in Belleville, Illinois
Probate of Estate of Nathan Titus (1822).

ILLINOIS STATE ARCHIVES

Illinois Servitude and Emancipation Records. http://www.cyberdriveillinois.com/departments/archives/databases/servant.html.

ILLINOIS SUPREME COURT CASES

Jarrot v. Jarrot, 2 Gilman 1 (Ill. 1845).

United States Supreme Court Cases

Johnson v. M'Intosh, 21 U.S. (8 Wheat.) 543 (1823).
Dred Scott v. Sandford, 60 U.S. 393 (1856).

Other Court Cases

Somerset v. Stewart, 98 ER 499 (1772).
The Slave, Grace, 2 Hag Adm 94 (1827), 166 ER 179, 2 State Trials NS 273.

Miscellaneous Government Records

Revolutionary War Pension Files of Peter Mcanelly, Indiana Number 13923.
Revolutionary War Pension Files of David Shipman, NARA number 54–4891.

Articles and Books

Ablavsky, Gregory. "Making Indians 'White': The Judicial Abolition of Native Slavery in Revolutionary Virginia and its Racial Legacy." *University of Pennsylvania Law Review* 159 (2011): 1457.
Adams, Alice Dana. *The Neglected Period of Anti-Slavery in America (1808–1831)*. Boston and London: Ginn, 1908.

Alvord, Clarence Walworth. *Kaskaskia Records, 1778–1790.* Collections of the Illinois State Historical Library, Vol. 5, Virginia Series, Vol. 2, 1909.

———, *Cahokia Records, 1778–1790.*

———, *The Illinois Country, 1673–1818.*

Arenson, Adam, *The Great Heart of the Republic: St. Louis and the Cultural Civil War.* Cambridge, MA: Harvard University Press, 2011.

Aron, Stephen, *American Confluence: The Missouri Frontier from Borderland to Border State.* Bloomington: Indiana University Press, 2006.

Association of Graduates U.S.M.A. et al. *Annual Register of Graduates and Former Cadets 1802–1990.* West Point, NY: West Point Alumni Foundation, 1990.

Baker, H. Robert. *The Rescue of Joshua Glover: A Fugitive Slave, the Constitution, and the Coming of the Civil War.* Athens, Ohio: Ohio Univ. Press, 2007.

Banks, Taunya, *Dangerous Woman: Elizabeth Key's Freedom Suit - Subjecthood and Racialized Identity in Seventeenth Century Colonial Virginia,* 41 Akron Law Review 799 (2008).

Banner, Stuart. *Legal Systems in Conflict: Property and Sovereignty in Missouri, 1750–1860.* Norman: University of Oklahoma Press, 2000.

Baudissen, Graf Adelbert. *Der Ansiedler im Missouri-Staate.* Iserlohn: Julius Baedeker, 1854.

Bay, W. V. N. *Reminiscences of the Bench and Bar of Missouri.* St. Louis: F. H. Thomas, 1878.

Beale, Howard K., ed. *The Diary of Edward Bates 1859–1866.* Washington: U.S. Government Printing Office, 1933.

Beckwith, Paul. *Creoles of St. Louisy.* St. Louis: Nixon-Jones Printing, 1893.

Berlin, Ira. *Generations of Captivity: A History of African-American Slaves.* Cambridge, MA: Harvard University Press, 2003.

———. *Many Thousands Gone: The First Two Centuries of Slavery in North America.* Cambridge, MA: Harvard University Press, 1998.

———. The Making of African America: The Four Great Migrations. New York: Penguin Books, 2010.

Berlin, Ira, and Philip Morgan, eds. *Cultivation and Culture: Labor and the Shaping of Slave Life in the Americas.* Charlottesville: University Press of Virginia, 1993.

Billon, Frederic Louis. *Annals of St. Louis in Its Early Days under the French and Spanish Dominations* (1886). Reprint, Bowie, MD: Heritage Books, 1971.

———. *Annals of St. Louis in Its Territorial Days from 1804 to 1821: Being a Continuation of the Author's Previous Work, the Annals of the French and Spanish Period.* St. Louis: Frederic Billion, 1888.

Blackstone, William. *Commentaries on the Laws of England,* Vol. 1. New York: W. E. Dean, 1832.

Blassingame, John W., ed. *Slave Testimony: Two Centuries of Letters, Speeches, Interviews, and Autobiographies.* Baton Rouge: Louisiana State University Press, 1977.

Boggess, Arthur Clinton. *The Settlement of Illinois, 1778–1830.* Chicago: The Society, 1908.

Bornstein, Heinrich. *Memoirs of a Nobody: The Missouri Years of an Austrian Radical, 1849–1866.* Translated by Steven Rowan. Detroit: Wayne State University Press, 1997.

Bowditch, William I. *The Rendition of Anthony Burns.* Boston, MA: R. F. Wallent, 1854.

Breckenridge, William Clark. "Biographical Sketch of Judge Wilson Primm." *Missouri Historical Collections* 4, no. 2 (1913): 127–159.

Breese, Sidney, *The Early History of Illinois; From Its Discovery by the French, in 1673, until Its Cession to Great Britain in 1763, including the Narrative.* Chicago, IL: E. B. Myers & Co., 1884.

Brink, McDonough, & Company, *History of St. Clair County, Illinois.* Philadelphia: Brink, McDonough, 1881.

Brophy, Alfred F. "Humanity, Utility, and Logic in Southern Legal Thought: Harriet Beecher Stowe's Vision in Dred: A Tale of the Great Dismal Swamp." *Boston University Law Review* 79 (1998): 1113–1161.

———. "A Revolution which Seeks to Abolish Law, Must End Necessarily in Despotism": Louisa McCord and Antebellum Southern Legal Thought." *Cardozo Women's Law Journal* 5, no. 33 (1998).

Brown, Margaret Kimball. *History as They Lived It: A Social History of Prairie du Rocher, Ill.* Toole, UT: Patrice Press, 2005.

Brown, William Wells. *From Fugitive Slave to Free Man: The Autobiographies of William Wells Brown.* Edited by William Andrews. Columbia: University of Missouri Press, 2003.

Browne, Martha Griffith. *Autobiography of a Female Slave* (New York: Redfield, 1857). Reprint, Jackson: University of Mississippi Press, 1998.

Buchanan, Thomas C. *Black Life on the Mississippi: Slaves, Free Blacks, and the Western Steamboat World.* Chapel Hill: University of North Carolina Press, 2004.

Burke, Diane Mutt: On Slavery's Border: Missouri's Small-Slave holding Households, 1815–1865. Athens: University of Georgia Press, 2010.

Burnet, Jacob. *Notes on the Early Settlement of the North-Western Territory.* New York: D. Appleton; Cincinnati: Derby, Bradley, 1847.

Bynum, Victoria E. *Unruly Women: The Politics of Social and Sexual Control in the Old South.* Chapel Hill: University of North Carolina Press, 1992.

Cashin, Joan. "Black Families in the Old Northwest." *Journal of the Early Republic* 15 (1995): 449–475.

Catterall, Helen Tunnicliff. *Judicial Cases concerning American Slavery and the Negro.* New York: Octagon Books, 1968.

———. "Some Antecedents of the Dred Scott Case." *American Historical Review* 30 (1924): 56–71.

Cayton, Andrew R. L., and Frederika J. Teute. *Contact Points: American Frontiers from the Mohawk Valley to the Mississippi, 1750–1830.* Chapel Hill: University of North Carolina Press, 1998.

Chatman, Samuel L. "'There Are No Slaves in France': A Re-examination of Slave Laws in Eighteenth Century France," *Journal of Negro History* 85, no. 1 (2000): 144–153.

Chetlain, A. L. *Recollections of Seventy Years.* Galena: Gazette, 1899.

Chittenden, Hiram Martin. *The American Fur Trade of the Far West,* Vols. 1 and 2. Lincoln, University of Nebraska Press, 2006.

Christian, Shirley. *Before Lewis and Clark: The Story of the Chouteaus, the French Dynasty that Ruled America's Frontier.* New York: Farrar, Straus and Giroux, 2004.

Clamorgan, Cyprian. *The Colored Aristocracy of St. Louis.* Edited by Julie Winch. Columbia: University of Missouri Press, 1999.

Cobb, Thomas R. R. *An Inquiry into the Law of Negro Slavery in the United States of America* (T. and J. W. Johnson, Negro Universities Press, 1858). Reprint, Athens: University of Georgia Press, 1968.

Cockrum, William Monroe. *Pioneer History of Indiana: Including Stories, Incidents and Customers of the Early Settlers.* Oakland City, IN: Press of Oakland City Journal, 1907.

Conard, Howard Louis, ed. *Encyclopedia of the History of Missouri: A Compendium of History for Ready Reference.* New York and Louisville: Southern History, 1901.

Corbett, Katharine T. *In Her Place: A Guide to St. Louis Women's History.* St. Louis: St. Louis Historical Society Press, 1999.

Cotter, William R. "The Somerset Case and the Abolition of Slavery in England." *History* 79, no. 255 (1994): 31–56.

Cover, Robert M. *Justice Accused: Antislavery and the Judicial Process.* New Haven: Yale University Press, 1975.

Cranch, William. *Reports of cases, civil and criminal in the United States Circuit Court of the District of Columbia: from 1801 to 1841.* Boston: Little, Brown, 1852.

Cullum, George Washington. *Biographical Register of the Officers and Graduates of the U.S. Military Academy, United States Military Academy Association of Graduates,* 3rd ed. West Point, NY: United States Military Academy, 1891.

Darby, John Fletcher. *Personal Recollections of Many Prominent People Whom I Have Known* (1880). Reprint, New York: Arno Press, 1975.

Davidson, Alexander, and Bernard Stuvi. *History of Illinois from 1673 to 1873; Embracing the Physical Features of the Country; Its Early Explorations; Aboriginal Inhabitants; French and British Occupation; Conquest by Virginia; Territorial Condition and the Subsequent Civil, Military and Political Events of the State.* Springfield: Illinois Journal, 1874.

Davis, Adrienne D. "The Private Law of Race and Sex: An Antebellum Perspective," *Stanford Law Review* 51 (1999): 221–288.

Davis, David Brion. The Problem of Slavery in the Age of Emancipation, New York: Knopf 2014.

Davis, David Brion. "The Significance of Excluding Slavery from the Old Northwest in 1787." *Indiana Magazine of History* 84, no. 1 (1988): 75–89.

Davis, Marion M. *Judge George Turner (1750–1843) Portrait with Biographical Data*. Philadelphia: Historical Society of Pennsylvania, 1932.

de la Fuente, Alejandro. "Slaves and the Creation of Legal Rights in Cuba: Coartación and Papel." *Hispanic American Historical Review* 87, no. 4 (2007): 659–692.

Delaney, Lucy. "From the Darkness Cometh the Light or Struggles for Freedom." In *Six Women's Slave Narratives* (1891). Reprint, New York: Oxford University Press, 1988.

Delany, Martin R. *The Condition, Elevation, Emigration and Destiny of the Colored People of the United States*. Amherst, NY: Humanity Books, 2003.

Dexter, Darrel. *Bondage in Egypt: Slavery in Southern Illinois*. Cape Girardeau, MO: Center for Regional History, Southeast Missouri State University, 2011.

Deyle, Steven. *Carry Me Back: The Domestic Slave Trade in American Life*. New York: Oxford University Press, 2005.

Dillon, John B. *A History of Indiana, from Its Earliest Exploration by Europeans to the Close of the Territorial Government in 1816....* Indianapolis: Bingham & Doughty, 1859.

Dorsey, Bruce. *Reforming Men and Women: Gender in the Antebellum City*. Ithaca, NY: Cornell University Press, 2006.

Drumm, Stella M. "Robert E. Lee and the Improvement of the Mississippi River," *Missouri Historical Society Collections* 6, no. 2 (1829): 157–171.

Dunn, Jacob Piatt. *Indiana: A Redemption from Slavery*. Boston: Houghton Mifflin and Co., 1888.

———. *Indiana and the Indianans: A History of Aboriginal and Territorial Indiana and the Century of Statehood*. Chicago and New York: American Historical Society, 1919.

———. *Slavery Petitions and Papers*. Indianapolis: Bowen-Merrill, 1894.

Durst, Dennis L. "The Reverend John Berry Meachum (1789–1854) of St. Louis: Prophet and Entrepreneurial Black Educator in Historiographical Perspective." *The North Star: A Journal of African American Religious History* 7, no. 2 (Spring 2004). https://www.princeton.edu/~jweisenf/northstar/volume7/durst.html.

Early, Sarah J. W. *Life and Labors of Rev. Jordan W. Early, One of the Pioneers of African Methodism in the West and South*. Nashville: Publishing House of the A.M.E. Church Sunday School Union, 1894.

Eastman, Zabena. The Black Code of Illinois, unpublished, unfinished text, Illinois Historical Survey, Library Of The University Of Illinois.

Edwards, Laura F. *The People and Their Peace*. Chapel Hill: University of North Caroline Press, 2009.

Edwards, Ninian. *The Edwards Papers: Being a Portion of the Collection of the Letters, Papers, and Manuscripts of Ninian Edwards*. Chicago: Fergus Print. Co., 1884.

Edwards, Ninian, and William Wirt. *History of Illinois, from 1778–1833; and Life and Times of Ninian Edwards*. Springfield: Illinois State Journal, 1870.

Edwards, Richard, and M. Hopewell. *Edwards's Great West and Her Commercial Metropolis, Embracing a General View of the West, and a Complete History of St. Louis*. St. Louis: Edwards's Monthly, 1860.

Ehrlich, Walter. *They Have No Rights: Dred Scott's Struggle for Freedom*. Westport, CT: Greenwood Press, 1979.

Ekberg, Carl. *Colonial Ste. Genevieve: An Adventure on the Mississippi Frontier*. Gerald, MO: Patrice Press, 1985.

———. *Stealing Indian Women: Native Slavery in the Illinois Country*. Champaign: University of Illinois Press, 2010.

Eliot, William Greenleaf. *The Story of Archer Alexander: From Slavery to Freedom*, March 30, 1863.

Elliott, Joseph Peter. *A History of Evansville and Vanderburgh County, Indiana: A Complete and Concise Account from the Earliest Times to the Present....* Evansville, Indiana: Keller Print, 1897.

Ellsberry, Elizabeth Prather. *Mason County, Kentucky, Marriage Records 1804–1811 Vol II.* Chillicothe, MO: Elizabeth Prather Ellsberry., 1965.

Esarey, Logan. *A History of Indiana from Its Exploration to 1850.* Indianapolis: W. K. Stewart, 1915.

"Famous Dred Scott Case: Mrs. Chaffee, Owner of Old Slave, Still Living in Springfield." *New York Times,* December 22, 1895.

Fede, Andrew. *Roadblocks to Freedom: Slavery and Manumission in the United States South.* New Orleans, LA: Quid Pro Books, 2012.

Fehrenbacher, Don E. *The Dred Scott Case: Its Significance in American Law and Politics.* New York: Oxford University Press, 1978.

Fehrenbacher, Don E., and Ward M. Mcafee. *The Slaveholding Republic: An Account of the United States Government's Relations to Slavery.* New York: Oxford University Press, 2002.

Fiedler, George. *The Illinois law courts in three centuries, 1673–1973; a documentary history.* Berwyn, Ill.: Physicians' Record Co., 1973.

Fields, Barbara Jeanne. *Slavery and Freedom on the Middle Ground.* New Haven, CT: Yale University Press, 1985.

Finkelman, Paul. "The Crime of Color," *Tulane Law Review* 67, no. 6 (1993): 2063, 2085.

———. *An Imperfect Union: Slavery, Federalism, and Comity.* Chapel Hill: University of North Carolina Press, 1981.

———. *Slavery and the Founders: Race and Liberty in the Age of Jefferson,* 2nd ed. Armonk, NY: M. E. Sharpe, 2001.

———. "Slavery and the Northwest Ordinance: A Study in Ambiguity." *Journal of the Early Republic* 6 (Winter 1986): 343–370.

Fisher, George. "The Jury's Rise as Lie Detector." *Yale Law Journal* 107 (1997): 575.

Foley, William E. *The Genesis of Missouri: From Wilderness Outpost to Statehood.* Columbia: University of Missouri, 1989.

———. "Slave Freedom Suits before Dred Scott: The Case of Marie Jean Scypion's Descendants." *Missouri Historical Review* 79, no. 1 (October 1984): 1–23.

Foley, William E., and C. David Rice. *The First Chouteaus: River Barons of Early St. Louis.* Champaign: University of Illinois Press, 1983.

———. "Pierre Chouteau: Entrepreneur as Indian Agent." *Minnesota Historical Review* 72 (1978): 365–387.

Franklin, John Hope. *From Slavery to Freedom: A History of Negro Americans.* New York: McGraw-Hill, 1974.Frazier, Harriet C. *Runaway and Freed Missouri Slaves and Those Who Helped Them, 1763–1865.* Jefferson, NC: McFarland, 2004.

Frazier, Helen C. *Runaway and Freed Missouri Slaves and Those who Helped Them, 1763–1865.* Jefferson, N.C.: McFarland, 2010.

Fuller, Melville W. *Biographical Memoir of Sidney Breese.* Chicago: New Library Press, 1884.

Galanter, Marc. "Why the "Haves" Come Out Ahead: Speculations on the Limits of Legal Change." *Law & Society Review* 9, no. 1 (1974): 95.

Gardner, Eric. *Unexpected Places: Relocating Nineteenth-Century African American Literature.* Jackson: University Press of Mississippi, 2009.

Gardner, Eric. "'You Have No Business to Whip Me': The Freedom Suits of Polly Wash and Lucy Ann Delaney," *African American Review* 41, no. 1 (2007): 33–50.

Gaskell, Judith. "Illinois Legal Research before Statehood in 1818: A Bibliographical Guide." In *Prestate Legal Materials: A Fifty-State Research Guide, Including New York and the District of Columbia.* Binghamton, NY: Haworth Information Press, 2005.

Genovese, Eugene. *Roll, Jordan, Roll: The World the Slaves Made.* New York: Pantheon Books, 1974.

Gillmer, Jason. "Suing for Freedom: Interracial Sex, Slave Law, and Racial Identity in the Post-Revolutionary and Antebellum South." *North Carolina Law Review* 82, no. 2 (2004): 535.

Gitlin, Jay. *The Bourgeois Frontier: French Towns, French Traders, and American Expansion* Yale University Press, 2010.

Gitlin, Jay, Adam Arenson, and Barbara Berglund. *Frontier Cities: Encounters at the Crossroads of Empire*. Philadelphia: University of Pennsylvania Press, 2013.

Golay, Michael. *The Tide of Empire: America's March to the Pacific*. New York: John Wiley, 2003.

Goodell, William. *The American Slave Code in Theory and Practice: Its Distinctive Features Shown by Its Statutes, Judicial Decisions, and Illustrative Facts* (1853). Reprint, Ann Arbor: University of Michigan Press, 2005.

Grant, Ulysses S. *Personal Memoirs of Ulysses S. Grant, 1822–1885* (1885). 2 vols. Reprint, New York: Random House, 2002.

Griffiths, Martha. *Autobiography of a Female Slave*. New York: Redfield, 1857.

Grivno, Max L. "'Black Frenchmen' and 'White Settlers': Race, Slavery and the Creation of African-American Identities along the Northwest Frontier, 1790–1840." *Slavery and Abolition* 21 (December 2000): 75–93.

Gross, Ariela. *Double Character: Slavery and Mastery in the Antebellum Southern Courtroom*. Princeton, NJ: Princeton University Press, 2006.

———. *What Blood Won't Tell: A History of Race on Trial in America*. Cambridge, Mass.: Harvard University Press, 2008.

Hafen, Le Roy Reuben, and Harvey Lewis Carter. *Mountain Men and Fur Traders of the Far West: Eighteen Biographical Sketches*. Lincoln: University of Nebraska Press, 1982.

Hahn, Steven. *A Nation under Our Feet: Black Political Struggles in the Rural South from Slavery to the Great Migration*. Cambridge, MA: Harvard University Press, 2004.

Harris, N. Dwight. *The History Of Negro Servitude In Illinois And Of The Slavery Agitation In That State 1719–1864*. Chicago: C. McClurg 1904.

Harrison, William Henry, et al. *Messages and Letters of William Henry Harrison*, Vol. I. Edited by Logan Esarey. Indianapolis: Indiana Historical Commission, 1922.

Heitman, Francis B. *The Historical Register and Dictionary of the U.S. Army from Its Organization, September 29, 1789, to March 2, 1903*. 2 vols. (1903). Reprint, Champaign: University of Illinois Press, 1965.

Hempstead, Stephen, and Dana O. Jensen, eds. "I at Home, by Stephen Hempstead, Sr., the Diary of a Yankee Farmer in Missouri, 1811–1814." *Bulletin of the Missouri Historical Society* 13 (October 1956): 31–32.

Henderson, Madison, et al. *Confessions of Madison Henderson, alias Blanchard, Alfred Amos Warrick, James W. Seward, and Charles Brown, murderers of Jesse Baker and Jacob Weaver: as given by themselves and likeness of each, taken in jail shortly after their arrest*. St. Louis: Printed by Chambers & Knapp, Republican Office, 1841.

Higginbotham, A. Leon. *Shades of Freedom: Racial Politics and Presumptions of the American Legal Process*, Vols. 1 and 2. New York and Oxford: Oxford University Press, 1996.

Higginbotham, A. Leon, and F. Michael Higginbotham. "'Yearning to Breathe Free': Legal Barriers Against and Options in Favor of Liberty in Antebellum Virginia." *New York University Law Review* 68 (1993): 1213–1271.

Higginbotham, A. Leon, and Barbara K. Kopytoff. "Property First, Humanity Second: The Recognition of Slave's Human Nature in Virginia Civil Law." *Ohio State Law Journal* 50 (1989): 511–545.

Higginbotham, A. Leon. "Justice Thurgood Marshall: He Knew the Anguish of the Silenced and Gave Them a Voice." *Georgetown Journal on Fighting Poverty* 3(1996): 163–167.

History of Jo Daviess County, Illinois.... Chicago: H.F. Kett, 1928.

History of Madison County, Illinois, with Biographical Sketches. Edwardsville: W.R. Brink, 1882.

Hodder, Frank H. "Some Phases of the Dred Scott Case." *Mississippi Valley Historical Review* 16 (1929): 3–22.

Hopkins, Vincent C. *Dred Scott's Case* (1951). Reprint, New York: Atheneum, 1957.

Houck, Louis. *A History of Missouri: From the Earliest Explorations and Settlements until the Admission of the State into the Union*. 3 vols. Chicago: R.R. Donnelley & Sons, 1908.

———. *The Spanish Regime in Missouri: A Collection of Papers and Documents Relating to Upper Louisiana*.... Chicago, Illinois: R. R. Donnelley & Sons, 1909.

Houston, Horace K. Jr. "Another Nullification Crisis: Vermont's 1850 Habeas Corpus Law." *New England Journal Quarterly* 77, no. 2 (2004): 252–272.

Hurd, John Codman. *The Law of Freedom and Bondage in the U.S.* 2 vols. Clark, NJ: Lawbook Exchange, 1858. Reprint, New York: Little, Brown, 2006.

Hurt, R. Douglas. *Agriculture and Slavery in Missouri's Little Dixie.* Columbia: University of Missouri Press, 1992.

Hyde, Anne Farrar. *Empires, Nations, and Families: A New History of the North American West, 1800–1860.* Lincoln: University of Nebraska Press, 2011.

Jackson, Mattie J. *The Story of Mattie J. Jackson; Her Parentage—Experience of Eighteen Years in Slavery—Incidents during the War—Her Escape from Slavery. A True Story.* Lawrence, MA: Sentinel, 1866.

Jackson, Ronald Vern. *Iowa 1836 Territorial Census Index.* Bountiful, UT: Accelerated Indexing Systems, 1976.

———. *Iowa 1838 Territorial Census Index.* Bountiful, UT: Accelerated Indexing Systems, 1981.

———. *Iowa 1840 Territorial Census Index.* Salt Lake City, UT: Accelerated Indexing Systems, 1979.

———. *Michigan 1830 Index Census.* Bountiful, UT: Accelerated Indexing Systems, 1976.

———. *Minnesota 1840.* North Salt Lake, UT: Accelerated Indexing Systems, 1982.

———. *Wisconsin 1836 Census Index.* Bountiful, UT: Accelerated Indexing Systems, 1976.

———. *Wisconsin 1838 Census Index.* Bountiful, UT: Accelerated Indexing Systems, 1984.

———. *Wisconsin 1840 Census Index.* Bountiful, UT: Accelerated Indexing Systems, 1978.

Jackson, Ruby West, and Walter T. McDonald. *Finding Freedom, the Untold Story of Joshua Glover, Runaway Slave.* Madison: Wisconsin Historical Society Press, 2007.

Jacobs, Harriet A. *Incidents in the Life of a Slave Girl: Written by Herself.* New York: Cambridge University Press, 1987. Reprint, New York: Dover, 2001.

Johnson, Walter. *Soul by Soul: Life inside the Antebellum Slave Market.* Cambridge, MA: Harvard University Press, 1999.

———. *River of Dark Dreams: Slavery and Empire in the Cotton Kingdom.* Cambridge, MA: Harvard University Press, 2013.

Jones, Martha. "Time, Space, and Jurisdiction in Atlantic World Slavery: The Volunbrun Household in Gradual Emancipation New York." *Law & History Review* 29, no. 4 (2011): 1031–1060.

Kargau, Ernst D. *The German Element in St. Louis. A Translation from the German of Ernst D. Kargau's "St. Louis in Former Years: A Common History of the German Element.* Edited by Don Heinrich Tolzmann. Translated by William G. Bek. Baltimore: Clearfield, 2004.

Kaufman, Kenneth. *Dred Scott's Advocate.* Topeka, KS: Tandem Library, 1996.

Kennedy, Roger G. *Mr. Jefferson's Lost Cause: Land, Farmers, Slavery and the Louisiana Purchase.* New York: Oxford University Press, 2004.

Kennerly, William Clark, as told to Elizabeth Russell. *Persimmon Hill, a Narrative of Old St. Louis and the Far West.* Norman: University of Oklahoma Press, 1948.

King, Charles. *The True Ulysses S. Grant.* Philadelphia: J. B. Lippincott, 1914.

King, Wilma. *Stolen Childhood: Slave Youth in Nineteenth-Century America (Blacks in the Diaspora),* 2011.

Kinnaird, Lawrence. *Spain in the Mississippi Valley, 1765–1794.* Washington: U.S. Govt. Print. Off., 1946.

———. *Annual Report Of The American Historical Association For The Year 1945 Volume II.* Washington: U.S. Govt. Print. Off., 1949.

Konig, David. "The Long Road to *Dred Scott*: Personhood and the Rule of Law in the Trial Court Records of St. Louis Slave Freedom Suits." *UMKC Law Review* 75, no. 1 (2006): 53–79.

Körner, Gustav Philipp. *Memoirs of Gustave Koerner, 1809–1896: Life Sketches Written at the Suggestion of His Children, in Two Volumes.* Edited by Thomas Joseph McCormack. Cedar Rapids, IA: Torch Press, 1909.

Kutler, Stanley I. *The Dred Scott Decision.* Boston: Houghton Mifflin, 1967.

Lauber, Albon. *Indian Slavery in Colonial Times within the Present Limits of the United States.* New York: Columbia University, 1880.

LeCompte, Janet. "Pierre Chouteau, Junior." In *The Mountain Men and the Fur Trade of the Far West.* 10 vols. Edited by Leroy Hafen. Lincoln: University of Nebraska Press, 1997.

Leichtle, Kurt E., and Bruce G. Carveth. *Crusade Against Slavery: Edward Coles, Pioneer of Freedom.* Carbondale: Southern Illinois University Press, 2011.

Levinson, Sanford, and Bartholomew H. Sparrow, eds. *The Louisiana Purchase and American Expansion, 1803–1898.* Lanham, MD: Rowman and Littlefield, 2005.

Litwack, Leon F. *Been in the Storm So Long: The Aftermath of Slavery.* New York: Knopf: distributed by Random House, 1979.

———. *North of Slavery: The Negro in the Free States.* Chicago: University of Chicago Press, 1961.

Lyons, Mary E. *Letters from a Slave Girl: The Story of Harriet Jacobs.* Reprint, New York: Simon Pulse, 1996.

Mackey, Frank. *Done with Slavery: The Black Fact in Montreal, 1760–1840.* Montreal: McGill-Queen's Press, 2010.

MacKinnon, Catharine. *Feminism Unmodified: Discourses on Life and Law.* Cambridge, MA: Harvard University Press, 1987.

MacKinnon, Catharine, and Gilligan, C. *In a Different Voice.* Cambridge, MA: Harvard University Press, 1982.

Mahoney, Timothy R. *Provincial Lives: Middle-Class Experience in the Antebellum Middle West.* New York: Cambridge University Press, 2006.

———. *River Towns in the Great West: The Structure of Provincial Urbanization in the American Midwest, 1820–1870.* New York: Cambridge University Press, 1990.

Marshall, Anna Maria, and Scott Barclay. "In Their Own Words: How Ordinary People Construct the Legal World." *Law and Social Inquiry* 28 (2003): 617.

Martin, Jonathan D. *Divided Mastery: Slave Hiring in the American South.* Cambridge, MA: Harvard University Press, 2004.

Matthews, William. *American Diaries: An Annotated Bibliography of American Diaries Written Prior to the Year 1861.* Los Angeles: University of California Press: 1945.

McConnel, George Murray. "Some Reminiscences of My Father, Murray McConnell." *Journal of the Illinois State Historical Society* 18, no. 1 (1925): 40–50.

McDermott, John Francis. *The Early Histories of St. Louis.* St. Louis: St. Louis Historical Documents Foundation, 1952.

———. *Old Cahokia: A Narrative and Documents Illustrating the First Century of Its History.* St. Louis: St. Louis Historical Documents Foundation, 1949.

McDonough, J. L., et al. *Combined History of Randolph, Monroe and Perry Counties, Illinois....* Philadelphia: McDonough, 1883.

McFeely, William S. *Grant: A Biography,* New York: W.W. Norton, 2002.

McGinty, Brian. "Dred Scott's Fight for Freedom Brought Him a Heap O' Trouble." *American Illustrated* 16 (May 1981): 34–39.

McLaurin, Melton A. *Celia, a Slave.* New York: Perennial, 1993.

McMaster, S. W., *Sixty Years on the Upper Mississippi: My Life and Experiences.* Rock Island 1893.

Meachum, John B. *An Address to All the Colored Citizens of the United States.* Philadelphia: King and Baird, 1846.

Mersman, Joseph J. *The Whiskey Merchant's Diary: An Urban Life in the Emerging Midwest.* Edited by Linda A. Fisher. Athens: Ohio University Press, 2007.

"Missouri Broadside Collection, 75 pieces." Durham, NC: Duke University Libraries, 1836–1942.

Monks, Leander J., Logan Esarey, and Ernest V. Shockley. *Courts and Lawyers of Indiana, Volumes I & II.* Indianapolis: Federal, 1919.

Moore, Robert. *A Ray of Hope, Extinguished: St. Louis Slave Suits for Freedom. Gateway Heritage* 14, no. 3 (1993–1994): 4–15.

Morris, Christopher. *Becoming Southern: The Evolution of a Way of Life, Warren County and Vicksburg, Mississippi, 1770–1860.* New York: Oxford University Press, 1995.

Morton, Patricia. *Discovering the Women in Slavery: Emancipating Perspectives on the American Past.* Athens: University of Georgia Press, 1996.

Myers, Jacob, W. "History of the Gallatin County Salines," in Journal of the Illinois State Historical Society, Vol. 14, at page 342.

Nash, A. E. Keir. "Fairness and Formalism in the Trials of Blacks in the State Supreme Courts of the Old South." *Virginia Law Review* 56 (1970): 64–100.

———. "Reason of Slavery: Understanding the Judicial Role in the Peculiar Institution." *Vanderbilt Law Review* 32 (1979): 7–218.

———. "In Re Radical Interpretations of American Law: The Relation of Law and History." *Michigan Law Review* 82 (1983): 274–344.

Neal, Anthony W. *Unburdened by Conscience: A Black People's Collective Account of America's Ante-Bellum South and the Aftermath.* Lanham: University Press of America, 2009.

Neal, Anthony W. *Unburdened by Conscience: A Black People's Collective Account of America's Ante-Bellum South and the Aftermath.* University Press of America, 2011.

Nebelsick, Alvin Louis. *A History of Belleville.* Belleville, IL: Township High School and Junior College, 2010.

Norton, W. T. *Centennial History of Madison County, Illinois, and Its People: 1812–1912.* Chicago: Lewis, 1912.

Northup, Solomon. *Twelve Years a Slave,* 1853.

O'Donovan, Katherine. "Engendering Justice: Women's Perspectives and the Rule of Law." *University of Toronto Law Journal* 39 (1989): 127–148.

Oldham, James. "New Light on Mansfield and Slavery." *Journal of British Studies* 27 (1988): 45–68.

Olexer, Barbara. *The Enslavement of the American Indian in Colonial Times.* Milwaukie, OR: Joyous, 2005.

Palmer, Colin A., ed. *The Worlds of Unfree Labour: From Indentured Servitude to Slavery.* Aldershot, UK: Ashgate, 1998.

Palmer, Strange M. *Western Wisconsin in 1836.* Madison: Atwood & Culver, 1872.

Papin, Edward Villiere. "The Village under the Hill: A Sketch of Old St. Louis." *MHS Collections* 5 (1927): 18–37.

Patterson, Orlando. *Slavery and Social Death: A Comparative Study.* Cambridge, Mass.: Harvard University Press, 1982.

Payne, Daniel Alexander. *History of the African Methodist Episcopal Church.* Edited by C. S. Smith. Nashville, TN: Publishing House of the A. M. E. Sunday School Union, 1891.

———. *Recollections of Seventy Years.* Edited by C. S. Smith. Nashville, TN: Publishing House of the A. M. E. Sunday School Union, 1888.

Pease, Theodore Calvin. *The Frontier State, 1818–1848.* 1918. Reprint, Chicago: A.C. McClurg, 1922.

Peterson, Charles E. *Colonial St. Louis: Building a Creole Capital.* St. Louis: Missouri Historical Society, 1949.

Philbrick, Francis S. "Law, Courts, and Litigation of Indiana Territory (1800–1809)." *Illinois Law Review* 24, no. 1 (1929): 14–15.

———. *The Laws of Illinois Territory, 1809–1818,* Vol. XXV. Springfield: Illinois State Historical Library, 1950.

———. *The Laws of Indiana Territory 1801–09,* Vol. XXI; Law Series, Vol. II, at xli nn.100–01. Springfield: Illinois State Historical Library, 1950.

Pierce, Frederick Clifton. *Field Genealogy: Being the Record of All the Field Family in America....* Chicago: W. B. Conkey, 1901.

Phillips, Christopher. *Freedom's Port: The African American Community of Baltimore, 1790–1860.* Urbana: University of Illinois Press, 1997.

Podruchny, Carolyn. *Making the Voyageur Word: Travelers and Traders in the North American Fur Trade.* Lincoln: University of Nebraska Press, 2006.

Pooley, William Vipond. *The Settlement of Illinois from 1830 to 1850.* Madison: University of Wisconsin, 1908.

Pope, Nathaniel. *Pope's Digest, 1815.* Springfield: Trustees of the Illinois State Historical Library, 1938.

Primm, James Neal. *Lion of the Valley, St. Louis, Missouri, 1764–1980,* 3rd ed. Columbia: University of Missouri Press, 1981.

Rawick, George P. *The American Slave: A Composite Autobiography,* Vol. 11: Arkansas Narratives, Part 7, and Missouri Narratives. Reprint, Westport, CT: Greenwood Publishing Company, 1972.

Ress, David. *Governor Edward Coles and the Vote to Forbid Slavery in Illinois, 1823–1824.* Jefferson, NC: McFarland, 2006.

Reynolds, John. *My Own Times: Embracing also the History of Illinois.* Illinois, 1855.

Rodolf, Theodore. "Pioneering in the Wisconsin Lead Region." *Collections of the State Historical Society of Wisconsin* 15 (1900): 338–389.

Russell, Marion J. "American Slave Discontent in the Records of the High Court." *Journal of Negro History* 31 (1946): 418–419.

Salafia, Matthew. *Slavery's Borderland: Freedom and Bondage along the Ohio River.* Philadelphia: University of Pennsylvania Press, 2013.

Savage, William Sherman. *Blacks in the West.* Westport, CT: Greenwood, 1976.

Saxton, Martha. "Lives of Missouri Slave Women: A Critique of True Womanhood." In *Contested Democracy: Freedom, Race and Power in American History.* Edited by Manisha Von Eschen and Penny Sinha. New York: Columbia University Press, 2007.

Schafer, Judith Kelleher. *Becoming Free, Remaining Free: Manumission and Enslavement in New Orleans, 1846–1862.* Baton Rouge: Louisiana State University Press, 2003.

Scharf, J. Thomas. *History of Saint Louis City and County, from the Earliest Periods to the Present Day: Including Biographical Sketches of Representative Men.* 2 vols. Philadelphia: L. H. Everts, 1883.

Schwartz, Marie Jenkins. *Born in Bondage: Growing Up Enslaved in the Antebellum South.* Cambridge, MA: Harvard University Press, 2000.

Schweninger, Loren. "Prosperous Blacks in the South 1790–1880." *American Historical Review* 95, no. 1 (Feb. 1990): 31–56.

Scott, James C. *Weapons of the Weak: Everyday Forms of Peasant Resistance.* New Haven, CT: Yale University Press, 1985.

Scott, Rebecca J. *Degrees of Freedom: Louisiana and Cuba after Slavery.* Cambridge, MA: Harvard University Press, 2005.

Scott, Rebecca J., and Jean M. Hebrard. *Freedom Papers: An Atlantic Odyssey in the Age of Emancipation.* Cambridge MA: Harvard University Press, 2012.

Shepard, Elihu Hotchkiss. *The Early History of St. Louis and Missouri, from Its First Exploration by White Men in 1673 to 1843.* 8 vols. St. Louis: Southwestern Book, 1870.

Shipley, Alberta D., and David O. Shipley. *The History of Black Baptists in Missouri.* Nashville, TN: National Baptist Convention, 1976.

Smith, George Washington. *A History of Southern Illinois: A Narrative Account of Its Historical Progress, Its People, and Its Principal Interests,* Vols. 1–3. Chicago and New York: Lewis, 1912.

Smith, Hubbard Madison. *Historical Sketches of Old Vincennes, Founded in 1732: Its Institutions and Churches, Embracing Collateral Incidents and Biographical Sketches of Many Persons and Events Connected Therewith.* Vincennes, IN: Press of W.B. Burford, 1903.

Snyder, Charles E. "John Emerson, Owner of Dred Scott." *Annals of Iowa,* 3rd series, 21 (October 1938): 440–461.

Snyder, John Francis. *Adam W. Snyder, and His Period in Illinois History, 1817–1842.* Virginia, IL: B. Needham, Bookseller & Stationer, 1906.

Spangler, Mrs. George, "Will of David Shipman, A Revolutionary Soldier Buried in Tazewell County, Ill." *Journal of the Illinois State Historical Society (1908–1984)* 14, no. 1/2 (Apr.–Jul. 1921): 122–132.

Spencer, Thomas Edwin. *The Story of Old St. Louis.* St. Louis, MO, 1914.

Spivak, Gayatri Chakravorty. "Can the Subaltern Speak?" In *Markism and the Interpretation of Culture.* Edited by Cary Nelson and Lawrence Grossberg. Urbana: University of Illinois Press, 1988.

St. Clair, Arthur. *The St. Clair Papers: The Life and Public Services of Arthur St. Clair...*, 2 vols. Arranged and annotated by William Henry Smith. Cincinnati: R. Clarke. 1882.

Steiner, Mark, E., ed. "Abolitionists and Escaped Slaves in Jacksonville: Samuel Willard's 'My First Adventure with a Fugitive Slave: The Story of It and How It Failed.'" *Illinois Historical Journal* 89 (Winter 1996): 213–232.

Stevens, Frank E. "Alexander Pope Field." *Journal of the Illinois State Historical Society* 14 (1911–1912): 7–37.

Stevens, George E. *History of Central Baptist Church*. St. Louis: King, 1927.

Stevens, Walter B. *St. Louis: The Fourth City*. 3 vol. Chicago: S.J. Clarke, 1911.

Stoddard, Amos. *Sketches, Historical and Descriptive, of Louisiana*. Philadelphia: Mathew Carey, 1913.

Stowe, Harriet Beecher. *Uncle Tom's Cabin, Project Gutenberg EBook.*

Sweet, John Wood. *Bodies Politic: Negotiating Race in the American North, 1730–1830*. Philadelphia: University of Pennsylvania Press, 2007.

Thomas, James. *From Tennessee Slave to St. Louis Entrepreneur: The Autobiography of James Thomas*. Columbia: University of Missouri Press, 1984.

Tregilis, Helen Cox. *River Roads to Freedom: Fugitive Slave Notices and Sheriff Notices Found in Illinois Sources*. Bowie, MD: Heritage Books, 1988.

Trexler, Harrison Anthony. *Slavery in Missouri, 1804–1865*. Baltimore: Johns Hopkins Press, 1914.

Turner, Frederick Jackson. "The Significance of the Frontier in American History" (1893). In *The Frontier in American History*. New York: Henry Holt, 1921.

Turner, George. *Traits of Indian Character*, Vol. I. Philadelphia: Key & Bibble, 1836.

Tushnet, Mark. *The American Law of Slavery 1810–1860: Considerations of Humanity and Interest*. Princeton, NJ: Princeton University Press, 1981.

VanderVelde, Lea. *Mrs. Dred Scott: A Life on Slavery's Frontier*. New York: Oxford University Press, 2009.

VanderVelde, Lea, and Sandhya Subramanian. "Mrs. Dred Scott." *Yale Law Journal* 106 (1997): 1033, 1122.

Van der Zee, Jacob. Fur Trade Operations in the Eastern Iowa Country under the Spanish Regime, 12 Iowa Journal of History and Politics 355 (1914).

Volkman, Lucas P. Church Property Disputes, Religious Freedom, and the Ordeal of African Methodists in Antebellum St. Louis: Farrar v. Finney (1855), 27 Journal of Law & Religion 83 (2011–12).

Wade, Richard. *Slavery in the Cities: The South 1820–1860*. New York: Oxford University Press, 1967.

———. *The Urban Frontier: Pioneer Life in Early Pittsburgh, Cincinnati, Lexington, Louisville, and St. Louis*. Chicago: University of Chicago Press, 1959.

Waldrep, Christopher. *Roots of Disorder: Race and Criminal Justice in the American South, 1817–80*. Champaign, IL: University of Illinois Press, 1998.

Walker, Juliet E. K. *Free Frank: A Black Pioneer on the Antebellum Frontier*. Lexington: University Press of Kentucky, 1995.

Walsh, Edward P. "The Story of an Old Clerk" (originally printed in *St. Louis Weekly Reveille*, Oct. 15, 1848). Reprinted in *Glimpses of the Past*, St. Louis: Missouri Historical Society, Jefferson Memorial, 1934. www.umsl.edu/virtualstl/phase2/1850/events/perspectives/oldclerk.html.

Washburne, E. B. *Sketch of Edward Coles, Second Governor of Illinois and Slavery Struggle, 1823–24*. New York: Negro Universities Press, 1882.

Washington, Booker T. *Up from Slavery*. New York: Doubleday, Page, 1901.

Watkins, James. *Struggles for Freedom: or The Life of James Watkins....* Reprint, Manchester, UK: A. Heywood, 1860.

Weiner, Mark. *Black Trials: Citizenship from the Beginnings of Slavery to the End of Caste*. New York: Knopf, 2004.

White, Lucie E. "Subordination, Rhetorical Survival Skills and Sunday Shoes: Notes on the Hearing of Mrs. G." *Buffalo Law Review* 38 (1990): 1–58.

Whiteside, Bill Whiteside Family 9000 Geneology. at www.whitesideancestry.org

Whitman, T. Stephen. *The Price of Freedom: Slavery and Manumission in Baltimore and Early National Maryland*. Lexington: University Press of Kentucky 1997.

Williams, Michael Patrick. "The Black Evangelical Ministry in the Antebellum Border States: Profiles of Elders John Berry Meachum and Noah Davis." *Foundations* 21, no. 3 (1978): 225–241.

Wilson, George. *History of Dubois County from Its Primitive Days to 1910*. Jasper, IN, 1910.

Winch, Julie. *The Clamorgans: One Family's History of Race in America*. New York: Hill and Wang, 2011.

Yellin, Jean Fagan, Harriet Jacobs: A Life, Cambridge: Basic Ciritas Books, 2005.

Zaborney, John J., *Slaves for Hire: Renting Enslaved Laborers in Antebellum Virginia*. Baton Rouge: Louisiana State University Press, 2012.

Newspapers

Debow's Review, Agricultural, Commercial, Industrial Progress and Resources.

Frank Leslie's Illustrated Newspaper 4, no. 82 (June 27, 1857).

Missouri Republican, 1838–1856.

Northwestern Gazette and Galena Advertiser San Jose Telegraph, 1857.

Conversations

E-mail correspondence between Lea VanderVelde, University of Iowa law librarian John Bergstrom, and the Indiana Supreme Court and the Indiana State Historical Society (2012).

Correspondence between Lea VanderVelde and William Foley about records in the cases of the Scypion family.

Web Sources and Resources

Ancestry.com

Revised Dred Scott Case Collection, http://digital.wustl.edu/d/dre/.

Illinois Secretary of State for Illinois State Archives, http://www.cyberdriveillinois.com/departments/archives/databases/servant.html.

U.S. Government Bureau of Land Management General Land Office Records, www.glorecords.blm.gov/.

Mason County, Kentucky Marriage Records, 1804–60 Vol. II-VI. Ancestry.com

Missouri Supreme Court database, Missouri State Archives, http://www.sos.mo.go/archives/judiciary/supremecourt.

Digital Library on American Slavery, library.uncg.edu/slavery/.

Wabash Valley Visions & Voices: Digital Memory Project, http://visions.indstate.edu.

St. Louis Legal Encoding Project, digital.wustl.edu/legalencodingproject/.

St. Louis Probate Court Digitization Project, 1802–1900, www.mo.gov/archives/mojudicial/stl_history.asp.

Special Collections of Private Individuals

Robert Hansen and Alfred Mueller, Galena Lead Mining Permits, Galena Public Library.

Vital Statistics from Galena newspapers.

1826 Tax List for Jo Daviess County.

St. Louis Manumission List prepared by Robert Moore, U.S. Park Service for the Old Courthouse, St. Louis.

City Directories for St. Louis

1836–1837, 1838–1839
Keemles 1842, 1845, 1847, 1848, 1851, 1852 1854–1855
St. Louis Directory of Citizens and a Business Directory 1857, 1858, 1859 1860
Kennedy's 1864
Edwards 1865, 1866, 1867, 1870, 1871, 1872
Gould & Aldrich's 1873
Gould's 1875, 1876

INDEX

Abuse of slaves, 32, 64, 200; overwork, 92, 96, 104, 168; physical abuse, 139, 200; psychological abuse, 131; rape and sexual, 131, 139; *see also* murder; retribution; worst abuse often took place in private, 197–98, 261, n. 15

Abolitionism, *see* Anti-Slavery

Abolitionist Societies, 9, 19, 207

"Act Concerning Freed Negroes and Mulattos," 67, 160

Adams, Calvin: ran a Mississippi river ferry, 99; lost his wife to Robert Duncan, 99; sued Robert Duncan for assault, 238 n. 12; litigious, 238 n. 13

Adams, Sally, 99, 238 n. 12–13

Adams, Swanzey (also known as Swansey or Swanston) slave of Duncans, disposition in will, not identified by name Swanzey, 97; confusion over name, 241 n. 57; brother of Shadrach Duncan, 99, 241 n. 56; worked at the Illinois salt mines, 103; mined in Galena, 106; sued James Duncan for freedom, 107; kidnapped, 107, 240 n. 48; transferred, 243 n. 93; emancipated by Shadrach, 109, 240 n. 48, 241 n. 63; may have worked for levy, 243 n. 95; married, 243 n. 94; death, 240 n. 48, 243 n. 94; image, 115

Advertisements for runaway slaves, 5, 203; for sale of slaves, 168–69, 174, 185

African American, 7, 19, 48, 57, 74, 76, 114, 128, 204, 208; kidnapping of, *see* kidnapping men, occupations of, 16, 96, 103, 137; women, occupations of, 121, 138, 150

African Church, attendance by Leah, 127, 127–28; participation by John Berry Meachum, 121–22; participation by Jonathan Duncan, 114, 117; participation by Jordan Early, 141

Age of slaves; at which children were put to work, 68–69, 163, 167, 172, 205; elderly considered a burden, 72, 138, 167, 178; of majority, 141, 149; at end of indenture, 67, 76, 85, 89, 103, 161, 184

Alcohol, 99, 120

Ambiguous legal status, 87, 133

American Fur Company, 177, 208

Ann, daughter of Milly Duncan, 113; disappearance, 113, 242 n. 83; slave petitioner, 242 n. 80–81

Antislavery, sentiment, 9, 119, 159, 207; absence of critique of slavery in Missouri, 9, 245 n. 30; advocacy outlawed, 9, 122, 245 n. 30

Archibald, son of Leah Charleville, slave petitioner; 117; lived with Reverend Meachum, 120; sued for freedom, 120

Arson, 2, 99, 127, 129

Assault, actual, 77, 99, 108, 151, 238 n. 12; fictive, 197; as a necessary element to a freedom suit, 196–97

Attorneys in St. Louis, 73–74, 86, 106, 109–10, 141, 168, 171–75, 185, 208

Attorneys for slaves, appointment of, 8, 67; *see also* specific individuals by name

Auctions, of slaves, 4, 48–49, 148, 166–68, 172, 174, 185, 221 n. 48; where held, 47, 49, 148, 150, 165–67, 189

Back wages, 54, 64

Bank notes, 17; at issue in Milton Duty's estate, 170–71

Baird, Joseph, kidnapped Peter and Queen, 29

Baptismal records, Catholic, 43–44, 50–51, 131, 220 n. 25, 221 n. 34

Bark, Perry, purchased Eliza Tyler, 133; deceived and sold Tyler, 134; sued by Nelson Campbell, 213 n. 21; 247 n. 9